Islam, Securitization, and US Foreign Policy

"Viewing Islam as a security issue did not happen by accident. Erdoan Shipoli's book sheds light on how for decades Islam has been constructed as a security threat by a variety of actors. This book gives a theoretical base to the securitization of Islam in America and its implications in global peace and security. This research will pave the road for more discussions on the role of religion in politics and international affairs. A must-read for students of security, politics, religion, and international affairs."
—Ihsan Yilmaz, *Professor of Islamic Studies, Alfred Deakin Institute of Globalisation and Citizenship, Deakin University, Australia*

"Dr. Erdoan Shipoli has argued, convincingly in this book, that the complex web of networking between extremist lobbies on the right, in Congress, academia, media and strategic think-tanks have collectively manipulated Islamophobia and its discourse to scare and alienate large swathes of the American public from engaging with Islam and Muslims.

This network has succeeded in securitizing Islam as a religion by politicizing its value system, and pushing it to the forefront of the American national security agenda. They have adroitly marshaled billions of dollars for this purpose from those hell-bent to demonize Islam and Muslims.

President Bill Clinton's and President Barack Obama's liberal reasoning have been outwitted by the gullible rhetoric of President George W. Bush and the opportunism recklessness of President Donald Trump.

Dr. Shipoli's elaboration and emendation of the Securitization Theory is, by itself, worth the price of the entire volume."
—Mohamed Bakari, *Professor and Vice-Chancellor Designate, RAF International University, Kenya*

"Erdoan Shipoli has written a must-read primer for anyone interested in securitization of Islam in US foreign policy . . . a very important guide full of important information for those of us who want to discover and understand the role of Islam in United States' political discussions."
—Savaş Genç, *Ph.D. Visiting Scholar, Department of Political Science, University of Heidelberg, Germany, and Researcher at Stockholm University (SUITS), Sweden*

"Erdoan Shipoli has written two books expanding the Copenhagen School's theory of securitization beyond the domestic domain. This current study carefully analyzes the discourse that US foreign policy makers have used to construct Islam as a security concern worldwide. With his detailed history that linked democracy promotion, intervention, and cold war mentality, Erdoan has contributed to the understanding of new rivalries and polarizations in global politics. This is a must-read for policy makers as much as for students of political science."
—Gokhan Bacik, *Professor of Political Science, Palacky University, Czech Republic*

"Shipoli provides an important analysis of how vocabulary and conceptualizations influence policies. His study of how U.S. policy is shaped by the ways Islam is conceived by policy makers is a model for understanding the dynamics of policy formulation in general as well as providing insights into the specifics of American policies relating to Islam."
—John Voll, *Professor Emeritus of Islamic History, Georgetown University, USA*

"*Islam, Securitization, and US Foreign Policy* provides a much-needed research on how fear influences and shaped policies, both domestic and foreign. The securitization of Islam has affected not only US policies but the lives of US citizens, as well as lives of Muslims around the globe. This work shows how fear and discourse can construct an enemy, polarize the world, and lead to unprecedented results. It is essential to understand how Islam is securitized and what we need to do to counter it. Want proof? See the 2016 elections, which affected not only Muslims but also other minority communities as well. This is a well-researched book that should be read by policy makers concerned about the security of America."
—Wajahat Ali, author of *The Domestic Crusaders* and co-author of *Fear Inc.*

Erdoan A. Shipoli

Islam, Securitization, and US Foreign Policy

palgrave
macmillan

Erdoan A. Shipoli
Visiting Scholar at the Center for
Muslim Christian Understanding
Georgetown University
Washington, DC, USA

ISBN 978-3-319-71110-2   ISBN 978-3-319-71111-9 (eBook)
https://doi.org/10.1007/978-3-319-71111-9

Library of Congress Control Number: 2018935256

© The Editor(s) (if applicable) and The Author(s) 2018
This work is subject to copyright. All rights are solely and exclusively licensed by the Publisher, whether the whole or part of the material is concerned, specifically the rights of translation, reprinting, reuse of illustrations, recitation, broadcasting, reproduction on microfilms or in any other physical way, and transmission or information storage and retrieval, electronic adaptation, computer software, or by similar or dissimilar methodology now known or hereafter developed.
The use of general descriptive names, registered names, trademarks, service marks, etc. in this publication does not imply, even in the absence of a specific statement, that such names are exempt from the relevant protective laws and regulations and therefore free for general use.
The publisher, the authors, and the editors are safe to assume that the advice and information in this book are believed to be true and accurate at the date of publication. Neither the publisher nor the authors or the editors give a warranty, express or implied, with respect to the material contained herein or for any errors or omissions that may have been made. The publisher remains neutral with regard to jurisdictional claims in published maps and institutional affiliations.

Cover Design by Fatima Jamadar

Printed on acid-free paper

This Palgrave Macmillan imprint is published by the registered company Springer International Publishing AG part of Springer Nature.
The registered company address is: Gewerbestrasse 11, 6330 Cham, Switzerland

Foreword

Islamophobia is a social cancer that threatens the very fabric of America and Europe and the religious freedoms, security, and civil liberties of its Muslim citizens and residents. Islamophobia has also fed the securitization of Islam and the securitization of Islam has in turn fed Islamophobia.

The securitization of Islam did not happen suddenly with the 9/11 and the war on terror. In the aftermath of the Iranian Revolution, a decade before Samuel Huntington's acclaimed book, Edward Said warned of the clash of civilizations. The Iranian Revolution, hijackings, hostage taking, acts of terrorism in the 1980s and 1990s, attacks of September 11, 2001, attacks in Europe, the war on terror, and the terrorist attacks in America, Europe, and the Muslim world have been catalysts in affecting how many Americans and Europeans view Islam and Muslims. As a result, today Islam is securitized in both domestic and foreign policy.

While al-Qaeda, ISIS, and other terrorist groups continue to threaten the West, we often overlook the fact that the vast majority of Muslims reject the barbaric acts of terrorists and are the majority of militant jihadists' victims. We also forget that most of the violence committed in America is not driven by Islam and Muslims, but by far-right, white, anti-government groups, as documented in FBI and Southern Poverty Law Center reports.

There are many actors that have contributed in defining Islam on security terms. In America and in Europe this is largely a well-engineered and strategized campaign. This campaign includes pundits, bloggers, authors, lobbyists, and elected officials who have meticulously cultivated an ideologically, agenda-driven, anti-Muslim polemic (not simply anti-extremism but anti-Muslim and anti-Islam), and in social media Islam and Muslims, not just Muslim extremists, are the problem.

Political candidates and elected officials have played major roles. Polling data show that during election campaigns there is an increase in anti-Muslim and anti-Islam sentiments. In the recent American presidential elections, when a candidate said something against Muslims or Islam, their donations and numbers went up.

Mass media and social media are the biggest enablers. Media Tenor did a study of ten years, from 2001 to 2011, where they analyzed 975,000 pieces of media from major European and American sites. In 2001, 2% of the analyzed media pieces were devoted to Islamic extremism and 0.1% to mainstream, ordinary, Muslims. In 2011, the 2% jumped to 25% and the coverage of the mainstream Muslims remained to 0.1%. That statistic has continued to grow. In the most recent study in 2015, Media Tenor found that the coverage of Islam in 2014 was worse than after the 9/11 attacks, reaching the peak with the emergence of ISIS. While Christianity, Judaism, and other religions received considerable positive coverage, Islam's coverage was almost exclusively negative.

Studies using Internal Revenue Service (IRS) tax returns have shown that more than $180 million has been donated from different philanthropies to major anti-Islam and anti-Muslim websites and media outlets. A 2011 Fear Inc. study, a ten-year study of seven American foundations, reported that $42.6 million flowed only from these philanthropy foundations to Islamophobic authors and websites. A 2013 CAIR Report, "Legislating Fear: Islamophobia and its Impact in the United States", reported $119,662,719 in total revenue between 2008 and 2011. This number continues to increase every year, making Islamophobia a very lucrative industry for pundits, bloggers, authors, journalists, lobbyists, and elected officials.

What Are the Main Drivers of Violent Extremism?

Combating violent extremism simply by focusing on religion and ignoring the root causes that are political, economic, and ethnic is a dead end. Even when they speak about the failures in the Middle East, American officials speak about how the invasion of Afghanistan and Iraq did not get us anywhere, they speak about how "winning hearts and minds" strategy did not get us anywhere, and they speak about how we are not winning the war against ISIS. But most of the time they fail to mention the root causes of violent extremism and how we are addressing them. They fail to speak about political and economic situation in the region, about the Arab Spring, and the fallout of the Arab Spring.

The main drivers in violent extremism today are political, economic, and ethnic grievances, some of which are framed in the name of religion. Wars; occupation; authoritarian regimes and oppression; poverty and economic inequality; national, regional, ethnic and tribal rivalries; and proxy wars and militias are all drivers of violent extremism and recruitment. Other drivers that make for the anti-Americanism in the mainstream societies in many parts of the world, which then become adopted by extremists, are the US double standards in promoting democracy and human rights, support for infringed regimes, military assistance, and arms sales. If we look at the narrative of the leaders of terrorist organizations in the Middle East, they talk against the US foreign policy, but more than that they talk about the situation in the Middle East, the authoritarian regimes in the Middle East, the role of the USA and the west in forming the Middle East, and their role in supporting the authoritarian regimes in the region. So, context becomes a primary driver, whereas texts become a way to legitimize.

In countries that the democratic means of expressing political discontent are closed, there is lack of or limited possibility for significant political representation and reform, and since there is government repression, there will be a search for alternative means and options for expression and power share. For ISIS-like groups religion becomes a tool to legitimate a narrative of marginalization and discontent, and to recruit on global scale, in the name of Islam. Major polls have consistently reported that Islam is a significant component of religious and cultural identity for Muslims. Violent extremists use that as an instrument for legitimation and mobilization, but if you look at their rhetoric and practices, they are much more concerned with political power legitimated in the name of religion. In the old days, it would have been legitimated in the name of Arab nationalism or Arab socialism, but today it is Islam.

Where Do We Go from Here?

Moving forward, America faces overwhelming challenges. The USA continues to be seen as siding with authoritarian regimes, despite its rhetorical commitment to democracy. The USA justified its interventions, invasions, and occupations in the name of bringing democracy to Afghanistan, Iraq, and the Arab world, while at the same time it used regional violence, and the terrorism of ISIS and al-Qaeda, to justify its support for authoritarian Arab regimes. The real need is to move beyond a narrative that emphasizes self-determination, governmental accountability, rule of law, and human rights, to promoting them in practice, everywhere in the Middle East.

Failure to address these root causes legitimizes the widespread beliefs in the Arab world that America has double standards when it comes to the promotion and support for democracy and human rights. It also reinforces anti-Westernism and anti-Americanism, as well as the mantra of militant extremism that neither the Arab regimes nor Western allies will allow real people in power, and therefore will fuel greater radicalization and recruitment by terrorist organizations. Unless we address the root causes, which are there for more than 50 years, the pressure level by authoritarian regimes will only cause a pressure cooker effect and at a certain point of time it will blow the top off. The vast majority won't turn to terrorism but the terrorist factor will continue to be there, in that society.

The perception of American foreign policy is of utmost importance both in the Muslim world and for the American Muslims, and here is where Erdoan Shipoli's *Islam, Securitization, and US Foreign Policy* could not be more timely and critical. Most so-called homegrown jihadist terrorists have said, or wrote, that they see the war on terror as a war against Islam, as a war against Allah and Muslims, and that each and every Muslim knows that America is at war with Islam. So, there is that projected image, not of a selective war with terrorists but that broad-based image that brushstrokes Islam and Muslims.

In this work, Erdoan answers the questions of how do we talk about Islam in context of US security? How does language we use to describe Islam influence the way we imagine it? And how is Islam constructed as a security issue? The narrative toward Islam does affect not only America's foreign policy but also its image abroad, global polarization, and international security. It is particularly important that Erdoan looked at the four recent US Presidents' speeches directly and made a latent analysis of the key terms and phrases used in these speeches to construct Islam as a security issue, why they used these terms, and what were the consequences in America and abroad.

Washington, DC John L. Esposito
November 2017

Preface

This book is about the construction of Islam as a security issue, by American policymakers, in their discourse. Since Buzan and Waever have been writing about the securitization theory, it has become a dominant theory to security. This theory analyzes how an issue becomes a security issue, mainly through discourse. It is the belief of this work that the place of Islam in US foreign policy can be better explained by the securitization theory than by liberalism and realism.

Islam has been dealt with as a security issue, and this has its consequences, both domestic and international. For America, the securitization of Islam has resulted in two invasions, instability in the Middle East, alienation of the Muslim community in America, many terrorist attacks in its soil, and a polarized, tired, and scared American population. I have tried to compare the latest administrations and their approach toward Islam. They are very different, starting from Clinton who refused to securitize Islam, Bush who used the securitization of Islam, Obama who understood that it was not the right policy and tried to desecuritize Islam, and Trump, who is a result of that securitization.

This work also contributed to the securitization theory. A considerably new theory, securitization theory needs to be developed further and many distinguished scholars have contributed to that. What I have found during the study of why and how Islam was securitized is that there are different levels of securitization, which use different actors, audience, and methods and take different amounts of time. The systematic securitization, where the securitization of Islam fits, is a longer campaign that needs a strategy and involves everyone. Only few issues make it to the systematic securitization and the world is divided into poles as "with us" or "against us". This type of securitization is very difficult to be desecuritized and can also be misused by the political elite. What we see today as the rise of the Christian right, white supremacists, racism, and anti-Semitism has been made easier with the securitization of Islam. When one issue is securitized at the systematic level, it is easier to substitute that issue with others, like substituting Muslims with Jews, immigrants, or people of color, or substituting Islam with Judaism, liberalism, or socialism, just as Islam was securitized to fill the gap left over from communism.

This is a work of more than six years of my PhD work, started in Turkey and finished in the USA. It is also the continuation of my Master's research where I analyzed how Kosovo became a security issue and realized that international securitization is different from domestic securitization. In this journey, there are so many people that have supported, lifted, encouraged, and kept me on the right track. It will be impossible to mention all of them here as I know that I will forget some whose support has been very valuable. But it is important to mention that I feel forever in debt to Fatih University as an institution and to everyone that worked there, from the administration, to the professors, to the supporting staff. My years at Fatih University were the best in my life. Moreover, I thank Georgetown University, especially the Center for Muslim-Christian Understanding, who has hosted me to make my PhD research and continue my work to finish this manuscript. They have opened their doors and have shared their resources in the most difficult times of my academic life. Finally, I must thank Palgrave Macmillan for trusting in me and this work. It goes without saying that any mistake is solely mine and they cannot be blamed for anything I did, or didn't do, with their comments, support, and encouragement.

Washington, DC   Erdoan A. Shipoli

Acknowledgments

This book is a product of more than eight years of research. I started with the securitization theory during my Master's program and then continued in my PhD. During this time, there have been many people who have inspired, encouraged, supported, and taught me. However hard I try, most probably I will forget to mention all of them. But, I am grateful to everyone who has contributed to my academic journey. First of all, I am forever grateful to my family, for their sacrifice, encouragement, and trust. I am forever grateful to my wife, who had to support me through academic struggles, and her family who have always supported us.

Most importantly I am grateful to everyone at Fatih University, from professors, to administrators, to the supporting staff. I spent my best years at Fatih University and I never regret one day of that time. In particular I have to mention Professors (in alphabetical order) Ahmet Arabaci, Ebru Altinoglu, Gokhan Bacik, Ihsan Yilmaz, Mohamed Bakari, Ozguc Orhan, Ozlem Bagdonas, Sammas Salur, Savas Genc, and many others, who have followed me through my studies from day one of my PhD.

I am especially grateful to the Center for Muslim-Christian Understanding at Georgetown University who have accepted me as a visiting researcher to conduct the research for this book, in the most difficult time of my academic life. In particular I must thank professors John L. Esposito and John O. Voll, who have been my biggest supporters and encouragers to do this work. It could not have been done without their help. But everyone at the center, starting from professor Jonathan Brown and his team, as well as other affiliated scholars, have been very helpful and have contributed to this work. Thank you very much.

Friends, colleagues, professors, and family have all supported me and I will skip mentioning names because the space here will be insufficient but also because I am scared that I will forget someone. But know that I am grateful to all of you.

Finally, I want to thank my editor at Palgrave Macmillan, Anca Pusca, for believing in this project and supporting it to the end; her assistant Katelyn Zingg, who has given me her assistance any time I needed it; my copy editor, Michael Seyfert, who has worked tirelessly; Numan Aksoy, who has helped me since the beginning of this work; and anonymous reviewers, whose feedback have strengthened this book. Any mistake in this book is solely mine and no one mentioned above is to blame for any shortcoming of this book.

Contents

1 Introduction   1
    1.1 Structure of the Book   8
    References   12

2 Theoretical Approaches to US Foreign Policy   13
    2.1 Doctrines, Actors, and Current State   14
       2.1.1 Cold War   15
       2.1.2 9/11   17
       2.1.3 Doctrines of US Foreign Policy   18
       2.1.4 Actors in US Foreign Policy   27
    2.2 Realism   33
       2.2.1 Realism in America   35
       2.2.2 Realists' Main Arguments   36
       2.2.3 US Foreign Policy Built on Both Idealism and Realism   40
    2.3 Liberalism   42
       2.3.1 Post-Cold War Liberalism   44
       2.3.2 Liberal Arguments of Intervention   46
    2.4 Democratic Peace Theory   49
       2.4.1 Wilsonianism and the Democratic Peace   52
       2.4.2 Wilsonian Legacy Among the US Presidents   55
       2.4.3 Democratic Peace Today   58
    References   61

3 The Securitization Theory — 71
3.1 Building Blocks of the Securitization Theory — 73
3.2 The Evolution of the Securitization Theory — 78
3.3 Securitization of Religion: New Sectors in the Securitization Theory — 85
3.4 Securitization: Domestic, International, and Systematic—An Alternative to Liberalism and Realism to Explain US Foreign Policy — 91
References — 96

4 Islam in US Politics — 101
4.1 Islam in America and American Foreign Policy — 104
    4.1.1 Early History of Islam in America — 105
4.2 Islam in America Today Is Defined by Islamophobia — 114
References — 126

5 Securitization of Islam in US Foreign Policy: The Clinton Administration — 133
5.1 Democracy, Security, and Religion — 134
5.2 Pre-Clinton Administrations — 136
    5.2.1 Cold War Foreign Policy — 137
    5.2.2 The USA and the Muslim World During the Cold War — 140
5.3 Clinton Administration — 144
    5.3.1 Democracy Promotion and Islam: From Yugoslavia to the Middle East — 145
        5.3.1.1 The Jordan Speech — 155
    5.3.2 Terrorism and the Securitization of Islam — 157
References — 162

6 Securitization of Islam in US Foreign Policy: The Bush Administration — 167
6.1 George W. Bush Administration — 167
    6.1.1 The USA After 9/11 — 171
    6.1.2 War on Terror: From Weapons of Mass Destruction (WMDs) to Democracy Promotion — 175

    6.1.3 *Bringing Back the Cold War and Securitizing Islam*   185
         6.1.3.1 The Axis of Evil Speech   194
    6.1.4 *The Result of the War on Terror and the Securitization of Islam*   197
References   206

7 Desecuritization and Resecuritization of Islam in US Foreign Policy: The Obama and the Trump Administrations   211
7.1 *Obama Administration*   212
    7.1.1 *Obama's Approach Toward Islam*   214
         7.1.1.1 The Cairo Speech   214
         7.1.1.2 The Killing of bin Laden   220
         7.1.1.3 Obama's Speech at the Baltimore Mosque   221
    7.1.2 *Obama's Practice in What He Preached*   225
7.2 *Trump Administration*   233
    7.2.1 *National Security and Terrorism Speech*   236
    7.2.2 *Making Islamophobia Great Again*   239
References   252

8 US Democracy Promotion   259
8.1 *Development of the Democracy Promotion Policy in the USA*   260
8.2 *Tools, Methods, Types, and Controversies of Democracy Promotion*   265
8.3 *Democracy Promotion for Post-Cold War America: Clinton's Balkans and Bush's Middle East*   272
References   299

9 Conclusion   309
9.1 *What Next?*   315
References   319

Index   321

CHAPTER 1

Introduction

The concept of "security" is very broad, and many scholars have explained it differently. There are those who explain security only as the absence of threats to the existence of the nation and the state, as well as the core values; and there are ones who explain security as something more, including to maintain these values, the nation, or the state by victory even when they are challenged and when the war is unavoidable. For this study, the definition of the concept of security is that it is something constructed, which makes people feel safe in the absence of threats to their life, conscience, property, comfort, and thoughts, by assuring them that even if these values are threatened, they will be maintained by victory.

Securitization is a widely used concept in economics, finance, information technology (IT), and other fields, but the usage of this concept here is political only. Securitization prioritizes the issue by naming it a security issue, bringing it above politics, as an existential issue that shall be dealt with immediately. An issue is securitized when it is presented as existentially important and when the public agrees (usually by a silent consent) that the referent object shall be protected by any means.

There are three levels of dealing with political issues: the first one is *non-politicization*, undermining the issue, constructing it as unimportant; the second one is *politicization*, which brings up the issue to the discussions in the public realm; and the third level is *securitization*, which prioritizes the issue by naming it a security issue, bringing it above politics, as an existential issue that shall be immediately dealt with.

© The Author(s) 2018
E. A. Shipoli, *Islam, Securitization, and US Foreign Policy*,
https://doi.org/10.1007/978-3-319-71111-9_1

Politics is directed by security "threats", and they command people's way of life. Securitized issues determine the political agenda and highly affect the political, social, and economic life of the countries and the international community. There are some important issues that cannot be negotiated for, but there are some others that are only constructed as such. It is important to understand these issues and to understand what lies behind the idea of securitizing an issue. It is also important to understand the intentions of the ones that construct these issues as so special that they cannot be negotiated. By understanding the intentions of the actors, one can decide for themselves the importance of those issues.

The Copenhagen School of Security Studies has developed a critical theory of "securitization". This theory explains how some issues become security issues and some do not and who categorizes those issues as such (Waever 1995; Buzan et al. 1998). This book aims to develop the theory of securitization further by analyzing how and why Islam is being dealt with at the "security level" of US foreign policy.

For a referent object to be securitized, one shall argue the existential importance of that referent object. Securitization is done by uttering fragile words (such as "security", "threat", and "danger", among others) when either talking about the referent object (such as nation, state, etc.) or the threat (in this case Islam). The securitizing actors want to be able to use extraordinary means, which would not normally use, to deal with the issue at stake.

There are indicators that US foreign policy follows the Wilson doctrine, where there are "zones of shared values" (Ikenberry 2000: 120) in the world and where the USA has a grand strategy of democracy promotion. But this "promotion" of democracy during the President George W. Bush administration backfired, as Bush wanted to promote democracy in the Middle East by getting more engaged and intervene in the Middle East. The Obama administration saw the results and tried to promote democracy by looking more distantly on the idea of further intervention and instead by trying to build broader coalitions in the Middle East and in the world. In all this promotion-of-democracy politics, Islam and how they dealt with Islam played a crucial role.

Islam has always been an issue of discussion in American politics. How do we talk about Islam, its place, and relationship within the context of US security? How does the language we use to describe Islam influence the way we imagine it? How is Islam constructed as a security issue? These and similar questions are answered in this book.

This book argues that Islam has been securitized, especially during the W. Bush administration, when it was considered as a threat and as the "other" in US foreign policy. American politics had once securitized communism, race, weapons of mass destruction, and now Islam. This securitization is done through the association of Islam with security words in speeches of foreign policy and national security. By analyzing the four recent US presidents' discourses on Islam, this work sheds light on how they viewed Islam. Islam is analyzed in this work as a religion and a social reality. The current work analyzes how the US policymakers have used Islam in their discourse and how they viewed it as an ideology, because we see that for some it is an ideology that conflicts with what America stands for, whereas for others it is an ideology that aligns with America's values. This work does not analyze particular relations of the USA with Muslim majority countries or groups, but these relations are analyzed in a broader spectrum as the view toward Muslims and not toward particular groups or states.

Previously, President Clinton decided to hold back from using Islam in his foreign policy discourse, especially in his second term. Only when necessary would he include Islam in the solution and not the problem. On the contrary, President W. Bush securitized Islam in order to legitimize the promotion of democracy, the war on terror, and the invasion of Iraq. He made security a religious issue, and then he increased the security alert in America by fear, thereby constructing Islam and Muslims as the "other" and the rival. Islam was securitized by association rather than directly, increasing polarization, terror, and chaos in the world and undermining US national security that it aimed to protect. The Obama administration wanted to desecuritize Islam, by claiming that America doesn't see Islam as an enemy/rival. The administration thought that desecuritizing Islam and trying to show how Islam is compatible with democracy is the right method of democracy promotion and fight against extremism. Nevertheless, the desecuritization of Islam has remained only in discourse, whereas in practice very little progress has been made. The biggest indicator of the lack of desecuritization of Islam is the election of President Trump. In his campaign speeches, he made it clear that he and his administration see Islam as a security issue only. Although we cannot analyze his approach toward Islam now, because it is only his first year, but we can predict his approach by analyzing who he hired in senior position at the White House and his initial speeches. Today, America is in the most securitized state since the end of the Cold War. Many issues have been securitized since the new administration, and a separate study needs to be made to analyze that rapid escalation. We believe that the securitization of Islam has helped in bringing up the security atmosphere in America, and the new administration has just amplified it by including more issues.

Because there are three levels of dealing with politics—the domestic, the international, and the system level—an issue can be securitized at different levels as well. It is different in method, in what one wants to achieve, in the actors involved, and in the impact that it has.

Analyzing the securitization of Islam has shown that securitization theory needs to be developed further. Different issues are securitized at different levels, and Islam, like communism, was securitized on a global level that we called the "systematic securitization", which is a longer campaign that involves many more actors. The actors, speeches, audiences, and methods involved in "systematic securitization" are different from traditional securitization.

The leaders of the states securitize domestic political issues so that they can protect their interests, including their position and ideologies. The leaders who resort to international securitization usually want the position of their states, or groups, to remain high, so that their individual position is high as well, in international platforms. The actors at the system level securitize an issue because they want to spread their own doctrine or ideology as the right one and to promote that doctrine or ideology. This has benefits to the leaders themselves, but it also has ideological meaning, where those groups (states, organizations, interest groups) that securitize in the systematic level want to spread their ideology. Although securitizing actors do not mention their interests directly, interests play an important role when an issue is securitized.

The actors of international securitization try to maintain and benefit their interests and the interests of their group. International issues are securitized against international threats, which usually threaten internationally accepted values, security, humanity, and international peace. By securitizing internationally, a leader or a state justifies intervening in another state, to the international public, and also by engaging in "someone else's businesses" to the domestic public, which includes military, financial, or political engagements (Shipoli 2010). International securitization is also done in order to protect the idea of "what we stand for", including the responsibility to protect and to defend the values that these leaders, or states, hold dearly. For example, an American leader may argue that an intervention in a developing country is necessary to protect and promote democracy, which is what America stands for. This also is an interest to protect the ideology and the values of a particular identity.

Systematic securitization, or macro-securitization as Buzan and Waever (2009) call it, is done in order to securitize an issue to the worldwide public and engage everyone to deal with it. Differently from international securitization, in the systematic securitization the issues that concern the whole globe are securitized, and this usually divides the international politics into poles, like communism-liberalism, east-west, and recently Islamic-western. This type of securitization is usually done by a large group spread throughout the world, or a super and unitary power, not by few leaders in a particular region.

Securitization is a process that is constructed by the actors of securitization; thus it was important for this study to analyze their narrative, speech, writing, and visual. In the systematic securitization, where the securitization of Islam fits, the number and scope of the securitizing actors change. While in domestic securitization there are the political elite, governmental officials, local officials, activists, and influential local persons as securitizing actors, in the systematic securitization, this category of securitizing actors includes ideologically driven persons, religious and faith leaders, international political leaders, influential international persons, international organizations, interest groups, multinational corporations, and international media.

The most important idea of the existence of state is the security of life and property of the people, in Hobbesian terms; but today it is obvious that the state's main goal is to ensure the national security and guarantee national interest. In Wilsonian terms, to be able to ensure the national security and interests, enlarging the zones of democracy is very important, because democracies don't fight with each other, and as many democratic states as there are, the threat against the USA will decrease. This study shows that securitization is used as a tool in this context. To be able to do this, they need to name someone as a rival as "other". One comes to think that everyone needs a rival or an "other" to be able to define "self". The big states, big organizations, big interests, and big people need bigger rivals and bigger "others", so when they securitize the system they usually divide the globe into a few poles. In systematic securitization, despite the individual and state political and economic interests, there lies an interest of identifying an idea as "evil", so that the idea of securitizing actors can be defined as "the right" one. Constructing a "rival" or an "other" is not enough while securitizing, presenting them as a threat is as important. In American foreign policy, communism once held that place and after the Cold War it was about to be replaced by Islam, but it wasn't replaced until the Bush administration, when the securitization of Islam was completed.

This study has looked for the indicators of securitization in foreign policy, security, and democracy speeches of presidents and their senior officials. But most importantly this work has made a latent content analysis of the foreign policy speeches, State of the Union speeches, and speeches given by the presidents on visits to foreign countries, but that had to do with the subject of security, Islam, US foreign policy, democracy, and terrorism. We have also looked at some speeches of the high-ranking foreign policy decision-makers, such as the Secretaries of State or Presidents' Chiefs of Staff, but very limited, when they directly focused on this topic.

Some of the decision-makers, such as Vice President Cheney, directly said that Islam is totalitarian and a threat to the USA and democracy, and they directly associated Islam with such words; but most of them were latent, as they were avoiding directly framing Islam as a threat, but were doing so through association and meaning.

For President Clinton, the main doctrine on how he sees Islam in US foreign policy was the Jordan speech, a speech that has been analyzed in depth; President Bush did not have such a one-speech doctrine because he talked about Islam in most of his foreign policy speeches, especially the ones that had to do with security, so they were all analyzed. In particular was his "Axis of Evil" speech, his second State of the Union address, which was analyzed in detail, as it was directly relevant to the topic; President Obama also had a one speech that outlined his doctrine of how the USA will engage Islam in its foreign policy, the speech he made in Egypt at the beginning of his presidency. Because President Obama tried to avoid talking about Islam in most of his speeches, the speech he gave in Cairo University was analyzed as his doctrine on this issue. We have also analyzed his speech at a Baltimore mosque, as one of his latest speeches as president. These two speeches, one made at the beginning of his presidency and the other at the end, paint a good picture of how he wanted to engage with Islam when he came to power and how much he had achieved that at the end. Because this book is written at the very beginning of the Trump administration, and because he speaks about Islam and security in most of his speeches, any speech that we will analyze will be outdated by the time this book arrives to the reader. For this reason, we have analyzed President Trump's statements on Islam and security in his campaign and the first months of his administration, but we have also analyzed the backgrounds, ideologies, and views of his first senior officials toward Islam in more depth. This administration has more turnaround than any other, but people like Bannon, Gorka, Flynn, or

Miller have structured the White House, and even though some of them have left, they still have the ear of the president.

Official statements/reports of the US governmental institutions, especially the Department of State, Department of Defense, Department of Homeland Security, and Department of Justice, were analyzed for this work as well. Among others, the most analyzed official reports were the "Advancing Freedom and Democracy Reports", and "Patterns of Global Terrorism" reports, of the Department of State; "Defense Science Board" reports of the Department of Defense; "National Security Strategy" reports of the White House; and "Terrorist Research and Analytical Section" of the FBI. Why this work focused especially on these is because they are the reports that give the main information about how different institutions have viewed Islam, security, terrorism, Muslims, foreign policy strategy, and democracy. They also led to information about profiling and the construction of the "other".

We have also looked at visual records used by mainstream media, or referred to by some decision-makers, to understand how they used visuals in relation to Islam, Muslims, the Muslim world, and democracy, terrorism, security, and foreign policy.

Finally, we have used existing statistics and surveys to understand profiling and relate the discourse of the decision-makers to acts conducted in this direction. Among others, statistics on the profile of inmates and their crimes, hate speech crimes, and the profile of the people stopped for extra security check by law enforcement agencies are some of the statistics this book has used. For profiling of Muslims, Arabs, and Muslim-looking people, we found it very useful to examine the media stories of how they were portrayed, official reports of people that were banned from flying or were taken off of planes, and FBI's training materials that profiled Arabs and Muslims, among some other groups, as potential criminals to watch for.

This work has a twofold purpose. First, it analyzes whether Islam was securitized in the US foreign policy. This study has not focused on whether or not this threat, namely, Islam, is real or not, but if it was constructed as a threat that would be beyond this work, which analyzes only whether and why there was such a securitization of Islam, not if that threat was a real or an imagined security concern. Second, it aims to develop the security studies and the theory of "securitization" further. By explaining if, why, and how Islam was securitized in the US foreign policy, this study contributes to developing different levels of securitization, in terms of the scope of the issue and the actors involved.

This study also aims to understand the lessons from the Balkans and the Middle East, on the US foreign policy in both regions, and then make some speculative suggestions on how the USA shall engage in the conflicting regions.

1.1 Structure of the Book

What was the place of Islam in US political discussions from its inception within the USA? How did the US political elite come up with democracy promotion as the longest-standing foreign policy? Who are the US foreign policymakers? What is the "war on terror" policy after the 9/11 terrorist attacks? How did Islam become a security issue for the USA? How is this related to democracy promotion in the Middle East? These and similar questions are debated in this book. The introduction familiarizes the reader with the main concepts that will be talked about in the later chapters, cementing the basics for an analysis of the forthcoming chapters.

The second chapter, theoretical approaches to US foreign policy, analyzes the main theories that have guided US foreign policy. First, it introduces the main doctrines, actors, and current debates regarding US foreign policy. Second, it introduces the realist political thought and analyzes how much realism has guided US foreign policy. Afterward, it introduces the liberalist political thought and an analysis of the main debates within liberalism. A special place is given to the Democratic Peace theory, a liberal theory that has guided US foreign policy since Woodrow Wilson. Realism and liberalism are the main theories in international relations and political science, and it is important for this work to touch upon them in discussing US foreign policy. However, these theories are only analyzed in light of how much they have influenced the US policy making and not in much detail about theoretical concepts.

A special focus is made to the Wilsonian liberalism, the liberalism understood and explained by President Woodrow Wilson, which is more relevant to this study. Then this chapter talks about the notion of intervention as understood by liberalism in general and Wilson in particular. A branch of liberal ideals, democratic peace, has paved the way of the US foreign policy for decades. Based on Immanuel Kant's idea that democracies are more peaceful to each other and do not fight each other, this theory has been an important drive in the US quest for promotion of democracy abroad. In this context, we have elaborated on the formation of international organizations and a common security community initiated by the USA. Furthermore, the legacy of the democratic peace is discussed, what Wilson had in mind, and how it evolved over time by Wilson's successors.

Similar analysis is done for realism, trying to understand how much US foreign policy was influenced by realism and trying to measure if liberalism or realism was more influential. Starting from the history of realism, and continuing with its history in the USA, there is an important discussion and debate between realism and liberalism and realism and democratic peace theories. In these discussions, it is understood that US foreign policy cannot be attributed to any of the theories, and this is explained in the theoretical approach chapter.

The securitization theory, discussed in Chap. 3, is a relatively new theory, and this work argues that it is a better alternative to understand today's American foreign policy, especially toward Islam. The need to discuss the securitization theory as a separate chapter raises from the fact that this work makes an important contribution to the theory itself. The current literature on the securitization theory is limited and scattered mostly among articles in academic journals and edited books, so it will be beneficial to bring together the securitization literature, review and discuss the main debates, and state our contribution that derives from analyzing the place of Islam in US foreign policy. As it is a relatively new theory, this chapter will also serve the purpose of laying a foundation for better understanding the debates in the next chapters, where we engage the theory in explaining how Islam became a security issue for the USA and its implications.

The chapter on Islam in US politics, Chap. 4, explores the place of Islam in US politics, from history to the current times. It analyzes the encounter of Americans with Muslims; the relation of Islam, Muslims, and America during and after the Cold War; American foreign policy and Islam; Islamophobia; and finally, it introduces the campaign of the securitization of Islam in US politics, prior to going into analytical discourse of US presidents.

The following three chapters deal with the securitization of Islam in US foreign policy, and they constitute the main discussions of the book. Chapter 5 analyzes the Clinton administration's approach toward Islam and security. Before the in-depth analysis of the Clinton administration, Chap. 5 includes important discussions of administrations before Clinton and how they viewed Islam in their foreign policy. The importance of starting with this administration is because it marks the end of the Cold War, and we can argue that the securitization of Islam is a continuation of Cold War policies.

The securitization of Islam was a long campaign, especially after the Cold War. Nevertheless, while President Clinton and his administration decided to approach Islam and Muslims in a more constructive, political way, the Bush administration decided to make Islam a security issue and play along with the advocates who wanted to securitize Islam. This is discussed in Chap. 6, where we analyze how, through fear and media propaganda, the Bush administration increased the security alert in the USA within a religious context and then placed Islam as the "other", which stands opposite of what America stands for. This chapter argues that Bush and his administration securitized Islam by association rather than directly.

President Obama and his administration acknowledged that this was a wrong policy and that it threatened world peace and stability by polarizing the world into two. They decided to desecuritize Islam and bring it back into the abode of politics. But this has remained only in discourse, as it is very difficult and time-consuming to desecuritize an issue after it has already been successfully securitized. Finally, President Trump has turned back to securitizing Islam even more, with major consequences. The last two administrations are analyzed in Chap. 7 where we speak about desecuritization and re-securitization of Islam in US foreign policy. The chapter is more focused on the Obama administration because we are only in the first year of the Trump administration as we write this book. Although we can assess how the administration views Islam, it is not possible to predict the success of, or the lack of, the re-securitizing acts.

Chapter 8, on US democracy promotion, builds on the discussions of the previous chapters and argues that Islam was securitized by the Bush administration so that they can justify the "crusade" for democracy promotion in the Middle East, the war on terror, and the invasion of Iraq. It compares US policy of democracy promotion in the Balkans—namely, Bosnia and Kosovo during the Clinton administration—and the Middle East, during the Bush administration. Both regions where the USA intervened had a Muslim majority, and democracy promotion was a leading policy in both cases. Yet, they had opposite results, and how the USA viewed Islam played an important role in having two opposing results.

This chapter talks about the democratization policy during many of the US administrations, but it also talks about how this policy has evolved to be a keystone in US engagement abroad. The question of "how far is the USA ready to go for democracy promotion?" is an important debate in the political literature debate, and this chapter compared this in two regions, the Balkans and the Middle East, and identified their differences. While this chapter tried to include the debates of critics and supporters of democracy promotion, it has also put a spotlight on some of the US presidents who have used this policy vastly in their international engagements. Before the cases were discussed, the US tools and methods of democracy promotion and the type of democracy that the US promotes abroad were analyzed.

The change of discourse toward the Middle East after the Cold War is an interesting read to be able to understand the link between US foreign policy, democracy, Islam, and security. While trying to answer what most American people ask today, "why do they hate us?", this chapter has tried to understand the evolution of enmity between the Middle East and the USA.

This conclusion lays down the findings and broadens the securitization theory, on different levels of securitization, suggesting that as seen with the securitization of Islam, there are different levels of securitizing an issue. Traditional securitization, which we have called "domestic securitization", has fixed actors, audiences, and methods, which have been explained by valuable scholars. But, when an issue concerns the international community and multiple countries, we are talking about "international securitization", which includes more actors. Finally, as seen by the case of Islam in this book, or as was the situation of communism during the Cold War, there is another level of securitization, the "systematic securitization", that is the most complex form of securitization. It is a much longer campaign and includes many actors that were not visible, or were irrelevant in the previous two levels. Systematic securitization divides the whole globe into poles, and usually into two, as either "with us" or "against us".

This conclusion is different from Chap. 3 in that the previous chapter lays down the main debates and the evolution of the securitization theory and will be helpful in the main body of the book. The conclusion, on the other hand, will lay down the findings and discuss how they translate to broadening the securitization theory, which would not be understood if explained prior to Chaps. 5, 6, and 7.

The second part of the conclusion summarizes the main arguments of the book and gives some policy suggestions on how to rebuild US relations with Muslims. The USA needs to desecuritize Islam, seeing it as a religion that is not foreign to the USA and engaging Muslims as part of the problem-solving family, rather than as a security problem. As in former Yugoslavia, in the Middle East the USA needs to focus on a better strategy to rebuild the region and the relations that have been destroyed.

REFERENCES

Buzan, Barry, and Ole Waever. 2009. Macrosecuritisation and Security Constellations: Reconsidering Scale in Securitization Theory. *Review of International Studies* 35: 253–276.
Buzan, Barry, Ole Waever, and Jaap de Wilde. 1998. *Security: A New Framework of Analysis*. London/Boulder: Lynne Rienner.
Ikenberry, John G. 2000. America's Liberal Grand Strategy: Democracy and National Security in the Post-War Era. In *American Democracy Promotion: Impulses, Strategies, and Impacts*, ed. Michael Cox, G. John Ikenberry, and Takashi Inoguchi, 103–126. New York: Oxford University Press.
Shipoli, Erdoan. 2010. *International Securitization: The Case of Kosovo*. Saarbrucken: Lambert Academic Publishing.
Waever, Ole. 1995. Securitization and Desecuritization. In *On Security*, ed. Ronnie D. Lipschutz, 46–86. New York: Columbia University Press.

CHAPTER 2

Theoretical Approaches to US Foreign Policy

It has been argued that the USA has a tradition of foreign policy based on promoting democracy, which is rooted in a firm, intellectual debate. After the Cold War, the USA has had the need to find its opposite to be able to define itself. And while many ideologies, countries, or groups have taken this position, Islam has been the biggest applicant to become the new "red".[1] But this new "red" proved not to be as similar as the previous ones. With many differences, therefore, came many challenges. To be able to discuss this further, this chapter will put US foreign policy into a theoretical structure, in the theories that the US foreign policy is mainly rooted in, that is, realism and liberalism. This chapter will examine the securitization theory, the theory that this book will use to examine how Islam has become the new security issue in America. Theoretical roots and approaches show the continuous tradition of politics, which, from time to time, may have gone off limits or off the lines of those theories that the country's intellectual tradition is based on.

The USA is a relatively new country, and in comparison to the old world (Asia, Africa, and Europe), America is a newly found continent, but

---

[1] The "red" metaphor has been widely used to describe the substitution of the Soviet threat with that of Islamic threat. Authors such as Lewis (1990) and Pipes (1994), who held important positions in W. Bush's administrations, have often compared these two, and authors such as Esposito (1999), Hadar (1995), and Halliday (1995), among many others, have used the comparison of "red" versus "green" in their writings. We have elaborated more on this when we speak on the "US Foreign Policy and Islam".

© The Author(s) 2018
E. A. Shipoli, *Islam, Securitization, and US Foreign Policy*,
https://doi.org/10.1007/978-3-319-71111-9_2

with an established tradition of politics. There are three main patterns of US foreign policy that shape how she looks at the outside world: Westphalian, classical realist; anti-utopian, civilizational clashes; and Philadelphian, optimist, liberal (Cox et al. 2000: 15–16). The USA goes back and forth among the three. The tensions between American desires and the global realities will be the main factor in determining US foreign policy (Cox et al. 2000: 16). This chapter will discuss the patterns of US foreign policy and try to identify which theory it leans toward. US foreign policy has a pattern that it follows, but the methods and the amount of that pattern change from time to time. Let us first discuss the building blocks of US foreign policy in theoretical context.

2.1 Doctrines, Actors, and Current State

After a short overview of the theoretical approach of the Cold War and its continuation, along with some of the doctrines that have been directing US foreign policy ever since, this chapter will briefly discuss the main concepts, tendencies, and debates in US foreign policy. Discussing the main doctrines of the most influential US leaders and policymakers will help the reader understand that particular time's political mindset, as well as the evolution of US foreign policy. This chapter will also present the structure of how the US government is divided and the actors that have a role in US foreign policy, together with their level of influence. It is very important to understand what independent US foreign policy is, who changes its course, and what decides the legacy of the US foreign policy elite. Finally, this chapter is divided between liberalism, democratic peace, and realism, to simplify the main currents of US foreign politics. Yet, this does not mean that there are no views outside of these. A more encompassing theoretical analysis would be a work in and of itself, which is outside of this work's limits. These theories are first analyzed to define the theoretical framework. Second, they serve to help us understand how liberalism and realism—especially within the context of democratic peace—view the outside world, how they differ, and how similar they might become within particular policies.

Although there might be counterarguments, the Democratic Party in the USA is associated with liberalist thought, while the Republican Party is associated with realist thought. This is the common understanding, but it does not stand for every policy and every administration. For the sake of simplicity this chapter considers these two main theories that govern US foreign policy, and for the sake of clarification and analysis it also explains the Democratic Peace theory, not just as a new set and developed theory but also as a very influential one, especially in US foreign policy. Liberalism and realism are the two main theories that are discussed in US foreign policy with the affiliations they are made to the parties. This chapter will analyze how they see Islam in US foreign policy, their similarities and differences in theory, and then in practice according to which party is in the White House.

2.1.1 Cold War

The Cold War has been a cornerstone in US foreign policy decision-making. The Cold War marks an important pattern in US politics, where US foreign policy bases its identity, where the goal and aim of influence is clear, and where the enemy is known. With the end of the Cold War, the USA did not only remain without an enemy, but it remained without a foreign policy identity that it needed to construct again. While many policymakers and scholars argue that the USA will choose an imperial foreign policy, others think the opposite. Still, even today there is an ongoing debate of whether the USA has followed the paths to being an imperial power or not. In October 1999, Sandy Berger claimed that the first global power in history that is not imperial is the USA; nevertheless, American sovereignty is needed to overcome a world with no rules, no verification, and no constraints (Berger 2000). America sees itself as the "Great Example" that will be divided, lose its free institutions, and introduce anarchy if it becomes imperial (Geertz 1973: 12). In this sense, US policymakers see the country as a global power that could and should maintain its line without descending into despotism. In this case the USA's role would be to oversee global peace; otherwise it would be a place without rules. This idea is seen as problematic, as American policymakers consider that anything that must be done in the world must be in line with American values and American ideology.

Even though the Cold War was over by 1991, the same rhetoric continued during the 1990s and into the new century. American fear of foreign ideas—once communism, now Islamic fundamentalism—occupies the official thinking of US bureaucrats (Cameron 2002). In the USA, the official thinking is that there is a perceived need to stand against threats—previously the Soviet Union and now Iraq, Iran, and other Middle Eastern countries. Modern US political thought has been defined by the Cold War, or the securitization of communism. After the Cold War the USA needed another country or idea to define itself against, so the need to securitize another issue arose. This perceived need to fight against threats is not only limited to countries, it can be extended to ideas too: Communism after the First World War and Islam after 9/11, both of which have been securitized to be the perceived threats that the USA should stand against. The preference to use military power to fight these threats has always been an option for US policymakers in the post-Cold War era. While communism had its own economic, social, and political ideology and followers, Islam is different. One can find an economic, political, and social ideology based on Islam that will differ or oppose that of the USA. If it cannot be found, it can be constructed. The shared characteristics of "self-selecting, self-recruiting and self-perpetuating foreign and security policy elite" have continued the American Cold War and post-Cold War policy (Cameron 2002: 181).

After the Cold War, the USA had to rethink its foreign policy priorities and strategies by deciding how much it wanted to engage in global issues. During the Clinton administration, the USA became interested in global issues with Europe as its priority foreign policy focus, along with conflicts in the Balkans and the enlargement of North Atlantic Treaty Organization (NATO). While Bill Clinton paid more attention to the Middle East and Africa than any previous president, George W. Bush was much more limited to domestic issues, that is, until September 2001. After September 2001, the foreign policy that W. Bush focused on can be understood from its budget spending, when military spending exceeded the non-military spending abroad. The September 11 attacks changed US foreign policy focus from Europe, Latin America, and Africa to the Middle East, Asia, and the Persian Gulf. This new US foreign policy brought a new divided world where one is either with the USA or against the USA, according to US decision-makers. According to how countries responded to the demand of the USA to fight in the Middle East, they were judged as "among us" or "against us", and by doing so, the USA lost some of its longtime allies such as France and Germany (Gordon and Shapiro 2004; Newhouse 2001; Perry 2001; Blinken 2001; McWallace 2001). The discussions of US foreign policy priorities and how the USA should engage with the outside world are still a matter of debate as this work is being written.

The method of engagement of the USA in the Middle East, Asia, and the Gulf has opened ways to stereotyping of other cultures by Americans. Surely a very dangerous phenomenon, Islamophobia became a problem of racism, thus decreasing understanding or sympathy for other cultures or for something that is different from one's own. This increased alienation has pushed people to denigrate other cultures as backward and has constructed a perceived need to change them even by force if needed. This is not new in America, as it was very apparent in the relations with African and Native American people before. But today this stereotyping governs the American relationship with the peoples of the developing world in general. American foreign policymakers have at times used racial hierarchy to inform their decisions and have shown hostility toward whatever is outside American norms (Spellberg 2013; Hunt 2009). But most importantly, Americans believe that the nation's greatness is directly linked to the promotion of liberty, that is, to making the world safe for liberty. Middle Eastern people, and Islam, have been approached similarly. This approach and other methods of "otherizing" first and then securitizing the Middle East and Islam have been the methods that the USA used in its military war and psychological and public relations (PR) war after 9/11.

2.1.2 9/11

The 9/11 attacks in New York and Washington DC dragged the USA into an atmosphere that is not new in Asia, Africa, Latin America, or the Middle East. During the Cold War, the USA faced a Soviet-type specter challenging American values. Terror, random violence, class struggles, and other types of violence came to the USA, and the USA decided to collaborate and bargain even with dictators in different countries, believing that they would bring more security to the well-being of the USA (McMahon 1981; Thorne 1979; Louis 1978). The advantages and disadvantages of the collaboration or bargain of the USA with these dictators are debatable as to the national security of America. The US leaders' main concern was the security of the USA, and they showed that they are ready to do anything they saw necessary for this purpose. US foreign policy saw a bigger shift after 9/11 than after the Cold War. With the 9/11 attacks, the new paradigm of the US foreign policy was the war on terror. In this "new" era of US foreign policy the questions debated were not whether the system should be unilateralism or multilateralism, but rather the question of whether the USA should continue to play an international role or retreat from that to decrease threats against its soil. Even in this debate there was no question of isolationism, as the USA did not hesitate to answer the calls to intervene in other countries, to find terrorists in foreign lands (Cameron 2002: 174). The "new realism" of the Bush administration portrayed the world as bipolar, and the questions are, first, whether the USA will respond to the deeper causes of terrorism, and second, whether the USA will recognize the benefits of international cooperation beyond fighting terrorism.

2.1.3   Doctrines of US Foreign Policy

These important decisions and viewpoints of how the USA should be engaged, as well as how the USA sees the world, are a matter of doctrines that influential US political elites develop. To answer those questions, it is important to find doctrines of these political leaders that have shaped US foreign policy at particular times in its history. Fortunately, US foreign policy is filled with doctrines and this chapter will mention some of them to be able to understand the US theoretical approach to foreign policy and to answer those questions that were asked above. Having a doctrine has become a matter of prestige among American presidents first and then among other policymakers. A foreign policy doctrine is a belief system and statement on foreign policy, made by nation's chief executives, chief diplomats, or political thinkers. These doctrines provide rules of foreign policy and show the view of that administration, but in some cases the doctrines are formed, or named, after the end of that person's foreign policy engagement, to show the legacy of that person, or administration. Today these doctrines have been very ambiguous and mystifying, but they are important to show a roadmap of US foreign policy. Below are some analyses of some of the most important policies of the most important policymakers in US foreign policy.

President *James Monroe* made the first major presidential foreign policy doctrine. Uttered at his State of Union Address, he made it clear that his foreign policy legacy will be based on not allowing European powers to colonize American independent states. In return, Monroe promised to stay out of European wars (Monroe 1823).

Among the most important doctrines is that of President Theodore Roosevelt, whose vision of "world power" has guided US foreign policy since. Also known as the Roosevelt Corollary, he amended the Monroe Doctrine, to include the American struggle to help stabilize Latin American nations, economically and politically (Quinn 2013: 37–52). He believed in Latin America as being an agency for expended US commercial interests as well as keeping European hegemony limited. Roosevelt accused the doubters that America will be the rising world power as "not worth their salt," but he also made the same remarks for those who did not believe that this role should be given to the USA and that it is for the best of all the unfortunate people around the world. Roosevelt knew that national greatness is not done by words but by wars and struggles, because he acknowledged that the greatest nations were the fighting nations; thus the USA should take the responsibility to fight its rivals. But just as important is the responsibility to rescue declining nations. Only through these two actions can the USA build and maintain national greatness (Quinn 2013; Hunt 2009). Roosevelt also strongly believed in the difference of race and he claimed that the USA should help the Asians and Africans to get out of their chains, but they should not be left alone for several decades, until those nations can learn to stand on their own (Quinn 2013). Similarly, President Jackson claimed in his farewell speech that the USA and Americans have been blessed and have been chosen as the guardians of freedom, but for the benefit of the whole human race (Jackson 1837).

President Woodrow Wilson, although he recognized the power of the USA, was not focused on his nation's greatness and global might, but rather on the moral responsibility to help the weak and the suffering to refine the American spirit. From the 1890s Wilson saw as a moral obligation of America to transform Asia, but to do this only for their welfare and not any other hidden agenda (Thompson 2013; Link 1966). Even though Wilson was against imperialism and taking over other countries, in 1898 he claimed that it was better that Spain be taken by the USA than by other powers such as Germany or Russia (Link 1966). One of the most important milestones of the Wilsonian idea was the formation of the United Nations, created by President Franklin D. Roosevelt afterward. This doctrine marked the beginning of US engagement in multinational organizations to maintain peace and stability (Moore and Pubantz 2006: 49).

President Harry Truman believed in the need to build a new consensus that Roosevelt had put forth to fight against communism, and in a speech he made to Congress on March 12, 1947, he laid down the policy that became known as the "Truman Doctrine". He believed that the USA's policy should be to support nations who are fighting against subjugation by armed minorities or outside powers. If the USA fails to help them, world peace may be endangered, and the welfare of the American nation would be endangered (Hastedt 2015: 14–17; McLean 1986: 41). All of the above ideologies address the responsibility of the USA to help the less developed nations, but they all claim that even when liberated they needed to be taken under western tutelage in order to learn the steps of democracy. Otherwise, premature democracies may easily be fooled by Moscow, including the relevant countries of Greece and Turkey (Hastedt 2015: 13–25; McLean 1986). Under Truman the USA was prepared to send money, equipment, and even military force to the countries that were threatened by communism. In his own words, "the policy of the United States is to support free people who are resisting attempted subjugation by armed minorities or by outside pressures" (Truman 1947). Truman claimed that if Greece and Turkey fall to communism, this will have incredible consequences throughout the region. And in May 22, 1947, he granted $400 million in military and economic aid to Greece and Turkey.

President Eisenhower continued Truman's doctrine to help the countries threatened by Soviet Union, but he amended it to include countries that sought American help in this regard, which makes his doctrine different from that of Truman's. In his address to Congress he claimed that his doctrine in foreign policy is "to secure and protect the territorial integrity and political independence of such nations, requesting such aid against overt armed aggression from any nation controlled by international communism" (Eisenhower 1957). The doctrine did not target only the countries that were threatened by the Soviet Union—though that was its primary focus—because it was more general, especially as during this time there was the problem of the Suez Canal and similar possibilities of hostility in different regions (Crabb 1982; Cox et al. 2013: 1–12).

As for the doctrine of President John F. Kennedy, it is arguably a continuation of the Monroe Doctrine. He openly supported the containment and reversal of communism in the Western Hemisphere, especially in Latin America. He voiced his doctrine in his inaugural address on January 20, 1961, saying "Let every nation know, whether it wishes us well or ill, that we shall pay any price, bear any burden, meet any hardship, support any friend, oppose any foe, in order to assure the survival and the success of liberty", and he called for public support in "a struggle against the common enemies of man: tyranny, poverty, disease, and war itself" (Kennedy 1961). This address later made up most of his administration's mindset and evolved even further during the Cold War with an "us versus them" narrative, which has continued to the present day.

President Lyndon Johnson declared that "when the object is the establishment of a communist dictatorship" domestic revolution is not a local matter anymore (Johnson 1963) and he used this narrative to intervene in the Dominican Republic.

Addressing the nation regarding the Vietnam War, President Nixon explained in November 3, 1969, that the USA now expects that her allies take primary responsibility for their own military defense; that the USA will keep all her treaty commitments; that the USA will provide help if a nuclear power threatens any of her allies, or to nations that are vital to US security; and, finally, that the USA will provide economic and military assistance when requested from her allies, nevertheless the USA expects that those allies resume primary responsibility for their own defense and provide the manpower (Nixon 1969b). With this doctrine, the USA pulled out of Vietnam and it is often called as the "Vietnam Doctrine".

President Jimmy Carter set the US rules of engagement in the Middle East. In his State of the Union Address in 1980, President Carter set his doctrine in accordance with US interest in the Middle East, specifically the Persian Gulf, and the tone of the words in accordance with making the message clear for the Soviets to stay out of the Persian Gulf. In his own words, "The Soviet Union is now attempting to consolidate a strategic position, therefore, that poses a grave threat to the free movement of Middle East oil" and that America sees it "as an assault on the vital interests of the United States of America, and such an assault will be replied by any means necessary, including military force" (Carter 1980).

Among the most controversial doctrines was that of Ronald Reagan. His doctrine was a cornerstone in supporting guerilla groups in fighting communism, as was set forth in his fifth State of the Union Address, "We must not break faith with those who are risking their lives ... on every continent, from Afghanistan to Nicaragua ... to defy Soviet aggression and secure rights which have been ours from birth. Support for freedom fighters is self-defense" (Reagan 1985), America will financially and militarily support these groups. Reagan called for support to the Contras in Nicaragua, the mujahedeen in Afghanistan, and the National Union for the Total Independence of Angola (UNITA) in Angola, which brought many scandals and questions that today commentators still deal with, such as the Iran-Contra Scandal, or even the birth of Al-Qaeda. Nevertheless, many consider that it was the Reagan Doctrine that brought the Soviet Union to its downfall and the Cold War to an end.

President Bill Clinton did not have a clear doctrine, but that is common for the presidents after the Cold War. Their foreign policy legacy is now considered as their doctrine. President Clinton's doctrine is known as the doctrine of interventionism. He suggested that the USA should not stand aside when human rights are being violated in other places of the world because of someone's religious, racial, or ethnic backgrounds. Within this political ideology he intervened in Yugoslavia, Africa, and other places in the world. In his own words,

> It's easy ... to say that we really have no interests in who lives in this or that valley in Bosnia, or who owns a strip of brushland in the Horn of Africa, or some piece of parched earth by the Jordan River. But the true measure of our interests lies not in how small or distant these places are, or in whether we have trouble pronouncing their names. The question we must ask is, what are the consequences to our security of letting conflicts fester and spread. We cannot, indeed, we should not, do everything or be everywhere. But where our values and our interests are at stake, and where we can make a difference, we must be prepared to do so. (Clinton 1999)

Similarly, George W. Bush had no established doctrine, but what is considered as his legacy are his eight years of foreign policy as president. In this respect, President Bush's doctrine is constructed by the tragic events of 9/11, and everything around it. What we can consider as his doctrine are the policies of treating countries that harbor terrorists in the same way as the terrorists; preventive wars, considering that invading Iraq would prevent attacks to America; democratic promotion, even if it means by force (Lynch 2013: 178–193); and most importantly, "crusading" for democracy and American security.

After the Cold War, the US political ideology has focused on keeping America safe and prospering. These years find America very divided: unilateralism against multilateralism, free trade against protectionism, how to deal with the failed states and terrorism, and American values in general (Lynch 2013: 178–193; Cameron 2002: xii). President George H. W. Bush coined the phrase "New World Order" after the collapse of communism and vowed that the USA is the maker of this order; President Clinton constantly talked about the "expanding of democracy and free markets"; George W. Bush pledged in his first inauguration speech "to keep America strong and free", nevertheless the terrorist threats found America undecided on how to respond to this new phenomenon, which is itself a result of globalization.

Realists like George Kennan, on the other hand, argued that morality and the freedoms and liberty of nations are only superficial and that countries cannot conduct their foreign policy on these assumptions. He accused the experts of US foreign policy, and the policymakers they advise, of carrying no intellectual baggage (Kennan 1983, 1984) and thus being out of touch with reality. As an alternative to Kennan, William Appleman Williams redefined the foreign policy ideology in terms of economic interest. Contrary to Kennan, Williams claimed that the US foreign policy is sophisticated, strategically correct, and doable. But Williams claimed that this functional ideology is only a tool used by American capitalism to maintain its economic power and sociopolitical control. He argued that US foreign policy will be driven by the economic interests (Williams 2009; Siracusa 1973: 24–26). Like Kennan, Williams suggested that Americans learn to preserve democracy and prosperity without imperial expansion. William recommended that the USA should liquidate the Cold War, channel development aid through the United Nations, and reorder American domestic life, which is the most important point. Otherwise, the USA will continue to operate along well-established lines (Williams 2009: 210; 2001: 17).

Scholars still argue about what President Barack Obama's doctrine was. Some argue that he embraced a more collective security foreign policy doctrine. While approaching every problem differently, he was more focused on negotiation and collaboration rather than confrontation. President Obama expressed his reservations of a "doctrinated" foreign policy approach (Dionne 2009), but said that the USA should "view our security in terms of a common security and a common prosperity with other peoples and other countries" (New York Times 2007) when asked directly at a democratic presidential debate. In an interview for Brian Williams of NBC Nightly News, in March 19, 2011, President Obama tried to put an end to this "doctrine" debate by claiming that all the countries and regions need to be taken separately because they are very different, and therefore one cannot have rules of foreign policy that will be suitable for all of them (Dionne 2009). Although his doctrine is considered as a shift from that of George W. Bush, today Obama's foreign policy in the Middle East is remembered with failed attempts to move troops, more engagement of the USA in Middle Eastern wars, and a drastic increase in drone attacks (Rohde 2012). There is still not much written about the Obama Doctrine, because of the busy agenda in US politics with the new president. As far as his domestic doctrine and legacy, the Healthcare Bill is what Obama left behind. But, as far as the foreign policy doctrine is concerned, Obama preferred to stay out of trouble whenever he could; he over-calculated every move and wanted to engage only on issues that he could have a quick impact; he wanted to share the responsibilities with other countries and not act alone; he also wanted to decrease any potential risks by not spreading the USA too thin in foreign policy. His doctrine, or at least what we know for now, is analyzed more deeply when we speak about his foreign policy in Chap. 8.

While many debate the guiding principles and doctrines of US foreign policy, there are those who think that the USA has no foreign policy principles and that she is only running on the gas of the Cold War (Kupchan 2001: 29). Others define the US foreign policy guiding principles on the sets of ideas such as that of Hamilton, who emphasized strong government and support for businesses; that of Wilson, who emphasized America's democratic mission; that of Jefferson, who emphasized the importance of protecting American values at home; and that of Jackson, who emphasized the military and economic strength. According to this equation, Clinton demonstrated a Hamiltonian and Wilsonian mix, while W. Bush demonstrated a more Jeffersonian and Jacksonian one. Finally, the "examplarists" and "vindicators" agree that the USA has the responsibility to better the world. The first argue that interfering in the affairs of other states will not only do harm to those states but will also jeopardize American values at home, and therefore the USA should only serve as a humane, democratic, and prosperous example; the second argue that the USA has the responsibility to take active measures beyond being an example, to better the world (Morgenthau 1969; Cameron 2002: 175; Kupchan 2001). These doctrines or thoughts in US foreign policy were present for a long time and their common claim is that world politics is changing, is affecting US power, and so the USA should be ready for these changes and keep her eyes open in foreign policymaking.

The debate on how the USA should engage in this changing world has divided US scholars, including those that work on US foreign policy, in many camps. It has been difficult to put US foreign policy into a particular category. Some call it multilateralism, others unilateralism, some idealism, while others isolationism, but still there is no common definition of US foreign policy. Among the most commonly used terms to describe US foreign policy is multilateralism, which puts forward the importance of international/multilateral organizations and is promoted by the USA. Among the international organizations, the USA sees NATO as a far more important organization than the United Nations (Smith 2009: 60), and this has a lot to do with the conflicts in the Balkans, particularly Kosovo, where the USA failed to take the UN on board and acted with NATO for an effective campaign against the violation of human rights and peace. Not all of the organizations are seen as equally important for the

USA, as those organizations that promote democracy, the pillar of the US foreign policy, may not be dominated by market democracies and thus fail to protect peace.

After 9/11 many expected that the USA would lean more toward multilateralism, as not to act alone on issues that concern others. Nevertheless, President Bush proved these expectations wrong, and as the administration acted alone against the Taliban, it also did not conform to internationally important issues such as Kyoto, the International Criminal Court, or the Comprehensive Nuclear-Test-Ban Treaty (CTBT) and other arms control treaties. During the early 2000s the world saw that the USA is prepared to work with other countries and organizations if that is necessary to achieve US foreign policy goals, but the common preference would be to work with no international limitations or constraints (Cameron 2002; Ikenberry 2000; Buzan and Waever 2003; Buzan and Gonzalez-Pelaez 2009), and the USA would not conform with other organizations if they pose limits to the acts it wants to take.

The biggest ongoing debate about US foreign policy is done between multilateralists and unilateralists. Many argue that the George W. Bush administration had been more comfortable in its use of unilateralist foreign policy, especially when compared to Bill Clinton. Although there is no clear-cut line among the parties in the USA, on which one is unipolar and which one is multipolar, there is a common belief that there are more unilateralists among the Republicans and more multilateralists among the Democrats in the US Congress (Kupchan 2001: 29; Cameron 2002: 176). The main argument that the unilateralists make is that America should accept no limitations as she is so powerful and she should not trade the autonomy of decision-making with anyone (Berger 2000; Kissinger 2001: 19; Cameron 2002: 176). Scholars like Huntington argue that the USA is more welcomed, and thus less threatened, when she acts in cooperation with others, instead of being a "rogue superpower" perusing only her interests and not caring enough for the interests of others (1992, 1999). Similarly, Nye (2002) claims that the ones that focus only on the imperial role are neglecting the importance of ideological, economic, and cultural power, thus focusing only on one. It is wrong to suggest that multilateralism and unilateralism are opposing concepts (Smith 2009: 63), because their biggest debate revolves around similar examples of America's foreign policy. Currently the most debated are the policies of the USA during the crises in Bosnia, Kosovo, Afghanistan, or Iraq, and interestingly both camps portray these events according to their own views, and when they accuse the other camp for failure they still use the same examples.

Another camp is that of the isolationists, who argue that American foreign policy has tended to be more isolationist at many times, and thus US foreign policy has gone back and forth between greater extremes than those of multilateralism and unilateralism. They argue that US foreign policy has gone between globalism and isolationism, and they are very hostile to a middle ground, claiming that foreign policy should be seen as "either, or" (Morgenthau 1969; Kull and Destler 1999). This history of intervention abroad brings other debates among US foreign policy scholars who discuss the real role of the USA in the world. The ultimate question is whether the USA should be a reluctant sheriff, trying to mediate peace, or a "globocop" (Friedman 2001: 467; Buchanan 1999; Cameron 2002: 181–182; Johnson 2000). The interventionist camp, headed by Wolfowitz, Rumsfeld, Cheney, and similar American Enterprise Institute policy makers, is very loud among US policy makers, and although they might not agree to what extent the USA should intervene in foreign issues, they agree that the USA must intervene to ensure the well-being of the USA, and her interests, including the values that she upholds, such as free market, democracy, human rights, and others.

Usually when one speaks about the USA's "imperialism", they say it in an insulting way, but there are others from conservative circles who think that America should answer the calls and accept its hegemonic role sooner rather than later. Although the USA should decide on what kind of hegemony it will follow, her role is inescapable for the Pax Americanas. By accepting her role, the USA should impose her values and defend her interest, which are the best and most applicable in the world, according to this camp (Huntington 1992, 1999; Wittkopf and McCormick 1999). Among the most important defenders of this camp, the "Pax Americana", is Thomas Donnelly from the Project for the New American Century. He criticizes Bush for trying to create a more modest realist policy or balance of power while trying to recognize the new reality that the USA is a new empire and should be managed as such as soon as possible so that it can adjust the USA's military and foreign policy to fit this mission. Furthermore, this camp argues that pushing for this American perimeter in Europe, the Persian Gulf, and East Asia should be the priority and provide the main mission for the US armed forces in the decades to come (Baker 2001). Andrew Bacevich claims that the main US strategy, although unspoken of, lies in maintaining its global power, since there is hardly any public figure who questions maintaining this power until the end of times (quoted in Cameron 2002: 186). Most of this system was built during the Cold War

(Ikenberry 2001), where America was successful in building a world around her interests and core values. While conservative scholars rightly claim that most Americans are already used to America running the world and that it would be difficult for them to let this go, their critics call on the US administration to focus more on domestic issues that they are promoting abroad. America has many domestic problems that should be tackled too, such as poverty, illiteracy, crime, violence, or homelessness (Wittkopf and McCormick 1999: 5).

With the end of the Cold War, and the vacuum it created, it was very natural for liberal internationalist thought to gain importance. Arguing the benefits of the Wilsonian doctrine, the followers of this theory tend to embrace the ones that want to have a place among the free-market democracies, as well as the enlargement of the community of democracies, as stated by Clinton (Smith 2009: 65–66). They have also developed what is today known as the "Democratic Peace theory", and this chapter will speak more broadly about the liberal theories, specifically the Democratic Peace theory, below. Although the Democratic Peace theory is only one branch of liberal theory, it is an important branch as far as this work is concerned and as far as US foreign policy is concerned. For this reason, it has been given a separate section to be explained in depth, but it will be useful to first briefly introduce the actors of US foreign policy.

2.1.4 Actors in US Foreign Policy

Today there is a legacy of US foreign policy, and therefore one should not underestimate the importance of how the US government is divided and of the actors of US foreign policy. Their role is very important and to be able to understand a particular issue in a particular administration, one should also understand the role that the foreign policy influencers play in US politics, starting from the president to public opinion. It has been discussed above that American foreign policy has a long legacy and cannot be changed in the course of four to eight years of one president's mandate. US foreign policy has many actors that keep the checks and balances of this legacy, thus their influence and their role in the US foreign policy are of utmost importance. We must know who influences foreign policy and to what extent.

The US governmental system is characterized by the functionality of the separation of powers, as stated in the US Constitution, and is shared among the president, the Congress (the House of Representatives and the

Senate), and the Supreme Court. Depending on how favorable the president is in congress, and the partisan balance, the president can be the greatest influencer of the US politics (Neustadt 1960, 1990). On foreign policy matters the president is usually the decision-maker and has greater influence, and so the White House has been under the radar of foreign statesmen, lobbyists, interest groups, and media. Depending on the influence that the president's party has in congress, and the balances there, the president can have a more active or passive influence in US foreign policy. Nevertheless, president's mandate plays an important yet limited role, for US foreign policy. A four-year term is very short for big changes, calculations, or strategies in foreign policy. This is one of the reasons why the presidents of the USA choose to follow an ideology, to be more focused. The first year of a new president is consumed by adaptation to the office and its foreign policy, followed by up to two years for the US President to recover from the campaign, balance the promises of the campaign with the reality, and name senior foreign policy staff and ambassadors, which usually takes six months to get approved by the senate (Wittkopf and McCormick 1999: 108; Neustadt 1960, 1990).

The US Vice President usually plays a supporting role, as his foreign policy is usually limited to travels abroad for funerals, conferences, or visiting foreign countries. But the roles of the VPs are always arguable, and they change according to the interests, international recognition, and also the popularity of the VP (Woodward 2004: 175). There can be vice presidents who choose to remain more ceremonial and those who refuse to remain ceremonial and want a place in the field, for example, Cheney during the George W. Bush administration.

The National Security Council is the laboratory of the president's foreign policy mindset. Composed of the Vice President, the Secretary of State, the Secretary of Defense, the Director of the Intelligence (CIA), the Chairman of the Joint Chiefs of Staff, and the National Security Advisor, the National Security Council continuously advises the president on foreign policy and prepares briefings on US foreign policy. Some senior bureaucrats have come from the position of NSC National Security Advisor, including Condoleezza Rice, Sandy Berger, Zbigniew Brzezinski, Henry Kissinger, and many others (Cameron 2002: 41–44; Destler et al. 1984).

The State Department is the official foreign policy conductor, but its roles can be summarized as leading and coordinating US representation abroad; conducting negotiations and concluding agreements and treaties;

managing the international affairs budget; and coordinating and supporting international activities of other US agencies (Destler et al. 1984; Cameron 2002).

The Department of Defense, commonly referred to as the Pentagon, is responsible for military strategy and policy of the USA, and it is very much engaged in the USA's foreign policy. The role of the Department of Defense has always been a heated debate in American politics, especially when some secretaries of defense get more engaged in foreign policy statements, like Donald Rumsfeld's famous division of Europe into the "old Europe" and the "new Europe" (Clark 2001; Halberstam 2001; Destler et al. 1984).

The USA has 15 intelligence agencies that form the US Intelligence Community, which play an invaluable role in creating US foreign policy. Although they have been criticized a lot, for not being able to give accurate intelligence for issues such as Saddam's ownership of weapons of mass destruction (WMD) and sometimes for having too much influence on the US President, the USA's defense and foreign policy heavily rely on the work of the intelligence community (Bamford 2001, 2004).

President Bush established another department in 2002, that of Homeland Security, which controls the borders and transportation security, emergency issues, chemical, biological, and nuclear precautions, as well as information analysis and infrastructure protection (Cameron 2002: 64). A very debatable department from day one, the Department of Homeland Security has overlapped many times with the FBI and the CIA.

With the end of the Cold War, foreign policy actors such as the US Congress have been taking more active roles. Not just because Congress approves funding for the government's activities but also because Congress has used its power in regulating trade, approving presidential nominations, and ratifying treaties, and it is the power of the Congress to declare war (Cameron 2002: 66). The end of the Cold War has also brought to discussions the US values in the foreign policy. This shift has resulted in the visits of foreign statesmen who want to meet with key Congress members when they visit Washington DC and the focus of lobby groups of foreign countries in the Congress.

After the Cold War, there was an increase in the number of non-formal foreign policy actors in the USA, while the roles of the traditional ones that were mentioned above have declined. These actors have not been governmentally established, so their main roles are in creating influence and pressure on the decision-makers. Lobby groups, business interest groups, trade unions, non-governmental organizations, international organizations, think tanks, religious groups, and foreign governments are only a few of these actors. It is well known that lobby groups play a huge role on the decision-makers in Washington DC. Ethnic lobbies being among the most powerful (Kennan 1997: 4; Mearsheimer and Walt 2007), business lobbies are also very influential (Smith 2000: 48). Samuel Huntington in the March/April 1997 issue of Foreign Affairs claimed that it is of utmost importance to analyze and understand these lobby groups if one wants to understand US foreign policy. Most of the time these lobbies unite with each other in coalitions to increase their influence on specific issues. It is common for the Armenian lobby to unite with the Greek lobby when it comes to pressuring Turkey, for example.

Public opinion is another very important factor, and this has been true since the Vietnam War (Kull and Destler 1999). This factor is especially important for American domestic political actors, who target public opinion when they take a decision, first and foremost because they want to be reelected and second because they want to have the public on their side when pursuing their political agenda.

Media is another very important influential factor in the US foreign policy. We have left the media as a foreign policy actor for last because of its importance to securitizing an international and systematic issue. The media as an actor is given a larger portion of this work, and because the elite have used the media to make their speeches and securitization, the media has constructed the security in the USA and has helped to prioritize issues.

The "CNN Effect" is a great denominator of the USA's foreign policy equation. Some politicians have started using media coverage and images for their own goal after they saw how important the media coverage and reporting have been. Especially when dealing with an international issue, international threat, or a faraway enemy, media plays a very important role as a medium to get the information about that issue, threat, or enemy. What the media can do is bring an issue to the agenda, prioritize an issue, and challenge the governments and their decisions. Recalling the decision of George H. W. Bush to intervene in Somalia in 1992, one can understand how influential international media can be in pushing a decision-maker to take decisions that favor that medium's choice:

> Finally, in 1999, George Bush himself asserted that it was news media coverage that motivated him to intervene in Somalia: Former President Bush conceded Saturday that he ordered US troops into Somalia in 1992 after

seeing heart-rending pictures of starving waifs on television. ... Bush said that as he and his wife, Barbara, watched television at the White House and saw "those starving kids ... in quest of a little pitiful cup of rice", he phoned Defense Secretary Dick Cheney and General Colin Powell, chairman of the Joint Chiefs of Staff. "Please come over to the White House", Bush recalled telling the military leaders. "I – we – cannot watch this anymore. You've got to do something." (Hines 1999)

This is called the CNN Effect, which is not reserved for CNN alone because the Associated Press, BBC, Reuters, Agence France-Presse also have similar, some higher and some lower, influence. The CNN Effect refers to the effect that these big international media, altogether, have.[2]

Studies show that television is the primary source of information in the USA. The rate of Americans who consider television as their primary source has risen from 29% in 1962 to 51% in 1980 and skyrocketed to 81% after 9/11. Same studies show that this is a result of emotional reaction as the news that followed the attacks of 9/11 generally had an emotional impact on people's psychology (Robinson 2002). Continuous visual representation of 9/11 in US television afterward and also the live feeds of the Iraqi war were key factors in the US perception of threats and enemies and important building blocks of the construction of security in the USA (McDonald 2008). Images influence people to give their support to the government or the opposition; some countries are prioritized over others according to how much media time is given to them; images are also used

---

[2] The story behind how this turned out to be called the CNN effect is best explained by Babak Bahador (2007: 3): "At 2:38 am, on January 17, 1991, the residents of Baghdad were woken by the launch of the first Gulf War. [...] Later that same night, a senior officer at Pentagon Command Center checked his watch while speaking to those planning the air attack and stated, while watching one broadcast, 'If the cruise missile is on target ... the reporter will go off the air about ... Now!' He was right. At that moment, the American Broadcasting Company (ABC) and the National Broadcasting Company (NBC) reports from Baghdad stopped broadcasting. These networks were relying on Iraqi communications network, which had just been destroyed. Cable News Network (CNN), which was transmitted over a dedicated circuit set up before war, however, remained on air. For the next two weeks, CNN was the only American television network broadcasting from Iraq. As a result, this relatively new and renegade organization that promised to be different by delivering 24-hour news surged in recognition and prestige. Its subscription base, in fact, grew substantially over the period of the Gulf War. Its name also became synonymous with rapid image and information transmission from the scene of action and, more importantly, the implication of this phenomenon on politics and foreign policy."

to gain support for a particular decision that has already been taken or challenge a decision that has been taken so it is taken back.

It is no coincidence that we consider today as the communications and technology era, where there are mediums of different voices that compete for audience. The CNN Effect was present much earlier than Al-Jazeera. Nevertheless, Al-Jazeera became an alternative player in the international media market that brings up-to-date news from the Middle East, bringing the "other" side of the story and entering deeper into the field. During the war in Afghanistan, CNN and other western media outlets had communicated incredible information on the military strategy, precision of the strikes, and descriptions of the events, while Al-Jazeera brought up the human consequences of the war (Bahador 2007). The birth of Al-Jazeera and its coverage of the war in Afghanistan polarized international media: the CNN Effect being the effect of the western media, and the Al-Jazeera effect being the effect of the media on the ground, local and independent from the big media corporations of the west. Alternatively, today the fastest videos are produced by the amateur witnesses on the scene that need only a phone with a camera and Internet connection to send the video to the international audience. The pictures that were leaked from the Abu Ghraib prison have shown that simple and cheap technology can trigger an emotional response and be an important asset to the securitizing actors (Buzan and Hansen 2009).

The media effect is highest when there is uncertainty in the public and among the decision-makers; thus the greatest consequence of the CNN Effect is its influence on setting the agenda. Media frames an issue as priority and pushes the decision-makers to deal with that issue prior to others. After prioritizing the issue, the media then defines the course of action, especially when the decision-makers have started looking for solutions (Linsky 1986: 130–145; Robinson 2002: 38; Bahador 2007: 9). On the one hand, the role of the media is to "help" decision-makers make up their mind; help governments to gain support; enable the implementation of that decision; help pursue the course of action; and then build a domestic "constituency" who will support that decision (Robinson 2002: 12–40). On the other hand, public opinion can act as a mediator between the media and the government. They can pressure, question, and challenge the government through media. Some interest groups, for example, will target the public through media to pressure the government and the politicians who want to win the next elections or leave a legacy.

From the analysis above, one can understand how complicated US foreign policy is and how its legacy has continued. It is likely that the number of actors will continue to increase to include non-state actors like civil society organizations, transnational organizations and companies, non-governmental organizations, or international organizations; these dynamics have kept the consistency of US foreign policy as well as the checks and balances in the decision-making system of the USA. Today, with the Trump administration, we can see how the families of US presidents have begun to play a greater role in influencing decisions. Because of their proximity, the children of presidents are often more engaged in politics, and with the Trump administration we find his children running his business, his daughter having an actual position at the White House, and his son-in-law holding a key position within the administration. Previously, and especially with Clinton, we have seen First Ladies play a very important, non-official, role as well. It is crucial to understand these actors and the roles they play so one can better analyze who can securitize and to what extent and how they are related. It is the discourse that these actors use in securitizing an issue that brings the most important issues to the forefront of US politics.

This chapter has identified some of the main doctrines in US foreign policy; the main camps of debates on what should be the course of US foreign policy; and the main actors and influencers of US foreign policy. Now, we will discuss the main theories that lead US foreign policy, beginning with realism, followed by liberalism and the Democratic Peace theory, as the main theories that have shaped US politics. Then in the next chapter we will discuss the Securitization theory as the overarching theory of this book, which will be utilized in the analysis of the Securitization of Islam in US foreign policy.

2.2 Realism

Realism is a very important theory with which we can analyze the US foreign policy. Some of the loudest debates among the scholars of US foreign policy have been on whether the USA should follow a liberal path or a realist path. Briefly, this work will discuss the claims of realism, find the main differences between realist claims and those of democratic peace, and finish with some thoughts on both realist and liberalist US foreign policy approaches.

Realism is not homogenous; it has many branches and a very long history. Its classic founder is considered to be Thucydides, who developed the core ideas of realism. According to Thucydides, moral norms have no effect on the relations between states, and even during times of peace, war is very likely; a state of hostility will sooner or later break out, as did between Athens and Sparta, who experienced a period of great peace, only to be followed by the outbreak of war. Competition under anarchy will always keep this hostility, which was the cause of the Great War between Athens and Sparta, as Athens grew very powerful and Sparta's fear increased, according to Thucydides (Thucydides 1970: 46–49).

Later realists such as Morgenthau think that the best way to approach a country's foreign policy is to identify its national interest (Morgenthau 1985). Morgenthau has defined this national interest as power, while a state's main goal is to acquire wealth and ensure national survival. Nevertheless, he does not omit the states' moral or ideological significance in their actions, but he refuses, as does realism, to identify the moral and ideological grounds of a particular state and nation with the ones of the universe. Moral aspirations are not as universal as the aspiration to acquire power (Morgenthau 1985: 1–15). For realism, the scholars or experts of international relations who do not believe in the pursuit of power are like scientists who do not believe in the law of gravity (Nau 2000: 128–129). Hardcore realists like Morgenthau, Lippmann, Carr, Kennan, and Tocqueville are skeptical of the public opinion of a nation; instead, they are for a strong tradition of foreign policy, a long-term strategic vision on national interests, combined with the power to pursue those interests when they are endangered, with speech, secrecy, and flexibility (Lippmann 1995; Morgenthau 1985; Carr 1946; Kennan 1984; Tocqueville 1946). These considerations would be jeopardized if public opinion, which is a product of short-term, non-strategic, irrational, emotional drives, is to be considered seriously. They consider that the task of a leader is to overcome these constraints that might be put by the public opinion in the short term, and the leader should lead not follow (Morgenthau 1985: 558; Cohen 1973: 62). This realist view on public opinion, and the risk, is best put in this quote:

> The unhappy truth is that the prevailing public opinion has been destructively wrong at the critical junctures. The people have impressed a critical veto upon the judgments of informed and responsible officials. They have compelled the government, which usually knew what would have been

wiser, or was necessary, or what was more expedient, to be too late with too little, or too long with too much, too pacifist in peace and too bellicose in war, too neutralist or appeasing in negotiations or too intransigent. Mass opinion has acquired mounting power in this country. It has shown itself to be a dangerous master of decision when the stakes are life and death. (Lippmann 1995: 20)

Realists do not reject peace altogether. They argue that although peace can be mitigated, even a lasting one, it does not mean that the likelihood of war is overcome. Realists are against the monopolization of peace, liberty, or democracy by liberals, and for some of the most important realists like Machiavelli, both glory and liberty are considered to be important factors, while for others like Thucydides or Rousseau, glory and democracy are important factors but they will not have a pacifying impact (Paine 1995: 342; Doyle 1997, 2000: 22; Locke 1988; Schumpeter 1950).

2.2.1 Realism in America

Although they do not reject peace altogether, realists claim that it should be achieved by keeping the country safe at the first place. In America, realism has been present in the discussion of American republic from the beginning. US Presidents from Washington to Hamilton advocated for a policy to keep peace in the world until America gained power and becomes self-sufficient and uncontested. They pursued this policy by avoiding permanent alliances while recognizing the need to make only temporary alliances (Gilbert 1961: 122–130). According to President Washington, America's biggest advantage was her distance from Europe, which prevented involvement in European affairs or alliances. This view was shared by many other American political pioneers such as John Adams and Thomas Paine (McDougall 1997: 39–41).

As far as realism and the democratic peace are concerned, realists think that democratic peace is a utopian idea that is not possible in the real world. These counterarguments are not to be rejected altogether, even by hardcore liberals, because as good as an idea as the democratic peace might be, there are other grand strategies that deserve a second thought, many of them deriving from realism, such as the balance of power, realpolitik, or containment (Ikenberry 2000: 104), which have served as important strategies in many situations. Realists have accused the liberals of having misread world politics and of having put the country in danger with utopian ideas and moral appeals especially on the inability of the Wilsonian agenda to establish order after the First World War, the debacle of the League of Nations, and the rise of Germany and Japan in the 1930s (Link 1974: 13–14; Knock 1992). Realists warn the USA against looking at foreign policy from the lens of democratic peace, as that can have a disastrous effect on American power, strategic mistakes, disastrous engagements abroad, and great power challengers (Layne and Lynn-Jones 1998: 329; Mearsheimer 1995). Nevertheless, not all the realists reject democratic peace in total and warn against it, there are some who give credit to the democratic peace, because, according to these realists, not all threats are centralized in power. Intentions, capabilities, and domestic factors also play a role in the states' behaviors with whom to side and against whom to act (Walt 1987; Schweller 1994: 104; Rose 1998: 144–172; Vasquez 1997). Nevertheless, these factors are not enough to lead to perpetual peace among nations, because the main cause of conflicts in an anarchical international order will remain, where there will always be a struggle for power and influence in a world of scarcity (Schweller 2000: 43).

2.2.2 Realists' Main Arguments

The main realist argument is related to Hobbes and his three causes of war. It is very common to hear or read the realists' reference to Hobbes when they build arguments against democratic peace and liberalism. In Leviathan, Hobbes explains the violent human nature and its causes in these words:

> All men in the state of nature have a desire and will to hurt, but not providing from the same cause ... so that in the nature of man, we find three principal causes to quarrel. First, competition; secondly, diffidence; thirdly, glory. The first maketh men invade for glory; the second, for safety; and the third, for reputation. (Hobbes 1985: 184)

For Hobbes, safety of life and property is the first reason of the existence of governments, so diffidence is the main cause for conflicts in the state of nature as well. Distrust makes one want to use force because even if one is a pacifist and cares for nothing else other than their security and safety, knowing that there are "wicked" people out there that want glory and pride will make them act on a worst-case scenario and make preemptive attacks (Schweller 2000: 44–45). As in the prisoner's dilemma, states too can be in irrational conflicts even though they both want security and prefer peace over war (Fearon 1995). In an anarchical system of the security dilemma dynamism, uncertainty causes war, even though the parties would want nothing more than their survival and would prefer peace over war (Jervis 1978; Glaser 1997). The reason why there is no war between democracies right now is that there has not been a conceived "wicked" state among the democracies so far, and they have learned to trust each other for now, but as soon as there is one example of belligerence, then the whole system will change to one being based upon lack of trust and fight for survival (Schweller 2000: 44–45). So far, the number of liberal democratic states has been so small, and all of them are in the same line of allies, that a serious conflict has not yet arisen.

According to realists, the desire for political power and influence is one of the most important drives for conflict as well. This desire that is related to selfishness that Morgenthau suggests is not identical, because selfishness, as in food, shelter, or security, is related to the vital need of the individual's survival, whereas the desire for political power and influence is related not with one's vital need for survival, but with one's position in the society, among his fellows. The danger is that while the selfishness for vital need can be satisfied, the desire for political power and influence can never be satisfied unless that person becomes God. Thus, men cannot be good in nature, the best one can hope for is to be "not too evil" (Morgenthau 1946: 192–193). Usually status or position is more important than wealth and physical well-being for human beings (Shubik 1971: 117). As domestically, so too internationally, status is achieved in various ways and the criteria for status change over time (Morgenthau 1985: 174–183). To gain this status recognition, states have engaged in various competitions over the years, such as the acquisition of sacred relics in ancient Greece, acquisition of lands in the ages of empires, palace building in the eighteenth century, colonialism and industrial revolution in the nineteenth century, and competitive space programs in the twentieth century (Luard 1976: 207).

Similar to individuals, competition is inevitable for states as well. Competition is the most common drive for war according to one of the forefathers of realism, Hobbes, where many parties want the same thing that cannot be shared and/or divided. At the same time, the strongest must have it, acquiring it by "sword" (Hobbes 1985: 184). The modern forefather of realism, on the other hand, Morgenthau, explains that in a competitive environment one wants something that the other one already possesses or wants too, and this leads to war (Morgenthau 1946: 192). The issue of indivisible scarce goods is especially important for the weak states. In a world of extreme scarcity there will be selfishness, non-cooperation, and war will be rational. Securing these scarce resources might be a matter of power for some, but for weak states it is a matter of life and death, effecting their vital interests, security, and prosperity (Schweller 2000: 49). But, even though in today's world everyone wants security and survival, primacy and power to influence still matters, and this is why the balance of power and military competition is very important. As long as there is politics there will always be a struggle over who gets what, how they get it, and when they get it (Waltz 1959: 203–204; Laswell 1950). Politics has been so integrated into the quest for power that scholars like Huntington suggest, "if power and primacy did not matter, political scientists would have to look for other work" (1993: 68–69).

When speaking about competition, another element that democratic peace speaks so dearly about, and one that the realists criticize, must also be covered: the free market. Free market or free trade, in fact, only increases competition, which produces winners and losers. In this sense, it is unexpected that weak democratic states adopt free-market policies instead of protectionist policies. Instead, the opposite is expected, so domestic producers are favored and not overtaken by the big corporations of the global superpowers (Krasner 1985). The problem in the newly independent states that came out of communism is exactly this, which has pushed too hard for a fragile democracy in these countries (Schweller 2000: 53). Also important is that while liberal democracies require market economies, capitalism doesn't require liberal democracy. Even in non-democratic states, capitalism has penetrated and functions in most cases better than in weak democratic states, or the democratic states per se. Such a pattern can be seen in countries such as Chile, South Korea, Panama, or Singapore, but most importantly in one of the least democratic countries: China, the world's biggest market economy with limited integrated capitalism (Barber 1996: 14). In market economy competition, the main question is not "how much do I gain?" but rather "who will dominate who?", and so conflicts arise, until one party is destroyed and/or dominated by the other one (Waltz 1971: 464). As a result, economic growth and market economy increase the demand for the scarce good and decreases the amount of that good. It increases the desire to have that good but it also increases the prestige and status of the good that is acquired (Schweller 2000: 59–60).

Finally, glory plays a very important role in realist thought of competitiveness and the criticism against democratic peace, whom they accuse of not including glory in their equation. For Hobbes, human nature includes glory as a cause of war, and man is by nature equipped with the willingness to destroy those who undervalue him (Landesman 1989: 146). Realists argue that the biggest hegemonic wars happened for glory or lack of. The rising powers while challenging the established system feel undervalued and are dissatisfied. They are of the belief that the territory distribution, political influence, and the influence and ownership of global economy do not reflect and value their increased power (Schweller 2000: 50; Gilpin 1981). In relation to economy, glory, and pride, the worst dictator of all times, Hitler, was partially right to claim that it is easier to unite people through common hate than common love: "For the liberation of a people more is needed than an economic policy, more than industry: if a people is to become free, it needs pride and willpower, defiance, hate, hate and once again hate" (quoted in Lukacs 1997: 126). If one cannot think of a completely harmony-of-interests' world, and certainly realists cannot, then promotion of democracy will not alienate the drive for competitiveness and war (Schweller 2000: 49).

As a result, the realist stand is that the promotion of democracy cannot eliminate war, although it can minimize it to a certain extent, first and foremost by increasing your own military capacity; second, by balance of power; and third, by having some sort of limited cooperation that would be of relative interest to the parties involved. A world full of liberal democracies will most probably be more peaceful; nevertheless, to claim that it will finish all wars and conflicts is utopian, according to realists. Although realists recognize the fact that states are not identical to humans, Hobbes' analogy of war-prone human nature shall be used with caution in reference to states in an anarchical system (Bull 1977: 46–51). Schweller believes that the real test for democratic peace has yet to come (2000: 60), as there is strong evidence to support democratic peace among mature democracies, but because they are very few in number one cannot say for sure, and there is much testing that must be done.

As for the denominators of foreign policy in general, and US foreign policy in particular, it must be mentioned that the foreign policy of a country is the reflection of internal policies and self-image. Every country behaves abroad according to domestic ideals and politics. A nation's economic, societal, religious, wealth, trade, investment, and military organization reflect in its foreign policy. It is common for countries that have similar self-images to ally and relate with each other; and the ones that do not have similar self-images, although they may tolerate one another, they usually fight each other (Nau 2000: 128–131).

The USA's domestic ideals are the ideals of a democratic society, and this influences the USA's foreign policy organization toward other states and how it perceives other states. The American self-image is not more important or sometimes as important as the national interest or power of the USA, but it says something about the mobilization or legitimization of US foreign policy actions (Nau 2000: 128).

2.2.3 US Foreign Policy Built on Both Idealism and Realism

Both idealists, or liberal peace thinkers, and the realists that are known for thinking in terms of power struggle direct US foreign policy. Among the liberalists there are two foreign policy perspectives: isolationism, which defends the thesis that democracy should play a very important role in US foreign policy and that the USA should perfect democracy at home and stay out of the affairs of other countries, and internationalism, which defends the thesis that again democracy should play a great role in US foreign policy by promoting democracy abroad and transforming international relations. Still, the realists claim that international relations are only power politics, and the USA should balance the power among the states and prevent other values to dominate America's foreign policy; thus democracy should play a very minor role in USA's foreign policy. It has been suggested that a new approach that combines these two extremes in conducting foreign policy is needed (Nau 2000: 127–128). Foreign policy needs to be conducted according to the realities of time and place, although the USA has tended to go one way more than the other at different times, shifting from one extreme to the other, but never being completely one-sided.

While it has been spoken of two extremes in US foreign policy, some administrations tend to follow other paths that sometimes one might argue are more extreme and sometimes they are only different. The George W. Bush administration and today's hardline Republicans tend to be more conservative in their thinking.

The main actors of the W. Bush administration may all be considered as conservatives. Conservatives trust and share the belief that they have a strong military, but they differ on the time and amount of military power to be used, as well as on the cooperation they should seek from allies.

There are two main camps: the neoconservative hardliners such as Rumsfeld, Wolfowitz, and Cheney, who are intellectually supported by the American Enterprise Institute's publications and who supported a unilateral and active US foreign policy to maintain American hegemony and omit any alternative or rival. Another camp is the camp of traditional conservatives, like Secretary Rice, Powell, and Hadley, who supported a more reluctant use of military power, limited only to threats by the big powers to America instead of engagements in distant and small wars. This "New Realism", as described by Rice, brings together both camps in their claim that the USA should seek an extensive network of alliances that would follow an American lead and would not question or be an obstacle to its freedom of action (Rice and Zelikow 1997). Bush tended to favor the more reluctant, traditionalist conservative view, but after the 9/11 attacks he switched to a neoconservative, interventionist, unilateral foreign policy, with America's obligation to fight global terrorism (Buchanan 1999; Johnson 2000).

Since the Cold War, the line between liberalist and realist scholars has faded continuously. It has faded among the politicians and the administrations in the USA. But despite this faded division, it is still interesting that these views are treated as opposites. In no other field is this faded line so obvious than in foreign policy, where presidents of different views have followed the same policies after the Cold War, like exporting American domestic policy to foreign policy. As President Johnson claimed: "The overriding rule which I want to affirm today is this: that our foreign policy must always be an extension of this Nation's domestic policy. Our safest guide to what we do abroad is always take a good look at what we are doing at home" (1966). This had a devastating effect when it was first tried in Vietnam in the 1960s (McDougall 1997: 190). Historically, America has followed both liberalism and realism in her foreign policy. Importantly, she had her greatest moments when the advantages of both were combined (Gilbert 1961: 136), but unfortunately in the latest wars in Iraq and Afghanistan, US politicians have decided to combine both of these theories, using the most dangerous and misconnected claims, which turned out to have great consequences in American foreign and domestic policy.

It can be concluded that the debate over which one is more influential, liberalism or realism, has been present in US politics for many years, and it seems that it will continue to be so for many more years to come. Nevertheless, liberalism, and especially democratic peace, has been one step ahead of the debate, in that it has shaped US foreign policy more than any other theory or ideology. In the debates, usually the means have been much more argued, whereas the ideology of the promotion of democracy has always been a cornerstone. What has changed is the rhetoric and tactics, which are only tools to justify the actions, instead of changes in the ideology itself. As can be seen in Chaps. 5 and 6, where we speak more about promotion of democracy in former Yugoslavia and the Middle East, this policy has never been questioned as a policy in and of itself; rather, it has been the priority that has been argued. Especially after the Cold War, even though most of the administrations have vowed to get less involved, they ended up getting more involved every time.

2.3 Liberalism

Liberalism is one of the most common theoretical approaches to US foreign policy, with all its sub-theories, including democratic peace. Democratic peace is left as a separate sub-title in this book because of its relevance to the subject. This part will analyze the liberal theoretical approach to US foreign policy and its debates in a chronological order.

Liberalism in America has its root in the twentieth century, specifically with the Cold War. After the twentieth century, American liberal thinkers had a hard time establishing a theory of such idealism. Realism sounded much more consistent with the conditions of the time.

One of the pioneers of American liberalism was President Woodrow Wilson, who defined liberalism as having three main aspects: promotion of liberal democracy abroad at the nation-state level, open market economy, and establishment of international institutions to regulate conflicts—political, military, and economic. What Wilson would later call "national self-determination" was based on the policy of encouraging a politically plural world (Talbott 1996; Smith 2000: 90) that was later manifested in the promotion of democracy and promotion of free markets and of liberal values. In the wake of the collapse of world empires—the Russian, Austro-Hungarian, and Ottoman Empires—Wilson recognized that the USA should do more than sympathize with the nations who want self-determination. For the first time in US political history he proposed a version of world order based on American liberalism. Wilson's new world order can be summarized in three main points: firstly, he believed that democratic states are more peace loving and stable, which made them the most appropriate building blocks for the global system and where it was not enough that this system be composed only of sovereign states;

secondly, that there should be some international organizations established to control and prevent the occurrence of wars, as for the moment they are not preventable, but these organizations should regulate interactions between states; and finally, America should take a leading role for the first time as the country that has designed the system, and this is how American national security liberalism unfolded (Talbott 1996; Smith 2000). Not everything went according to his plan, however, as terrible events in the twentieth century brought doubts to the Wilsonian vision. Out of the Versailles conference only Czechoslovakia emerged as an example of what president Wilson had envisioned, as many other new countries did not emerge in the same force. In fact, bolshevism and fascism followed world nationalists in many years to come (Smith 2000: 94). These events have put to question Wilson's liberalism in American minds as realism gained momentum, at least up until the Cold War. During the First and the Second World Wars liberalism remained nothing more than arguments, assumptions, and constructs that were never put into a full theory or practice.

With the end of the Second World War, Europe needed to be reconstructed and rearranged, and so did the USA. She needed a foreign policy, a different one. New institutions had to be formed and the global economy to be established. Although Wilsonian principles, of liberal internationalism, were over shadowed by the Cold War (Ikenberry 2000: 107–108), the mid-twentieth century was a better period for liberal ideas than the beginning of twentieth century. The end of the Second World War produced two sentiments in US foreign policy. The first one was the view of competition with Soviet Union in political and ideological terms, deteriorating relations with the Soviet Union. The second sentiment was what is called the "liberal democratic order" based on economic openness, political reciprocity, and an American-led liberal political order based on global institutions (Ikenberry 2000: 108). These debates about what role the USA should take are as old as the USA itself. Liberals have very often argued the level of US involvement in global issues, though they all agreed for involvement. Wilson's claims that the USA should encourage democratic governments, open economies, and multilateral institutions rest on the belief that what is good for America, and most importantly American security, was also good for all the world (Smith 2009: 64–65). Wilson was the first president to argue that the promotion of democracy and the enlargement of democratic territories serve best for the national security of America, which directly serves the common good of world peace.

It was not until the 1940s that Wilson's views could be put to practice. Under the presidency of Franklin Roosevelt and Harry Truman, the USA helped establish initiatives and organizations that would serve this purpose. With the Marshall Plan the USA would promote this vision to Eastern Europe. Similarly, the idea of European Union was an idea that came out of this vision. NATO is the best example of the Wilsonian vision of a military organization that would control and prevent wars among the western countries but also organize the interactions of countries with each other (Smith 2009: 64–65). In this way, America became the leading actor in this vision of promotion of democratic governments, open economies, and multilateral institutions and organizations. With the Cold War, all these great ideas did not let liberal internationalism be the leading policy of the USA, as it gave in to a containment policy with the Soviet Union. Still, although secondary, liberalism remained in the political atmosphere of the nation.

Whenever something went wrong with US foreign policy and war erupted, liberals, or Wilsonianists, have been the scapegoats to whom one of the pioneers of liberalism in America, Norman Angell, answered, "War is not impossible … it is not the likelihood of war which is the illusion, but its benefits" (Angell 1910: 386–387). They were also accused of being materialists rather than idealists (Kahler 1997: 23). There are two main critics of liberals in America: those who think that America needs not such a soft policy as it will be misunderstood and misused by her rivals and those who accuse the early American liberals as being materialists instead of idealists.

2.3.1 Post-Cold War Liberalism

With the end of the Cold War, Wilsonianism, liberal internationalism, or neoliberalism, evolved. While containment was left in the past, the Soviet Union collapsed, and the USA became the sole leader of the new world, while other, smaller countries explored ways to be part of the American vision. The collapse of the Soviet Union created a vacuum and the international order needed to be redefined, based on liberal values as opposed to nationalism. American academia and some political figures were ready to redefine the new international relations where the enlargement of the "community of democracies", as coined by Clinton, would take charge (Fukuyama 2006; Levy 1988; Smith 2009; Moravcsik 1997). The Democratic Peace theory is covered in detail below. But for now, it suffices to say that by the 1990s the Democratic Peace theory was as acceptable as it could get and the neoliberals had an established theory out of the Wilsonian vision, which was previously seen as too idealistic.

Among the most prominent scholars of this new doctrine, Anne Marie Slaughter drew three main elements of neoliberalism: The Democratic Peace theory, whose "empirical father" Michael Doyle advocated that there are no two democracies that went to war with each other (Doyle 1983), basing the data on Kant's famous perpetual peace (Doyle 1986; Cox et al. 2000: 8) to whom Doyle feels associated with. Slaughter (2009) claims that the Clinton administration borrowed the Democratic Peace theory as their grand strategy to expand the community of liberal democracies, and Bush's neocons have abandoned it; the second element is the "great men" approach to democracy transition, suggesting that great men and great ideas can make history. This element in the neoliberal theory suggests that not all the transitions to democracies do it correctly, and that in some of them, such as the ex-Yugoslavian countries, transition is bloody, while the dissolution of the Soviet Union did it in a smoother way by having great men with great ideas. The final element that Slaughter talks about is the right to intervene. According to Slaughter the neoliberal argument has transformed the meaning of sovereignty and has changed from the *right* to intervene to the *duty* to intervene. Although Slaughter herself does not agree with these arguments, especially when arguing that the "responsibility to protect" is humanitarian and it is neither realist nor neoliberal in nature, she summarized the arguments of neoliberalism in these three elements (2009: 98–100).

After the Cold War, American liberal internationalism has become an idealistic vision synchronized with a strategy on how to make America and American interests safer by becoming engaged in global issues and foreign countries. Smith refers to the post-Cold War liberalism as "liberal imperialism", which is a dangerous departure from liberalism of the twentieth century, mainly because "liberal" policymakers now believe that all liberal ideals can be achieved by military means and that undemocratic countries can be turned to democratic ones in an unrealistic time frame, by any means. The other two beliefs that made liberal imperialism questionable are that democracy is a universal value and the belief in the Democratic Peace theory (Smith 2007). After the Cold War, liberalism became bigger and more complicated than Wilsonian ideas (Steigerwald 1994: 169–171).

This idealism did not remain only liberal, or neoliberal, as today's American neoconservatives also want to promote these values abroad, thereby expanding the abode of democratic states and only differ on the constraints. While conservatives such as Dick Cheney see this era as American exceptionalism, they argue that America needs no constraints and that weaker states welcome America's preeminence, making her a great, not a predatory, nation (Beinart 2008: x–xi). For Liberals, economic development secures the well-being of liberty because liberty alone—not economic development and difference in wealth distribution—can make any country, including America, vulnerable, and this would undermine American values and security (Beinart 2008: ix). For this reason, it is wrong to claim that the promotion of democracy by the USA is an idealistic and unachievable goal for the USA. Democracy promotion, as seen from the USA, is a pragmatic vision, even a necessity, to create a stable international political system to ensure America's global security environment. America feels more comfortable in pursuing her interests and security in a democratic world rather than a non-democratic one (Ikenberry 2000: 103–104). Nevertheless, today the USA faces other threats that it needs to address, which sometimes threaten America more than a non-democratic country on the other side of the ocean. Among those are cyber threats, disease, environmental degradation, weapons of mass destruction, to name a few, which came about mostly through the effects of globalization pioneered by the USA. Even in democracies, when they do not improve the lives of the people, they may turn into vacuums of anarchy (Beinart 2008: 192). Radical terrorist groups today, such as the so-called jihadists, threaten the USA from the inside, and abroad, using the power of globalization (Beinart 2008: xi–xii), which shows that the USA should reconsider all prior strategies and come up with a strategy of dealing with the consequences of democracy promotion.

2.3.2 *Liberal Arguments of Intervention*

There are many arguments that the advocates for USA's intervention abroad use, but they can be sorted into a few main categories. First, it can be said that the aim is to make the USA safer. Democracies do not go to war with each other, as war becomes a very costly adventure, which is why it is of utmost importance to expend the territories of democracy for America to be safe. Also, the power transitions from one place to another cause war and this can be prevented if everyone accepts USA's leadership role (Friedman 2001: 195–217; Doyle 1986, 2000: 22; Ikenberry 2000: 104). Second, the USA bears a responsibility that comes together with her power. The tragedies in Bosnia, Somalia, Rwanda, Kosovo, Burundi, and elsewhere, where vast number of people were killed or suffered, showed that there is a need for peace-enforcing institutions against these tragedies—which trigger immigration, chaos, and flow of weapons and threaten American national interests—so the USA has the responsibility to be a leader rather than an observer (Gholz et al. 1997; Mandelbaum 1996: 16–32; Kennan 1993). Third, democracy promotion is fully consistent with American values. Democracy promotion is the "right-thing-to-do" and the "smart-thing-to-do", and this is consistent with American values of liberty, democracy, as well as of morality (Doyle 1986, 2000: 22; Smith 2000: 85; Cameron 2002; Ikenberry 2000). Alternatively, fascism and communism can destroy the free world, and if the USA is not there to promote democracy then the expansion of fascism and communism is inevitable (Smith 2000: 92). Although the threat of communism and fascism has decreased, the USA uses the same arguments to argue for the promotion of democracy, against an alternative "clash of civilizations" including religious fundamentalism and other extremist ideas. Fourth is a notion of national greatness. Promotion of democracy is linked to showing the national greatness of America (O'Sullivan 1839: 429; Hunt 2009: 30; LaFeber 1965: 37). This is one of the few ways of preserving American liberty as well, which can be endangered and be bounded to the fate of Europe if it remained passive.[3] This argument is mostly rejected by liberals, who want to promote democracy because it is the right thing to do, in the sense of promoting American system and values.

The aim of liberal intervention is to unite democratic nations around a common goal: promotion of democracy for the common security. This grand strategy has united American political camps like never before (Ikenberry 2000: 104), especially with the turn of the century, when the Republicans took over the White House but Congress was in the hands of the Democrats, who together decided on invading Afghanistan and Iraq. The differences in foreign policy between the parties in America were very vivid during the course of the Cold War. Although these differences were not new, with the turn of the century these bipartisan differences decreased. The Republican White House did not seek support from the people and

---

[3] Speeches made by many congressman and senators of that time can be reached at Graebner (1968).

Congress for the American interests, but rather asked for support in making the world a better place, referring to the Wilsonian vision of replacing the current system of balance of power with the community of powers and organized peace. A Democratic Congress, on the other hand, embraced this call as it suits its vision of democracy promotion as well (Cameron 2002: 3–6; Smith 2009: 66; Ikenberry 2009: 5). According to Tony Smith (2009), the neoconservatives implemented neoliberals' ideology, and this is why even if Al Gore had been elected as the US president, Afghanistan would still have been invaded, but doubtfully Iraq. Nevertheless, Americans also learned that one cannot ask for a global leadership role without being prepared to be evil (Beinart 2008: xi) at times when one cannot be good.

Before discussing and analyzing in depth the Democratic Peace theory, let us summarize how US foreign policy and democracy promotion should be studied, as there are big debates among scholars today. The lessons can be summarized into three points: Firstly, scholars have not understood US democracy promotion, and this can be seen in the literature of the last decade, which highly differs from what the reality and the literature is today. Concepts and names such as "idealism", "utopianism", or "moralism" that were used to connote liberalism have changed and even those critics have sided with the advocates of democracy promotion (Smith 2009: 86–87; Fukuyama 2006; Levy 1988; Moravcsik 1997; Russett and Oneal 2001). Secondly, there has been a striking continuity of US foreign policy since its founding. In fact, one can even argue that liberalism is more a continuity of the founding vision than the vision that was used in mid- or late twentieth century, and this tradition is based on Wilson's 14 points (Link 1966; Kissinger 1994; Ikenberry 2009: 6). Finally, democracy promotion is not an easy or a likely task in the near future. There are many reasons for this, among them being that America must understand that it has limits to its power and consequences for these ambitions (Smith 2009: 88). The scholars who support a one-fit-all democracy promotion should not underestimate local traditions, nationalist sentiments and pride, interests, political culture, or cultural values.

For this work the Democratic Peace theory is the most related branch of liberalism, and because of this it has been given a special place, to understand why the promotion of democracy in Yugoslavia and the Middle East was such an important policy.

2.4 Democratic Peace Theory

The current international system, based on the balance of power, is shown to lack stable guarantees of long-term peace. Except in limiting the ability of countries to dominate and decrease the scope of conflicts, the balance of power was unable to avoid conflicts and even wars. The goal of peace is substituted by short-term stability, and it aimed at keeping the dissatisfaction of states with the international order below the level of aggression (Kissinger 1994: 21). This system needs amendments or a new approach that will produce long-lasting peace, because according to liberals, overthrowing the world order would be very costly and unwise.

For liberals, states that run on the principle of the rule of law, equality of law, free speech, and other civil liberties, and have an elected representation, are liberal states and fundamentally oppose war. The citizens who elect their governments bear the consequences of war, and ultimately, they do not want to go to war when they can choose peace (Doyle 2000: 22). To claim that there is only one type of liberalism, or realism, is to miss the many points of what is to be offered in international relations. Doyle, whose name is mostly associated with Kant's view on liberal peace, divides liberals into three categories: the Lockeans, the commercial pacifists, and the liberal internationalists. To be able to understand liberal peace, where Kant argues that democracies do not go to war with each other but are more war-prone to the undemocratic states (Kant 1983), one needs to study all three of these categories that Doyle has talked about.

Lockeans agree that peace cannot be achieved by purely ideological and normative commitments and that there is a need for institutions to guarantee these commitments under international law and to be able to regulate international peace. The government should also be representative of the people living under that government, according to Lockeans (Doyle 2000: 35–36). The commercial pacifists agree that when the burden of war is upon the citizens who elect their governments, peace becomes a better option than war. They claim that by commerce, a more stable peace is built. War is inevitable to people, but when it becomes very costly then the system of war will be swapped for a system of peace, based on commercial interdependence, as war does not pay for commercial manufacturing societies (Doyle 2000: 29–30). Today's capitalist systems, including that of Adam Smith's philosophy, are based on this view, and economists such as Joseph Schumpeter even call it a capitalist pacification.

A special relation based on peace exists among liberal states for Kant, when they are representative, when they have liberal respect, and when they have transnational interdependent economies, which then makes it sufficient to enter into the liberal peace agreement with each other. Nevertheless, only and only if these three conditions are shared can they reach this point; a single element will not assure this peace treaty, as it will not be possible if any one of them is missing (Doyle 2000: 30–31). According to Kant, a liberal republic must achieve three conditions to be built: it should be a republic with an elected legislature, act on the rule of law, and consist of a separation of powers (Kant 1983: 116–175). Nevertheless, this type of government will not assure peace if it does not fulfill the other conditions: respect for human rights and non-discrimination. Individuals have innate rights that deserve respect, so this should assure respect for the citizens of other liberal republics, who represent free citizens. But it approaches non-liberal republics with suspicion because they cannot be trusted, as they do not even trust their own citizens; and finally, social and economic interdependence will form a mix of conflict and cooperation, but because they are less subject to single conflicts and tend to be more varied, they strengthen the relations and interests between the liberal republics, while breaking further the bonds with non-liberal ones (Doyle 2000: 31–32; Kant 1983).

These ideas of Kant have been developed further by many analysts and international relations scholars and hold that liberal democracies have peaceful relations with each other because of their internal structures and their shared norms and values (Kant 1983; Doyle 1983, 1986). In these structures, the types of conflicts with which democratic leaders can mobilize their citizens are limited, while the norms of peaceful resolution of conflicts limit the use of violence and also, similarly important, the effect of institutionalized government will push for more accountability toward the citizens (Ikenberry 2000: 111). These ideas came to be known as the "Democratic Peace theory", whose main claim is that democracies do not go to war with each other; thus the territory of democracies must expand. Although no one can give full credit to any of the above written elements alone for why democracies do not go to war with each other, the institutionalized internal structure, economic interdependence, and shared membership in international institutions all play a role (Russett et al. 1998; Nau 2000: 139; O'Neal and Russett 1997). However, because democracies are only more common since the Second World War and because they had a shared threat—the Soviet Union—it cannot be empirically proven, or yet surely considered, that democracies will not fight with each other if the Soviet Union had not existed or that democratic countries would be in majority (Nau 2000: 139; Spiro 1994; Gowa 1995). The belief among liberals stands that liberal democracies do not fight with each other and for the moment one can see more peaceful, continuous, institutionalized and legitimate relations between the liberal democratic countries than with non-liberal ones.

Although US policy makers have debated this view for centuries, it was explicitly put forward by the USA in 1995 by National Security Council Director, Anthony Lake, when he explained US foreign policy after the Second World War as a policy of expanding the pool of democracies for America's own security and prosperity because democracies are less likely to go to war with the USA or other nations, as they do not abuse their people's rights. They will also be better trading partners for the USA; thus they are all potential allies for struggles against ethnic and religious conflicts, reducing nuclear threats, combating terrorism and organized crime, as well as overcoming environmental degradation (Lake 1995).

For the American postwar policy, common identities among states facilitate stable and long-lasting peace and order. Not just power and interest, values and a sense of community matter and states with similar political values and social purposes will be more likely to cooperate with each other as they will understand each other better, while common liberal and democratic values specify expectations on how the conflicts should be resolved if there should be any (Ikenberry and Kupchan 1990; Beugel 1966; Fromkin 1995; Huntley 1980). The backbone of the democratic peace is the open market economy, as it reinforces democracy. The logic is simple: open market economy establishes free trade, which leads to prosperity that paves the way for democracy and results in peace. This order is "self-reinforcing" (Irwin 1996; Volgy and Schwarz 1997; Longregan and Poole 1996). Lipset advanced this relation between economic development and democracy in the 1950s, and he built the relations between economic development and maintenance of democracy. He stresses two factors: the fact that education increases with economic development, which then produces a more democracy-prone political culture, and the fact that economic development produces a middle-class-dominated social structure, which decreases class struggles and the likelihood for antidemocratic ideologies while increasing the popular support for democratic ideas (Lipset 1959). In this view, the increase in size of the middle class can only be done with economic growth and development, and this increase is the key to stable democratic institutions (Rueschemeyer et al. 1992). Another firm argument related to free markets is that despite economic development and democracy, free markets encourage interdependence between states and a common vision toward bigger interests that foster stability in international relations (Eckes 1971: 52). In this light, the American liberals think that open markets of free trade are the precondition for a prosperous international system. This led Truman to suggest tariff reductions and common rules and institutions of trade and investments in the world, which he called "economic peace" (Keynes 1920; Markwell 2006; Ikenberry 2009). Finally, for the American democratic peace thinkers, one of the strongest held views is that institutions matter. States tend to act differently when they operate within international institutions, and the conflicts that might occur are more likely to be handled quickly and with less violence. Coming together in international institutions, states agree to reshape, reconstruct, and limit their actions according to the common goal. The relationship between states increases, their interest increases, and a common logic of conflict resolution is created (Richter 1977).

Nevertheless, similar to the importance of the international institutions, internal institutions are also important, if not more so. Institutionalized separation of power and civil rights will lead to more accountability and checks and balances. In newly democratized countries, membership to international institutions will trigger internal institutionalization, but stronger internal institutions are needed to create long-lasting international institutions. Institutions will also prevent the concentration of power and the possibility of tyranny (Richter 1977) out of the guarantee of civil liberties, rule of law, and the insurance of the durability of the democratic political order. America has been a pioneer in institutionalizing what it can in the first opportunity. American political leaders have been ready to institutionalize just about everything domestically, as well as establishing the League of Nations, the United Nations, NATO, to institutionalize security, monetary relations, trade, aid, dispute resolution, and peacekeeping (Murphy 1994; Richter 1977; Gilpin 1975; Lake 1991).

2.4.1 Wilsonianism and the Democratic Peace

Attracted by this liberal view, American foreign policy thinkers considered building a common identity and community as an answer to what happened in the First World War. Wilson mentioned the "community of power" where he associated the common identity with democracy. He wanted to build a universal democratic community, but the problem was that Russia moved to the opposite direction, and Europe was not as firm as Wilson expected in 1919 (Ikenberry 2000: 120). In his first State of the Union address, on December 2, 1913, Wilson laid down the foundation of what came to be known later as Wilsonianism. Based on universal law and national trustworthiness this new international order aimed to change the logic of international disputes by bringing up binding arbitration instead of the use of force (Kissinger 1994: 44–45). In his own words, Wilson saw this new international order as "Our [America's] own honor and our [America's] obligations to the peace of the world" (Wilson 1913). Furthermore, in a speech before Congress in 1917, Wilson declared war against Germany on the basis of "making the world safe for democracy" in reference to liberal peace where he asserted that democracies make peace while non-democracies make war (Ikenberry 2009: 10). According to Wilson, speaking in front of Congress on April 2, 1917, only in the partnership of democratic nations can peace be maintained, as no autocratic government can be trusted to observe the agreements of peace, and a new international organization should be a league of honor and a partnership of opinions. Only free people will prefer the common good in the interest of mankind instead of their own narrow interests (Link 1966). After the war, in 1918–1919, Wilson authored his famous 14 points where he told the Europeans that the international system should abandon the balance of power and instead build on ethnic self-determination and that their security should be built on collective security instead of military alliances. He also argued that their diplomacy should be built on open agreements that have been openly arrived at, instead of through secret deals (Link 1966; Kissinger 1994: 19).

With Anglo-Saxon supremacy as its core, Wilson imagined America as the new game changer. Promoting self-determination, open economy, open diplomacy, and cooperation, Wilson's aim was to put empires down and establish foundations for a long-lasting peace (Hunt 2009: 134). Wilsonianism's intellectual origin is with no doubt the same as that of liberal peace, nevertheless, his project cannot be narrowed down only to open market and democratization, although they are the most important. Wilson called for the enlargement of the territories of democracy, where rule of law, representation, accountability, internal checks and balances, and transparency would need to prevail domestically first and then followed up internationally. It was thought that not only do democracies not go to war with each other but also that they engage in more far-reaching goals and cooperation (Smith 2009: 57; Ikenberry 2009: 11). Second,

Wilson called for open international markets, where internationally integrated markets would bring more prosperity, and interdependence would promote peace among these countries. The removal of all economic barriers and equality in trade opportunities would help in the integration of international trade and markets and foster interdependence. Together, democracy and open markets make peace more likely for Wilson (Smith 2009: 58; Ikenberry 2009: 11). Third, international multilateral institutions should be built to provide for collective security and cooperation and also mediate conflicts. Organizations such as the League of Nations, the United Nations, the North Atlantic Treaty Organization, the World Bank, or the International Monetary Fund (IMF), and many others, are the fruits of this vision, which bring commitments to collective security, prosperity, conflict resolution, equality, and liberty (Smith 2009: 58; Ikenberry 2009: 12). Finally, Wilson argued that America needs to take responsibility and lead for this vision to be successful. This was not an imperialistic thought, although it has been widely criticized as such, but rather a hegemonic one, where America had tried this formula on a smaller scale and needed to distribute the know-how. For Wilson, more important than the know-how, America had the responsibility to take this role (Smith 2009: 59; Ikenberry 2009: 13). Today, American political leaders have put these ideas into their agenda and shaped American foreign policy according to this theoretical approach.

Elaborating more on the last point, Wilson saw this mission of changing the international order as a messianic role given to America by God. To the liberalist thought Wilson gave it a moral twist, and he envisioned the American foreign policy as being more concentrated on human rights instead of property rights. For him this vision was a synchronization of material interests bounded to superior ethical, moral, and spiritual standards and purposes (Link 1974: 13). Wilson had faith in the goodness of man, the law of organic life, and the divine plan where he believed that one day democracy would be the ultimate universal rule (Link 1974: 14). In one of his speeches he defined this messianic role of the USA as "the light which will shine unto all generations and guide the feet of mankind to the goal of justice and liberty and peace" (Wilson 1914), where God gave this moral role to America to spread this new international order thought for world peace and prosperity (Kissinger 1994: 30–47; Ikenberry 2000: 105–106; Knock 2009: 31).

Most interestingly, analysts of Wilson tend to agree that his main goal was the promotion of democracy, but in his 14 points he never mentioned the word democracy (Slaughter 2009: 92–96). Instead, he mentioned self-determination and the right of the people to be free to determine their own fate. Wilson mentioned democracy on many other occasions, and analysts of Wilson agree with his vision of democracy promotion, but they link the absence of the term "democracy" in his 14 points on his great ability of using grammar and linguistics to impress the Congress, and anyways speaking about self-determination in an era of empires is broader in meaning than democracy alone (Cooper 2008: 26).

Regarding war, Wilson was a president who tried to avoid it at any cost. But when there was no other way he went to the Congress to ask for counsel and permission to enter into the First World War. One might argue that even though he made the case of fighting for values and principles such as peace and liberties, he did not ask permission to go to war to spread those principles (Slaughter 2009: 89), as he did not believe in spreading these principles, or democracy per se, by going to war. But one can also claim that a holy war for democracy would only mean America neglecting her own democracy to intervene in the affairs of others (Hunt 2009: 135).

The biggest benefaction of the Wilsonian legacy was the channeling of nationalism in liberal democracy, which produces governments that respect their citizens and their neighbors (Smith 2007: 67). Although one cannot speak of one single ideology that has affected world politics more than another after the First World War, one can argue that Wilsonianism is among the top, especially after the Second World War. Not only did America use these principles, but they helped Germany, Japan, and even Russia, to reform (Smith 2007; Dueck 2003). These principles that Dueck calls "low-cost internationalism" have been followed by nearly all of the twentieth- and twenty-first-century US presidents (2003).

2.4.2 Wilsonian Legacy Among the US Presidents

Wilson's principles have been the foundation of American foreign policy thought and game changers of the twentieth century (Kissinger 1994; Smith 2007; Dueck 2003). Although the extent of their influence has changed over time, they were always present. Wilson did not succeed in bringing on board the people and politicians of his time, but their successors have embraced Wilson's principles more and more ever since. Regardless of party lines, both Republicans and Democrats have embraced Wilsonian principles, and this is what makes the Wilsonian vision the most influential ideology in US foreign policy. From Roosevelt to Truman to

Reagan, Clinton, H. W. Bush, and W. Bush, most of Wilson's successors have embraced these principles to different extents. Roosevelt's view of the global issues reminds us of Wilson's and of liberal peace. For Roosevelt, democracy remains the hope of a peaceful world because of democratic states' peace-loving instincts, but the threat comes from the uncertainty of the despotic and militaristic regimes, against whom democracies must unite and where the USA should stand in the forefront (Divine 1969: 9; Nixon 1969a: 520). Roosevelt's vision included building institutions that would guarantee peace, and he learned from the failures of both the "realist" lessons from the League of Nations and the "liberal" lessons from regional imperialism and mercantilist conflict (Ikenberry 2000: 124). In this course, together with Winston Churchill, Roosevelt established the Atlantic Charter, a new league that would be a safeguard against another outbreak of aggression, based on just peace, the right of self-determination for all nations, and free trade (Hunt 2009: 147; Rosenman 1950: 6). Similarly, the Committee to Defend America by Aiding the Allies, encouraged by Roosevelt himself, was established in May 1940 (Hunt 2009: 149; Rosenman 1950: 638).

Arguably no other successor of Wilson embraced and put into practice his principles more then President Truman. The Second World War demonstrated that disregarding some specific relations between states and their citizens did not secure a long-lasting international peace and domestic well-being. This is why the domestic social compromise in the USA during Wilson's presidency, and more broadly during Roosevelt, needed to be diffused on a broader scale. With the end of the Second World War a similar organization to that of the League of Nations needed to be formed but it needed to be backed up by economic and security organizations and agreements, and most importantly the USA needed to have a more engaging role. The United Nations was formed with the Security Council giving the great powers "more equal" rights than the others, backed up by Wilsonian platform of Universal Declaration of Human Rights, IMF, and the General Agreement on Tariffs and Trade (GATT) (Slaughter 2009: 107; Ruggie 1982). Truman championed the Wilsonian adoption of the Marshall Plan. When he asked the Congress to give aid to Greece and Turkey, he also asked the American people to be ready and accept the great responsibilities in the struggle against communism. Truman believed that aggression anywhere in the world would endanger America both directly and indirectly. He also acknowledged that this role would not come at a cheap price (Hunt 2009: 158), but the USA had an obligation to make the international system hospitable for "free institutions, representative government, free elections, guarantees of individual liberty, freedom of speech and religion, and freedom from political oppression" (Truman 1947).

Starting from the Wilsonian vision, Roosevelt's Atlantic Charter served the purpose of establishing international institutions for the democratic community continued by Truman and other US presidents. With the establishment of the UN, international relations, diplomacy, and security became more organized. Economic, trade, and finance institutions organized the free markets, but the UN did not satisfy the Wilsonian or the Liberal Peace vision of bringing together the democratic community only, as Russia and China were there also. On the other hand, there was a lack of western/democratic community security institutions. This opened a way to establish the North American Treaty Organization, which is a fruit of the Atlantic Council, and the compilation of Wilsonian vision, where the USA's hegemonic power and leadership would come into play (Link 1954). Following this line from Wilson to Roosevelt to Truman, and others, Ronald Reagan asserted that the regime types of other states matter and that democracies are less threatening to the USA than non-democracies. This view of Reagan's went further with the pursuit of human rights and promotion of democracy taking the place of the "coexistence" approach of Nixon toward the Soviet Union. Reagan, and then H. W. Bush, engaged in many foreign territories to pursue this goal, such as the engagements in El Salvador, the Philippines, Chile (Ikenberry 2000: 125), to name a few countries that the USA pushed for democracy, open markets, and rule of law. President George H. W. Bush spoke of the "zone of democratic peace" on many occasions in the post-Cold War where he argued that America and her allies are not only a defensive alliance but also promoters of values and liberties (Huntley 1998; Fromkin 1995).

The 1990s are considered the most liberal moments of the twentieth century, with the Cold War coming to an end and globalization flourishing and the international organizations prospering. Clinton made the same arguments as George H. W. Bush for the expansion of NATO, promotion of the business of internationalism, markets, and management of international security, by professing these values even in countries like China, which led to the Clinton doctrine being labeled as the "doctrine of enlargement" (Wittkopf and McCormick 1999: 3–9; Kupchan 2001; Ikenberry 2009, 2000: 117–126; Cameron 2002: 183–192). President Clinton was accused several times by the Republicans of being "excessive illusory Wilsonian". But Republican George W. Bush put the Wilsonian democratic peace to the forefront of his policies. Meeting with Tony Blair in November 2004 after his reelection, Bush stated his firmness to promote peace on his firm belief in democracies, as democracies do not go to war with each other (quoted in Cameron 2002: 190). Yet, despite using Wilsonian discourse and framing struggle for the dominance of either liberty or evil and constructing the invasion of Afghanistan and Iraq as important for the advancement of liberty and democracy, Bush focused on military and security buildup, thereby failing to tackle other important issues for liberal peace and Wilsonian doctrine, including human rights, sustainable development, economic integration, and non-military foreign assistance (Wittcopf and McCormick 1999: 3–9; Cameron 2002: 190; Kupchan 2001). This does not mean that he broke out of the Wilsonian legacy, but that he continued the worst features of that legacy (Dueck 2003: 7).

2.4.3 Democratic Peace Today

Did everything work out great for the advancement of Wilsonian ideology in the USA? The rise of nationalism, ethnic conflicts, violence of all kinds, and the economic crackdowns all worked against the arguments of Wilson. But, the international system succeeded in stopping Slobodan Milosevic's destruction of nations, starving in Somalia, and further genocide in Rwanda. New roles have been given to the international community, with the USA as its hegemonic leader: that of the responsibility to protect. Although an argument can be made for a need of quicker interventions with less casualties, still, the interventions happened, they stopped atrocities at a point of time, and the non-existence of these international institutions would have made things much worse.

Today, Wilsonian ideas face many challenges that did not exist during the lifetime of Woodrow Wilson, but they need to be addressed by his fellow liberals. The world is not bipolar anymore, and no one can say for sure if it is unipolar or multipolar. The security problems have shifted from great powers threatening each other and smaller states, to terrorism and small/rogue/poor states threatening each other and the big powers. The growing American power is another challenge, as the international order is shifting toward a one-player game instead of an "international community" as envisioned by Wilson, which leads to the last challenge of the lack of control against abuses of intervention (Ikenberry 2009: 21–24), which is arguably what has happened during the W. Bush administration. These are all challenges to be tackled but in no way does this mean that Wilsonianism, or liberal peace, or democratic peace, has failed, or should be abandoned; rather, it means that in the years to come these challenges will be tackled and scholars will be writing much more about the compatibility of Wilsonianism with these, and other, challenges.

The ideas of democratic peace have remained a cornerstone for American foreign policy, and the USA is doomed to follow a liberal grand strategy, engaging and enlarging the international community but also raising the interdependence and institutionalization in international relations (Brinkley 1997; Ikenberry 2000: 126). America's engagement in this grand liberal democracy is seen as a source of a stable, peaceful, and prosperous international order where democratic states can establish a peaceful order only if they cooperate with each other, have open economies with each other, increase their economic interdependence for stable and continuous relations, and establish international institutions to shape and control conflicts (Cox et al. 2000: 11). Nevertheless, liberal democracy is not homogeneous, and it is not a simple straightforward entity (Sorensen 2000: 297–301). Democracy is not under the monopoly of liberals. It has been considered as a government model for centuries (Doyle 2000: 37) and has undergone many changes ever since. These changes have shown that democracy is neither an easy task nor a cheap one. Many years of American struggle have cost the US fortunes (Ikenberry 2000: 121), and still there is no guarantee except in the firm belief that the enlargement of territories of democracies will lead to a perpetual peace. It might minimize the causes of war but it will not eliminate them completely (Cox et al. 2000: 9) as the circle of democracies has always been small, so there are no satisfactory implications that democracies will not go to war with each other, on separate interests, when that circle becomes bigger. The other concern is that the promotion of democracy, sometimes by force, may backfire and give long-lasting damages to the international order, as it did in the Middle East to a smaller extent.

Today there are certain types of democracies or certain elements of democracies that have been pushed forward to the third world by the western powers. They are important to achieve but also very challenging, and they also bear risks when pushed too hard. The liberal market, the election model, and the strong state model have been the models that have been pushed on to the third world. Nevertheless, both the liberal markets and the election models contain weaknesses, usually bounded to the political culture and the economic strength of the country, whereas for the strong state it contains confusion on how one can define it as such (as in some places strong states already exists but there is no separation of power) and to change this considerable time is needed (Sorensen 2000: 297–301). The USA chose only a particular type of democracy, that of free markets and free elections, to be exported to the third world (Cox et al. 2000: 9–10; Kissinger 1994: 33–34), which is not always suitable where it is implemented and causes many problems in return. Contrary to Cox et al. and Kissinger, it is debatable that what the USA has exported to the third world is free market and free elections; instead, it is controlled markets by the USA and free elections to choose anyone that the USA puts forward or approves, but that is another subject of discussion.

Liberalism and democratic peace have been very important in the US foreign policy engagement with the world, as discussed above. As far as this book is concerned, democratic peace has been a driving force in the US engagement with the Balkans and the Middle East, and it has been a driving force in the US view of Islam. Democracy promotion as part of the Democratic Peace theory has been a cornerstone in America's relation with Islam and the Muslim world, and as it has been argued at the end of this chapter as well as at the conclusion of this work, democratic peace and democracy promotion have also been the cornerstones of the securitization of Islam in US foreign policy.

The democratic peace and liberalism have been present in US foreign policy from the beginning of its engagement with the world, and they have shaped US foreign policy throughout this engagement, sometimes more sometimes less. Nevertheless, the most important intellectual rival, another theory that has shaped the US foreign policy too, is realism. Liberalism and realism are both very important in understanding the debates in US foreign policy, which have developed America's intellectual legacy. But, to be able to understand the role of Islam in US foreign policy, as constructed by US foreign policy makers, we believe that the securitization theory is a better theory. Thus, the following chapter will analyze it in detail. The securitization theory is a relatively new theory, and the following chapter will also serve the purpose of bringing together the most important debates about the theory and the most important criticisms as well as the need for the theory to expand, which is one of the contributions of this work: to expand the securitization theory theory by analyzing Islam in US foreign policy.

References

Angell, Norman. 1910. *The Great Illusion: A Study of the Relations of Military Power to National Advantage*. New York/London: G. Putnam and Sons.
Bahador, Babak. 2007. *The CNN Effect in Action: How the News Media Pushed the West Toward the War in Kosovo*. New York: Palgrave Macmillan.
Baker, Kevin. 2001. The Year in Ideas: A to Z.: American Imperialism, Embraced. *New York Times*, December 9.
Bamford, J. 2001. *Body of Secrets*. New York: Doubleday.
———. 2004. *A Pretext for War: 9/11, Iraq and the Abuse of America's Intelligence Agencies*. New York: Doubleday.
Barber, Benjamin. 1996. *Jihad vs. McWorld*. New York: Ballantine Books.
Beinart, Peter. 2008. *The Good Fight: Why Liberals – and Only Liberals – Can Win the War on Terror and Make America Great Again*. New York: HarperCollins.
Berger, Samuel R. 2000. A Foreign Policy for the Global Age. *Foreign Policy*, November/December. http://www.foreignaffairs.com/articles/56625/samuel-r-berger/a-foreign-policy-for-the-global-age. Accessed 28 Nov 2014.
Beugel, Ernst H. Van Der. 1966. *From Marshall Plan to Atlantic Partnership*. Amsterdam: Elsevier Publishing.
Blinken, A. 2001. The False Crisis Over the Atlantic. *Foreign Affairs*, May/June.
Brinkley, Douglas. 1997. Democratic Enlargement: The Clinton Doctrine. *Foreign Policy* 106: 111–127.
Buchanan, Patrick J. 1999. *A Republic, Not an Empire: Reclaiming America's Destiny*. Lanham: Regnery Publishers.
Bull, Hedley. 1977. *The Anarchical Society*. London: Macmillan Press.
Buzan, Barry, and Ana Gonzalez-Pelaez. 2009. *International Society and the Middle East: English School Theory at the Regional Level*. Hampshire: Palgrave Macmillan.
Buzan, Barry, and Lene Hansen. 2009. *The Evolution of International Security Studies*. New York: Cambridge University Press.
Buzan, Barry, and Ole Waever. 2003. *Regions and Powers: The Structure of International Security*. Cambridge: Cambridge University Press.
Cameron, Fraser. 2002. *US Foreign Policy After the Cold War: Global Hegemon or Reluctant Sheriff?* London/New York: Routledge.
Carr, E.H. 1946. *The Twenty Years' Crisis, 1919–1939*. New York: Harper & Row.
Carter, Jimmy. 1980. *The State of the Union Address Delivered Before a Joint Session of the Congress*, January 23. http://www.presidency.ucsb.edu/ws/?pid=33079. Accessed 17 Oct 2015.
Clark, Wesley K. 2001. *Waging Modern War: Bosnia, Kosovo, and the Future of Combat*. New York: Public Affairs.
Clinton, William J. 1999. *Remarks by the President on Foreign Policy*, February 26. https://www.mtholyoke.edu/acad/intrel/clintfps.htm. Accessed 17 Oct 2015.

Cohen, Bernard C. 1973. *The Public's Impact on Foreign Policy*. Boston: Little Brown.

Cooper, John Milton. 2008. Making a Case for Wilson. In *Reconsidering Woodrow Wilson: Progressivism, Internationalism, War, and Peace*, ed. John Milton Cooper Jr., 9–24. Washington, DC: Woodrow Wilson Center Press with Johns Hopkins University Press.

Cox, Michael, et al. 2000. Introduction. In *American Democracy Promotion: Impulses, Strategies, and Impacts*, ed. Michael Cox, G. John Ikenberry, and Takashi Inoguchi, 1–17. New York: Oxford University Press.

Cox, Michael, Timothy J. Lynch, and Nicolas Bouchet, eds. 2013. *US Foreign Policy and Democracy Promotion: From Theodore Roosevelt to Barack Obama*. London/New York: Routledge.

Crabb, Cecil V., Jr. 1982. *Doctrines of American Foreign Policy: Their Meaning, Role and Future*. Baton Rouge: Louisiana State University Press.

de Tocqueville, Alexander. 1946. *Democracy in America*. London: Oxford University Press.

Destler, I.M., L.H. Gelb, and Anthony Lake. 1984. *Our Own Worst Enemy: The Unmaking of American Foreign Policy*. New York: Simon and Schuster.

Dionne, E. J. Jr. 2009. The Obama Doctrine in Action. *Washington Post*, April 16. http://www.washingtonpost.com/wp-dyn/content/article/2009/04/15/AR2009041502902.html. Accessed 17 Oct 2015.

Divine, Robert A. 1969. *Roosevelt and World War II*. Baltimore: The Johns Hopkins University Press.

Doyle, Michael. 1983. Kant. Liberal Legacies, and Foreign Policy. Parts 1 and 2. *Philosophy and Public Affairs* 12: 205–235 and 323–353.

———. 1986. Kant's Perpetual Peace. *American Political Science Review* 80: 1115–1169.

———. 1997. *Ways of War and Peace*. New York: W. W. Norton.

———. 2000. Peace, Liberty and Democracy: Realist and Liberals Contest a Legacy. In *American Democracy Promotion: Impulses, Strategies, and Impacts*, ed. Michael Cox, G. John Ikenberry, and Takashi Inoguchi, 21–40. New York: Oxford University Press.

Dueck, Colin. 2003. Hegemony on the Cheap: Liberal Internationalism from Wilson to Bush. *World Policy Journal* 20 (4): 1–11.

Eckes, Alfred E. 1971. *A Search for Solvency: Bretton Woods and the International Monetary System, 1944–1971*. Austin: University of Texas Press.

Eisenhower, Dwight D. 1957. *Eisenhower Doctrine*, January 5. http://millercenter.org/president/eisenhower/speeches/speech-3360. Accessed 17 Oct 2015.

Esposito, John. 1999. *The Islamic Threat: Myth or Reality?* New York: Oxford University Press.

Fearon, James D. 1995. Rationalist Explanations for War. *International Organization* 49 (3): 379–414.

Friedman, Thomas L. 2001. *The Lexus and the Olive Tree*. New York: Anchor Books.
Fromkin, David. 1995. *In the Time of the Americans: The Generation that Changed America's Role in the World*. New York: Alfred Knopf.
Fukuyama, Francis. 2006. *America at Crossroads: Democracy, Power, and the Neoconservative Legacy*. New Haven: Yale University Press.
Geertz, Clifford. 1973. *The Interpretation of Cultures*. New York: Basic Books.
Gholz, Eugene, Daryl G. Press, and Harvey Sapolsky. 1997. Come Home America: The Strategy of Restraints in the Face of Temptation. *International Security* 21: 79–108.
Gilbert, Felix. 1961. *To the Farewell Address: Ideas of Early American Foreign Policy*. Princeton: Princeton University Press.
Gilpin, Robert. 1975. *U.S. Power and the Multinational Corporation: The Political Economy of Foreign Direct Investment*. New York: Basic Books.
———. 1981. *War and Change in World Politics*. New York: Cambridge University Press.
Glaser, Charles L. 1997. The Security Dilemma Revisited. *World Politics* 50 (1): 171–201.
Gordon, P.H., and J. Shapiro. 2004. *Allies at War: America, Europe, and the Crisis Over Iraq*. Washington, DC: Brookings Institution Press.
Gowa, Joanne. 1995. Democratic States and International Disputes. *International Organization* 49 (3): 511–523.
Graebner, Norman. 1968. *Manifest Destiny*. Indianapolis: Bobbs-Merrill.
Hadar, Leon T. 1995. Political Islam Is Not a Threat to the West. In Paul A. Winters. Ed. *Islam: Opposing Viewpoints*. San Diego: Greenhaven Press.
Halberstam, D. 2001. *War in a Time of Peace*. New York: Simon and Schuster.
Halliday, Fred. 1995. *Islam and the Myth of Confrontation*. London: I. B. Tauris.
Hastedt, Glenn P. 2015. *American Foreign Policy: Past, Present, and Future*. Lanham: Rowman & Littlefield.
Hines, Craig. 1999. Pity, not US Security, Motivated Use of GIs in Somalia, Bush Says. *The Houston Chronicle*, October 24.
Hobbes, Thomas. 1985. *Leviathan*. Baltimore: Penguin.
Hunt, Michael H. 2009. *Ideology and U.S. Foreign Policy*. New Haven/London: Yale University Press.
Huntington, Samuel. 1992. *The Third Wave Democratization in the Late Twentieth Century*. Norman: University of Oklahoma Press.
———. 1993. Why International Primacy Matters. *International Security* 17 (4): 68–83.
——— 1999. The Lonely Superpower. *Foreign Affairs*, March/April.
Huntley, James Robert. 1980. *Using the Democracies: Institutions of the Emerging Atlantic-Pacific System*. New York: New York University Press.

———. 1998. *Pax Democratica: A Strategy for the Twenty-First Century*. London: Macmillan.

Ikenberry, John G. 2000. America's Liberal Grand Strategy: Democracy and National Security in the Post-War Era. In *American Democracy Promotion: Impulses, Strategies, and Impacts*, ed. Michael Cox, G. John Ikenberry, and Takashi Inoguchi, 103–126. New York: Oxford University Press.

———. 2001. *After Victory: Institutions, Strategic Restraint, and Rebuilding of Order After Major War*. Princeton: Princeton University Press.

———. 2009. Woodrow Wilson, the Bush Administration, and the Future of Liberal Internationalism. In *The Crisis of American Foreign Policy: Wilsonianism in the Twenty-First Century*, ed. John G. Ikenberry et al., 1–24. Princeton: Princeton University Press.

Ikenberry, John G., and Charles Kupchan. 1990. Socialization and Hegemonic Power. *International Organization* 43 (3): 283–315.

Irwin, Douglas A. 1996. *Against the Tide: An Intellectual History of Free Trade*. Princeton: Princeton University Press.

Jackson, Andrew. 1837. *Jackson's Farewell Address*. http://www.nationalcenter.org/Jackson'sFarewell.html. Accessed 17 Oct 2015.

Jervis, Robert. 1978. Cooperation Under the Security Dilemma. *World Politics* 30 (2): 167–214.

Johnson, Lyndon B. 1963. *The President's New Conference*, December 18. http://www.presidency.ucsb.edu/ws/index.php?pid=26465. Accessed 17 Oct 2015.

———. 1966. *Remarks Upon Receiving an Honorary Degree at the University of Denver*, August 26. http://www.presidency.ucsb.edu/ws/?pid=27809. Accessed 20 Aug 2015.

Johnson, Chalmers. 2000. *Blowback: The Costs and Consequences of American Empire*. New York: Metropolitan Books.

Kahler, Miles. 1997. Inventing International Relations: International Relations Theory After 1945. In *New Thinking in International Relations Theory*, ed. Michael Doyle and G. John Ikenberry. Boulder: Westview Press.

Kant, Immanuel. 1983. *Perpetual Peace and Other Essays*. Trans. Ted Humphrey. Indianapolis/Cambridge: Hackett Publishing Company.

Kennan, George. 1983. Memoirs 1925–1963. *Pantheon*.

———. 1984. *American Diplomacy*. Chicago: University of Chicago Press.

Kennan, George F. 1993. Somalia, Through a Glass Darkly. *New York Times*, September 30.

———. 1997. *The Cloud of Danger: Some Current Problems of American Foreign Policy*. Boston: Little, Brown.

Kennedy, John F. 1961. *Inaugural Address*, January 20. http://avalon.law.yale.edu/20th_century/kennedy.asp. Accessed 28 Nov 2014.

Keynes, John Maynard. 1920. *The Economic Consequences of the Peace*. New York: Harcourt, Brace and Howe.

Kissinger, Henry. 1994. *Diplomacy*. New York: Simon and Schuster.
———. 2001. *Does America Need a Foreign Policy? Toward a Diplomacy for the Twenty-First Century*. New York: Simon & Schuster.
Knock, Thomas J. 1992. *To End All Wars: Woodrow Wilson and the Quest for a New World Order*. New York: Oxford University Press.
———. 2009. Playing for a Hundred Years Hence: Woodrow Wilson's Internationalism and His Would-Be Heirs. In *The Crisis of American Foreign Policy: Wilsonianism in the Twenty-First Century*, ed. John G. Ikenberry et al., 25–52. Princeton: Princeton University Press.
Krasner, Stephen D. 1985. *Structural Conflict: The Third World Again Global Liberalism*. Berkeley: University of California Press.
Kull, Steven, and I.M. Destler. 1999. *Misreading the Public: The Myth of a New Isolationism*. Washington, DC: Brookings Institution Press.
Kupchan, Charles A. 2001. *The End of the American Era*. New York: Knopf.
LaFeber, Walter, ed. 1965. *John Quincy Adams and American Continental Empire*. Chicago: Times Books.
Lake, David. 1991. British and American Hegemony Compared: Lessons for the Current Era of Decline. In *History, the White House, and the Kremlin: Statesmen as Historians*, ed. Michael Fry, 106–122. New York: Columbia University Press.
Lake, Anthony. 1995. Remarks on the Occasion of the 10th Anniversary of the Center for Democracy. *Washington, DC*, September 26.
Landesman, Charles. 1989. Reflections on Hobbes: Anarchy and Human Nature. In *The Causes of Quarrel: Essays on Peace, War, and Thomas Hobbes*, ed. Peter Caws, 139–148. Boston: Beacon Press.
Laswell, Harold Dwight. 1950. *Politics: Who Gets What, When, How*. New York: Smith.
Layne, Christopher, and M. Lynn-Jones. 1998. *Should America Promote Democracy?* Cambridge: MIT Press.
Levy, Jack S. 1988. Domestic Politics and War: Realism, Liberalism, and Socialism. *Journal of Interdisciplinary History* 18 (4): 653–673.
Lewis, Bernard. 1990. The Roots of Muslim Rage. *Atlantic Monthly*, September.
Link, Arthur S. 1954. *Woodrow Wilson and the Progressive Era, 1910–1917*. New York: Harper and Row.
———, ed. 1966. *The Papers of Woodrow Wilson*. Princeton: Princeton University Press.
———. 1974. *Wilson the Diplomatist*. New York: New Viewpoints.
Linsky, Martin. 1986. *Impact: How the Federal Press Affects Policy-Making*. New York: W. W. Norton and Company.
Lippmann, Walter. 1995. *Essays in the Public Philosophy*. Boston: Little, Brown.

Lipset, Saymour Martin. 1959. Some Social Requisites of Democracy: Economic Development and Political Legitimacy. *American Political Science Review* 53: 69–105.

Locke, John. 1988. *Two Treaties on Government.* New York: Cambridge University Press.

Longregan, John B., and Keith Poole. 1996. Does High Income Promote Democracy? *World Politics* 49: 1–30.

Louis, Roger. 1978. *Imperialism at Bay: The United States and the Decolonization of British Empire, 1941–1945.* New York: Oxford University Press.

Luard, Evan. 1976. *Types of International Society.* New York: The Free Press.

Lukacs, John. 1997. *The Hitler of History.* New York: Alfred A. Knopf.

Lynch, Timothy. 2013. George W. Bush. In *US Foreign Policy and Democracy Promotion: From Theodore Roosevelt to Barack Obama*, ed. Michael Cox, Timothy J. Lynch, and Nicolas Bouchet, 178–195. London/New York: Routledge.

Mandelbaum, Michael. 1996. Foreign Policy as Social Work. *Foreign Affairs*, January/February. http://www.foreignaffairs.com/articles/51618/michael-mandelbaum/foreign-policy-as-social-work. Accessed 28 Nov 2014.

Markwell, Donald. 2006. *John Maynard Keynes and International Relations: Economic Paths to War and Peace.* Oxford: Oxford University Press.

McDonald, Matt. 2008. Securitization and the Construction of Security. *European Journal of International Relations* 14 (4): 563–587.

McDougall, Walter. 1997. *Promised Land, Crusader State.* Boston: Houghton Mifflin.

McLean, David. 1986. American Nationalism, the China Myth, and the Truman Doctrine: the Question of Accommodation with Peking, 1949–50. *Diplomatic History* 10: 25–42.

McMahon, Robert J. 1981. *Colonialism and Cold War: The United States and the Struggle for Indonesian Independence, 1945–49.* New York: Cornell University Press.

McWallace, W. 2001. Europe, the Necessary Partner. *Foreign Affairs*, May/June.

Mearsheimer, John J. 1995. Back to the Future: Instability in Europe After the Cold War. In *The Peril of Anarchy: Contemporary Realism and International Security*, ed. Michael E. Brown, Sean M. Lynn-Jones, and Steven E. Miller, 5–56. Cambridge, MA: The MIT Press.

Mearsheimer, John J., and Stephen M. Walt. 2007. *The Israel Lobby and U.S. Foreign Policy.* New York: Farrar Straus Giroux.

Monroe, James. 1823. *Monroe's Seventh Annual Massage to Congress*, December 2. http://avalon.law.yale.edu/19th_century/monroe.asp. Accessed 17 Oct 2015.

Moore, John Allphin, and Jerry Pubantz Jr. 2006. *The New United Nations: International Organization in the Twenty-First Century*. Upper Saddle River: Pearson Prentice Hall.

Moravcsik, Andrew. 1997. Taking Preferences Seriously: A liberal Theory of International Politics. *International Organization* 51 (4): 513–553.

Morgenthau, Hans. 1946. *Scientific Man vs. Power Politics*. Chicago: The University of Chicago Press.

———. 1969. *A New Foreign Policy for the United States*. New York: Praeger.

———. 1985. *Politics Among Nations: The Struggle for Power and Peace*. New York: Alfred A. Knopf.

Murphy, Craig. 1994. *International Organization and Industrial Change*. New York: Oxford University Press.

Nau, Henry. 2000. America's Identity, Democracy Promotion and National Interest: Beyond Realism, Beyond Idealism. In *American Democracy Promotion: Impulses, Strategies, and Impacts*, ed. Michael Cox, G. John Ikenberry, and Takashi Inoguchi, 127–148. New York: Oxford University Press.

Neustadt, R. 1960. *Presidential Power: The Politics of Leadership*. New York: Wiley.

———. 1990. *Presidential Power and the Modern Presidents: The Politics of Leadership from Roosevelt to Reagan*. New York: Maxwell Macmillan.

New York Times. 2007. *Democratic Debate on NPR*, December 4. http://www.nytimes.com/2007/12/04/us/politics/04transcript-debate.html?pagewanted=7%27s%20Changed&sq=Nothing&st=cse&scp=7&_r=0. Accessed 17 Oct 2015.

Newhouse, J. 2001. The Missile Defense Debate. *Foreign Affairs*, July/August.

Nixon, Edgar B., ed. 1969a. *Franklin D. Roosevelt and Foreign Affairs*. Cambridge: Harvard University Press.

Nixon, Richard. 1969b. *Address to the Nation on the War in Vietnam*, November 3. http://www.pbs.org/wgbh/americanexperience/features/primary-resources/nixon-vietnam/, Accessed 17 Oct 2015.

Nye, Joseph. 2002. *The Paradox of American Power: Why the World's Only Superpower Can't Go It Alone*. Oxford: Oxford University Press.

O'Neal, John, and Bruce Russett. 1997. The Classical Liberals Were Right: Democracy, Interdependence, and Conflict, 1950–1985. *International Studies Quarterly* 41 (2): 267–294.

O'Sullivan, J.L. 1839. The Great Nation of Futurity. *The United States Democratic Review* 6 (23): 426–430.

Paine, Thomas. 1995. The Rights of Man. In *Complete Writings*, ed. E. Foner. New York: Oxford University Press.

Perry, W. 2001. Preparing for the Next Attack. *Foreign Affairs*, November/December.

Pipes, Daniel. 1994. Same Difference: The Islamic Threat Part I. *National Review*, November 7.

Quinn, Adam. 2013. Theodore Roosevelt. In *US Foreign Policy and Democracy Promotion: From Theodore Roosevelt to Barack Obama*, ed. Michael Cox, Timothy J. Lynch, and Nicolas Bouchet, 37–52. London/New York: Routledge.

Reagan, Ronald. 1985. *Address Before a Joint Session of the Congress on the State of the Union*, February 6. http://www.presidency.ucsb.edu/ws/?pid=38069, Accessed 17 Oct 2015.

Rice, Condoleezza, and Philip D. Zelikow. 1997. *Germany Unified and Europe Transformed: A Study in Statecraft*. Cambridge: Harvard University Press.

Richter, M. 1977. *The Political Theory of Montesquieu*. Cambridge: Cambridge University Press.

Robinson, Piers. 2002. *The CNN Effect: The Myth of News, Foreign Policy and Intervention*. London/New York: Routledge.

Rohde, David. 2012. The Obama Doctrine. *Foreign Policy*, February 27. http://foreignpolicy.com/2012/02/27/the-obama-doctrine/. Accessed 17 Oct 2015.

Rose, Gideon. 1998. Neoclassical Realism and Theories of Foreign Policy. *World Politics* 51 (1): 144–172.

Rosenman, Samuel I. 1950. *The Public Papers and Addresses of Franklin D. Roosevelt*. New York: Random House.

Rueschemeyer, Dietrich, Evelyne Huber Stephens, and John D. Stephens. 1992. *Capitalist Development and Democracy*. Chicago: Chicago University Press.

Ruggie, John Gerard. 1982. International Regimes, Transactions, and Change: Embedded Liberalism in the Postwar Economic Order. *International Organization* 36: 379–415.

Russett, Bruce, and John Oneal. 2001. *Triangulating Peace: Democracy, Interdependence, and International Organizations*. New York: Norton.

Russett, Bruce, John Oneal, and David R. Davis. 1998. The Third Leg of the Kantian Tripod for Peace: International Organization and Militarized Disputes, 1950–1985. *International Organizations* 52 (3): 441–469.

Schumpeter, Joseph. 1950. *Imperialism and Social Classes*. New York: Harper.

Schweller, Randall L. 1994. Bandwagoning for Profit: Bringing the Revisionist State Back In. *International Security* 19 (1): 72–107.

Schweller, Randall. 2000. US Democracy Promotion: Realist Reflections. In *American Democracy Promotion: Impulses, Strategies, and Impacts*, ed. Michael Cox, G. John Ikenberry, and Takashi Inoguchi, 41–62. New York: Oxford University Press.

Shubik, Martin. 1971. Games of Status. *Behavioral Sciences* 16 (3): 117–129.

Siracusa, Joseph. 1973. *New Left Diplomatic Historians and Histories: The American Revisionists*. New York: Regina Books.

Slaughter, Anne-Marie. 2009. Wilsonianism in the Twenty-First Century. In *The Crisis of American Foreign Policy: Wilsonianism in the Twenty-First Century*, ed. John G. Ikenberry et al., 89–117. Princeton: Princeton University Press.

Smith, Tony. 2000. National Security Liberalism and American Foreign Policy. In *American Democracy Promotion: Impulses, Strategies, and Impacts*, ed. Michael Cox, G. John Ikenberry, and Takashi Inoguchi, 85–102. New York: Oxford University Press.

———. 2007. *A Pact with the Devil: Washington's Bid for World Supremacy & the Betrayal of the American Promise*. New York: Routledge.

———. 2009. Wilsonianism After Iraq: The End of Liberal Internationalism? In *The Crisis of American Foreign Policy: Wilsonianism in the Twenty-First Century*, ed. John G. Ikenberry et al., 53–88. Princeton: Princeton University Press.

Sorensen, Georg. 2000. The Impasse of Third World Democratization: Africa Revisited. In *American Democracy Promotion: Impulses, Strategies, and Impacts*, ed. Michael Cox, G. John Ikenberry, and Takashi Inoguchi, 287–307. New York: Oxford University Press.

Spellberg, Denise A. 2013. *Thomas Jefferson's Qur'an: Islam and the Founders*. New York: Knopf.

Spiro, David. 1994. The Insignificance of Liberal Peace. *International Security* 19 (2): 50–87.

Steigerwald, David. 1994. *Wilsonian Idealism in America*. Ithaca: Cornell University Press.

Talbott, Strobe. 1996. Democracy and the National Interest. *Foreign Affairs* 74 (6): 47–63.

Thompson, John A. 2013. Woodrow Wilson. In *US Foreign Policy and Democracy Promotion: From Theodore Roosevelt to Barack Obama*, ed. Michael Cox, Timothy J. Lynch, and Nicolas Bouchet, 53–68. London/New York: Routledge.

Thorne, Christopher. 1979. *Allies of a Kind: The United States, Britain, and the War Against Japan, 1941–1945*. New York: Oxford University Press.

Thucydides. 1970. *History of the Peloponnesian War*. Trans. Rex Warner. London: Penguin.

Truman, Harry S. 1947. *President Harry S. Truman's Address Before a Joint Session of Congress*, March 12. http://avalon.law.yale.edu/20th_century/trudoc.asp. Accessed 17 Oct 2015.

Vasquez, John A. 1997. The Realist Paradigm and Degenerative Versus Progressive Research Programs: An Appraisal of Neotraditional Research on Waltz's Balancing Proposition. *American Political Science* 91 (4): 899–935.

Volgy, Thomas J., and John E. Schwarz. 1997. Free Trade, Economic Inequality and the Stability of Democracies in the Democratic Core of Peace. *European Journal of International Relations* 3 (2): 239–253.

Walt, Stephen M. 1987. *The Origins of the Alliances.* Ithaca: Cornell University Press.
Waltz, Kenneth N. 1959. *Man, the State and War: A Theoretical Analysis.* New York: Columbia University Press.
———. 1971. Conflict in World Politics. In *Conflict in World Politics*, ed. Steven L. Spiegel and Kenneth N. Waltz. Cambridge, MA: Winthrop.
Williams, William Appleman. 2001. *History as a Way of Learning: Articles, Excerpts, and Essays.* New York: Franklin Watts.
———. 2009. *The Tragedy of American Diplomacy.* New York: W.W. Norton & Company: 50th Anniversary Edition.
Wilson, Woodrow. 1913. Annual Message to Congress on the State of the Union. 2 December. In *The Papers of Woodrow Wilson*, ed. Arthur S. Link, vol. 29. Princeton: Princeton University Press 1966.
———. 1914. *Address at the Independence Hall: "The Meaning of Liberty".* July, 4. http://www.presidency.ucsb.edu/ws/?pid=65381. Accessed 15 Aug 2015.
Wittkopf, Eugene R., and James McCormick. 1999. *The Domestic Sources of American Foreign Policy.* Lanham: Rowan and Littlefield.
Woodward, R. 2004. *Plan of Attack.* New York: Simon and Schuster.

CHAPTER 3

The Securitization Theory

Securitization theory is mainly associated with the Copenhagen School. An alternative approach to traditional security theories, securitization includes the society and identity in the set of security referent objects (Buzan and Hansen 2009: 30–45 and 212–217). Relatively new, in comparison to other international relations and political science theories, there are still debates about whether securitization is a theory, a method, a concept, a philosophy (Williams 2015: 114), or just an idea that explains what is already known. We, as many other scholars, consider it to be a theory that analyzes current international security events accurately. Based on the speech act and the speech act theory, securitization theory is also a part of the Schmittian debate of exceptional politics and security (Buzan and Hansen 2009). This theory draws on different international relations theories, such as constructivism, poststructuralism, and critical theory, explicitly trying to understand how an issue becomes a security problem (Balzacq 2011b: 1). Securitization is the third level of dealing with political issues. The non-politicization level includes issues that are not important, that are not worth discussing. The politicization level includes political issues for the public to discuss and to express their opinions. In the security level, one takes the political issues from the public discussion to a higher level of politics where the highest-level politicians and institutions deal with them, giving them an exceptional importance and emergency to deal with (Buzan et al. 1998; Waever 1998; Buzan and Hansen 2009) but not by the public.

© The Author(s) 2018
E. A. Shipoli, *Islam, Securitization, and US Foreign Policy*,
https://doi.org/10.1007/978-3-319-71111-9_3

Uttering security keywords when talking about a political issue securitizes it. This is done in a speech act by politicians and decision-makers who attach an existential importance to that issue to deal with immediately and ask to use extraordinary means to deal with that issue, means that would not be used in everyday politics (Waever 1995, 1998; Williams 2003). The literature of the securitization theory analyzes who securitizes, what are the referent objects, with what results, and under what conditions. These answers are not the same in domestic securitization, international securitization, and systematic securitization. They differ in scale, nature of the threats, nature of the referent objects, as well as in the importance of different sectors and conditions of the time (Shipoli 2010). This book shows how these actors change when an ideology, religion, or a greater identity is securitized, in this case Islam.

Common misconceptions that have to do with securitization are the concepts of desecuritization and asecuritization. Briefly, desecuritizing an issue does not mean that the threat does not exist anymore; it only means that one brings it to the low politics for the public to discuss and the government to build its policies accordingly. Like in the case of EU membership, the countries have taken off their label of security in their relations with each other, but this doesn't mean that there is no security threat between these countries. When an issue is successfully politicized that it cannot be securitized anymore, one can say that the issue has been asecuritized (Waever 1998; Williams 2003). It is important to understand these concepts, as they will be used later in this work.

Securitization can be considered as a "more extreme version of politicization" (Buzan et al. 1998: 23). It is considered to be a continuation of politics in a more radical form when normal politics does not work. The theory has a large field of application, from human and public security to the military and state security. A securitized issue needs to be dealt with immediately according to the securitizing actor, because if we do not tackle it now we will either not exist to deal with it later or we will not be free and able to deal with it anymore (Buzan et al. 1998; Waever 1998). An issue that is being securitized is presented as existential and the threat toward that issue is presented as a threat to one's own existence. This does not always mean that the securitized issues are socially constructed and they are not real. Most of them, in fact, are real. But the point here is that for an issue to be securitized, despite the fact if it is a real security issue or not, it needs to be constructed and presented in a particular way.

What the securitization theory tends to find out is: Why do we call an issue a security issue? What are the implications of calling it so—or of not calling it so? (Waever 1999: 334) Why some issues become security issues while others do not? Where do security and politics collide, and how do threats determine politics? (Balzacq 2011a: xiii) What is a real security problem and what is a perceived one?

3.1 Building Blocks of the Securitization Theory

There are some particular must-have building blocks for securitizing an issue and building it as existential. These concepts might change for domestic, international, and systematic securitization (Shipoli 2010).

Referent object is the most important element in the securitization theory in particular but also in the security studies in general. The referent object is the object that has the right to survive and the object that should be defended by all means. Whatever means needed to secure the referent object are legitimate. It is also essential that measures to secure the survival of the referent object should be taken immediately. The idea is that if the referent object does not survive, all other issues will be irrelevant and we will not be who we are at the moment. Traditionally the state and the nation have been the referent objects in the security studies (Buzan et al. 1998), but today the scope of referent objects has included environment, human rights, cyberspace, and many other fields. The scale of the referent object is an important factor in the success of the securitization act. Sometimes a referent object for one party can be a threat to another. Take for example Kurdistan or Catalonia: while one party sees it as a national cause and a referent object, the other party sees it as a threat.

Securitizing actors are similarly important. They are the ones that make the speech act, attach the existential importance to the referent object, identify the threats, and present the security issue to the public. The securitizing actors can be individuals or groups, but they must be influential, mainly political leaders, government, lobbyists, interest groups and bureaucrats (Buzan et al. 1998; Buzan and Hansen 2009), or experts on the referent object. An important detail here is that the securitizing actors need to be appropriate when securitizing an issue to be able to gain legitimacy (Williams 2003); the health minister cannot securitize the nuclear power of a country, but can securitize the healthcare system of a country. Thierry Balzacq calls this the linguistic competence (2011b: 25), where we should analyze who is allowed to speak for that matter of security and who is competent to debate it. The person or persons that have the linguistic competence to talk about that particular security issue commend trust, competence, knowledge, and guidance. Looking at who is the speaker for that particular issue determines the importance of that issue as well. If one wants to understand the weight of an issue in the eyes of senior government officials, they can look at the assigned official who declares and talks to the public about that particular issue or policy. More powerful officials deal with priority issues and vice versa. Also, a securitizing actor cannot be a referent object. It is not logical to argue your own survival in front of the public and ask for extraordinary means to secure your survival or the survival of your position in the society. Rather, one argues the securitization of the nation, state, principles, or values instead.

There must be a *threat* to be able to securitize an issue, and this threat must be eliminated for the survival of the referent object. Threats should be carefully picked. The threat needs to be such that it should touch the lives of the people if not dealt with immediately. Buzan et al. (1998) identify two types of threats in the securitization process: the existential and the non-existential threats. The existential threats are the ones that are present to the historical or geographical rivalry between neighbors or states. Non-existential threats, on the other hand, are constructed threats to serve the purpose of the elite or the pressure group, who make a securitization act. Although different sectors of security have different existential threats, the biggest challenge is to recognize and separate existential and non-existential threats. While threats posed to the sovereignty or the ideology of the state are existential threats to the political security sector, the identity of groups, the nation, the values, or the principles are threats in the societal security sector. But sometimes these sectors are not so clearly divided. Religion, although present in the societal sector, can sometimes be a threat (or constructed as such) to the ideology of the state. Turkey, for this matter, has securitized secularism (and Kemalism) against Islam and for years the state ideology was securitized against the threat of religion, in this case Islam (Bilgin 2008). Extraordinary means, like coups, imprisonment of political leaders, or closure of parties, were taken to guard secularism against conservatism.

Despite the direct involvement of actors in the securitization process of an issue, there are *functional actors* that influence the process of securitization. Such actors are the building blocks that do not securitize an issue or are not the referent objects, like factories in the environmental security sector or religious parties in the societal and political sectors, with the condition that they do not take direct role in securitizing an issue, or being the referent object (Buzan et al. 1998). The group of factional actors can be limitless, depending on the scope of the issue that is being securitized.

Without the audience accepting an issue as a security issue, one cannot talk about a successfully securitized issue. When there is a referent object whose existence is being threatened, functional actors and securitizing actors, then one can speak of a *securitizing move*. This is a very important element in the securitization process as it is the final process before going to the public and declaring the need for securitizing an issue.

The consent is expected from the public, also referred to as the *audience*, toward whom the securitizing act is being made. The public needs to accept it, not necessarily in a referendum but a silent consent is also acceptable (Buzan et al. 1998), and give permission for the use of extraordinary means, which would not be used in normal circumstances. Their consent gives the right to the security actors to use any means to make sure the survival of the referent object. The audience also validates the acts of the securitizing actors. But, it is important to note that the audience needs to be an "enabling audience", which has a direct connection with the securitized issue and has the right and ability to empower the securitizing actor to take measures to secure the referent object (Balzacq 2011c: 34). Audience is the most distinguished building block between domestic, international, and systematic securitization.

One of the most important building blocks in securitization is the *speech act*, which is theorized by Jane Austin (1962) in her book *How to Do Things with Words*. Austin argues that the speech act is neither true nor false; it is a performed action, like when you say, "I bet" you actually "act", or when you say, "I do" in a marriage, you actually "perform" something and your status changes, and even when you "declare war" you perform an act and you are in the state of war. In such cases there is no further action needed to finish these acts, they are final. Security is also a communicative act (Waever 1995), which affects the audience and drives them to act accordingly. Speech act is equated to action, not only communication (Austin 1962; Waever 1995; Buzan et al. 1998; Booth 2007), and this is why, by labeling an issue as a "security" issue, one preforms an act, such as naming a baby, naming a ship, getting married, or declaring a war. This case only updates the "speech act" into the "security speech act", where a political significance and an existential importance are given to the issue that is labeled as "security" (Waever 1995). When labeling an issue as a security issue, usually the word "security" is uttered. But that is not always a must, as words such as "defense, offense, or attack" have a similar effect as the word "security" (Waever 1995; Buzan et al. 1998). In politics, a security-labeled issue is equated to existence; this is why it becomes a priority policy for the government and the people. When an issue is profiled as a security issue then the action has already happened. There is no true or false, it immediately becomes a security issue, which is later discussed by the audience to issue the legitimacy to use the extraordinary means, that would not be used in normal circumstances, just to ensure the wellbeing of the securitized issue.

Language is always very important in politics, but especially in constituting a threat and a security atmosphere, language becomes even more important. Bourdieu (1999: 170) argues that there is a magical symbolic power of words, as they make people see and believe a particular vision of the world and make them act and mobilize in that world, as almost an equivalent of force. German philosopher, Jurgen Habermas (1984: 289), explains the relation between language and action as follows: "to say something, to act in saying something, to bring about something through acting in saying something".

Equally important is *framing*. To securitize an issue, the utterance of the word security is not always necessary. It can be substituted with other security words or with visuals that depict a security situation. Nevertheless, the framing of the securitization is important because there should be a correct securitizing move, toward a correct referent object, in front of the right audience (Vultee 2011: 77) in order to be relevant and successful. Framing is a construction process that involves entertainment, news, headlines, pictures, and the words that are used in media (Vultee 2011: 78). For example, the securitization of the war on terror did not happen through security keywords and speeches, but by constantly showing terrorist attacks, setting the agenda, and increasing fear in the public. When framing, sociological and psychological realities are very important. Constant coverage and framing of terrorism has allowed the securitizing actors and the audience to accept stereotypes, actors, and immediate solutions, easier and much faster, without much prior information (Norris et al. 2003: 11). Media can also be used to address different types of audiences, the public, the political establishment of the country, the international leaders, and other audiences, who are addressed differently because the support they give to the securitizing actor is different. The public gives a moral support, the political establishment a more formal support, and the international leadership needs to justify the discourse and the actions that will be taken.

Sometimes identity carries much higher weight than anything else, because it defines who "we are" and what "we stand for". Thus, framing a threat toward identity rather than the state per se has shown to be more lucrative for the securitizing actors. For example, when President Bush stated that "freedom itself was attacked this morning" on his first statement on 9/11 terrorist attacks, he named "freedom" as the victim of these terrorists (Anker 2005) and made "freedom" the core American national identity (Vultee 2011: 81). Securitization of sovereignty is important for state security, but securitization of identity is important for societal security, as it implies survival (Waever 1995: 67). This is why people react much faster when immigrants are framed as a threat to the identity of the society, or other threats to the identity and wellbeing of the society. America's "hyper-patriotism" (O'Reilly 2008: 69) has let the societal securitization be in high alert, and it is much easier to securitize any identity issue that resonates with American society. The 9/11 attacks, and their coverage and framing afterward, stripped American journalists and policymakers from ethical responsibility of objectivity, because we were witnessing a tragedy, the public was in danger, and the national security was threatened (Schudson 2002). In the next presidential elections, no one could question the administration's terrorism policies or argue anything against the war on terror (Bishop 2004). Now, more than ever, we should be careful what we consider as "sacred", because accordingly everything else can be framed as a threat.

Securitizing the "sacred" has become a real issue today; thus there is a need to study the securitization of religion deeper. This work will contribute to this, as it analyzes how Islam was constructed as a security issue, but there is a need for further scholarly analysis on the issue. Political actors have been using religion to justify their acts for ages. This is not a new trend, but what is new is that even secular leaders have started using religion, mostly with negative connotations, for their own purposes. You can see an increasing far-right movement in Europe and America, who use religion in their discourse to gain followers and make a point. But, the use of religion has not been exclusive to political actors. Non-state actors have also been using religion for their own gains—from Muslim terrorist organizations using Islam and Islamic discourse to far-right, Christian supremacy American groups using Christian discourse for their own purposes against governments, against minority groups, immigrants, or other religious communities. Secessionist armed groups in the USA often justify their acts with religious discourse. Religion is used as much by Buddhists in Myanmar in their genocide of the Rohingya Muslim community as by the ISIS terrorists against the Yezidi population in Iraq.

3.2 The Evolution of the Securitization Theory

Securitization is vaguely defined, as another level of dealing with political issues. Different scholars give different definitions. Thierry Balzacq for example defines it as,

> an assemblage of practices whereby artefacts ... are contextually mobilized by a securitizing actor, who works to prompt an audience to build a coherent network of implications, about the critical vulnerability of a referent object, that concurs with the securitizing actor's reasons for choices and actions, by investigating the referent subject with such an aura of unprecedented threatening complexion that a customized policy must be undertaken immediately to block its development. (Balzacq 2011b: 3)

There are many definitions of securitization today. Sometimes it feels that the definition of securitization has moved out of its initial Copenhagen School definition, and now it only means that an issue is a matter of debate in security terms (Croft 2012: 78). This evolution is productive because we can better understand the securitization of political issues, their negative and positive sides, as well as how to solve them.

Many scholars consider the securitization theory as part of the Schmittian debate of exceptional politics and security (Buzan and Hansen 2009; Waever 2011) with the sense of exceptionality and urgency for the securitized issues. Williams (2015) brings the securitization theory further than Schmittian exceptional politics to the politics of extraordinary, arguing that securitization is wider than the view of enmity, emergency, exceptionality, and negativity that has been attributed to the theory, because of looking at it as a theory of exceptional politics. Rather, he argues, securitization is a wider perspective that includes the negative dimension as well as the positive dimension of security and politics. Borrowing from Andreas Kalyvas (2008), Williams expands securitization to the "politics of extraordinary", focusing on the potential of a positive securitization as a process of democracy, self-determination, and openness. He argues that like the politics of the extraordinary that describes the power of the people to make positive and sovereign change, with popular mobilization and consensus (Kalyvas 2008: 164–165), securitization also has the potential of positive mobilization of the sovereign, for democratic processes; thus defining it in terms of friend-enemy terms is very limiting. This develops the securitization theory further to explain what we argued at the conclusion of this book, that securitization is a process and it is neither bad nor good, it is what one makes of it. While it can be misused by demagogues to securitize issues for their interests, others will have to use it to securitize issues that are of real existential importance, otherwise people would not know about them.

When analyzing and researching securitized issues, how one designs the research is of utmost importance. The differences of research design have also contributed to the evolution of the securitization theory, as more case studies are analyzed, the more securitization theory has been developed. What the students of securitization need to focus on while they design their research is what they are going to analyze: the threat, the referent object, the speech act, or other building blocks of securitization. Most focus on case studies, which is very productive because one can analyze different elements of securitization in a case study, and it is easier to understand. Balzacq argues that there are three types of case studies in securitization: typical, which shed light on the already known, given phenomenon. They serve more informative goals; critical cases, whose main aim is to test the application of the theory on those cases; and revelatory cases, which analyze cases that were previously out of sight (2011c: 32–34).

As for the methods of analysis, there are four methods of analyzing securitization that Thierry Balzacq (2011c) identifies. Discourse analysis is the first method that most students of securitization theory use. It is the oldest method as well, because the Copenhagen School had initially limited securitization to speech act, and only later did it evolve to include visuals, writing, and context. Although the methods have evolved, we have used mainly discourse analysis in this work as it is the most relevant for our cases. But we have also looked into images, visuals, and context, with lesser focus.

Ethnographic research is the second method. This research method is the most sensitive to the sociological variant of securitization. Taken from Clifford Geertz (1971), ethnographic research is characterized as the study of a concrete, microscopic case. In short, it is the miniature study of the whole, like taking a particular event and amplifying to explain the whole event. We have used this method, among others, when we analyzed particular speeches of presidents, to amplify the doctrine toward Islam and security in American political discourse. For this method, open-ended interviews can also be helpful, with the "insiders" of that particular issue, such as administration members of a particular presidency, who had to do with security and Islam.

Process-tracing is the third methodology proposed. Based mainly on qualitative data, this method is based on tracing the process that the securitization move has gone through, and if it produced a successful or an unsuccessful securitization. We consider a securitization move to be successful when the audience accepts it. An audience has the power to grant the securitizing actors the right to use the means to secure the referent object. If we analyze securitization through the process-tracing methodology, then we are analyzing the scope and conditions under which a securitization has succeeded or failed. We analyze the social mechanisms that have affected that success or failure. However, we need to investigate both successful and unsuccessful securitization cases (George and Bennett 2005; Salter 2008), as they both have different lessons to teach. The two main focuses are audience and the co-dependency of agency and the context. Circumstances are very important and the power of persuasion by the agents is equally important. Using this method will produce a detailed narrative, analytical explanation, a more general explanation, and generalizations (George and Bennett, 2005: 210–211).

Finally, it is the content analysis method, which we have used mostly for this work, but not limited to it. With this method, the researchers use content analysis to understand what the audience responds to and whether it is independent from the context or not (Hermann 2008: 167). Moyser and Wagstaffe (1987: 20) explain the content analysis as a method to explain the ways that the agents use symbols to communicate and as a meaning for their own purpose. These methods don't have to be exclusively used. They can be combined and the best results were drawn when they were combined. For this work, we have used all of them at different points to get the best of them and analyze the securitization of Islam in US foreign policy as best as we can.

The primary debate and development on the securitization theory revolves around the "audience". Who the audience is, what its role is, and similar questions are constantly debated, and this has developed the securitization theory since Waever first wrote about it. Waever recognized the need to study audience more to come to "a better definition and probably differentiation" (2003: 26). The problem with the audience is that we cannot judge exactly when the audience is persuaded (Stritzel 2007: 363) and that there are different types of audiences at different points. The securitizing actors must address them at different levels on different occasions. For example, while the leaders of international organizations might be the audience for a global security issue, they become securitizing actors when they securitize that issue toward their domestic audience, their nations (Shipoli 2010). Salter (2008: 322–328) argues that there are four types of audiences: popular, elite, technocratic, and scientific. They all must be addressed differently.

Other scholars categorize the audience in other categories. Michael Williams (2011) gives another perspective on the audience and the securitizing actors. He argues that the audience of the securitization theory does not necessarily exist prior to securitization, and it can be constructed by the securitizing actor, bringing together an audience that is interested in that issue but didn't exist before as unified. Furthermore, he argues that the element that will bring together and unify this audience in the security domain is fear, because "security appeals to what we don't know: to fears of the unknown, the unforeseen, and the perhaps unforeseeable" (215). In the case of President Bush securitizing Islam, we see that fear played a major role in unifying American public on the one hand and international leaders on the other. In fact, fear is the most overplayed sentiment for securitization, because when there is fear people act less rationally and they are more likely to give the right of utilizing extraordinary means to the government in order for them to guarantee their security.

Most scholars that deal with securitization theory agree that it is under-theorized. Much more research, with different examples, needs to be made to understand the audience, when securitization happens (McDonald 2008: 573) and how it happens at different levels. Understanding the audience, its role and impact, is important because for the securitization act to become successful there is a need for the audience to accept it, and this is why the securitizing actors need to identify with the audience, through feelings, needs, and interests (Balzacq 2011b: 9). The securitizing actor needs to persuade the audience by speech, gesture, tone, image, attitude, by sympathizing and identifying with them. The consent of the audience is also very much debated. What kind of consent should be given to the securitizing actor so we can understand that an issue was successfully securitized? While most scholars agree that silent consent is enough, it is also important that the audience has the ability and the power to let the securitizing actors use any means to secure the referent object and that they have a relation with the issue that is being securitized (Balzacq 2011c: 34). In the different levels of securitization the audience is very important as is the consent that they give.

Securitization is used by political leaders for different purposes. The most common uses of securitization theory are agenda setting, deterrence, legitimizing past actions, control (Vuori 2008: 76), preserving the status quo, and defining "self" against a different "other". The idea of the development of the securitization theory is that there are no security issues in themselves; they are constructed as such (Buzan et al. 1998: 21). These issues are constructed as security issues and then transformed into policy as security problems. These issues are moved from the political level to the security level by speech (Waever 1995: 55). The audience is convinced that the problem is indeed a security one (Leonard and Kaunert 2011: 66) and this way the agenda is set for that issue to be taken as a security issue in public discourse and the policy is built accordingly. Another indicator of successful securitization is policy formation. When the securitizing actors have set up the agenda and persuade the audience, they then measure the approval and disapproval from the public. When they feel that the approval rates have increased, they form policies that reflect the securitization of that issue.

After the agenda is set, and the audience is persuaded, the securitizing actors look for bargains and build winning coalitions, because some people (audience) may have been convinced, and some may have not. The ones that are not yet convinced have to be given something in return (Leonard and Kaunert 2011: 67; Kingdon 1984: 160). Securitization is also a negotiating process between different audiences. While the public can give moral support, there is a need of political support from the political establishment (Balzacq 2005; Roe 2008). Leonard and Kaunert use the analogy of Kingdon, who used to explain how policy is done and adopted, to explain how the securitizing actors, who they have equated with Kingdon's "policy entrepreneurs", have to act fast to use the "policy window" to adopt a policy toward that securitized issue (2011: 68–69). These "policy entrepreneurs" that in securitization are better known as securitizing actors have the social capital and the position authority for securitizing that particular issue (Buzan et al. 1998: 33), but they also have the expertise, the ability to speak for others, a decision-making position, political connections, negotiation skills, and are persistent (Kingdon 1984: 180). The "policy windows", on the other hand, are the time frames that policy entrepreneurs use to adopt policies. When such an opportunity is opened it is best to securitize an issue and adopt a policy then, but also the policy window being open for an issue means that there is a higher probability that policies for other, similar, issues can be adopted. The policy entrepreneurs can sense the opening of the policy window for a popular issue, and they see an opportunity to push for the adaptation of another, related, policy (Kingdon 1984: 168–190; Leonard and Kaunert 2011: 68–69). Patriot acts are results of these policy windows that policy entrepreneurs used to adopt policies that have limited liberties of Americans and have securitized Islam. This is because they sensed the policy window of terrorism as a popular issue, and then they pushed for their own agenda.

Another very much debated topic in securitization is timing. The securitizing actors need to choose critical times when they try to persuade the audience for securitizing an issue (Balzacq 2011b: 13). Also, issues at different levels—domestic, international, or systematic—need different periods of time to be securitized. International securitization takes more time, has more agents, than domestic securitization (Shipoli 2010). But, systematic securitization is a longer campaign, has a larger scope, has more agents, and takes more time than securitization of an international issue. The bigger the issue is, the more actors it involves. The experience of the securitizing actors, the policy entrepreneurs, is also important. How fast can they frame the security issue and what powers they have in hand are very important. Similarly important is if they have securitized any issues before. It will be difficult for Finland to securitize an international conflict, whereas for America that is much easier. They know how to do it, what arguments to use, who to go to, and they have done it before. If Finland tried to securitize the conflict in Kosovo and make it an international security issue, it would have been unlikely to evolve to NATOintervention. But when America did it, in a matter of months NATO intervened in Kosovo.

Scholars of international relations and security studies have identified varieties of securitizations. Thierry Balzacq (2011b), for example, argues that there are differences in analyzing securitization from the philosophical and sociological perspectives. The differences that he sees are three: first, from the philosophical perspective, securitization is reduced to a "conventional procedure" where the conditions must fully occur, such as marriage or betting, for the act to happen. For the sociological perspective, on the other hand, securitization is a more pragmatic process, where circumstances, contact, the power and mindset of the audience, and speaker all influence the act. Second, from the sociological view, agents' "habitus" mediate performatives; they inform the perception and the behaviors (Bourdieu 1990, 1999). Thus, these performatives are analyzed as results of power games. The third distinction is the audience, where the philosophical view takes the audience as formal, given; whereas the sociological view sees both the securitization actors and the audience as constructed.

For Balzacq, these differences are important because "Securitization can be discursive and non-discursive; intentional and non-intentional; performative but not 'an act in itself'" (2011b: 2). This adds to Pouliot's claims that social actions are not necessarily results of premeditated design, and sometimes they happen without an initial intention for that social action (Pouliot 2008: 261). Balzacq (2011b) ultimately criticizes the power of the speech act in security, claiming that it is not an act in itself, and urges the scholars to look at circumstances and sociological realities, which play an equally important role as the speech act. For him, to claim that securitization is a speech act is to reduce securitization and miss the larger scope it can cover in analyzing security issues.

Securitization is a process, a campaign, that can succeed and can fail at the end. There are successful and unsuccessful securitized issues in world politics. Kosovo and Islam are successfully securitized issues at their respective levels. According to Mark Salter, the process that defines if a securitization move was successful or not in securitizing an issue must answer these four questions: First, how much is the issue discussed in the wider political debate? Second, is the threat accepted as existential or not? Third, is the solution accepted or not? And fourth, are the new emergency powers given to the securitizing actors? (2011: 120) Furthermore, Salter argues that possible securitizable issues need to be within the scope of political discussions; that the threat must be accepted as existential because if it is accepted as a temporary panic then it cannot be securitized; that the solution put forward by the securitizing actors must be accepted by the public; and that the emergency powers need to be granted to the securitizing actors, such as a policy change, budget, or the actual right to intervene by force. While we agree with most of these assessments, we don't believe that acceptance of the solution is necessary. Salter himself says that the American public has questioned Bush's counterterror policies, although the war on terror was successfully securitized; but when we look at it we see that those policies went forward and it didn't matter that the public did not accept them, challenged them, and finally rejected them.

While we argue in the last part of this chapter that there are three levels of securitization—domestic, international, and systematic—Thierry Balzacq identifies three other levels of analysis: agents, in which we analyze the actors involved on securitizing the issue, such as securitizing actors, audience, functional actors, referent objects, threats, and alike, their drives, intentions, and power; acts, in which we analyze the methods used to construct the security (Williams 2003; Wilkinson 2007, 2011); and context, where we analyze the context where the discourse happens, as neither the discourse nor securitization happens in vacuums, but within a specific context (Fairclough and Wodak 1997). This level deals more with discourse analysis, and it explains the relationship between what is being said, when it is being said, and where it is being said (Crawford 2004).

3.3 Securitization of Religion: New Sectors in the Securitization Theory

There have been many criticisms addressed toward the securitization theory and its authors, Barry Buzan and Ole Waever. The main criticisms, some of which we discussed above, pointed out different perspectives of the theory, challenges, as well as its limits. But we must give credit to Weaver and Buzan, because they never said that the theory was complete. In fact, on many occasions they argued that the theory is underdeveloped and that it needs more scholars to study and contribute to it. In their book with Jaap de Wilde, which most consider to be the foundation of the securitization theory, *Security: A New Framework of Analysis*, they initially distinguished between sectors: political, economic, military, societal, and environmental. While some critics have argued that there are some sectors that don't fit in any of the initially identified sectors, both Buzan and Waever argued for other sectors to be included (Buzan and Albert 2011; Waever 1999). Buzan argues that sectors are only lenses, and there is a need for new lenses in the securitization theory. Law should be differentiated from the political sector and so do gender and religion from the societal one (Buzan and Albert 2011). And there have been new studies that have separated these sectors into new lenses, or some have merged, for example, religion with both a societal and political lens. As Buzan and Albert (2011: 415) point out, "Sectors are thus seen as analytical devices that are used to shed light on the diverse practices and dynamics of securitization. ... [They] are identified simply from the existing usages in the discourse of security", and that the number and type of sectors will be defined by the security discourses.

One of the main sectors that needs to be studied further is religion. This sector is also very relevant to this book, and this is why it is important to analyze the evolution of religion into security discourse in world politics. As we said before, religion is vastly used in political disocurse and the time to study it in relation to security is overdue. It is time to bring religion back from exile, which is where it went after the Treaty of Westphalia, when the nation-state became the standard. This nation-state was understood as a secular nation-state and religion had no place in it (Shipoli 2017). In fact, for most secular states their essence of existence was in conflict with religion. By omitting religion from political discourse the problem has grown, and today religion has become a security issue instead. Vendulka Kubálková (2003) rightly argues that the time has come for an "International Political Theology" discipline, similar to the international political economy or international security. But that is beyond the scope of this book. What is in the scope of this book, however, is to analyze how religion is securitized and how there is a need of further studies on religion and security.

It is assumed that since the end of the Cold War, conflicts and wars are motivated by identities and cultures. Huntington's idea that the re-emerging of the importance of religions will reinforce cultural and ideological differences (Huntington 1997) has been adopted as a mainstream idea. Today, wars are less driven by classical drives of power and territorial gains; they are labeled more as ethnic, religious, or cultural (Laustsen and Waever 2000). These assumptions and the claims of many violent non-state actors of being religiously driven have brought religion to the security level. In the area of security studies, this assumption has been supported by the alleged threat from fundamentalism, primarily assumed as Islamic fundamentalism (Esposito 1999), but then evolved into evangelic fundamentalism in the USA (Laustsen and Waever 2000: 705–706). This has not been more eminent than today, when we speak about the American far-right, and far-left, even more than Islamic fundamentalism. Suddenly, scholars who neglected religion from international relations, politics, and security studies started talking about religion and its threat toward the established secular states. Often considered as political moves, the religious dimension of the discourse of fundamentalism and security should not be downplayed. But how are we going to analyze the securitization of religion?

Securitization theory argues that the character of the referent object is important and makes a big difference. Therefore, we need to firstly characterize the nature, logic, and importance of securitized religious beliefs and objects. Then we need to understand how what we might think is specific to religion may be present in other political ideologies (Laustsen and Waever 2000: 706–707). Here is where sectors, once more, enter in the debate. Religion has been considered as part of the societal sector, according to the initial sectors defined by the Copenhagen School, where nations, minorities, clans, and other ethnonational identities are included besides religion. However, this categorization does not analyze religion as religion, but as a community, in the similar fashion as the nation, minorities, clans, and other ethnonational identities; whereas, religious discourse is about a transcendent, about faith, truth, worship, and belief, rather than defending a particular identity or community (Laustsen and Waever 2000: 709). So, we need to understand the characteristic of the objects that we are analyzing to be able to analyze them correctly and do them justice.

Another debate about religion being a separate sector is that we know what is the referent object for the military, economic, and societal sectors, but for religion that is debated. Usually it is "faith" or "being" that are the referent objects. Referring to sacred referent objects as threatened directly implies that one's faith and being is threatened, and thus they are securitized. It is easy to securitize religion because associating a threat to the referent object directly implies a threat to its existence; thus the securitizing move toward a religious referent object is much more successful and quick than another political or societal object. But, it is never automatic that association of threat will need to be done in the political realm (Laustsen and Waever 2000: 719). Today what we often see is the use of religious discourse, as a fast way of securitization, for political referent objects. Al-Qaeda's threat was considered as a threat toward America as a state and as a nation. But also, the invasion of Afghanistan and Iraq was considered as "crusade" or a "call from God" by the Bush administration. So, most of these sectors cannot be thought as independent, and here is where religion is mixed with the political sector; thus considering it only from the societal sector lens will not do it justice. It is best if religion is considered as a separate sector that contributes and takes from other sectors, but is not under another sector altogether. Religion is unique in security discourse and thus needs to be treated uniquely. Even in public life, religion claims to be unique, the oneness of God and the message, the divine, and the transcendent.

How religion can be involved in international politics and security is categorized in three by Laustsen and Waever, in one of the early articles about securitization "In Defence of Religion: Sacred Referent Objects for Securitizations" in 2000. They are:

1. A religious group is considered to be a threat to the survival of the state.
2. Faith is seen as threatened by whoever or whatever "non-religious" actor or process (states, technology, industrialism, modernism, etc.).
3. Faith is seen as threatened by another religious discourse or actor.

Interestingly, not much has been written about securitization and religion after that, although this has been one of the earliest scholarly works on securitization.

For this work, we are mainly focusing on the first category. In this category, the threats are defined as fundamentalisms against the secular state, and the enemy is not only from abroad, it can be from within as well. The struggle between secular state and fundamentalism is not only political, in fact it is a religious struggle as well, defined by the "modernist" view toward religion by the seculars versus the "pre-modern" view toward religion by the fundamentalists. In this case, fundamentalism as a term is sufficient, it is a keyword, of securitization. The secular state leaders use this, and other keywords, to securitize religion against the secular state. Very little has been written about the secular pressure and hatred toward religion, in comparison to how much has been written about the religious, or fundamentalist, pressure and hatred toward secularism. In fact, many secular governments, such as the USA, France, or Turkey, have violated liberal and democratic processes to counter what they considered as "fundamentalist [religious] threat" (Juergensmeyer 1995: 353; Laustsen and Waever 2000: 720–721). This discourse was used extensively by George W. Bush to justify the invasion of Afghanistan and Iraq. He claimed that America knows what fundamentalism could do so they needed to be stopped right away. In fact, he even went further to claim that America has seen this before, with fascism, and that America knows how dangerous it is. Many US policymakers before Bush have labeled the threat against America as Islamo-fascism, but Bush has adopted it as a policy, beyond the discourse. We will discuss this further in the upcoming chapters.

The second category is the category of faith being threatened by non-religious actors. This type of securitization of religion is not directly linked to this book, but it is important to remember that crusades were such a war, where there was a need to fulfill God's will and where religion was threatened (Laustsen and Waever 2000: 722–723). Why it is important to point this out is because the invasion of Iraq and Afghanistan was labeled as both: a crusade and a call from God. In this category, it is not religion that acts, but some political leaders act for religious purposes, or religiously labeled purposes.

And the third category is about the clash of two religious discourses, which is usually the type of conflict that first comes to mind that involves religion as a security issue. Nevertheless, especially after Westphalia, this is the most uncommon conflict, where a religion clashes with another religion. It is more common that religion conflicts with state or with secularism (Laustsen and Waever 2000: 723; Juergensmeyer 1995: 2). The three categories of securitization of religion are present and are used from time to time by different political actors, both religious (such as Iran) and secular (such as America).

These discussions alone are sufficient for claiming that there is a need to consider religion as a sector on its own. However, these sectors are linked, and they cannot always be analyzed separately. Today, we can see even more that religious discourse and the securitization of religion are used more often in politics. But how does this securitization affect religion? Laustsen and Waever correctly argue that "securitizing religion means impoverishing it" (2000: 726) because religion stops being about the divine, and becomes about politics, be it about the state, the leader, or the political ideology. Ideology is the one that does harm to religion. Thus "de-securitization then means de-securitizing ideology, or in other words respecting religion as it is" (Laustsen and Waever 2000: 726) and letting religion be religion. In many cases, ideologies abuse religion, posing as religions themselves, using similar components as religion in discourse to gain more legitimacy. Securitization of religion because of ideological purposes leads to violation of liberal and democratic rights of citizens, nations, and sovereign countries.

In some countries, like in Turkey, both the secularists and the conservatives have securitized religion. The secular Kemalist elite have seen and constructed religion as a threat to the wellbeing of the secular state. Policies were adopted accordingly and political actions, such as military coups, were taken because of this. Conservatives, on the other hand, securitize religion as being threatened by the state; by the previous, mostly secular, elite; by other religious groups; and by foreign powers. The defense and the wellbeing of Erdogan as the leader of the ideology have been constructed as the wellbeing of religion itself. Belief and religion have become less about the divine, about the sacred, about nature, or humanity, and more about the ideology, the leader, and the wellbeing of the present status quo. Interestingly, their discourse is also similar. Secularists used to frighten the audience into believing that if they lose power the country will go back to the dark ages of religious governance, where women were oppressed, where the state will decide how you look, where you go, how you practice your religion, or your style of life. Whereas conservatives today frighten the audience by claiming that if they lose the power the country will go back to the dark ages of secular state where state will decide what you wear, where you go to school, how you practice your religion, and discriminate against the conservatives. It is not important if these claims are true or not; what is important is that the claims were very similar to one another, and religion played an important role in constructing these claims, realities, and the discourse of both sides.

The question is not whether religion is another sector of securitization, as in today's security discourse religion is an inescapable element of that discourse. But the question is what are we going to do about it? When diplomats are deployed in other countries, for example, they are trained on the culture, the language, and the traditions of those places. They are also trained on protocol, universal manners and etiquettes, communication skills, and even listening. But they don't learn about that country's religious beliefs, and sometimes the religious values and sensitivities are not even taken into consideration. Spiritual and emotional life is also important in peacemaking and conflict resolution, but they are usually ignored, too.

As per the topic of this book, we must point out that the securitization of Islam has developed further the securitization theory in general and the sector of religion in particular. The otherness and the demonization of Muslims and Islam are done not only through speech act but also with images and videos. Muslims and Islam are the "radical other", the "oriental other" (Croft 2012: 247), or the "fundamental other". America and European countries have depicted Islam and Muslims as the fundamentalist threat to their survival and have vowed to do everything in their power to stop it (Cesari 2010). Jocelyne Cesari raises an important point: the securitization of Islam is not only done by the discourse of the leaders, and the media propaganda, but very often Muslim spokespeople are depicted to talk against Muslims and Islam (2010: 14), both in Europe and in America. The likes of Ayaan Hirsi Ali and Maajid Nawaz are only few examples. By securitizing Islam, European countries and America have restricted the liberties and democracy of their citizens, which explains Laustsen and Waever's claims under the first category of securitization of religion. Nevertheless, as we will speak below about different levels of securitization, the securitization of Islam in US foreign policy has transcended its implications form the USA to the world. That is because Islam was securitized in the systematic level and this securitization of Islam has been used in the discourse of different leaders around the world, like the Serbian leaders against the Bosnians and the Kosovo Albanians. They increased their rhetoric against Muslims and Islam by referencing to Bush's speeches (Erjavec and Volcic 2007), to justify their acts against the Muslims in ex-Yugoslavia.

For the securitization of Islam in US foreign policy we will speak in depth in the following chapters; thus it suffices for now to stop here, as the main goal was to make a point about the securitization of religion, as both a political fact and a contribution to the expansion of the securitization theory.

3.4 Securitization: Domestic, International, and Systematic—An Alternative to Liberalism and Realism to Explain US Foreign Policy

Similar to the need for different analytical lenses, there is a need for different levels of analysis. We propose three different levels of analysis in securitization: domestic, international, and systematic. They change in scope, actors, aims, and methods. Let's first look at the differences between domestic and international securitizations.

Domestic and international securitizations are very different (Shipoli 2010). Domestic securitization is closer, is more defined, and has less but better-known actors, and usually the issues are related to a particular country or nation, whereas international securitization is done in the international arena for an international issue that concerns more than two countries or nations. It is much more difficult, it is open to different voices, and includes more but less-known actors. The elite of a country, the interest groups in that country, the government, or the political leaders usually securitize a domestic issue to preserve the status quo and prevent change, because domestic change usually means instability (Buzan 1991: 303), whereas security means the protection of the position of leaders, interest of the interest groups, the government, or the elite of the country, that is, the status quo. In international securitization, however, there are many actors that are not present or not as influential in the domestic securitization. Besides the leaders and the elite of the states, the international securitization includes leaders of international organizations, such as the General Secretary of the United Nations or NATO (Buzan et al. 1998; Buzan and Hansen 2009), and also other experts on that particular issue. International non-governmental organizations, international leaders, and some international institutions replace the power of states or state leaders in securitizing an issue internationally. The UN, for example, can securitize an issue by declaring it as "a threat to international peace and security" (Buzan et al. 1998: 149–151). Different organizations have different impacts when securitizing an issue. The World Health Organization, for example, will not have the same effect on securitizing an historic site, as UNESCO would have; or, UNESCO would not have the effect of securitizing a global health issue as it has in securitizing a historical site as a "world heritage".

Territory, ideology, and nation are the usual referent objects in domestic securitization. Territory is the most "sacred" referent object for domestic securitization because most of the wars in history have been waged to secure this referent object (Buzan 1991: 92–96). In international securitization, state-based issues lose the monopoly of the referent objects. The development of security studies and security concerns in the world has diverged the attention of security studies to other, non-state, issues. Environmental issues, global economic issues, poverty, and natural disasters are only some of the international, non-state concerns that are tackled today (Buzan and Waever 2003: 360). With the new global problems that we face today, internationally securitized referent objects have increased. Just recently there have been more discussions about the importance to tackle cybersecurity more seriously as a common threat.

Media is an important platform on which to perform the speech act, both in domestic and international securitizations. Nevertheless, they differ in this as well. Because the securitizing actors are more limited in domestic securitization, and because the media outlets are owned by a small circle of people, they are more effective and easier to use for securitization in the domestic realm, whereas using media in the international securitization is much more difficult for the securitizing actors because of the different voices and point of views that the international media might have. Where the media is state controlled, one is usually able to see what the government wants them to see, which serves their purpose in securitizing an issue (Buzan 1991: 347–353), whereas the international media do not concern only one country and are typically privately owned media outlets. The effect of the international media, often labeled as the CNN effect, has an important role. It prioritizes an issue, sets the agenda, draws solutions, and is a platform for the leaders to perform their speech act internationally (Shipoli 2010: 58–61).

In fact, one cannot speak of a united audience in international securitization as one does in domestic securitization. The people are usually the targeted audience in domestic securitization, and they are the ones that give the permission to use the extraordinary means to secure the survival of the referent object. The relationship between the audience and the securitizing actor is less clear in international securitization (Fierke 2007). Domestic securitization is a one-layer process, where the securitizing actor securitizes an issue toward the people. International securitization, on the other hand, is a multi-layered process, where first the securitizing actors in international securitization (including the actors that cannot securitize a domestic issue but are present among the securitizing actors of international issues) securitize an issue toward the elite or the leaders of every country/government that he/she wants to be involved, and only afterward they together securitize that issue toward the people of those governments or of those security communities (Shipoli 2010). Here it can be seen that in international securitization the audience can change the role and be a securitizing actor afterward.

International securitization is more scattered and lacks a formal road map of securitization (Buzan et al. 1998: 152), with different and changing actors, objects, and methods. Unlike in domestic securitization, in international securitization one requires a better organization and more collective actors of securitization, rather than individual actors (Bahador 2007). International securitization, thus, is a more complicated process than that of domestic securitization.

Buzan and Waever (2009) have developed another concept, that of "macrosecuritization", which analyzes the construction of threats beyond the individual and regional platform. Macrosecuritized events include the Cold War, nuclear proliferation, climate change, and the global war on terror. These are issues that concern the whole globe and are beyond international securitized issues, which include many states and regions (Shipoli 2010). What we have referred to as "systematic securitization" is a wider version of Buzan and Waever's "macrosecuritization". The main problem remains: who shall take actions against such threats, and how they should be securitized. Although Fierke (2007) claims that it is up to the governments to act on them, these roles are not very clear. Analyzing issues in the scope of the Cold War, climate change, or nuclear proliferation will certainly develop the securitization theory further, because these are issues that concern the whole globe, not only one country or one region. This work aims to develop the securitization theory toward this direction, from domestic to international securitization and then to the systematic securitization where only a few issues, such as the Cold War, nuclear proliferation, and ideological competitiveness, make it to that level. It argues that Islam has been securitized at that level.

The case for the systematic securitization will be made while we analyze the securitization of Islam in US foreign policy, and we will have a clearer differentiation between the three levels in the conclusion, but to introduce the reader to the systematic securitization, as a third level of analyzing securitized issues, it will be beneficial to make some points here. When one analyzes the engagement of US foreign policy with Islam, one can see that most of these steps were taken to securitize Islam. These claims will be argued in the following chapters, but for now it suffices to say that Islam has been constructed as the most imminent "threat" to the USA and beyond, as the main issue worldwide, where the world is polarized between two: with us or against us.

As far as US foreign policy toward Islam is considered, and how they have dealt with Islam, neither liberalism nor realism or any other mainstream theory can explain the US engagement and view toward Islam completely. There is a need for another theory that can explain this particular policy, something that would be outside of the debated box, and this work shows that the securitization theory is that theory. Liberalism and realism, as has been seen, are very important and have an enormous legacy in US foreign policy, but in the policies toward Islam they both collide and go outside their boundaries. The securitization theory can explain this particular issue better. What makes the securitization theory different and more authoritative in explaining security issues is that unlike the mainstream theories, securitization is concerned with analyzing insecurities together with the available shared knowledge. While mainstream theories analyze insecurities as an objective threat toward an objective entity, securitization analyzes the construction of these threats and how they threaten other entities. How threats are perceived and how they are defined are equally important for the securitization theory, whereas in the mainstream theories, such as realism, threat is perceived as a unit that affects other actors (Balzacq 2011a: xiii), not analyzed deeper as a dependent variable.

The USA needed the "other" after the Cold War. The mentality that has developed in 40 years since the Cold War has trained many experts and policymakers, who have seen the world from the "us" versus "them" perspective. In many other attempts America could not locate that rival; China, weapons of mass destruction, ethnicities, and others, did not fulfill the criteria that the USA was looking for. Societies are created by threats and global societies needed global threats (Beck 2002), so what America needed in order to construct a global society was a global threat. When 9/11 happened, it was natural that the Muslims be in the "other" category toward the USA and what it stands for. Islam, with all of its influence, geographical reach, and differences, fits the frame. The US policymakers brought Islam to be a securitized issue, an issue that only they can deal with, and that normal people should fear, so they give all their rights to them. US foreign policy and security elite's self-selecting policy of foreign policy and security issues (Kegley and Wittkopf 1996: 7) have selected Islam to become the new actor in the security level of America especially after the Cold War, as a continuation of the Cold War mentality, just with different actors, where the new "red" is now "green" and the new "Cyrillic" is now "Arabic".

US securitizing actors, policymakers and especially the president, securitized Islam toward the American public but also toward the other global leaders. Religion was used to justify this securitization, so security was religionized. Muslims were depicted as enemies, and Islam was depicted as something that stood opposite of American values, namely democracy. Women and women's rights were depicted as something that resonates with America and that needed protection. The result was intervention in Afghanistan and Iraq in the name of democracy, to protect and save the women and find the weapons of mass destruction. The world was divided into two poles: with us or against us. This is what we call systematic securitization.

Islam was successfully securitized during the George W. Bush presidency, but the problems increased, America was not more secure, it was less secure. The next administration recognized this failed policy and accepted that Islam had been securitized during the previous administration. They saw that to ensure the wellbeing and security of America, as well as democracy promotion, human and women's rights, and international cooperation, they need to desecuritize Islam. Many steps were taken but they were not enough. Desecuritization is a much harder process than securitization. The failure of the desecuritization of Islam, and other issues, has produced the Trump presidency: a direct result of the unsuccessful desecuritization in American politics.

America has gone between liberalism and realism multiple times in foreign policy, but the great historical moments have happened when both of these theories, ideologies, were combined (Gilbert 1961: 136). And for this particular issue, this combination has left space for new, alternative theories. In relation to Islam, the US foreign policymakers decided to approach it in security terms, bringing Islam to a security level, dividing the world into poles, associating Islam with security keywords, and constructing it as an ideology that would be an obstacle for the US grand strategy of democracy promotion, the view that for America to be safe, the territories of democracy needed to expand.

After all these studies on securitization, the theory has yet to be fully developed, and it has a lot of potential. Religion will be an important sector that will contribute to further development of securitization theory, firstly by bringing it back from exile and then normalizing and analyzing it as religion, rather than being associated by ideologies.

Among other things, securitization theory students will also have to find the answer of "who can resist securitization?" and "how?". We are aware that securitization is used for good and ill purposes, but how can we resist securitizing moves, is still unknown.

References

Anker, Elisabeth. 2005. Villains, Victims, and Heroes: Melodrama, Media, and September 11. *Journal of Communication* 55 (1): 22–37.

Austin, Jane L. 1962. *How to Do Things with Words*. Oxford: Clarendon Press.

Bahador, Babak. 2007. *The CNN Effect in Action: How the News Media Pushed the West Toward the War in Kosovo*. New York: Palgrave Macmillan.

Balzacq, Thierry. 2005. The Three Faces of Securitization: Political Agency, Audience and Context. *European Journal of International Relations* 11 (2): 171–201.

———. 2011a. *Securitization Theory: How Security Problems Emerge and Dissolve*. London/New York: Routledge.

———. 2011b. A Theory of Securitization: Origins, Core Assumptions, and Variants. In *Securitization Theory: How Security Problems Emerge and Dissolve*, ed. Thierry Balzacq, 1–30. London/New York: Routledge.

———. 2011c. Enquiries into Methods: A New Framework for Securitization Analysis. In *Securitization Theory: How Security Problems Emerge and Dissolve*, ed. Thierry Balzacq, 31–53. London/New York: Routledge.
Beck, Ulrich. 2002. The Terrorist Threat: World Risk Society Revisited. *Theory, Culture & Society* 19 (4): 39–55.
Bilgin, Pinar. 2008. The Securityness of Secularism? The Case of Turkey. *Security Dialogue* 39 (6): 593–614.
Bishop, I. 2004. Nuisance Nonsense: Rudy Rages at Kerry's Crack on Slashing Level of Terror. *New York Post*, October 12.
Booth, Ken. 2007. *Theory of World Security*. Cambridge: Cambridge University Press.
Bourdieu, Pierre. 1990. *The Logic of Practice*. Cambridge: Polity Press.
———. 1999. *Language and Symbolic Power*. Cambridge, MA: Harvard University Press.
Buzan, Barry. 1991. *Peoples, States, and Fear: An Agenda for International Security Studies in Post-cold War Era*. Colorado: Lynne Rienner.
Buzan, Barry, and Lene Hansen. 2009. *The Evolution of International Security Studies*. New York: Cambridge University Press.
Buzan, Barry, and Mathias Albert. 2011. Securitization, Sectors and Functional Differentiation. *Security Dialogue* 42 (4–5): 413–425.
Buzan, Barry, and Ole Waever. 2003. *Regions and Powers: The Structure of International Security*. Cambridge: Cambridge University Press.
———. 2009. Macrosecuritisation and Security Constellations: Reconsidering Scale in Securitisation Theory. *Review of International Studies* 35 (02): 253–276.
Buzan, Barry, Ole Waever, and Jaap de Wilde. 1998. *Security: A New Framework of Analysis*. London/Boulder: Lynne Rienner.
Cesari, Jocelyne. 2010. Securitization of Islam in Europe. In *Muslims in the West After 9/11: Religion, Politics, and Law*, ed. Jocelyne Cesari, 9–27. London/New York: Routledge.
Crawford, X. 2004. Understanding Discourse: A Method of Ethical Argument Analysis. *Qualitative Methods* 2 (1): 22–25.
Croft, Stuart. 2012. *Securitizing Islam: Identity and the Search for Security*. Cambridge: Cambridge University Press.
Erjavec, Karmen, and Zala Volcic. 2007. 'War on Terrorism' as a Discursive Battleground: Serbian Recontextualization of G.W. Bush's Discourse. *Discourse and Society* 18 (2): 123–137.
Esposito, John. 1999. *The Islamic Threat: Myth or Reality?* New York: Oxford University Press.
Fairclough, N., and R. Wodak. 1997. Critical Discourse Analysis. In *Discourse as Social Interaction*, ed. T. Van Dijk, 258–284. London: Sage.

Fierke, K.M. 2007. *Critical Approaches to International Security*. Cambridge/Malden: Polity Press.
Geertz, Cliford. 1971. *Islam Observed: Religious Development in Morocco and Indonesia*. Chicago: University of Chicago Press.
George, A.L., and A. Bennett. 2005. *Case Studies and Theory Development in the Social Sciences*. Cambridge, MA: MIT Press.
Gilbert, Felix. 1961. *To the Farewell Address: Ideas of Early American Foreign Policy*. Princeton: Princeton University Press.
Habermas, Jurgen. 1984. Theory of Communicative Action. In *Reason and Rationalization of Society*, vol. 1. Boston: Beacon Press.
Hermann, M.G. 2008. Content Analysis. In *Qualitative Methods in International Relations: A Pluralist Guide*. New York: Palgrave Macmillan.
Huntington, Samuel P. 1997. The Erosion of American National Interests. *Foreign Affairs* 76 (5): 28.
Juergensmeyer, Mark. 1995. Antifundamentalism. In *Fundamentalisms Comprehended*, ed. Martin A. Marty and R. Scott Appleby. Chicago: University of Chicago Press.
Kalyvas, Andreas. 2008. *Democracy and the Politics of Extraordinary*. Cambridge: Cambridge University Press.
Kegley, C.W., and E.R. Wittkopf. 1996. *American Foreign Policy: Pattern and Process*. New York: St. Martin's Press.
Kingdon, J.W. 1984. *Agenda, Alternatives, and Public Policies*. Boston: Little Brown.
Kubálková, Vendulka. 2003. Toward an International Political Theology. In *Religion in International Relations: The Return from Exile*, ed. P. Hatzopoulos and F. Petito, 79–105. New York: Palgrave Macmillan.
Laustsen, Carsten Bagge, and Ole Waever. 2000. In Defence of Religion: Sacred Referent Objects for Securitization. *Millennium: Journal of International Studies* 29 (3): 705–739.
Leonard, Sarah, and Christian Kaunert. 2011. Reconceptualizing the Audience in Securitization Theory. In *Securitization Theory: How Security Problems Emerge and Dissolve*, ed. Thierry Balzacq, 57–76. London: Routledge.
McDonald, M. 2008. Securitization and the Construction of Security. *European Journal of International Relations* 14 (4): 563–587.
Moyser, G., and M. Wagstaffe. 1987. *Research Methods for Elite Studies*. London: Allen and Unwin.
Norris, Pippa, Montague Kern, and Marion Just, eds. 2003. *Framing Terrorism: The News Media, the Government, and the Public*. New York: Routledge.
O'Reilly, C. 2008. Primetime Patriotism: News Media and the Securitization of Iraq. *Journal of Politics and Law* 1 (3): 66–72.
Pouliot, V. 2008. The Logic of Practicality: A Theory of Practice of Security Communities. *International Organization* 62 (2): 257–288.

Roe, P. 2008. Actor, Audience(s) and Emerging Measures: Securitization and the UK's Decision to Invade Iraq. *Security Dialogue* 39 (6): 615–635.

Salter, Mark B. 2008. Securitization and Desecuritization: A Dramaturgical Analysis of the Canadian Air Transport Security Authority. *Journal of International Relations and Development* 11 (4): 321–349.

———. 2011. When Securitization Fails: The Hard Case of Counter-Terrorism Programs. In *Securitization Theory: How Security Problems Emerge and Dissolve*, ed. Thierry Balzacq, 116–132. London: Routledge.

Schudson, Michael. 2002. What's Unusual About Covering Politics as Usual. In *Journalism After September 11*, ed. Barbie Zelizer and Stuart Allan, 36–47. New York: Routledge.

Shipoli, Erdoan A. 2010. *International Securitization: The Case of Kosovo*. Saarbrucken: Lambert Academic Publishing.

———. 2017. Bringing Religion Back from Exile. *HuffPost*, January 4. https://www.huffingtonpost.com/entry/bringing-religion-back-from-exile_us_586bdbfee4b068764965c499. Accessed 7 Aug 2017.

Stritzel, H. 2007. Towards a Theory of Securitization: Copenhagen and Beyond. *European Journal of International Relations* 13 (3): 357–383.

Vultee, Fred. 2011. Securitization as a Media Frame: What Happens When the Media 'Speak Security. In *Securitization Theory: How Security Problems Emerge and Dissolve*, ed. Thierry Balzacq, 77–93. London: Routledge.

Vuori, J.A. 2008. Illocutionary Logic and Strands of Securitisation – Applying the Theory of Securitisation to the Study of Non-democratic Political Orders. *European Journal of International Relations* 14 (1): 65–99.

Waever, Ole. 1995. Securitization and Desecuritization. In *On Security*, ed. Ronnie D. Lipschutz, 46–86. New York: Columbia University Press.

———. 1998. Insecurity, Security, and Asecurity in the West European Non-war Community. In *Security Communities*, ed. E. Adler and M. Barnett. Cambridge: Cambridge University Press.

———. 1999. Securitizing Sectors?: Reply to Eriksson. *Cooperation and Conflict* 34 (3): 334–340.

———. 2003. Securitization: Taking Stock of a Research Program in Security Studies. *Mimeo*.

———. 2011. Politics, Security, Theory. *Security Dialogue* 42: 465–480.

Wilkinson, C. 2007. The Copenhagen School on Tour in Kyrgyzstan: Is Securitization Theory Unseable Outside Europe? *Security Dialogue* 38 (1): 5–25.

———. 2011. The Limits of Spoken Words: From Meta-Narratives to Experiences of Security. In *Securitization Theory: How Security Problems Emerge and Dissolve*, ed. Thierry Balzacq, 94–115. London: Routledge.

Williams, Michael C. 2003. Words, Images, Enemies: Securitization and International Politics. *International Studies Quarterly* 47: 511–531.

———. 2011. The Continuing Evolution of Securitization Theory. In *Securitization Theory: How Security Problems Emerge and Dissolve*, ed. Thierry Balzacq, 212–222. London: Routledge.

———. 2015. Securitization as Political Theory: The Politics of the Extraordinary. *International Relations* 29 (1): 114–120.

CHAPTER 4

Islam in US Politics

This chapter explores the place of Islam in US politics. It analyzes the early encounters of Americans with Muslims and the relation of Islam, Muslims, and America during and after the Cold War. In particular this chapter analyzes the places of Islam in US foreign policy, from history to the present time. Although this book will focus on the foreign policymakers, US foreign policy is a product of domestic realities (Quandt 1986: 6–29), influenced by public opinion, media, interest groups, Congress, and other institutions. For this reason, even though this work will focus on the executive branch and presidents' closest policymaking elite, it cannot turn a blind eye to the domestic actors, when necessary.

Since the end of the twentieth century, especially by the beginning of the twenty-first, the USA has had the largest economy, unequaled military power, with the longest history of democracy, political stability, and educated population. This makes the USA the only superpower, or in the words of the former French Foreign Minister Hubert Vedrine, a "hyperpower". But the first year of the twenty-first century showed that even this superpower, or hyperpower, could not be immune to the terrible terrorist attacks (Cameron 2002: xi) on its political and financial capital cities. The USA today has the largest and most technologically advanced military, with a global reach (Brzezinski 1997: 23) and presence of 725 bases all around the globe, out of which 17 are full-powered bases, and a quarter million deployed servicemen, one-and-a-half million of which are active ones. This military power is much more effective when considered together

© The Author(s) 2018
E. A. Shipoli, *Islam, Securitization, and US Foreign Policy*,
https://doi.org/10.1007/978-3-319-71111-9_4

with the USA's power in international organizations starting from the UN, the IMF, the World Bank to NATO, WTO, and other regional and global organizations.

Nevertheless, US intelligence failed to predict the 9/11 attacks (Fouskas 2003: 125) and the attacks afterward. With all the strategists and the artificial and technological intelligence it possesses, the USA failed to predict the outcomes of the wars in the Middle East, the next terror attacks, and the next steps it needs to take to maintain its national security.

Studying American foreign policy in particular and American politics in general has been difficult but also very important. Even though it is very difficult to define what foreign policy is, and it is far beyond the scope of this work, it is considered as a policy of how a nation/country deals with another nation/country, region, and globally, over mutual issues of interest or international issues. Driven by values, interests, national objectives, foreign policy is a combination of many external and domestic factors. In fact, it is a very complex equation of economic, military, ideological, social, cultural, political, and legal components (Cameron 2002: xvi; Fouskas 2003: 116), where most if not all of these factors must be incorporated in most if not all of the foreign policy decisions. In fact, even war is the continuation of foreign policy by other means (Clausewitz 1976). Traditionally, foreign policy has focused on governments, but recently there has been a shift in its focus to international concerns of climate change, global warming, genetically modified organisms, investment regimes, human rights (Cameron 2002: xvi), aviation regulations, pollution, and many other issues, which have a small share of foreign policy just to break the monopoly of the focus on governments' political, economic, and military issues. This shift has made foreign policy much more difficult.

When analyzing the world's diplomatic history, it can be seen that every century has a new power, which shaped the politics of that century according to its values. The seventeenth century was shaped by France's nation-state and national interest as the ultimate purpose. The eighteenth century was shaped by Great Britain's concept of balance of power, which lasted for the next 200 years. The nineteenth century came back and forth between Austrian and German influence, which shaped European diplomacy into a "cold-blooded game power politics". The twentieth century, on the other hand, has been heavily shaped by the US foreign policy of engagement in other countries' domestic affairs while promoting its own values as universally applicable (Kissinger 1994: 17–18). NATO and its transformation from a defense to a political pact have supported this new mission of the USA by projecting her hegemony of values promotion in the zones that during the Cold War were influenced by the Union of Soviet Socialist Republics (USSR) (Fouskas 2003: 13–15). Today America can neither withdraw from world affairs nor dominate them, and this is the new phenomenon of the new world order (Kissinger 1994: 19) that no great power can stay out of world affairs, and no single great power can dominate the world.

While there is a consensus among foreign policy analysts that the promotion of democracy is the goal of the USA's engagement in world affairs, there is also an agreement that the US foreign policy has changed with the September 11, 2001, terrorist attacks in New York and Washington DC. This period has been associated with planes crashing the twin towers of World Trade Center, a symbol of American economic power (Parmar et al. 2009: 1), and Pentagon, the symbol of American security power. Furthermore, the American power is on trial for the invasion of Afghanistan and Iraq. The post-Bush era foreign policy is often compared to the post-Vietnam foreign policy, but it is early to decide if they are the same (Parmar et al. 2009: 1–2). Although it is early to make the link between the post-Vietnam era and the post-Iraq era, Vassilis Fouskas (2003: 24–25) makes a link between Vietnam and Kosovo, when he explains the Camp Bondsteel that the US army built in Kosovo, which he claims is the biggest American military camp after Vietnam.

Speaking of US foreign policy and the Balkans, there are many international relations commentators, like Chomsky, who constantly question the USA's national interests and the intervention in Kosovo and Bosnia. Some analysts claim that the reason was the expansion of NATO eastward and improving the USA's political image by supporting Kosovo Muslims, counterbalancing its pro-Israeli politics in the Middle East. The post-Cold War US foreign policy had a strategy of unifying the Balkans with the Middle East, to serve a geostrategic purpose for the USA, which could not be achieved during the Cold War (Fouskas 2003: 26). This includes the US grand strategy of stability and the creation of areas of stability all around the world.

American foreign policy's lean toward democracy promotion is based on the firm confidence that the USA has internalized this system and shines as the brightest example for others to follow. In many cases, including the speech he made on the eve of the NATO intervention in Kosovo, President Clinton claimed that the character of a nation's foreign policy is a reflection of its values, and democracy is definitely America's value (Clinton 1991). Making references to American values, US presidents have legitimized their actions in foreign lands on the ground of defending and promoting those values.

Understanding the patterns of the US foreign policy and the mentality behind it will help us to examine the role and the place that Islam played in US foreign policy but also in the discourse of the US foreign policymakers. Understanding the role of democracy in establishment of the USA, and the role that democracy promotion plays in America's foreign policy, is crucial to understanding American political culture and American foreign policy. When talking about Islam and how Islam should be engaged, usually there is a tendency to associate those discussions with democracy promotion, which is equally important to understand in order to analyze the place of Islam in US foreign policy.

4.1 Islam in America and American Foreign Policy

Even though Islam has been present in America for a long time, not so much has been written about it. As for the time being, the literature on Islam in the USA is limited but growing rapidly.[1] We need to analyze the place of Islam in the US history, to be able to understand the place of Islam in US politics and foreign policy today.

Today, Islam and the Middle East dominate the news in American media. Especially associated with the negative news, Islam is viewed as the cause for radicalism, extremism, and terrorism (Esposito 2012: x). This view is present despite the fact that Islam is the third largest religion in the USA. Islamophobia has become the new orientalism in today's modern world.

The US politics has been influenced by different sources on Islam, but orientalists have occupied the biggest part. Scholars like Bernard Lewis and Samuel Huntington were the closest to the White House in the turn of the twenty-first century, while liberal and pluralist scholars were mostly kept isolated from the policymakers. This century's study of Islam by the policymakers is very biased, taking in consideration that Bernard Lewis advises that "Muslims and Islam have not changed over the centuries" and therefore to be able to understand today's Muslims it suffices to read the

---

[1] A group of 80 literary agents have released an open call for submission from Muslim authors after Donald Trump was elected the US president. More by Antonia Blumberg, Dozens Of Literary Agents Release Open Call From Muslim Authors, http://www.huffingtonpost.com/entry/open-call-muslim-authors_us_589b9b79e4b04061313b778e

ninth-century manuscripts (Lewis 1993; AbuKhalil 2002: 18–19). It is during such crisis as the Iranian Revolution and hostage crisis, the Gulf War, or the 9/11 terrorist attacks that Americans show more interest toward Islam. Qur'an becomes the best seller, and the media puts it in focus. People rush to study Qur'an when they see it as a threat, and even though it might be a coincidence Tony Blair's declaration that he is studying Qur'an just after the "new war on terrorism" links Islam with terrorism, and only then arises the will to educate the public about Islam (AbuKhalil 2002: 19). This is not something new. During the seventeenth-century America and Great Britain, Islam was used as a tool to criticize or protest everything: Catholicism, violence, American revolution, the Pope, British tyranny (in America), and more. British officers associated the American revolutionaries with Muslim soldiers that fought beside the Muslim Prophet (Spellberg 2013: 32), to condemn the enemy and also show anti-Islamic sentiments. On the other hand, others have used Islam in their debates in association with anti-Trinitarianism, thus being tolerant toward Islam (Spellberg 2013: 69). Islam has been a topic of debate whenever there was a conflict, unfortunately depicting only parts of it, or prejudices toward Islam, for their own interests.

4.1.1 Early History of Islam in America

From the beginning of migration to North America, Protestant preachers have brought across the ocean the European prejudice against Islam, and in the USA they found a ready audience. They demonized Islam, or the Prophet of Islam, as one of the heads in the twin-headed manifestation of Antichrist, one being Islam and the other being Catholicism, or one being the Prophet Mohammed (or the Sultan) and the other being the Pope (Marr 2006; Kidd 2009: 8; Quinn 2008: 24–43; Spellberg 2013: 20). They claimed that both Catholicism and Islam were violent and spread by sword (Scouten 1961: 1104; Spellberg 2013: 30). American Protestants inherited their hostility toward Islam from protestant reformers from Europe in the sixteenth century, who defined Antichrist in terms of Islam (Fuller 1995). For Europeans, Islam presented three main threats to its wellbeing: a challenge to Europe's stability as Islam was both a religion and a social institution; a challenge to Christian expansion, as Islam was a pluralist religion; and finally, the claim that Islam was the last Abrahamic revelation might supersede Christianity and confine it to the spiritual, theological, and social wilderness (Allen 2010: 26). Up until the end of the eighteenth century Americans thought of Islam as an invention of Muhammad, as tyranny, and the antithesis of Anglo-Britain political ideals and values, as this was preached to them by books, theater shows, and sermons at churches (Allison 2000: 35–59; Kidd 2009: xii–xiii; Marr 2006: 5–9).

Among the biggest influencers of the American Protestants is the German protestant reformer, Martin Luther (1483–1546), who wrote that the person of Antichrist is both the Pope and the Turk (referring to the Ottoman Sultan, who was depicted—incorrectly—as the head of Muslims, just as Pope is for the Christians) and only later changed to the claim that the spirit of the Antichrist is the Pope whereas the flesh is the Turk (Scribner 1994: 150–183). French Protestant reformer, John Calvin (1509–1564), one of the biggest influencers of American Protestantism, also depicted the Antichrist in terms of Islam, but he did not refer to the Sultan but to the Prophet himself, as the twin of the Pope (Slomp 1995: 134). In lighter accusations, Anglican clergyman Humphrey Prideaux (1648–1724) wrote that the Muslim Prophet has forged chapters of the Qur'an on Jewish and Christian sources and has not received any revelations from the angel Gabriel (quoted in Spellberg 2013: 18). This was the highly circulated view on Islam by the seventeenth-century English clergymen, and although Prideaux claims he knew Arabic, taught in Oxford at that time, his book showed little knowledge on the Arabic scriptures, rather it showed most references to the Latin translations of Arabic scriptures. Prideaux became very popular with many editions of his book in England and three editions published in America (Spellberg 2013: 14–19).

Stereotyping and profiling of Muslims and Islam in Europe was not only done through books and preaching; theaters also played a big role. The first play about Islam performed in America was written by Francois-Marie Arouet, better known as Voltaire (1694–1778). It was first written in French as "Le Fanatisme, ou Mahomet le Prophete". It was first staged in Paris in 1742, then in England in 1744, and in America in 1776. This play depicted the Muslim Prophet as a religious and political fanatic. He degraded Islam by associating it with religious violence, intolerance, and religious prosecution. After its premier in Paris it was forbidden by the Catholic clergy as they claimed that Voltaire did not want to explain Islam but rather wanted to explain Catholicism, because at that time the violence of Catholics toward Protestants was a national French policy, and Voltaire used the Islamic context to avoid censorship from clergy and the government, a tactic which did not work as he was prosecuted afterward

(Allison 2000: 43–46; Matar 1999: 169–183; Spellberg 2013: 27–29; Schueller 1998: 49–58; Gunny 1996: 134–141; Elmarsafy 2009: 81–84). Voltaire was known for his criticism of religion in general, so for him it didn't matter if it was Islam or Catholicism that he depicted in these plays, but it is important to note that such stereotypes of Islam and Muslims were promoted in eighteenth-century Europe.

There were some terms that were used to depict the Muslims in sixteenth- and seventeenth-century Europe and then America. The term "Turk", for example, was very popular in Europe and was used to depict Muslims. Coming from the Ottoman conquest, Turk was used instead of the term "Muslim" despite the fact that Turks constituted only a portion of the Muslim population in the world. In the sixteenth century it was used in English to mean "a cruel, rigorous, or tyrannical man", and these negative connotations continued to be widely used in America during the seventeenth and eighteenth centuries (Spellberg 2013: 25). The term "Mohametan" was another term used in sixteenth-century Europe as a misconception that Muslims are worshipers of Mohammet, not God alone. This term and its similar spellings were used in America in reference to Islam as the faith of "Mohametanism", which shows how these misconceptions were imported from Europe to America and how little they knew about Islam (Battistini 2010: 141 Marr 2006: 6). Another term was "Moor", meaning someone with darker skin, a connotation for Arabs and Berbers in North Africa and used by American Protestants in reference to Muslims (Battistini 2010: 473–474; Spellberg 2013: 26). Finally, the term "Alcoran" was used for the holy book of Islam. The problem with this word is that it used the Arabic prefix "al", meaning "the", and the French word "Coran", so that the meaning of Alcoran would literally be "the Coran" instead of the correct "Qur'an", meaning "Recitation". In America, the problem was bigger because they used to call Qur'an as the "Alcoran of Mahomet", wrongly claiming that the Prophet was the author (Spellberg 2013: 26; Gunny 1996: 156).[2] These terms were developed by orientalist writers, some of whom have not traveled to the Muslim lands but have written from their imagination. It is not only that these names

---

[2] According to Islamic beliefs the Qur'an was revealed to Prophet Muhammad, but it was not codified during the Prophet's time. The Qur'an was written only after the Prophet's death, by his close friends who memorized the Qur'anic verses from Him. The revelations that came to the Prophet were taught by Him to the people in his closest circle, and after his death the verses that were unanimously agreed on were codified into the book that we know today as the Qur'an.

were grammatically wrong, they were misleading too. The orientalists' imagination of the Muslim world that reflected in their paintings, plays, and history books (Said 1978) is far from reality. Many paintings of the Middle East and North Africa of that time are sexually oriented, showing orientalists imagined something they didn't see.

Despite these negative depictions and prejudices against Islam, there were some philosophers, even though using degrading language toward Islam, still gave some credit to the religion. Puritan minister and author Cotton Mather claimed in his book *The Christian Philosopher* that the Christians should have more devotion to philosophy than the Muslims, in many ways denigrating Islam but in many other ways using it as an example of the reconciliation of natural science and philosophy (Marr 2006: 97–103; Quinn 2008: 24–43; Kidd 2009: 8). Written in 1721, it is believed that he read Ibn Tufayl's translation of the 1185 "Islamic Treatise" manuscript, demonstrating that human reason alone leads to belief in the existence of God (Attar 2007; Allison 2000: 7; Spellberg 2013: 20). In an angry manner Mather says that even a Muslim knows and demonstrates that reason alone leads to the Almighty and finally argues that God has taught a Muslim, but wishing that he would have found this solution instead of a Muslim scholar (Mather 1994: 11–12). This book that Mather praised had previously influenced John Locke to develop one of the first ideas of enlightenment (Spellberg 2013: 20).

In 1584 a miller from a town near Venice, Italy, known as Menocchip, told the Inquisition that Jesus commanded all to "Love God and Thy Neighbor", claiming that no Church holds favorites in salvation and that all Christian branches, and other religions, will be saved equally. This was a radical claim but a great step toward religious tolerance, although he never used that word. He was later imprisoned and then banned from his village and from speaking about his belief (Ginzburg 1992). Similarly, in 1529 Sebastian Franck also talked about tolerance between faiths in Protestant and Catholic context, to criticize the existence of differences between Christians, but unintentionally praising Islam as well. He claimed that one superiority of Muslims in comparison to Christians is that they do not force anyone to their faith (Spellberg 2013: 52). These were not authors who wanted to change the common views toward Islam; in fact, most of them wanted to degrade Islam but ended up praising it instead, in one way or another, and presented its features accurately, unlike previous authors who had misinterpreted the Qur'an, to attack Islam and Muslims.

Not all that was written about Islam during the seventeenth century was negative. In fact, it was during the mid-1600s that some western authors wrote positive things about Islam. Although small in number, and highly isolated, these scholarly manuscripts circulated by hand. One of them was Henry Stubbe, who wrote a treatise on Islam in 1671, and although it was never officially published it was widely circulated. He portrayed the Prophet of Islam in a positive light and declined the claim that Islam was spread by sword (Garcia 2012: 30–59). His manuscript was the first positive writing in English, defending Islam, claiming that it was more tolerant than his faith, Christianity. He was accused of not knowing Arabic and making things up and so his book was never published, although his influence was widespread, including some enlightenment intellectuals such as John Locke (Spellberg 2013: 67).

By the end of eighteenth century stories that depicted Islam as a religion, in a positive light, were circulated among the Europeans and Americans. In 1791 New York Magazine published a story, "Mohamet: A Dream", where they accused the Prophet as an impostor at the beginning, as was depicted in most of that time's discourse. But alter in the story they called him a "great man" and by the end of the story they defined Islam as a faith promising salvation and morality (Reynolds 1981: 17). "The Algerian Captive", another novel with a positive view toward Islam and Muslims, was published in 1797. In this novel, Royal Tyler claimed that the stories are based on real American experiences. In the story, an Algerian Muslim frees an American captive and then this is done every year. Unlike Voltaire, Tyler allows his Muslim characters to talk about Islam in a positive way, and Tyler accused Europeans for bigotry against Islam. Tyler condemns slavery by both Americans in North America and Muslims in North Africa (Matar 1999: 169–183; Schueller 1998: 49–58; Allison 2000: 35–59; Marr 2006: 7–8; Battistini 2010: 446–473). In 1801, another novel, "Humanity in Algiers", was published and this novel also depicted Muslims positively (Allison 2000: 94–96; Spellberg 2013: 27–40; Reynolds 1981: 17–18).

The first English translation of the Qur'an is recorded by Robert Ketton in 1143, entitled "Lex Saracenorum", or the Law of the Saracens (Spellberg 2013: 84; Elmarsafy 2009; Burman 2007). This source tells us that from the early twelfth century up until the eighteenth century the debate about Islam among Christians was on polemics, instead of scholarly interest of how Islam should be covered. This first translation of Qur'an was published as an attempt to convert Muslims into Christianity, after the failure of the crusades, and it was commissioned by a British Anglican Protestant group whose mission was to promote missionary education, called the Society for Promoting Christian Knowledge (Elmarsafy 2009: 1; Spellberg 2013: 85; Kidd 2003: 767). British and American scholars, mostly from Anglican Church, when debating about Islam considered it as a school of law rather than what it is, a religion. The first dated translation of Qur'an, present in America, was by George Sale (c. 1696–1736), a lawyer and an Anglican, and he described Prophet Muhammad as the legislator of Arabs, while Qur'an as the text of the Islamic law (Elmarsafy 2009: 1–2; Spellberg 2013: 84; Burman 2007).

It is believed that it was Sale's translation of Qur'an that made it first to the American continent, and it was this version that Jefferson and the missionaries read. This version is considered relatively accurate, in comparison to the version of Ketton, and it contained information on Islamic history, law, and Islamic rituals. Sale was himself a missionary so by this translation his thought was the conversion of Muslims to Christianity, but he wanted to try it by reason, and he wrote this for the missionaries to use in the Middle East (Spellberg 2013: 86–87). His translation was not the most accurate, however. In the Qur'anic verse 2:256 where it is stated that "there is no compulsion in religion", he translated it to "there is no violence in religion" adding in the footnote that this was only true during the Prophet's time and not afterward (Spellberg 2013: 86–87), but he also added that Christians have "shown a more violent spirit of intolerance" than either Jews or Muslims (quoted in Spellberg 2013: 88). He was the first one to refute John Leland's claim that "Mohamet called in the use of law and the sword, to convert people to his religion; but Jesus did not – does not" (quoted in Spellberg 2013: 250).

Maybe it was because of the time and place that Sale lived, or maybe it was because of his missionary ideas, or maybe both, but one can argue that Sale's translation had some very accurate information about Qur'an and many flaws in translation and understanding that we see even today in different translations of the Qur'an. But, Thomas Jefferson was intellectually affected by Sale's translation of the Qur'an, as he owned this version, although his goal with Muslims was not to convert them, as Sale's goal, but to get their acceptance. Jefferson's first Qur'an might have been this, but Jefferson had known about Islam even earlier, by European authorities on religion and law (Spellberg 2013: 92–93) such as John Locke.

By the eighteenth century, America started debating religious toleration and Muslims were mostly included in these debates. Muslims were considered as individuals who should be given rights as all others. The American founding fathers, all of them Protestants, saw Muslims as potential inhabitants, although at the beginning there were no Muslims that the founding fathers were aware of. This is the time when slavery was legal, and even though there might have been Muslim slaves from Africa, they were not citizens. Nevertheless, the founding fathers debated about the right of Muslims as potential inhabitants. The main debate that went on during the sixteenth and seventeenth centuries was on whether America should be a Protestant country or there should be religious pluralism, and if the latter then what are its limits, should the non-Protestants be able to hold highest offices or should those individuals be held to a "religious test" (Spellberg 2013: 4). These were all questions of debate among the founding generation that we haven't overcome even today.

George Washington was among the founding fathers that professed religious pluralism. In a letter sent to a friend in 1784 seeking a carpenter and a bricklayer to help at his Virginia home, he claimed that the worker's belief, or lack of belief, was no problem at all for him, that the workers can be Jews, Christians, Mahometans, or Atheist, although he would not expect that there would be any Muslim candidate (quoted in Spellberg 2013: 5). In another instance George Washington publicly declared that he is not among the ones that thinks that people should be judged for what they believed or their denomination (quoted in Spellberg 2013: 211). In fact, a decade before he publicly declared openness to Muslim laborers in 1784, Washington had listed two slave women from West Africa among his taxable property. "Fatimer" and "Little Fatimer" were a mother and daughter, and these were the names usually used for Muslim slave women of Africa, named after the daughter of Prophet Mohammed (Thompson 2010: 392). Like Washington, many of the founding fathers may have had Muslim slaves, which had been taken from West Africa. Although they professed religious rights, Washington, Madison, Jefferson, and others may not have been aware that they are denying those rights to the Muslims that are already present in the USA, including their practice of religion. Unknown in numbers, Muslim slaves might have numbered in tens of thousands, which would exceed the number of Jews or Catholics present in America. There are records of two American Muslim slaves, Ibrahim Abd al-Rahman and Omar ibn Said, who were literate, and Omar even wrote an autobiography in Arabic. Their presence shows us that there might have been many Muslim slaves in America by the eighteenth century (Spellberg 2013: 7–10).

There are very few records of first Muslims in the USA, but their presence is traced back to slavery, or sometimes even back to the first expedition of Columbus in 1492 (Curtis 2009: 4). The presence of Muslims from Spain in this expedition is estimated, but it is not known if they were practicing or had already converted to Christianity. Nevertheless, what we have in record is the presence of Muslims in America in the sixteenth century, as European converts and Spanish merchants, who were trying to find new trading routes (Ghanea Bassiri 2010: 9). Muslim names such as Hasan, Osman, Amar, Ali, or Ramadan figure in Spanish colonial documents as expeditors to find the new world (Curtis 2009: 5–6; Austin 1997).

They were not residents; they were travelers who came to America in search of a new, and better, life. But, the first residing Muslims were African Muslims who came here as slaves (Mazrui 2004: 124). They lived under hard conditions and many of them were forced to convert to Christianity; nevertheless, they have managed to at least keep their Islamic culture and traditions, by speaking to each other in Arabic, sewing their clothes and jewelries with Islamic motives, and calling each other by their Muslim names (Diouf 1998: 1–2, 77–82; Ghanea Bassiri 2010: 14; Curtis 2009: 1).

In 1797 the USA ratified a peace treaty with Tripoli, signed by John Adams, which stated that the USA is not founded on the basis of Christian religion and that there is no enmity against anything that Islam holds. Furthermore, there should not be any hostility between parties arising from religious difference of opinions (quoted in Spellberg 2013: 197). Later on, the US Senate again ratified the same treaty with minor changes in April 17, 1806, after Thomas Jefferson signed it in Tripoli. The change that they made in this treaty was that they omitted where it stated the USA was not founded on Christian religion but the part that America has no hostility with the laws or principles of Islam remained intact. A new amendment was added, and it stated that Muslims should be able to practice their religion in private and that even the slaves should not be impeded from going to each nation's consuls' houses in hours of prayer (Spellberg 2013: 216–218).

The first Muslims that Jefferson encountered were the Turkish Ambassadors of North African states, whom he met in London, where John Adams was the Ambassador, while Jefferson was the Ambassador in Paris. Adams has met the first Muslims a month ago, and he had invited Jefferson to negotiate a treaty with Tripoli, where it is the first time, in March 1786, that Jefferson knowingly met with Muslims, who were neither black nor dark skinned. Jefferson was not interested in their ethnicity, race, or religion; he was only interested in the treaty, which would guarantee safety for the American shipmen against the pirates in Tripoli and Tunisia (Spellberg 2013: 8; 124–125). Jefferson's view on religion was very private, but he did not stay back from declaring that the salvation of an individual is not a state concern but a personal concern of the individual himself (Spellberg 2013: 108). When Jefferson bought the Sale's translation of the Qur'an in 1765, he was a passionate law student who had curiosity about other peoples' laws and religion (al-Hibri 1999: 499–500). Among his few references to religion, Jefferson claimed that there is no enmity between Protestantism and Jews, or Muslims, as they are all creatures of God, and that hurting any individual would be a sin for the Protestants (Spellberg 2013: 93). Jefferson had no good feelings about Islam, and in many occasions, he associated Islam with Catholicism, brutality, and alike, but what he was preaching was individual rights that included everyone and he was giving credit to Islam when needed, trying to be accurate for the religion as much as he could (Spellberg 2013: 102–105).

Another important period for America, where we encounter the Muslims, is the Civil War. When the University of Alabama was set on fire in 1865, librarian Andre Deloffre was allowed to save one volume of his choice. He chose to save a copy of Qur'an in English, *The Koran: Commonly Called the Alcoran of Mohammed*. Today, that copy of the Qur'an is present at William S. Hoole Special Collections Library, in the University of Alabama. In the registers of Civil War soldiers, we can encounter names such as Captain Moses Osman, Nicholas Said, Max Hassan, Haj Ali, and others (Holland 2010; Curtis 2010: 561), who seem to have been converts because of using their Christian names first and then their adopted Muslim names. We can understand the early presence of Islamic manuscripts and the presence of Muslims in major American historical events.

Eisenhower made similar remarks to Jefferson nearly a century later, in the opening ceremony of the first Islamic Center in Washington DC on June 28, 1957. He stated that under American constitution, tradition, and hearts, the Islamic mosque is as welcoming as religious centers of other religions and that America would do whatever it needs to protect it and the right of Muslims to worship according to their own conscience. He called this an American value that America would not be what it is if this value was not present (Eisenhower 1957; Ghanea Bassiri 2010: 152).

4.2 Islam in America Today Is Defined by Islamophobia

Fast forward to today. Although there have been debates about accommodating all people equally, Muslims have not been fully welcomed. During the founding decade Muslims were not present in the public discourse, and thus the prejudice against them was imaginary and constructed. Today, on the other hand, political attacks, prejudices, and propaganda against Muslims are real, political, and directed toward US-born American Muslim citizens. The 9/11 and the war on terror have ignited an anti-Muslim discourse and deprived them from full equal citizenship rights that led scholars like John Esposito to ask, "What are the limits of this Western pluralism?" (Esposito 2011b: 228). It became a common practice during election campaigns to hear comments about Muslim candidates that they are not real Americans, referring to the candidate's origin, religion, race, and what not. To be labeled as a Muslim is not new, it happened to Jefferson as it did to President Obama. Similarly, the first Muslim member of Congress, Keith Ellison, was accused of many things because of his religion. He was called a non-American and an enemy of American foundation (Dietz 2006). This image is helped by television and Hollywood, where the common depiction of Muslims is arrogant, ignorant, money-greedy, terrorist, aggressive, and radical fanatics (Shaheen 1997, 2001, 2008).

What defines the current approach toward Islam in America is something different. It is something that has evolved into a "phobia" or even "racism" and this is why it is important to analyze it. Understanding Islamophobia, where it comes from, and what purpose it serves, will help the reader to understand how Islam has been demonized and made a security threat in the USA. This is a very important phenomenon to be able to understand the construction of Islam in the US media, public, and foreign policy, but also, it is an important measurement to analyze the discourse of US policymakers toward Islam.

Islamophobia is a phenomenon that has been on the rise in the last two decades, but it has been present for many decades before. What many consider "the fear of Muslims and Islam", Islamophobia has been fueled in the USA and Europe by many factors, such as what is happening in the Muslim world, the western media coverage of Muslims, Islam, and the Middle East, and even the discourse of political candidates. There are many definitions of what Islamophobia is, but in a more concise definition it is considered as "dread, hatred, and hostility towards Islam and Muslims perpetuated by a series of closed views that imply and attribute negative and derogatory stereotypes and beliefs to Muslims" to quote the most commonly referenced report on Islamophobia, the Runnymede Report of 1997 (quoted in Esposito and Kalin 2011: xii–xiii). The term and this particular report have been widely discussed and criticized, but it still remains the most used term and referenced report on Islamophobia. The main goal of Islamophobia has been "prejudice, falsehoods, stereotypes, and myths that incite people to conflict" according to Anas Al-Shaikh Ali (2011: 147). Islamophobia, commonly associated with prejudice, harassment, and stereotyping of Muslims and Islam, has different consequences and results. Among the consequences of these stereotypes are physical harassments, discrimination, verbal assaults, and demonization of Muslims. All these acts are justified after Islam is portrayed as an identity that it has no common values with other cultures, is violent to others, and has a political ideology.

The same report described Islamophobia as a construct by others, targeting Muslims and Islam. This report is considered as the first report that has been written on Islamophobia. In 2002 the European Monitoring Center on Racism and Xenophobia (EUMC) released the Summary Report on Islamophobia in the EU after September 11, 2001. In 2004 the Runnymede Trust released the follow-up of their first report, while the Council on American-Islamic Relations documented in many reports during 2004 and 2005 the increasing hate crimes toward Muslims. In 2004 the UN called a conference on Confronting Islamophobia: Education for Tolerance and Understanding. Similarly, Gallup Poll made numerous studies on the increase of Islamophobia in the USA (Esposito and Kalin 2011: xxiii–xxiv; Kalin 2011: 8–10). Different scholars refer to different sources on the definition of the term, and the roots. Some argue that the root comes from two French West African scholars, Maurice Delafosse and Alain Quillien (circa the 1910s) (Allen 2010; Lopez 2011; Cesari 2011: 21), while others argue on the similarity of Islamophobia and anti-Semitism (Said 1985; Bunzl 2007; Nussbaum 2012; Lean 2012; Vakil 2010), comparing the two and claiming that both have the same genesis and are similarly dangerous. Islamophobia is considered as another racist bigotry (Modood 1997; Purkiss 2003; Sayyid 2014; Vakil 2010; Allen 2010; Larsson 2005; Lean 2012; Cesari 2011). This "industry of hate", in Nathan Lean's words, is a network of racist politicians, bloggers, and religious leaders, fueled by Fox News pundits (Lean 2012). But these fears of "taking over America" are not new and they have been present in the

American narrative during the revolution war with illuminatis, late nineteenth century with Catholicism, as well as communism in McCarthy era (Lean 2012). While Lean and Allen consider this phenomenon of hate as a step to construct "the other", Sayyid (2014) argues that Islamophobia is wrongly described for its purpose, because the purpose of Islamophobia is not to raise fear and hostility toward Muslims, it is a phenomenon to de-Islamize Muslims, just like slavery did to African Muslims who were brought to the USA and had to forget their Islamic traditions, or what communism did to countries like Albania, composed of dominantly Muslim population who have been secularized and now do not associate themselves with Islam as a religion but as a culture. This, for him, is another wave of such intentions.

Islamophobia is considered the new racism of the twenty-first century, just as the twentieth century was defined by problems of race and color (Shryock 2010: 20–21). It is considered as racism because Islamophobia is not an attack on Islam, it is an attack on the people, the Muslims (Allen 2010: 135–138). If one wants to tackle and solve this problem, then one should consider it as a social problem toward a group of people with a particular identity. Deepa Kumar (2012) draws a comparison between the Islamophobia "industry" and McCarthyism, which she defines as a political system where Democrats and Republicans participated, to create a system of fear and punish the dissidents during the Cold War. It was a system of cooperation between the security apparatus, the political system, academia, think tanks, and the media to inflict fear. Similarly, this system is constructed to inflict fear against Muslims and Islam today. The main groups who fuel Islamophobia are neocons, Zionists, Christian Right, and former Muslims (Kumar 2012: 176–184). A very interesting point has been raised by Andrew Shryock (2010), who talks about the strategy of dividing the "good Muslims" with the "bad Muslims", as another piece of Islamophobic propaganda, and he terms it "Islamophilia", which includes constructing images of "a good Muslim". This is not only done by the Islamophobia industry but rather by Muslims who want to distance themselves from the Islamophobic features that exist in public. Nevertheless, they accept those stereotypes to be embedded in Islam and among Muslims, but just that themselves they are not Muslims like "that". What do these selective positive images of Islamophilians include? It will be of interest to quote Shryock in full as he explained this best:

The "good Muslim", as a stereotype, has common features: he tends to be a Sufi (ideally, one who reads Rumi); he is peaceful (and assures us that jihad is an inner, spiritual contest, not a struggle to "enjoin the good and forbid the wrong" through force of arms); he treats women as equals, and is committed to choice in matters of hijab wearing (and never advocates the covering of a woman's face); if he is a she, then she is highly educated, works outside the home, is her husband's only wife, chose her husband freely, and wears hijab (if at all) only because she wants to. The good Muslim is also a pluralist (recalls fondly the ecumenical virtues of medieval Andalusia and is a champion of interfaith activism); he is politically moderate (an advocate of democracy, human rights, and religious freedom, an opponent of armed conflict against the U.S. and Israel); finally, he is likely to be an African, a South Asian, or, more likely still, an Indonesian or Malaysian; he is less likely to be an Arab, but, as friends of the "good Muslim" will point out, only a small proportion of Muslims are Arab anyway. (Shryock 2010: 9-10)

Different authors bring up different theories on Islamophobia, but they do not question the fact of the existence of Islamophobia, they just argue the reasons, results, and different variations or definitions.

Islamophobia has a long history that dates back to the crusades, but it has never been as large a part of the public discourse as after the 9/11 attacks, when Islam was equated with al-Qaeda, claiming that they take their motivation from the religion (Schwartz 2010), and then this became a new industry in the USA (Lean 2012; Schwartz 2010). One of the first, modern, encounters of American public with Muslims was the Iranian Revolution of 1978, where American diplomats were taken hostage for more than 400 days, and this resulted in the American interest to know more about Muslims and Islam (Lean 2012: x), but it was not an interest to know a friend, rather it was an interest to know an enemy.

How real is Islamophobia or anti-Muslim prejudice in the USA? The presence of Islamophobia is documented by studies that show that anti-Muslim hate crimes have been in constant rise since 9/11. These sentiments do not spike only after terrorist attacks, but have a constant increase, due to Islamophobic discourse and hate speech. A Pew Research conducted in August 2010 found that more Americans had unfavorable than favorable views toward Islam (Pew research Center for the People and the Press 2010). Also, Muslims are more likely to earn lower income and feel more alienated than the Christians in the USA and the west, which makes Muslims less likely to vote too (Wuthnow and Hackett 2003; Model and Lin 2002). A USA Today-Gallup Poll of 2006 showed that most of

Americans favor more tightened security measures with Muslims, including issuing a special ID card for them. Nearly half of the responders think that Muslims are not loyal to the USA; around 20% would not want a Muslim neighbor; and more than one third said that they would feel nervous to have a Muslim on their flight (Esposito 2012: xii). USA Today also reports that since 9/11 Muslim communities have had more difficulties in opening mosques. In New Jersey, for example, anti-mosque advocates distributed fliers that "warned" the citizens that people with possible relations to terrorists will be worshiping in such places (Majid 2000). Similarly, prosecutions of Arabs and Muslims all over America have increased tremendously since 9/11. Different ads were run on TV to dehumanize Muslims and categorize them all as terrorists, while the picture of an Arab always appears when "terrorism" is mentioned (Salaita 2006: 33–34). Over 60 incidents of discrimination by airline crew members in the USA have been spotted from September 2001 to 2004. It has become a common news that Arab-looking men are accompanied to the gate by the pilot or the crew member and then told that they cannot board because the crew, or the passengers, do not feel safe with him on board (Salaita 2006: 107–108). Similarly, over 688 Arab and Muslim Americans filed charges of discrimination at work after the events of 9/11 and up to 2004 (Pollitt 2004; Sussman 2004). An annual FBI report in 2002 showed that hate crimes against Muslims have risen 1600%, where only 28 incidents were reported in 2000 and 481 in 2002 (Schevitz 2002). The polls conducted after 9/11 found that negative sentiments toward Muslims have risen sharply and continuously. While in the first two years after 9/11, 14% of Americans believed that Islam is a religion of violence, in 2008 that number rose to 48%, whereas in 2010 this number skyrocketed to 50% (ABC News – Washington Post Poll 2006; Lean 2012: 39). Especially during election cycles, trends of anti-Muslim hate crimes increase, but the highest level was just before the invasion of Iraq. The year 2016 was among the worst years in anti-Muslim hate crimes. The 2016 elections were built on 2015 tensions where there were more than 174 reported incidents of anti-Muslim hate crimes, including murders, physical assaults, threats against individuals and institutions, vandalism and destruction of mosques, arson attacks, and also shootings and bombings toward Muslims and Islamic institutions such as mosques (The Bridge Initiative 2016). The number of violent acts against Muslims in America during 2015 is not only higher than in 2014 but also higher than after 9/11 horrible terrorist attacks. This shows that the constant increase of hate crimes against

Muslims was a result of the constantly increasing anti-Muslim stereotyping in the media and in the political discourse. President Trump made anti-Muslim statements both when he was a candidate for the US president from the Republican Party and when he became the president. This has normalized anti-Muslim rhetoric, stereotypes, and hate acts toward American Muslims. These and other examples have shown how real Islamophobia in the USA is, how it became part of the everyday discourse, and how dangerous and destructive Islamophobia is.

Media portrayal of Islam plays a very important role. Usually the keywords that are associated with Islam in the media are terrorism, fundamentalism, fascism, fanaticism, radicalism, extremism, violence, militant, Islamist/Islamism, backward, closed-minded, strange, and jihadist (Gibbon 2005; Mohideen and Mohideen 2008), which makes it clear how Islam and Muslims are associated with all things negative in the media, and how Islam is brought to the discussion of security, as all these words are representative of the need for security. ThinkProgress released a study that shows how Fox News manipulates its viewers. In only three months Fox used shariah 58 times, while CNN used the same term 21 times and Microsoft News Broadcasting Company (MSNBC) 19; Fox pundits talked about radical Islam or extremist Islam 107 times in a three-month period, whereas CNN 78 and MSNBC 24 times for the same period; and also, Fox used the term jihad 65 times, whereas CNN 57 and MSNBC used it 13 times (Seitz-Wald 2011).

There are many ways that Islamophobia is promoted. Mainly through media and public speeches, Islamophobes inject these prejudices and fears into discourse. Among other traditional forms, the most interesting and worth mentioning is how Islam and Muslims have been framed in America's mainstream media caricatures.[3] Cartoons, which are supposed to pass a message through satire, have an incredible power of portraying someone, or something, in a particular way. Because they are "only joking" and their popularity is so high, cartoons are much more effective in the consciousness of the people, and because they are short and don't involve a lot of text, they stay in mind. As the editor of Time once wrote: "Cartoons suck the air out of the editorial pages because they are the one thing many people gloom onto. In other words, they get in the way of people reading the paper more closely" (quoted in Gottschalk and Greenberg 2008).

---

[3] Peter Gottschalk and Gabriel Greenberg compiled a wonderful manuscript on *Islamophobia: Making Muslims the Enemy*, where they show how Islam is portrayed and how Islamophobia is propagated in American mainstream media.

Symbols are very important. All the ideologies, groups, and states have symbols that identify that group, state, or ideology. In American media, especially in cartoons and caricatures, Muslims and Islam have been present by certain symbols, mostly negative, and most importantly they have been compared to American symbols, such as liberty, as different and conflicting. Peter Gottschalk and Gabriel Greenberg (2008) divide the symbols used against Muslims into four. One of these symbols is the scimitar. The sharply curved scimitar became a symbol related to Muslims and Islam and a weapon of difference between the westerners and the Muslims. It is showed in the hands of barbaric characters, depicted as Muslims to symbolize Muslim barbarity. Second is the mosque. They use the mosque as a symbol of otherness when they depict Muslims, as a symbol of Islam that the Muslims pray in, although many Muslims pray at home instead of a mosque. When a violent and unwanted character, Middle Eastern or Muslim, is drawn, they usually draw him in the mosque, or in a picture where a mosque is present, to show the otherness. Third is the crescent. Like the mosque, the crescent is used as a symbol to associate a place or the people to the otherness that is not American. Fourth are the Muslim men. The figure of men is usually used to denote Islam. To portray Islam as very patriarchic, Muslim women are mostly used when they want to show them as oppressed, otherwise Muslim men are the symbol of Islam. Fifth is the veil. The generalized image of Islam is a man, but when oppression is symbolized then a veiled woman does the job. The invisibility of the woman is what symbolizes oppression and Islam. Also, in American caricatures these Islamic or Muslim symbols are mainly portrayed as conflicting with US symbols, such as in conflict or in "war" with American "Lady Liberty" or "Uncle Sam".

In American movies, while the good guys, FBI agents, police, or the heroes, refrain from doing anything related to Islam even if they are identified as Muslims, the bad guys, thieves, terrorists, or murderers, perform acts that derive from religion, such as the Islamic prayer (salaat), when they want to commit bad acts, like kill someone. In the movie *The Siege*, there is a good Muslim, the FBI agent, and a bad Muslim, the terrorist. While the terrorist prays before killing someone, the FBI agent, as a good Muslim, does not perform prayers, or does not do anything that is related to Islam, that he can be associated with Islam, only when the agent talks about "not being a Muslim like the terrorist" do the viewers understand that he is a Muslim. The association here is made that American Muslims who do not perform any Islamic ritual are good, normal, Muslim, and

American; while the ones that practice Islam are bad Muslims and ready to commit crimes against America. In the American entertainment industry, these depictions and construction of these stereotypes did not start and will not end with Muslims. For decades, African Americans were only poor, criminals, or slaves; Mexican Americans were illegal immigrants, soldiers, or banditos; women were only mothers, sisters, lovers, wives, prostitutes, or victims; while the typical police officer, a main character soldier, lawyer, doctor, reporter, or an FBI agent was a white European American male of an uncertain religion (Gottschalk and Greenberg 2008). These and similar depictions were done toward communists as well, and in many instances, it is easy to see how Islam replaced communism and how Muslims replaced communists.

The stereotypes are constructed to depict the negative "them" in such a way that they would be different from the positive "us". In short, America's enemies define what America is not. By depicting Muslims as untrustworthy, they define Americans as truthful; by depicting Muslims as regressive and backward, they define Americans as progressive; by depicting Muslims as medieval, they define Americans as modern; by depicting Muslims as evil, they define Americans as good; and so on.

Firstly, politicization of Islam has made it a part of politics, which is a fundamental component of dividing "friends" and "enemies". Muslims then have become the "enemy" who neglects "our" way of life, so they must be fought in order for "us" to maintain "our" existence (Schmitt 1996: 27). Secondly, the people in the west, "us", needed to be convinced that even if there are Muslims who look like "us", who were born and raised and live in "our" countries, among "us", they in fact are not "us", they are different and they are "them". So, Islamophobia is not strictly based on fear, anger, or hate, it is also based on difference, enmity, or a potential enmity (Shryock 2010: 8–9), because one does not need to be an Islamophobe to fear or to hate what al-Qaeda is doing, so fear or hate is not the only measurement. In every point of time there has been an "enemy", someone different that threatened "our" way of life. Jews, Catholics, Protestants, Africans, Gypsies, homosexuals, and many others have fit into this category. Today, with the fall of the Soviet Union, and the end of the Cold War, Islam and Muslims fit in this category. As anthropologists point out, human societies work best by opposition, "us" versus "them", independently of how big the human society is (Bowen 2012: 3–4; Shryock 2010: 3), from families to empires. After the Cold War the new "red" is now "green".

Islamophobia raises the sentiment of "us" versus "them", where "us" is threatened by "them". These can be realistic or symbolic threats toward values, morals, culture, or worldview (Stephan et al. 2000; Stephan and Stephan 2000). These prejudices of threat perceptions from minority groups have been made toward African Americans, Latin Americans, and other immigrants before (Stephan et al. 1998, 1999, 2000, 2002). As for Muslims and Islam, dignitaries, including Pope Benedict XVI and George W. Bush in the "war on terror" campaign, have fueled these portrayals of Islam (Kopansky 2000; Mohideen and Mohideen 2008). US presidential hopefuls do not refrain by publicly condemning and denigrating Islam or Islamic values in each election cycle. Newt Gingrich and Rick Santorum have prescribed Islamic duties upon every Muslim as an existential threat to America, and Gingrich has compared the Park 51 organizers to Nazis (Siddiqui 2011; Feffer 2012: 8–9). President Bush even threatened the sympathizers of "them", when he claimed that if you are not in the side of the USA you are on the other side. This narrative of categorizing "us" and "them" and also the ones that are sympathetic to "them" is the second level of increasing prejudices. The "them" became even a bigger set, including all Arabs, regardless if they are Muslim or not (Hirsh 2002). Even though anti-Muslim sentiments were present far before the organized industry of Islamophobia (Edgall and Hartmann 2006; Kalkan et al. 2009), it was during the latest narrative that this open categorization is constructed. Today Islamophobia is used as a phenomenon to distinct the "superior life of America" against those who "do not like our way of life" or "hate us because of who we are", mainly the Muslims and Arabs (Echebarria-Echabe and Fernandez-Guede 2007; Pratto et al. 1994). Blaming multiculturalism for letting Muslims infiltrate, Islamophobes accuse the liberals for "open[ing] the back door to the adversary" (Feffer 2012: 22).

Islamophobia has a huge effect in the US government policies and foreign policy. During election campaigns candidates do not try to hide their suspicion of Muslims' loyalty to America, but also at other times there are on-duty administrators who share these suspicions openly. Similarly, the "war on terror" was constructed on the vilification of Muslims as "terrorists", legitimizing torture under interrogation without conviction or accusations; infiltration of agents into mosques, youth centers, or even cafés that are mainly populated by Muslim youth; as well as the use of Islamophobic literature to train the security enforcement personnel for action (Lean 2012; Kundnani 2014). Islamophobia also leads to social divisions and violent actions. The effect of the Islamophobia industry can be seen in the terrorist attack of Anders Breivik, where 69 teenagers were killed in a shooting spree at a youth camp of the Norwegian Labor Party, and he bombed several government buildings in Oslo where 8 other people were killed (Bowen 2012: 5–6). Before the attack Breivik wrote a "manifesto", which had a hate language against all foreign things that "threaten" the Norwegian way of life, such as Islam and multicultural politics. He vowed to free Europe from Islam by a killing spree. His manifesto was filled with Islamophobic quotations from Pamela Geller, Robert Spencer, and Bat Ye'or, among other Islamophobia pioneers (Allen 2010; Lean 2012: 166–168; Bowen 2012; Kumar 2012: 175). The rise of Islamophobia has affected the rise of anti-Americanism among the Muslims as well. These two, similar in many ways, are the hatred of a people just for being who they are, Muslim or American, and they have fueled each other (Nimer 2011: 77).

There have been two important Islamophobic campaigns in the USA. The first was the campaign against "Park 51", a youth center containing a mosque that was going to be built and managed by Muslims, five blocks away from the twin towers. Approved by local boards, the Mayor's office, and families of 9/11 victims, this center was going to be used to strengthen the understanding of Muslims and people of other faiths and beliefs (Lean 2012: 41; Kumar 2012: 161–169). But, led mainly by Pamela Geller, Islamophobic crusaders used this campaign as a holy war against Muslims.

The second one was the campaign to pass anti-shariah laws in the USA, led by the Republican presidential candidate Newt Gingrich, in which case there has never been an attempt to ask for shariah compliance laws in the USA (Lean 2012; Kumar 2012: 161–169). Legislators in more than 20 states have passed or proposed bills banning shariah law, since November 2010. This campaign was led by Oklahoma, where a massive turn out of people voted to ban state courts to use or consider shariah or international law. It was sponsored by Rex Duncan, who said he was motivated to sponsor such a measure because of the "cancer" of shariah spreading in Britain, and because he learned that a New Jersey judge enforced shariah in a case (Bowen 2012: 99). It turned out the New Jersey case was a misinformation and no New Jersey judge enforced shariah in any case, ever.

The most common negative, and wrong, Islamophobic opinions toward Muslims and Islam include the perception that Islam is a monolithic entity rather than diverse and dynamic; a fixed entity that leaves no option to change or develop; Islamic culture and values are in conflict with other cultures and values so Islam is an enemy not a partner; characterization of Islam and Muslims as barbaric, irrational, manipulative, and violent; Islam is a sexist religion; Muslims are incapable of democracy and self-rule; and also the sentiment that anti-Muslim prejudice is normal and natural so discrimination against Muslims is defended rather than challenged (Runnymede Trust 2004; Allen 2010: 69–73; Kumar 2012; Gottschalk and Greenberg 2011: 196), which brings to the famous motto "Islamophobic and proud" that is not uncommonly used in today's US media outlets such as Fox News. Portraying Islam like this made it easier for George W. Bush to twist the "search for weapons of mass destruction in Iraq" to the "quest for democratization of Muslims and Islam", and the "liberation of Afghani women".

The vilification of Muslims has limited American liberties, such as the right of movement or the right to speak. Muslim foreign scholars have been banned from entering and giving speeches in the USA, limiting the right of information to American citizens as well as the right of movement of foreign scholars (Figueroa 2012). Also, American Muslims are constantly "randomly" selected for further security checks in airports or are denied the right to travel. In the words of Esposito, Islamophobia "is becoming a social cancer ... and is a threat to the very fabric of our democratic pluralistic way of life" (2011a: xxxiv). Although Islamophobia is associated with 9/11 and the war on terror, it has been present long before, and although today it is mainly spoken about Islamophobia in the USA and Europe, it is present in India, China, some African countries (Shryock 2010: 1–2), and even some Muslim majority countries such as Albania, Kosovo, Turkey, and others.

These Islamophobic portrayal of Muslims and the inflicting of fear against Islam and Muslims have brought Islam to the security level in America and globally. Islamophobia has been the front-runner of a securitizing speech act, and the Islamophobic discourse of US policymakers will be analyzed in the following chapters.

For now, it suffices to conclude that Muslims constitute a very important part of American society. The problems that Islam and Muslims face in the USA today are not new. Other religious and non-religious minority groups, such as Catholics, Jews, homosexuals, women, have had similar challenges before and they still struggle to overcome them. Although Islam has never had a positive image in the USA, in the last century Islam has been portrayed mainly with very negative connotations, stereotypes, and prejudices. This developed to a "phobia" and even "racism" against Islam and Muslims.

For security issues to be constructed there must be a system that propagates this. American hyperpower ambitions and democracy promotion goals have had the need of a new "other" after the Cold War. Islam best filled this gap, and then Islamophobic discourse and images have brought Islam to everyone's attention. This brought Islam to the level of a threat, and Islam has become an issue that should be dealt with immediately for the security of the USA. Fueled by fear, this issue raised too many debates and continues to be a challenge. The issue of how and why Islam became a security issue in the US foreign policy will be analyzed in the next three chapters, but socially Islam has been defined by Islamophobia in the USA.

Although the labeling of Muslims, and the labeling of political candidates as Muslims, thus unfit to serve, is a long-standing American political narrative, from Jefferson to Obama, today the stereotyping and targeting of Muslims is done in speeches and also in images. Television and Hollywood have contributed to this industry of Islamophobia. Muslims are depicted as arrogant, ignorant, money-greedy, terrorist, aggressive, and radical fanatics, who don't have honor, cannot be trusted, and who constantly lie. But the Islamophobia industry today is a multi-million-dollar industry in America and Europe. Islamophobia pioneers like Geller, Spencer, and Gaffney receive multi-million-dollar donations every year, speaking engagements, book contracts, and even government positions.

Historically, Americans wanted to learn more about Islam whenever there was a crisis or an attack. It started with the Iran hostage crisis, continued with Organization of the Petroleum Exporting Countries (OPEC) crises, and ultimately this interest spiked after the 9/11 attacks. After the 9/11 attacks all the orientalist, historians, and scholars of the Middle East became experts of Islam in one night. Orientalists and Islamophobes were celebrities, and they didn't hesitate to make things worse. The most important thing that happened was to construct Muslims as "them" versus Americans as "us", and "green" became the new "red". Muslims became the "enemy" who neglects "our" way of life and belief, so we must fight "them" to defend "us". Occasionally there were some good Muslims on TVs and movies. They usually were the ones who call for the abandoning of Islam and the Qur'an, calling for modernizing Islam, non-practicing Muslims. For this industry, the best practicing Muslims were the Sufis, who don't mingle in everyday life, politics, and only devote themselves to mysticism.

The effect of Islamophobia in US governmental policies and foreign policy is enormous. During the election campaigns candidates don't try to hide their views against Muslims, questioning their loyalty to America and their ability to do any normal job. When they get elected some don't share these suspicions openly but some others do, especially with the latest administration. This reflects in how they deal with Muslims in America, but also with Muslim countries abroad, how they view Muslims in Iraq and Afghanistan, and how much US foreign policymakers can trust Muslims. Muslims, on the other hand, are confused and scared, because they came to the USA for its pluralism and are made to ask, "What are the limits of this Western pluralism?" (Esposito 2011b: 228).

REFERENCES

ABC News – Washington Post Poll. 2006. Broad Skepticism of Islam Marks Post-9/11 Sentiment. March 5. http://abcnews.go.com/images/International/Islam_views.pdf. Accessed 26 Aug 2015.

AbuKhalil, As'ad. 2002. *Bin Laden, Islam, and America's New "War on Terrorism"*. New York: Seven Stories.

al-Hibri, Azizah Y. 1999. Islamic and American Constitutional Law: Borrowing Possibilities or a History of Borrowing? *University of Pennsylvania Journal of Constitutional Law* 1 (3): 492–527.

Ali, Anas Al-Shaikh. 2011. Islamophobic Discourse Masquerading as Art and Literature: Combating Myth Through Progressive Education. In *The Challenge of Pluralism in the 21st Century: Islamophobia*, ed. John L. Esposito and Ibrahim Kalin, 143–172. New York: Oxford University Press.

Allen, Chris. 2010. *Islamophobia*. Burlington: Ashgate.

Allison, Robert J. 2000. *The Crescent Obscured: The United States and the Muslim World, 1776–1815*. Chicago: University of Chicago Press.

Attar, Samar. 2007. *The Vital Roots of the European Enlightenment: Ibn Tufayl's Influence on Modern Western Thought*. New York: Lexington Books.

Austin, Allan D. 1997. *African Muslims in Antebellum America: Transatlantic Stories and Spiritual Struggles*. New York/London: Routledge.

Battistini, Robert. 2010. Glimpses of the Other Before Orientalism: The Muslim World in Early American Periodicals, 1785–1800. *Early American Studies* 8 (2): 446–474.

Bowen, John R. 2012. *Blaming Islam*. Cambridge, MA: MIT Press.

Brzezinski, Zbigniew. 1997. *The Grand Chessboard: American Primacy and its Geostrategic Imperatives*. New York: Basic Books.

Bunzl, Matti. 2007. *Anti-Semitism and Islamophobia: Hatred Old and New in Europe*. Chicago: Prickly Paradigm Press.

Burman, Thomas E. 2007. *Reading the Qur'an in Latin Christendom, 1140–1560*. Philadelphia: University of Pennsylvania Press.

Cameron, Fraser. 2002. *US Foreign Policy After the Cold War: Global Hegemon or Reluctant Sheriff?* London/New York: Routledge.

Cesari, Jocelyne. 2011. Islamophobia in the West: A Comparison Between Europe and the United States. In *The Challenge of Pluralism in the 21st Century: Islamophobia*, ed. John L. Esposito and Ibrahim Kalin, 21–43. New York: Oxford University Press.

Clinton, Bill. 1991. A New Covenant for American Security. *Speech Delivered at the Georgetown University School of Foreign Service*. Washington, DC, December 12.

Curtis, Edward E. 2009. *Muslims in America: A Short History*. New York: Oxford University Press.

———., ed. 2010. *Encyclopedia of Muslim-American History*. New York: Sheridan Books.

Dietz, Rob. 2006. CNN's Beck to First-Ever Muslim Congressman: "[W]hat I feel like saying is, 'Sir, prove to me that you are not working with our enemies'". *Media Matters for America*. November 15. https://www.mediamatters.org/video/2006/11/15/cnns-beck-to-first-ever-muslim-congressman-what/137311. Accessed 17 Oct 2017.

Diouf, Sylviane. 1998. *Servants of Allah: Muslims Enslaved in the Americas*. New York: New York University Press.

Echebarria-Echabe, A., and E. Fernandez-Guede. 2007. A New Measure of Anti-Arab Prejudice: Reliability and Validity Evidence. *Journal of Applied Social Psychology* 37 (37): 1077–1091.

Edgall, P., and D. Hartmann. 2006. Atheists as Other: Moral Boundaries and Cultural Membership in American Society. *American Sociological Review* 71: 211–234.

Eisenhower, Dwight D. 1957. Eisenhower Doctrine. January 5. http://millercenter.org/president/eisenhower/speeches/speech-3360. Accessed 17 Oct 2015.

Elmarsafy, Ziad. 2009. *The Enlightenment Qur'an: The Politics of Translation and the Construction of Islam*. Oxford: One World Press.

Esposito, John L. 2011a. Introduction. In *The Challenge of Pluralism in the 21st Century: Islamophobia*, ed. John L. Esposito and Ibrahim Kalin, xxi–xxxv. New York: Oxford University Press.

———. 2011b. *What Everyone Needs to Know About Islam*. New York: Oxford University Press.

Esposito, John. 2012. Foreword. In *The Islamophobia Industry: How the Right Manufactures Fear of Muslims*, ed. Nathan Lean, x–xiii. London: Pluto Press.

Esposito, John L., and Ibrahim Kalin, eds. 2011. *The Challenge of Pluralism in the 21st Century: Islamophobia*. New York: Oxford University Press.

Feffer, John. 2012. *Crusade 2.0: The West's Resurgent War on Islam*. San Francisco: City Lights Publishers.

Figueroa, Tiffani B. 2012. "All Muslims Are Like That": How Islamophobia Is Diminishing Americans' Right to Receive Information. *Hofstra Law Review* 41 (2): 467–502.

Fouskas, Vassilis. 2003. *Zones of Conflict: US Foreign Policy in the Balkans and the Greater Middle East*. Sterling: Pluto Press.
Fuller, Graham H. 1995. *A Sense of Siege: The Geopolitics of Islam and the West*. Boulder: Westview Press.
Garcia, Humberto. 2012. *Islam and the English Enlightenment, 1670–1840*. Baltimore: Johns Hopkins University Press.
Ghanea Bassiri, Kambiz. 2010. *A History of Islam in America: From the New World to the New World Order*. New York: Cambridge University Press.
Gibbon, J. 2005. *Unveiling Islamophobia; American Attitudes Toward Islam*. Working paper.
Ginzburg, Carlo. 1992. *The Cheese and the Worms: The Cosmos of a Sixteenth-Century Miller*. Baltimore: Johns Hopkins University Press.
Gottschalk, Peter, and Gabriel Greenberg. 2008. *Islamophobia: Making Muslims the Enemy*. New York: Rowman and Littlefield.
———. 2011. From Muhammad to Obama: Caricatures, Cartoons, and Stereotypes of Muslims. In *The Challenge of Pluralism in the 21st Century: Islamophobia*, ed. John L. Esposito and Ibrahim Kalin, 191–209. New York: Oxford University Press.
Gunny, Ahmad. 1996. *Images of Islam in Eighteenth-Century Writings*. London: Grey Seal.
Hirsh, Michael. 2002. Bush and the World. *Foreign Affairs*, September/October: 18–43.
Holland, Taylor. 2010. Copy of Quran Only Book Saved from Union's 1865 burning of UA. *The Tuscaloosa News*, September 10.
Kalin, Ibrahim. 2011. Islamophobia and the Limits of Multiculturalism. In *The Challenge of Pluralism in the 21st Century: Islamophobia*, ed. John L. Esposito and Ibrahim Kalin, 3–20. New York: Oxford University Press.
Kalkan, K.O., G.C. Layman, and E.M. Uslaner. 2009. "Bands of Others?" Attitudes Towards Muslims in Contemporary American Society. *The Journal of Politics* 71: 847–862.
Kidd, T. 2003. Is It Worse to Follow Mahomet than the Devil? Early American Uses of Islam. *Church History* 72 (4): 766–790.
Kidd, Thomas S. 2009. *American Christians and Islam: Evangelical Culture and Muslims from the Colonial Period to the Age of Terrorism*. Princeton: Princeton University Press.
Kissinger, Henry. 1994. *Diplomacy*. New York: Simon and Schuster.
Kopansky, Ataullah Bogdan. 2000. Orientalism Revisited: Bernard Lewis' School of Political Islamography. *Intellectual Discourse* 8 (2): 133–157.
Kumar, Deepa. 2012. *Islamophobia and the Politics of Empire*. Chicago: Haymarket Books.
Kundnani, Arun. 2014. *The Muslims are Coming! Islamophobia, Extremism, and the Domestic War on Terror*. New York: Verso.

Larsson, Goran. 2005. The Impact of Global Conflicts on Local Contexts: Muslims in Sweden After 9/11 – The Rise of Islamophobia, or New Possibilities. *Islam and Christian-Muslim Relations* 16: 29–42.

Lean, Nathan. 2012. *The Islamophobia Industry: How the Right Manufactures Fear of Muslims.* London: Pluto Press.

Lewis, Bernard. 1993. Islam and Liberal Democracy. *Atlantic Monthly*, February.

Lopez, Fernando Bravo. 2011. Towards a Definition of Islamophobia: Approximations of the Early Twentieth Century. *Ethnic and Racial Studies* 34 (4): 556–573.

Majid, Anouar. 2000. *Unveiling Traditions.* Durham: Duke University Press.

Marr, Timothy. 2006. *The Cultural Roots of American Islamicism.* New York: Cambridge University Press.

Matar, Nabil. 1999. *Turks, Moors and Englishmen in the Age of Discovery.* New York: Columbia University Press.

Mather, Cotton. 1994. In *The Christian Philosopher*, ed. Winton U. Solberg. Urbana: University of Illinois Press.

Mazrui, Ali A. 2004. Muslims Between the Jewish Example and the Black Experience: American Policy Implications. In *Muslims' Place in the American Public Square: Hope, Fears, and Aspirations*, ed. Zahid H. Bukhari, Sulayman S. Nyang, Mumtaz Ahmad, and John L. Esposito, 117–144. Walnut Creek: Altamira Press.

Model, S., and L. Lin. 2002. The Cost of Not Being Christian: Hindus, Sikhs and Muslims in Britain and Canada. *International Migration Review* 36: 1061–1092.

Modood, T. 1997. Introduction. In *The Politics of Multiculturalism in the New Europe: Racism, Identity and Community*, ed. T. Modood and P.J. Werbner, 1–25. London: Zed Books.

Mohideen, Haja, and Shamimah Mohideen. 2008. The Language of Islamophobia in Internet Articles. *Intellectual Discourse* 16 (1): 73–87.

Nimer, Mohamed. 2011. Islamophobia and Anti-Americanism: Measurements, Dynamics, and Consequences. In *The Challenge of Pluralism in the 21st Century: Islamophobia*, ed. John L. Esposito and Ibrahim Kalin, 77–92. New York: Oxford University Press.

Nussbaum, Martha C. 2012. *The New Religious Intolerance: Overcoming the Politics of Fear in an Anxious Age.* Cambridge, MA: Harvard University Press.

Parmar, Inderjeet, et al. 2009. Introduction. In *New Directions in US Foreign Policy*, ed. Inderjeet Parmar, Linda B. Miller, and Mark Ledwidge, 1–3. New York: Routledge.

Pew Research Center for the People and the Press. 2010. *Public Remains Conflicted Over Islam.* http://www.pewforum.org/2010/08/24/public-remains-conflicted-over-islam/. Accessed 23 Aug 2015.

Pollitt, Katha. 2004. Moore 1, Media 0. *The Nation*, July 19.

Pratto, F., J. Sidanius, L.M. Stallworth, and B.F. Malle. 1994. Social Dominance Orientation: A Personality Variable Predicting Social and Political Attitudes. *Journal of Personality and Social Psychology* 67: 741–763.
Purkiss, R. 2003. Islamophobia and European Identity. In *The Fight Against Anti-Semitism and Islamophobia: Bringing Communities Together*, ed. Anna Diamantopoulou, 61–64. Brussels: European Monitoring Center on Racism and Xenophobia.
Quandt, William B. 1986. *Camp David: Peacemaking and Politics.* Washington, DC: The Brookings Institution.
Quinn, Frederick. 2008. *The Sum of All Heresies: The Image of Islam in Western Thought.* New York: Oxford University Press.
Reynolds, David S. 1981. *Faith in Fiction: The Emergence of Religious Literature in American.* Cambridge, MA: Harvard University Press.
Runnymede Trust. 2004. *Islamophobia: Issues, Challenges, and Action.* London: The Runnymede Trust.
Said, Edward. 1978. *Orientalism.* New York: Pantheon.
———. 1985. Orientalism Reconsidered. *Race & Class* 27 (2): 1–15.
Salaita, Steven. 2006. *Anti-Arab Racism in the United States: When It Comes from and What It Means for Politics Today.* London: Pluto Press.
Sayyid, S. 2014. Measuring Islamophobia. *Islamophobia Studies Journal* 2 (1): 10–25.
Schevitz, Tanya. 2002. FBI Sees Leap in Anti-Muslim Bias Hate Crimes. *San Francisco Chronicle*, November 26. http://www.sfgate.com/news/article/FBI-sees-leap-in-anti-Muslim-hate-crimes-9-11-2750152.php. Accessed 26 Aug 2015.
Schmitt, Carl. 1996. *The Concept of the Political.* Chicago: University of Chicago Press.
Schueller, Malini Johar. 1998. *U.S. Orientalisms: Race, Nation, and Gender in Literature, 1790–1890.* Ann Arbor: University of Michigan Press.
Schwartz, Stephen. 2010. Islamophobia: America's New Fear Industry. *Phi Kappa* (Fall): 19–21.
Scouten, Arthur H., ed. 1961. *The London Stage, 16000–1800: A Calendar of Plays, Part 3: 1729–1747.* Carbondale: Southern Illinois University Press.
Scribner, R.W. 1994. *For the Sake of Simple Folk: Popular Propaganda for the German Reformation.* Oxford: Clarendon Press.
Seitz-Wald, Alex. 2011. Fox News Watchers Consistently More Likely to have Negative Views of Muslims. *Think Progress*, February 16. http://thinkprogress.org/media/2011/02/16/144856/fox-news-watchers-consistently-more-likely-to-have-negative-views-of-muslims/. Accessed 17 Aug 2017.
Shaheen, Jack. 1997. *Arab and Muslim Stereotyping.* Washington, DC: Center for Muslim-Christian Understanding, Georgetown University.
———. 2001. *Reel Bad Arabs: How Hollywood Vilifies People.* New York: Olive Branch.
Shaheen, Jack G. 2008. *Guilty: Hollywood's Verdict on Arabs After 9/11.* New York: Olive Branch Press.

Shryock, Andrew. 2010. Islam as an Object of Fear and Affection. In *Islamophobia Islamophilia: Beyond the Politics of Enemy and Friend*, ed. Andrew Shryock. Indiana: Indiana University Press.

Siddiqui, Habib. 2011. Shariah-Phobia in America. *IslamiCity*, June 22. http://www.islamicity.org/4349/shariah-phobia-in-america/. Accessed 27 August 2017.

Slomp, Jan. 1995. Calvin and the Turks. In *Christina-Muslim Encounters*, ed. Yvonne Yazbeck Haddad and Wadi Z. Haddad, 50–65. Gainesville: University Press of Florida.

Spellberg, Denise A. 2013. *Thomas Jefferson's Qur'an: Islam and the Founders*. New York: Knopf.

Stephan, W.G., and C.W. Stephan. 2000. An Integrated Threat Theory of Prejudice. In *Reducing Prejudice and Discrimination*, ed. S. Oskamp, 23–45. Mahwah: Lawrence Erlbaum.

Stephan, W.G., O. Ybarra, C.M. Martinez, J. Schwarzald, and M. TurKaspa. 1998. Prejudice Toward Immigrants to Spain and Israel: An Integrated Threat Theory Approach. *Journal of Cross-Cultural Psychology* 29: 559–576.

Stephan, W.G., O. Ybarra, and G. Bachman. 1999. Prejudice Toward Immigrants. *Journal of Applied Social Psychology* 29: 2221–2237.

Stephan, W.G., R. Diaz-Loving, and A. Duran. 2000. Integrated Threat Theory and Intercultural Attitudes: Mexico and the United States. *Journal of Cross-Cultural Psychology* 31: 240–249.

Stephan, W.G., K.A. Boniecki, O. Ybarra, A. Bettencourt, K.S. Erwin, L.A. Jackson, et al. 2002. The Role of Threats in the Racial Attitudes of Blacks and Whites. *Personality and Social Psychology* 28: 1242–1254.

Sussman, Peter. 2004. Fahrenheit 9/11: Firing up the Choir. *Alternet*. www.alternet.org/story/19139. Accessed 26 Aug 2015.

The Bridge Initiative. 2016. *When Islamophobia Turns Violent: The 2016 U.S. Presidential Elections*. Georgetown University: Alwaleed bin Talal Center for Muslim Christian Understanding. May 2. http://bridge.georgetown.edu/when-islamophobia-turns-violent-the-2016-u-s-presidential-elections/. Accessed 17 Aug 2017.

Thompson, Mary V. 2010. Mount Vernon. In *Encyclopedia of Muslim-American History*, ed. Edward E. Curtis. New York: Facts on File.

Vakil, Abdoolkarim. 2010. Is the Islam in Islamophobia the Same as the Islam in Anti-Islam; Or, When Is It Islamophobia Time? In *In Thinking Through Islamophobia*, ed. S. Sayyid and Abdoolkarim Vakil, 23–44. New York: Columbia University Press.

Von Clausewitz, Carl. 1976. *On War*. Louise Wilmot. London: Wordsworth (edt.). 1997.

Wuthnow, R., and C. Hackett. 2003. The Social Integration of Practitioners of Non-Western Religions in the United States. *Journal for the Scientific Study of Religion* 42: 651–667.

CHAPTER 5

Securitization of Islam in US Foreign Policy: The Clinton Administration

The next three chapters constitute the main discussions of the book. They argue that the securitization of Islam has been a long-standing campaign, especially after the Cold War. Nevertheless, while president Clinton and his administration (especially in his second term) decided to approach Islam and Muslims in a more constructive, political way, the Bush administration decided to make Islam a security issue and play along with the advocates who wanted to securitize Islam. Finally, President Obama and his administration acknowledged that this was a misguided policy tactic and that it threatened world peace and stability by polarizing the world into two opposing sides. They decided to desecuritize Islam and bring it back into the abode of politics. But this has remained only in discourse as it is very difficult and time-consuming to desecuritize an issue after it has been successfully securitized. With the new administration coming to the White House, unfortunately the progress made during the Obama administration was wiped out almost immediately. Islam became the number one issue in the discourse of the new administration being associated with security and fear.

For the next three chapters, we have analyzed the discourse and some policies of the recent four administrations. We have analyzed Clinton's Jordan speech as the main doctrine of Clinton toward how he sees Islam. In this speech, he laid down his views on what he thinks about Islam and how he thinks to engage it. For Bush, we have analyzed the "Axis of Evil" speech, although he spoke of Islam in most of his foreign policy and security

© The Author(s) 2018
E. A. Shipoli, *Islam, Securitization, and US Foreign Policy*,
https://doi.org/10.1007/978-3-319-71111-9_5

speeches, which we addressed in the next chapter. For Obama, we analyzed his speech in Cairo in the first year of his presidency, and his speech in a mosque in Baltimore in his last year of presidency. Although it is too early to determine which speech best captures President Trump's doctrine toward Islam, Muslims, America, and security, we have analyzed his National Security and Terrorism speech given while campaigning.

5.1 Democracy, Security, and Religion

Religion has always been a matter of debate in the society as a very controversial topic. Today, terrorists use religion to justify their terrorist acts and gain support. Nevertheless, how we accept it, how we understand it, and how we address it is very important. In the last few decades, one of the most concerning issues was how terrorists use religion, especially Islam, for their interests. The terrorists used religious camouflage to legitimize their acts toward anyone who doesn't think like them, while others who did not know anything about that religion attacked it. From declaring a "crusade" to declaring that "this is a war of us against them" or "they hate our freedoms and way of life", the discourse in the US foreign policy is very controversial. Among others, this has legitimized the false discourse of the terrorists, who have hijacked religion, in their claim that the west is fighting this war and many others against Islam as a religion. Secretary of State, Colin Powell, in an interview to Al-Hayat, and Arabic Daily, in September 26, 2001, called Muslims to free their religion from the influence of terrorists. This has never been heard before, even when abortion clinics were bombed, or when Christian criminals carried out violent acts, no one called for Christians or for the Pope to free Christianity from terrorists (AbuKhalil 2002: 22). No one should call any religious people to free any religion from terrorism, and no one should call terrorists or terrorist acts with any other name than that which they deserve: terrorists and terrorist acts.

As with many other policies, there are many voices in the US politics that have expressed their concerns of this narrative toward Islam. One can argue that most of them have the same goal in mind: security of the USA; but they've been differing in how to address Islam in this path. The American lawmakers seem to agree that democracy—mainly American version—is the answer to the wars and conflicts in the world in general and the Middle East in particular. Nevertheless, the hardliners, such as Bernard Lewis, Judith Miller, Samuel Huntington, Amos Perlmutter, Gilles Kepel, or Daniel Pipes, argue that unchecked democracy in the Middle East might bring Islamists to power, which will not be in the interests of America—thus it must be an American-dominated system—while liberals such as John Esposito, John Voll, Leon Hadar, Richard Bulliet, Scott Appleby, and Robin Wright (1995) think that working together with local politicians over time will bring the right governing system. Both camps give reference to the Cold War.

The hardliners claim that like communist totalitarians, Muslim political leaders are by instinct antidemocratic and anti-western, because Islam does not coexist with democracy, they will turn against democracy instinctually if they are given the right of "one man, one vote, once" (Lewis 1993: 91) because Islam, in the words of Amos Perlmutter, is "an aggressive revolutionary movement as militant and violent as the Bolshevik, Fascist, and Nazi movements of the past" (Perlmutter 1992; see also Pipes 1994; Miller 1993; Huntington 1984, 1991, 1993). They see this struggle between Islamic countries and democracy not as material or political interest conflicts but as a clash of cultures and civilizations, and thus to be able to democratize these countries, to make the USA safer, the Islamic ideology should be fought and changed (Huntington 1993; Lewis 1993). Bernard Lewis was appointed as an advisor to the George W. Bush administration on foreign policy, which explains Bush's stance toward the Middle East and the peak of securitization of Islam in his two terms.

On the other hand, liberals try to accommodate Islam and democracy together. According to this camp, democracy should be spread all around the world, but in the Muslim majority countries this should be done together with Islam, accommodating Islam. They see no clash of cultures or civilizations, just some groups' interests, with whom one should not generalize the whole religion or the whole Muslim population. They argue that the small group of extremists is being taken into the loop by academia and the media, and this has constructed the Islamic-Christian dispute, which omits many other factors and elements. These writers argue that like democracy, Islam is also not monolithic, and that putting Islam into a monolithic stance means that one has not taken into consideration the history of Islam and Islamic political unities, where there have been very conflicting views within the Islamic tradition (Esposito 1999; Hadar 1995; Appleby 1995; Bulliet 1994; Voll and Esposito 1994). This camp argues that what Muslims oppose are particular Western policies toward them, not the west itself. They oppose the western domination of Muslim societies' and the dictating of their political structure, including, but not limited to, the support of totalitarian Middle Eastern regimes, unconditional support for Israel, economic and military intervention, as well as the control of oil. Otherwise, the Muslim world admires and is fully integrated into western technology, education, concepts of liberty, human rights, rule of law, and improved standards for living (Hippler 1995; Fuller and Lesser 1995: 40–42, 102–103). Fuller and Lesser (1995: 109–112) further argue that American leaders can address and try to eliminate the obstacles and threats posed to the USA, but what they cannot afford is to ignore the hopes, aspirations, and fears of the Muslims toward and from the west. The synchronization of Islam and democracy, for this camp, is a challenge for the west rather than a threat as the hardliners argue. They call the US government to accept the ideological differences and argue that these confrontations are more perceived than real. They do not necessarily praise Islam per se but they are also concerned with the US national security and argue that a clash with Muslims can be avoided while democracy is promoted (Wright 1995; Esposito 1999; Hadar 1995).

Of course, these camps are categorized into groups and they have differences between themselves too. Even when Islam and Islamic extremism are sometimes put as different, they are not explained properly. This leads to the categorization of good versus bad Muslims or good versus bad Islam, which again does not desecuritize but in fact securitizes Islam even more.

5.2 Pre-Clinton Administrations

The end of the Second World War found the USA with a more determined mindset, knowing better what they want to do in world politics. The State Department had decided that the system they want to build in the new world order is a free trade system. The Treasury Department knew that it wanted to build a postwar economy governed by international institutions. US politicians wanted to emphasize building a United Nations that would focus on global political governance. The Department of Defense focused on the access of Asian and European raw materials. In other words, access to markets and resources, socioeconomic stability, and political pluralism were tied together to American security interests, while economic turmoil and political instability and upheaval possessed a threat to American security (Leffler 1984: 358; Ikenberry 2000: 123). This might be considered as the basis of the American liberal grand strategy, which was present in many historical occasions, but nevertheless came together after the Second World War and put the foundation of today's ideas and strategies (Ikenberry 2000: 123). These goals and policies toward global politics remain as intact today as they were in 1945, linking American security to the access to resources, socioeconomic and political stability, and pluralism.

Most of the Cold War was a dilemma between democracy promotion and Cold War allies. While it is considered that the USA wanted to expand the zones of democracy, most of it remained only in discourse. As in Washington's response to the East German Uprising in 1953 or the Hungarian Revolution in 1956, the USA needed to balance its politics toward authoritarian allies against the Soviet Union. The lack of trust of the governments to come, and the fear of radical leftists, limited the "democratization" and "human rights" promotion in US foreign policy (Holsti 2000: 157). These were the political realities; nevertheless, it would be unfair to claim that the USA was driven by these policies alone. If that was the case, then the end of the Cold War would result in the end of the western alliances as there is no Soviet threat anymore, but instead today there are still open economies, international institutions and agreements, or liberal ideas (Ikenberry 2000: 124; Talbott 1996; Smith 2000: 94–95) as driving forces of US foreign policy. One might argue that for the Western states, mainly the European countries, the USA has struggled yet succeeded to help build a liberal democracy and did not have a "common-threat" policy that brought them together. Whereas in countries nearer to Russia, especially the Middle East, the USA had to balance its policies, firstly, because they were fighting against a common enemy, and secondly, because they had no trust in the governments that could come after those authoritarian regimes.

5.2.1 Cold War Foreign Policy

The Cold War is associated with decades of the US-Soviet Union race. Clearly the USA has won the race with the end of the Cold War, but the question is whether or not it can overcome the mindset built after four decades of this race or what its consequences will be in the new post-Cold War world order. America has always had a dilemma between isolationism and internationalism, idealism and realism, and now that it is a sole superpower, the questions of the influence of the Cold War politics in new policies, especially terrorism, remain (Cameron 2002: 12). This is a more serious problem than we realize, because if the USA continues with its

Cold War mindset of the US-SU race, then many new problems will arise, which already have. For those who think that the USA has overcome that, it is enough to remember that Secretary Condoleezza Rice is a Soviet Union expert, and she led the US foreign policy for many years after the Cold War. The four decades of the US-SU race had their peak points, which were crisis points that show what the policy looked like, and these crisis points can be compared to the US crisis points after the Cold War.

One of the most dangerous points was the Cuban Missile Crisis in 1962, also known as the thirteen days' crisis, when President Kennedy and Soviet Leader Nikita Khrushchev raced over the placement of Soviet missiles in communist Cuba (Allison and Zelikow 1999; Kennedy 1966). Another crisis was during the presidency of Richard Nixon, when the USA engaged in a round of arms control with the Soviets (Kissinger 1979). Nevertheless, Soviet invasion of Afghanistan in 1979 and the US support of Afghani troops for independence is a crisis that has left its consequences even today. This has haunted the USA after more than two decades, where the Taliban transformed from a US-supported organization to a US-hate-centered terrorist organization (Cameron 2002: 10–11; Coll 2004). These policies have their consequences in today's politics, starting from an unstable Middle East, empowered by tribes and terrorist organizations, who were all American allies during the Cold War, especially with the Taliban and the al-Qaeda leadership during Carter and Reagan. It would be naïve to claim that the USA supported these organizations knowing of what they would or could become. America's focus on defeating the Soviet threat has led to many untraditional alliances, and these were some of them, with the intention to fight communism. Nevertheless, the empowering of these groups has backfired on the USA, and although the policies should be criticized, one cannot claim that the US decision-makers could have thought that one day the tables might turn.

After the Cold War America has been challenged with adapting to the new norms of unipolarity. Nevertheless, the search for a new world order after a major war is not new for America. After each of the great world wars the USA searched for a new world order that would shape global politics, each time aiming for a more democratic international system (Knutsen 1999; Hulsman 1997). While some analysts highly value this search of the USA, others argue that America's rhetoric and hegemonic ambitions are nothing more than dangerous American over-commitment after each great war (Cox 2000: 218). Similarly, the end of the Cold War found American politicians in search of a special role in world affairs. Many academics, such as Huntington, Lewis, and Fukuyama, were already there to give their advice on what should be the new role of the USA, including the question of who should be the new enemy and threat.

This comes after four decades of a Cold War, but filled with democracy rhetoric, followed by American presidents like Kennedy who stated that the USA "would pay any price and bear any burden, meet any hardship, support any friend, and oppose any foe" in the fight against communism (Kennedy 1961); or Carter proclaiming that the USA "ought to be a beacon for nations who search for peace, freedom, individual liberty and basic human rights"; or Reagan "the US was by destiny rather than a choice the watchman on the walls of world freedom" (quoted in Cameron 2002: 9). Over the course of four decades, the USA built up its power in competition with the Soviet Union on what is known as the Security Dilemma, having over 200 military bases all around the world, with hundreds of thousands of troops overseas (Ambrose and Brinkley 1997; Andrew 1995). The end of the Cold War found America as the sole superpower, searching for its global role and the new world order. Involved in peacekeeping and humanitarian interventions like in Somalia, Rwanda, Kosovo, Bosnia, and their national building, the waters were tested on what should the new doctrine of the USA be. We believe that after the Cold War America focused more on democracy promotion, but this was also a policy during the Cold War. The biggest difference is that the Soviet threat has led America to untraditional alliances with Middle Eastern, Latin American, and Asian undemocratic regimes.

Democracy promotion policy was as important during the Cold War as it was afterward. The challenge remained, how far the decision-makers could go to promote democracy, because the USA needed to keep good relations with other non-democratic leaders to keep them aligned against the Soviet Union. Even before the Cold War, US presidents have tried to take steps toward collective security and democratization. One cannot claim that they've succeeded, but they have tried and have paved the road toward making democratization a grand strategy. The Roosevelt administration was determined in promoting liberal democracy. While in the first term they promoted an open international economic system, in the second we saw the creation of Bretton Woods system and the United Nations. Truman urged western European powers to form what Wilson called Franco-German union based on peace without victory, and he saw the democratization of Japan and Germany (Smith 2000: 94). What Roosevelt and others learned is that they have to make an international system that will work, and the

League of Nations did not. This is why they built the post–Second World War system with a more realist approach than that of the 1920s and a more liberalist approach than that of the 1930s (Ikenberry 2000: 124). As President Carter said it in 1977, "I believe that we can have a foreign policy that is democratic, that is based on fundamental values, and that uses power and influence for humane purposes" (Carter 1977). Strikingly the liberal internationalism was as bipartisan as any issue can get in American foreign policy. Both Reagan and Bush pursued the expansion of democracy, markets, and the rule of law. Following the trend of Wilson, Roosevelt, Truman, and others before him, Reagan used the democratic peace argument, claiming that regime types matter, and that as many democracies there are in the world as less the USA is. On this policy, he got involved in El Salvador, the Philippines, Chile, and elsewhere (Ikenberry 2000: 125). H. W. Bush, on the other hand, did not believe that the USA should be the world's watchman, but advocated strongly that this is the USA's responsibility and opportunity to lead, after the Cold War as the sole remaining superpower (Cameron 2002: 17). He, like none other, saw the inauguration of many democratic states, from the fall of the Soviet Union to the fall of Yugoslavia. Especially for the Eastern European states, Bush was very much interested in getting involved with civil society and other institutions to ensure a good transformation to democracy, and in too many cases he used the European Union and the NATO cards (Smith 2000: 95; Ikenberry 2000: 122), referring to them as the "zone of democratic peace".

Nevertheless, the American leaders knew very well that a liberal policy alone will not prevail in the Cold War, so while they pursued a liberal-based foreign policy of democratization and liberal economy, they knew well the realities of balance of power and working with non-democratic regimes to fight communism.

5.2.2 *The USA and the Muslim World During the Cold War*

Double-standard policies sometimes increase US foreign policy opposition in the Arab world and the Middle East. While the USA talks about human rights violations of countries like Libya and Iran, violations and religious oppression by Saudi Arabia, a longtime US ally, get no criticism and no media coverage. Similar double standards exist in the US media and civil society, which shape the hearts and minds of the American people. While the media frequently criticizes some countries in the Middle East, there is no coverage of other countries such as Saudi

Arabia. Or there is no feminist group protest against the Saudi royal family for the right of women, as the American public and policymakers supported the war in Afghanistan to free the Afghani women from oppression (AbuKhalil 2002: 43–44). Although these double standards back up US interests in the Middle East, the US image as a pioneer of values is diluted, and the public opinion becomes one that sees the USA as hypocritical.

In the Middle East, the USA did not have much luck in choosing friends. It is now widely believed in the Middle East that the USA helped bin Laden build his al-Qaeda empire to fight the Russians. Nevertheless, it is also known that the US money in Pakistan helped the formation of Taliban. Pakistani CIA campaign director Zia ul-Haq turned to being a militant Islamist, funneling money and weapons to extremists and establishing schools where many Taliban leaders were trained. Benazir Bhutto, a secular US ally, also supported the Taliban at the beginning against the Iranian Shi'ite influence in Afghanistan, but then she toured the world to explain the wrong doings of the Taliban (Coll 2004). All three regimes that extended official recognition to Taliban, Saudi Arabia, United Arab Emirates, and Pakistan, were close allies to the USA (AbuKhalil 2002: 55–56). After 9/11 the USA committed itself to fighting the Taliban in Afghanistan. After the Afghanistan War, the most contested issue for the USA was the harboring of bin Laden in Afghanistan, and the cultivation of opium, which the Taliban has forbidden. In November 2001, the cultivation of drugs resumed in Afghanistan after the Taliban lost control.

Although there has been more focus on Islam, Muslims, and the Muslim world since the Cold War, Islam has always been in US politics—from Thomas Jefferson, who was "accused" of being a secret Muslim, to Obama, who is still "accused" of being a Muslim, and until today where one of the presidential campaign promises was the Muslim ban. Up until the 1990s, Islam was an issue that came up from time to time into politic debates. US presidents like Carter and Reagan, and especially George H. W. Bush, had relations with political Islamists, and they had their good days and their bad days. When a crisis with Muslims arose the discourse on Islam would get fierce, like during the Carter administration when most of his staff pushed hard for intervention and a military offensive against Iranian Islamist revolution (Gerges 1999: 37–58). Crises like the Iranian Revolution, or the hostage crisis, have shaped US policies and public opinion toward Islam.

Unfortunately, US high-level political elite would speak of Islam and Muslims only when there is a crisis or a "bomb". During the debates on acquiring nuclear weapons and the discussion of a Muslim bomb, or Iranian bomb, Reagan stated bluntly "I don't think that you can overstate the importance that the rise of Islamic fundamentalism will have to the rest of the world in the century ahead – especially if, as seems possible, its most fanatical elements get their hands on nuclear and chemical weapons" (Reagan 1990: 409). Furthermore, some of the US political elite, like President Reagan, President Bush or his Vice President Quayle, would not make a difference between extremist Muslims and Islam. When things got tougher, like when Reagan decided to bomb Libya, he announced that Libyan barbarism was a part of a bigger Muslim terrorist movement (Reagan 1986); and when he was president-elect he even uttered the possibility of "literally, a religious war – the Muslims returning to the idea that the way to heaven is to lose your life fighting the Christians or Jews" (Reagan 1980). Carter and Reagan administrations were preoccupied mostly with the Iranian Revolution and the hostage crisis, when it came to their engagement with the Muslim world. They had no other window at looking the Muslims from, but that of trying to prevent the other Muslim countries from getting influenced by the Iranian Revolution. That was their biggest threat after the Soviet Union.

While Carter and Reagan administrations were mostly dealing with the Iranian Revolution, H. W. Bush also had to deal with crisis in the Muslim world. His one term was the time of the Algerian crisis, which raised doubts about possible enlargement of Iranian-type theocracy and revolution. To combat this, Bush spent much of his effort empowering moderate Muslims against Iranian-influenced extremists. He and Clinton praised Islamic culture and religion and tried to portray America as a bridge of different beliefs. Bush and Clinton administrations rejected the "clash of civilizations" and stressed their commitment to common civilizational grounds (Gerges 1999: 3). Nevertheless, most of that discourse was only rhetoric. On many occasions Islam was equated to Nazism or Communism, by many high-level politicians, like Vice President Don Quayle, who drew a direct link between "the rise of Communism, the rise of Nazism, and the rise of radical Islamic fundamentalism" (Quoyle 1990). In 1994 a senior US official (quoted in anonymity by John Esposito 1999: 3) remarked that with the death of Communism, Islam is the new alternative.

It is important to note that in up to the 1990s America was in wars every couple of decades, and it took the US presidents several years to decide on the path they wanted to take in engaging with the world. The Cold War is known for the Soviet Union threat, which was a combination of ideology and fighting power, similarly to what religion, particularly Islam in Western Europe, posed centuries before the Cold War (Acheson 1969: 490). Islam would come later as a perceived threat, to take the place of the Soviet Union, but this time not only as a threat to Western Europe but also America, in fact America more than Western Europe.

Before and during the Cold War Islam was tackled as a security problem only occasionally and randomly. No organized thought of securitizing Islam was present that bared fruit. The biggest attempts to securitize Islam were during Reagan and H. W. Bush, and some during Carter, but with no major effect. Pre-Clintonian administrations' engagement with Islam, out of the election campaign accusations, was shaped by the Iranian Revolution, the Iranian hostage crisis, OPEC crisis, and nuclear weapons. The accusations made to Jefferson and others of being "hidden Muslims" were made to other candidates for being "hidden Catholics" or "hidden Jews" as well. Another important issue was the Israeli-Arab conflict, which some presidents wanted to solve. This is a hot topic even today, and this is one of the biggest issues that shape the prejudices toward Islam in the USA and the image of the USA among the Muslim majority countries. Prior to the twentieth century, prejudices against Islam were inherited from Europe, as many other things, and this is how Islam was viewed.

Let this subchapter be only as an introduction to the empirical data based on discourse that has to do with the US administrations toward Islam. So far, this chapter has touched briefly upon administrations prior to the Clinton one, to have a brief knowledge on what has happened before and what were the main situations that shaped USA's policies toward Muslims and their view toward Islam. This information is also important to understand that Islam did not come into American politics at once, it was there and the American politics has always tackled Islam as an issue, sometimes trying to unsuccessfully securitize it, sometimes taking it as a political or social issue, and other times using Islam to try to gain support for their fight against the Soviet Union. Many administrations have flirted with securitizing Islam before 9/11 and the war on terror.

5.3 Clinton Administration

The end of the Cold War resulted in America being the sole superpower, with unchallenged superiority in mainly four fields: the military, which is undoubtedly the biggest and best trained in the globe; the economy, with the highest global growth after the Cold War; the technology, pioneering in the latest developments in innovation; and the culture, an unchallenged field of influence after the Cold War, especially among the youngsters around the globe (Brzezinski 1997). It is this combination that made America the sole superpower, but the question remains if this is the ultimate guarantee for the USA.

When in the White House, for two years Clinton governed with a focus on domestic politics, as he had promised during the elections. On many occasions President Clinton stated that he came to the White House to deal with domestic policy rather than foreign policy, and so did his advisors comment that foreign policy doesn't take much of the president's time. Even when Clinton dealt with foreign policy it was mostly on economic issues, such as lowering tariffs and barriers with Japan, dealing with some decisions of the World Trade Organization, establishing American Free Trade Agreement, and alike. His war and peace policy was not present during the two years of his first term. Although Clinton advocated for America's role to spread democracy, he and his staffers commented that the spread of democracy is going to be natural, backed by changes in economy and technology (Beinart 2008: 81–82). This commitment to domestic politics had been influenced by his previous position as the governor of Arkansas, and for these two years he did much in improving domestic policies while remaining reluctant toward foreign policy engagements. But that did not go on for long; he understood at the time that foreign policy could not be avoided much longer.

When Clinton understood that he could no longer run away from foreign political engagement, he started with globalization and cyberspace first. He stated that his priority was to restore the American economy, increase the markets of trade for American businesses, take the lead in the global economy, help the developing countries to grow faster, and promote democracy in Russia and elsewhere (Cameron 2002: 19). As promised during his campaign, Clinton addressed the domestic issues as well as restoring America's economy and interests. Nevertheless, for the promotion of democracy Clinton himself did not have an idea how he wanted to do this at the beginning. The fact that Clinton won against

Bush on the criticism that Bush was too preoccupied with global affairs and not with domestic issues, and that Clinton certainly wanted to get reelected, challenged the situation even further (Jones 1995; Cox 1995, 2000: 223). This is a common challenge among many US presidents. They become more engaged in foreign policy during their second term rather than the first, unless unexpected things happen, because they don't have to think of reelection again.

5.3.1 Democracy Promotion and Islam: From Yugoslavia to the Middle East

The rhetoric of "democracy promotion" raised many questions, as it was not very understandable to what extent Clinton was committed to democracy promotion abroad. Analyzing his presidency, one can understand that Clinton wanted democracy promotion and he became involved in minor affairs, but he was never so committed to it; he was not a savior of liberalism searching for wars to fight. Even when he did commit to democracy promotion, he saw it as an instrument for advancing American security and economic interests, rather than as a moral duty (Cox 2000: 221). He had criticized his predecessor so much on the issue of foreign policy that he wanted to avoid it as much as he could. But, most importantly, Clinton did not have a clear vision of what is meant by democracy promotion, so he needed time to figure out what his democracy promotion legacy will be.

It was no secret that Clinton paid tribute to Wilson and his ideas, but he also was cautious with them and mostly leaned toward a more balanced politics like those of Kennedy and Truman. Nevertheless, Clinton considered Wilsonian ideas as valid and a great vision for the new world order. He praised Wilsonian ideals but did not think that the new world order could be reached by ideals alone. After the first three years of his administration, Clinton's foreign policy was clearer: he wanted to build upon Wilsonian legacy, but not as naïve, rather as a more cautious foreign policy. His staffers were promoting the spirit of the post–Second World War that they argued they needed to build after the Cold War (Cox 2000: 230–231). Focusing on collective security to decrease commitment abroad, Clinton was ready to work with anyone without escalating the situation and winning new enemies.

President Clinton wanted to build his doctrine based on enlargement of the zones of democracy, organized around international institutions and organizations, on business, economy, security, and democracy. Nevertheless, this new doctrine would not be very different from what the presidents from the other party, Bush and Reagan, were advocating for. In this sense, there is no radical ideological difference between the two parties in the USA (Ikenberry 2000: 125–126). The name used by Clinton and his administration, "democratic enlargement", was a good choice, especially taking in consideration that they wanted to keep any negative foreign policy news out of the media, as this phrase had positive connotations. Before he uttered this new choice in a keynote delivered to the UN on September 27, 1993, Clinton and his administration made sure to check the waters in academic circles, starting from the Secretary of State Warren Christopher in Columbia University, National Security Advisor Anthony Lake in the School of Advanced International Studies at Columbia University, and Secretary Madeleine Albright in the Naval War College (Cox 2000: 223–224), where they gave different speeches and engaged with faculty and students to discuss and brief them on "democratic enlargement". In February 1996, the White House published the "National Security Strategy of Engagement and Enlargement", which focused primarily on three US goals: to enhance the US security by military force, to bolster the US economy and economic interests through opening foreign markets and help global economic growth, and to promote democracy abroad. According to the document, "the more that democracy and political and economic liberalization take hold in the world, particularly in countries of strategic importance to us, the safer our nation is likely to be and the more our people are likely to prosper" (White House, February 1996). They made American foreign policy about America and Americans rather than about the "others". In this way, the Clinton administration made sure to get involved in global politics while also keeping the domestic engagement, doing what they had promised in the presidential campaign, and widening the base for reelection.

Clinton definitely refused to be a crusader for democracy; instead, he saw his policies toward democracy promotion only as a smaller part of the larger US grand strategy. In a speech at the University of Wisconsin in 1992, while criticizing Bush on not doing much to back up liberal democracies, and being very close to autocratic regimes, Clinton said that he doesn't want to upset the established US relations with other countries, especially China, as the USA cannot and should not force its ideals on others, but that the USA should act by prudence and common sense. According to Clinton, democracy promotion is an important goal for the USA, but it does not override the other goals (Clinton 1992). In the beginning, the idea that the way other countries govern themselves ensures the security of the USA was odd among the public, especially coming from someone as inexperienced as Bill Clinton. So, it was Clinton's aids that decided to be early promoters of the "democracy promotion" idea to the American public (Layne and Lynn-Jones 1998; Cox 2000: 225). Secretary of State Madeleine Albright proposed a "community of democracies" in the 1990s, to be established alongside the United Nations if the UN should be paralyzed by its system of decision-making. She proposed this system to be based on market democracies and include all the market democracies globally. It was supposed to be an alternative to NATO as well (Smith 2009: 60–61). UN and NATO were important institutions for the USA, but they could not be fully trusted, and US presidents have always looked for different ways to solve different issues at different times. At her Wilsonian best, Secretary Albright, in a speech at Harvard University for the 15th anniversary of the Marshall Plan, stated:

> American security and prosperity are linked to economic and political health abroad ... we must take advantage of the historic opportunity that now exists to bring the world together in an international system based on democracy, open markets, law and a commitment to peace. Today the greatest danger to America is not some foreign enemy; it is the possibility that we will fail to heed the example of [the postwar] generation; that we will allow the momentum toward democracy to stall, take for granted the institutions and principles upon which our own freedom is based, and forget what the history of this century reminds us: that problems, if left unattended, will all too often come home to America. A decade or two from now, we will be known as the neo-isolationists, who allowed tyranny and lawlessness to rise again, or as the generation that solidified the global triumph of democratic principles. (Smith 2000: 95)

Strobe Talbott advocated that democracy has become the political gold standard of the late twentieth century. In front of an Oxford University audience in England in 1994, Talbott argued that no dictatorship could resist the attractiveness of democracy; the evidence was that in 21 years the number of democratic countries rose from 44 in 1972 to 107 in 1993 (Cox 2000: 225; Layne and Lynn-Jones 1998). Similarly, Clinton believed and argued that American democracy is not only a success story but also an example that others should follow. He also considered that the nation's foreign policy should reflect its core values: the principle of democracy (Cox 2000: 226; Shin 1994). It was crystal clear now that Bill Clinton and his administration were heading toward a "democracy promotion" policy like no other president before.

Clinton began to be more engaged with the world outside of America, with many successes in the Balkans, and some failures, especially in Somalia and Rwanda. In fact, many scholars argue that these failures in Somalia and Rwanda made Clinton more decisive in the Balkans, especially in Kosovo. Clinton also got involved in the Middle East, but his involvement in the region was more about settling disputes, like the Palestinian-Israeli conflict, or containing the Gulf countries from using the oil card.

But, there was a difference. Clinton and his administration were committed to finding a new definition of democracy, especially in the Middle East, first not to be "hijacked" by local political groups (Islamist) so there will be no situation of one man—one vote—once; and second, to promote US values, where democracy should be measured by free elections, but also by an independent judiciary and the protection of human rights (Lake 1993). The engagement with the Muslim world, for Clinton, was the promotion of democracy, and this proved to be his policy toward engaging Islam as well. Here comes the question of what democracy the USA should promote. This is an important question that challenged Clinton during his presidency.

Clinton's democracy enlargement was not applauded by everyone. There were many supporters but there were many critics as well. The critics of the Republican realists toward Clinton were pretty harsh. In 2000 Condoleezza Rice, who took high-level positions in the W. Bush administration afterword, attacked Clinton's foreign policy as illusory in international politics. She said that a Republican administration would of course be internationalists, but it would pursue American national interests more firmly. She also criticized Clinton on the huge expenditures of the military abroad and advised the new president to have a lighter, more lethal, and more mobile force, which she called the force for the twenty-first century. Other issues she criticized Clinton for were the lack of acknowledgment to America's traditional allies, including European countries; NATO's enlargement, structure, and mission; a greater view of China, where she argued that trade liberalization was a necessity and also that China was not a partner but a "strategic competitor" with regional ambitions; strengthening of defense relations with Japan and South Korea; more assurance to Taiwan; and she criticized him on deterrence, or the lack of, in a possible event of the use of weapons of mass destruction (Rice 2000). All of these criticisms were forgotten as soon as Condoleezza Rice became Bush's National Security Advisor, and among the most powerful advisors on the team, especially after she became the Secretary of State. Ironically, she did the opposite of what she was arguing when she criticized Clinton, and she advocated for even more engagement than Clinton.

In an article, published in the Foreign Affairs magazine, another of Bush's foreign policy advisers Bob Zoellick criticized the economic policies of Clinton, mainly on the issues of drift on trade, erosion of credibility, on the inability to frame strategies, the uncertainty of when and how to use power, and on the many polls and politically driven calculations (Zoellick 2000). As can be seen, the Republicans never argued for a fundamental change on the foreign policy mentality of the USA, but on how to conduct it. This doesn't mean that they agree on everything with the Democrats. They agreed on the internationalist ideals meeting at the common basic principles that benefit the USA, like deterring aggression, resolving conflicts, raising standards, opening markets, and coming together with allies against common dangers that concern more than one country (Berger 2000). One of such common policies, democracy promotion remains the most criticized issue during the elections and then the most pursued policy when in power.

To be able to understand the Clinton administration's foreign policy vision, it is useful to see how they conducted foreign policy in practice. The democracy promotion that Clinton envisioned was to bring democracy where it did not exist before. After the debacle of the "Black Hawk Down" in Somalia, followed by pulling off from Somalia in 1993, Clinton had one chance to make it right, and although late, he got it right in Bosnia (Powell 2012: 206). In the Balkans, the USA was not ready and interested in the escalation of conflicts, they wanted to manage the situation and resolve it in the best way possible with as less burden as possible. This is why Washington rejected the Vance-Owen peace plan, designed by former US Secretary of State Cyrus Vance and former British Foreign Minister David Owen. This plan included the redrawing of borders, which would open ways to more conflicts and would be a very difficult job. The American administration was not interested in that (Cameron 2002: 25). Clinton's idea was to have the issues resolved in the best manner that would keep the borders as they are. He and his administration were not ready to enter into new adventures and open old wounds by drawing new borders.

Yugoslavian forces, under Serbian leadership, were conducting a violent suppression, ethnic cleansing, and genocide in Bosnia. Militarily, according to General Colin Powell, "there was no achievable political objective and no way to touch all the bases preferred by military doctrine" (2012: 206).

Nevertheless, Clinton wanted to take this opportunity to end the conflict, and although he needed two years to engage NATO, the bombing of the Serbian forces in Bosnia and Herzegovina finally started and proved Clinton right, because NATO succeeded (Powell 2012: 206–207). The Bosnian conflict made a radical shift of the US approach to foreign policy. Racist and dangerous Serbian nationalism was something that liberals would not tolerate, and the circumstances of Bosnia were very different: first, no American troops were going to be engaged, as the fight would be from the air; and second, it wasn't to secure oil but to prevent further genocide. Even the most anti-interventionist, anti-imperialist analysts in the USA have supported the intervention in Bosnia (Beinart 2008: 83–84). This conflict was also an opportunity for the leader of the free world to take his position, his role. With the atrocities going on the ground and the arms embargo punishing the Bosnians who had no weapons while the whole Yugoslavian arsenal was at the disposition of the Serbians, Clinton used political pressure. Nevertheless, with the massacre of around 8000 Bosnian men and boys in Srebrenica, Clinton decided to convince NATO to an airstrike, resulting in a partition plan and 60,000 NATO troops in the ground (Beinart 2008: 83). Although late, Bosnia was among the first, limited, collective actions of NATO and the UN. The USA played a crucial role in diplomacy and negotiations, but when those measures were exhausted, they were ready to intervene. The war in Bosnia was framed as a war of religious differences unlike the war in Kosovo, but what made the Clinton administration intervene was the genocide that was happening there.

Clinton's second term showed to be more difficult in terms of foreign policy, and more engaging. With Bosnia in a somewhat silent position, Serbian leader Slobodan Milosevic this time turned against Kosovo. Diplomatic measures were taken into action with no delay, headed by the new Secretary of State, Madeleine Albright. After a difficult job of convincing both parts to sit at the table in Rambouillet, Albright managed to make the Albanians agree on her peace plan, but the Serbs refused. Instead, they continued the ethnic cleansing, bringing more than half of the Kosovar Albanian population out of Kosovo and moving more than 40,000 troops on the border with Kosovo. This time, the USA decided not to wait for more atrocities and genocide to happen. They decided to convince NATO to conduct a military airstrike that lasted for 78 days (Beinart 2008: 84; Clinton 2004: 785–796). The airstrike had clear goals, which was very advantageous, and Clinton brought them down to three:

"to show Milosevic we were serious about stopping another round of ethnic cleansing, to deter an even bloodier offensive against innocent civilians in Kosovo, and, if Milosevic did not throw in the towel soon, to seriously damage the Serbs' military capacity" (Clinton 2004: 796). Clinton considered this successful airstrike of NATO in Kosovo as a turning point in the world's military history, which resulted in Serbian forces' retreat, Kosovar Albanians returning home, and later the independence of Kosovo, in February 2008.

The Kosovo crisis was handled fast mainly because of the failure to do so in Bosnia. As president Clinton said: "we learned that if you don't stand up to brutality and the killing of innocent people, you invite the people who do it to do more of it" (Clinton 1999). Clinton recalls in his autobiography that he and Albright were determined not to allow Kosovo to become another Bosnia. The intervention was the first collective intervention, unlimited airstrikes, of NATO allies in the 50th birthday of NATO. Unlike the conflict in Bosnia, the Kosovo War was purely ethnic, at least it was constructed as such, and so no religious flavor was associated with it. The minority Christian Albanians in the fight against the Serbian atrocities acted together with the majority Muslim Albanians, and religion has never been a subject of conflict among Albanians. Neither was it a subject of debate in the discourse of the world powers when they were debating to intervene.

The Kosovo crisis, and its ending, brought a New Liberalism to international relations and politics lexicon. Clinton's closest ally in the Kosovo crisis, British Prime Minister Tony Blair, visited Chicago in April 2000 and outlined a new neoliberal foreign policy doctrine that he called "a new doctrine of international community". Focusing on globalization, Blair proposed a new Bretton Woods-like system to stabilize international economy after the Asian crisis; he proposed new trade measures, pushing for free trade, relief of third-world debts, and promotion of global economic development. He also called for immediate combat of global warming, as an issue that no country can address alone (Blair 1999). But, most strikingly were his remarks on military force and the new system of the use of force:

> The principles of international community apply also to international security. ... When oppression produces massive flows of refugees which unsettle neighboring countries, then they can properly be described as "threats to international peace and security". (Blair 1999)

This speech was later referred to as the "Blair Doctrine". As was understood, the Kosovo intervention was just the beginning of a greater shift in international affairs. It meant that the world powers would intervene, even militarily, when a government commits domestic atrocities and destabilizes other countries. But, as in economic development, this new policy would be conducted together, in alliance, not alone (Blair 1999). Similar to this vision, Clinton argued in a conference in San Francisco in the same year that "the real challenge of foreign policy is to deal with problems before they harm our national security" (quoted in Beinart 2008: 85). During this time, the USA understood the need to act with other allies, not on its own, and to take the responsibility when things go wrong. Most importantly, the USA under the Clinton administration understood that first, it needs to let the other democracies have a say in the international community, and second, that America cannot be in love with its own democratic values. This would be very dangerous, and the USA should seek to keep itself sober from the overwhelming power, as not to enter into the corruption of power itself (Beinart 2008: 85). One can argue that these lessons were not learned, or at least not put into practice in the next administration, who overestimated American power and influence and recognized no limits.

As important as it was for the new neoliberal vision of international affairs, the Kosovo crisis and intervention opened a new way of theorizing politics in the USA. Kosovo was the first successfully securitized issue in the international arena (Shipoli 2010), and this brought a new theoretical component to the field of international relations. Outside of this, the Clinton administration used the Kosovo crisis as an opportunity to balance its foreign policy, especially in the Middle East, and change priorities of US foreign policy. Mainly due to the collapse of the Soviet Union, but not limited to that, the Balkans became a key geopolitical region for the USA in the 1990s. NATO's eastward expansion could provide necessary security environment to energy projects, but also it could provide a bridge between Western and Eastern regions (Fouskas 2003: 26). Similarly, the majority Muslim population of Kosovo was an important factor for mainly two reasons. First, the USA was able to counterbalance its pro-Israeli policy in the Middle East by offering help to a Muslim majority country (Fouskas 2003: 26). This was a big issue at the time, as the USA failed to provide the same help to Bosnia, again a Muslim majority ethnic group; and second, some radical Islamic groups infiltrated Bosnia, where and when the USA was not present and uninterested to help, so they did not want to make the same mistake in Kosovo. These are the main reasons this book argues that Kosovo plays an important role in the securitization of Islam in US foreign policy, although not crucial, which later would be much more constructed and would take a very different path.

When intervening in Kosovo there was no religion associated with the policies; nevertheless Clinton was highly criticized for non-intervention in Bosnia where the Bosnian Muslims were slaughtered, and for his pro-Israeli stand. Kosovo has served as a transition period to repair his and America's image toward the Muslim world. During the war in Bosnia the western countries did not agree to lift the arms embargo to Bosnians. The Serbian authorities, on the other hand, had at their disposition all the weapons that remained from Yugoslavia. At this time some Islamist groups, guerillas, and Iran offered help to Bosnia, which Bosnians were obliged to accept, as they had no other options. Nevertheless, these groups showed to be much more problematic than the USA had thought. This played a big role for the swift intervention in Kosovo, so there would be no place for such groups in Kosovo.

As far as the Middle East is concerned, the Clinton presidency solidified the US-Israeli relations. Although the relations were always close, Clinton tried to bring ties closer, by increasing intelligence ties and brining to life all Israeli demands except the release of the Israeli spy Jonathan Pollard. These unprecedented relations between the two countries irritated the Arab countries in the Middle East, which eventually had its consequences (AbuKhalil 2002: 31). Especially during the elections, Bill Clinton had a very pro-Israeli discourse, but when he was elected president he tried to balance his image with some symbolic gestures such as organizing the first Iftar dinner at the White House, and similar gestures. Nevertheless, Clinton did not make the mistake of associating all the Muslim countries with Iran; he did not categorize Algeria as extremist, or as a threat, unlike France; he cooperated with Islamists in Egypt, but later he gave full support to Mubarak against the Islamists; he supported and saw Turkey as an irreplaceable American ally after the Cold War, as Germany was during the Cold War, and which he considered a role model of Islamic and western world coexistence; he even supported a Turkish Islamist government, as long as US national interest and national security was not at stake (Gerges 1999). The US security interests drove President Clinton's policies, rather than categorization of countries as enemies and friends on ideological basis. When it was in the interest of the US security Clinton was willing to work with anyone that would deliver and defend these interests best. Change of ideology was not a prerequisite.

Clinton was a pioneer among those who thought that democracy should be promoted in the Middle East and in the world, but that could and should be done together with traditional values of the people in those countries, of Islam in the case of the Muslim world. He and his administration rejected the thesis of a clash of civilizations while making sure to denounce extremism and favor the moderates. The Clinton administration did not use the dichotomy of bad versus good Muslims, which today has become a problematic discourse. From mid-level officials to the highest-level officials in Clinton administration, including the President and the First Lady, everyone made statements on American misconceptions of Islam, whenever possible. National Security Adviser, Anthony Lake, pursued the logic that the choice for Middle Eastern countries is clear: they want either development or stagnation, extremism or democracy, weapons of mass destruction in the Middle East or security for all, and existential threats versus regional stability. He saw this struggle as the struggle for power, of evil versus good forces, where extremist and isolated states like Libya, Iraq, Iran, and Sudan would fall under evil, and the moderate states and allies of the USA and Israel share a similar vision when it comes to free markets, democratic enlargement, and control of WMD (Lake 1993). Nevertheless, he failed to mention the names of states that fall under the second category, who are democratic and prosperous, with free markets, that are US allies in the Middle East.

A few months later, President Clinton applied the same comparison in his speech in Jordanian Parliament, where he stated that he sees "a contest between tyranny and freedom, terror and security, bigotry and tolerance, isolation and openness … fear and hope" (Clinton 1994a). Nevertheless, they were very careful, especially the president, not to mention or associate Islam with any of these competing ideas. Anthony Lake stated that the fault line is not between civilizations or religions, it is between oppressive and repressive governments, between isolation and openness, and between extremism and moderation and that America will not choose between religious and secular guise, rather between those who want to advance their agenda through coercion, terror, oppression, intolerance, and extremism and those who want to advance their agenda through democratic means, openness, and moderation (Lake 1994). On the other hand, on occasions where he would need support for democratic enlargement, Clinton would refer to Islamic values and traditions in support of the "forces of good", which was a smart move to bring back Islam, and religion in general, to the political realm, instead of dealing with it in security terms. He often quoted messages of tolerance that the Prophet Mohammad professed to his people, and people of other faiths (Clinton 1994b, 1995a). Most importantly in the Jordanian Parliament he stated, "The traditional values of Islam – devotion to faith and good works, to family and society – are in harmony with the best of American ideals. Therefore, we know our people, our faiths, our cultures can live in harmony with each other" (Clinton 1994a). Not limiting himself to the statements abroad, President Clinton made similar remarks on the joint press conference with King Hussein of Morocco in the White House: "Islam can be a powerful force for tolerance and moderation in the world, and its traditional values are in harmony with the best of Western ideals ... the United States has great respect for Islam and wishes to work with its followers throughout the world to secure peace and a better future for all our children" (Clinton 1995b). A month later he praised Prime Minister Benazir Bhutto of Pakistan, as a figure who is leading a nation of 130 million Muslims to a moderate democratic Islamic country, to play a role in the Muslim world, by combining the best traditions of Islam with modern democratic ideals (Clinton 1995c).

When analyzing these statements, one understands that Clinton looked at the Middle East from the eye of bringing stability and securing US interest in the region, as he looked at the Balkans. He did not bring Islam to security discussions and he, as well as his administration, was generally careful not to target Islam as something that must change in order to achieve these goals in the Middle East. On the contrary, they tried to take Islam by their side when they wanted to make a point on the need for freedoms and democratic changes in the Middle East.

5.3.1.1 The Jordan Speech
The key speech where President Clinton addressed Islam in US foreign policy was his Jordan speech, made in Jordanian Parliament in Amman, October 26, 1994, to celebrate peace and cooperation between Jordan and Israel. This is considered the foremost speech that showed the view of Clinton and his administration toward Islam, equal to that of President Obama's address in Cairo, where he declared the change of the US approach toward Islam. Although he mentioned Islam only twice in his speech, Clinton praised the King of Jordan by calling him the descendent of Prophet Mohammed before thanking him for being an example of

bringing peace to the Arab world. He added, "You made a bold choice: You rejected the dark forces of terror and extremism. You embraced the bright promise of tolerance and moderation. ... The United States admires and supports the choice you have made. And we will stand with you in months and years ahead."

Touching on the long-standing Jordanian-American relations, Clinton praised those relations in such a fashion:

> My country, a nation of immigrants from every area of this world, respects your openness and your understanding that diversity is a challenge but it can be a source of strength. America's commitment to Jordan is as strong tonight as it was when Your Majesty traveled to the United States for the first time 35 years ago and met President Dwight Eisenhower, the first of eight Presidents you have known.
>
> The President and Your Majesty discussed the great threat that communism then posed to America and to the Arab world. And when President Eisenhower asked what America could do to help, Your Majesty said then, "We need more than anything else the feeling that we do not stand alone". Now, at a time when those who preached hate and terror pose the greatest threat to the cause of peace, President Eisenhower's response still holds true. Thirty-five years ago he told Your Majesty, "Our country knows what you have done. Believe me, we won't let you down."
>
> Both of us, Jordan and America, are fighting the same battle. Today, that battle is the struggle for peace. And I say again, on behalf of the United States, we will not let you down.

After promising economic development and economic help, he asked for these changes to affect for the better life of ordinary citizens. Clinton made sure to touch on the place of religion in this entire nexus, saying that:

> there are those who insist that between America and the Middle East there are impossible religious and other obstacles to harmony, that our beliefs and our cultures must somehow inevitably clash. But I believe they are wrong. America refuses to accept that our civilizations must collide. We respect Islam. Every day in our own land, millions of our own citizens answer the Moslem call to prayer. And we know the traditional values of Islam, devotion to faith and good works, to family and society, are in harmony with the best of American ideals. Therefore, we know our people, our faiths, our cultures can live in harmony with each other.

While calling the clashes in the Middle East "a contest of forces that transcend civilizations, a contest between tyranny and freedom, terror and security, bigotry and tolerance, isolation and openness ... age-old struggle between fear and hope ... [while] what we have in common is more important than our differences", Clinton did not miss to quote Prophet Mohammed on "There is no argument between us and you. God shall bring us together, and unto him is the homecoming" after he quoted the Prophet Moses on similar lines. Finally, he thanked God that the people of Jordan and people of Israel have reached across the Jordan River, and his last word was *Ilham du Illah* ("Thank God" in Arabic).

This speech represents his doctrine toward Islam, and it holds some important details. He did praise Jordan for choosing peace instead of terror, and he wished this for the whole Middle East; he refrained from over-mentioning Islam in a speech where he was talking about the need to bring peace instead of chaos; he rejected the clash of civilization theories; and he used Islam to support his arguments of peace, show his and the American people's respect for Islam, and to sound familiar and informed about Islam. He started the speech by praising Jordanian King for choosing peace, by also calling him the descended of the Prophet Mohammed. He finished his speech by a quote of Prophet Mohammed and finally saying *Ilham du Illah*. These symbolic gestures have a profound effect on how one addresses an issue, and the keywords that one associates with that issue are the greatest determiners if that issue is to be securitized, politicized, or non-politicized.

5.3.2 Terrorism and the Securitization of Islam

As far as terrorism is concerned, Clinton was aware of the dangers awaiting the USA. He devoted a considerable amount of resources to fight terrorism as the USA was engaged in a long-term fight of freedom against fanaticism and rule of law against terrorism. In a speech at the United Nations he even stated that terrorism makes the top agenda of US foreign policy so it should make the top agenda of the global politics as well (Cameron 2002: 135). In 1996, fighting terrorism was a top priority for Clinton. The strategy they drafted was about international cooperation in preventing serious incidents, stopping the money flow to terrorist organizations, limiting their communication, cutting off their accessibility to weapons and especially weapons of mass destruction, and imposing sanctions to countries that harbor terrorists. This strategy had brought many successes in the USA and abroad, from preventing alleged attacks in Lincoln and Holland Tunnels to preventing the blowing up of Philippine airplanes, while it also extradited many terrorists to the USA for trial. Nevertheless, as Clinton himself recalls, "it was more difficult to get at non-state terrorist organizations; the military and economic pressures that were effective against nations were not as easily applied to them" because the methods of economic, political, and military pressure that would work against nations would not apply to non-state terrorist organizations and it became clear that "terror is more than a form of international organized crime; because of their stated political objectives, terrorist groups often enjoy both state sponsorship and popular support" (Clinton 2004: 672), and this showed how challenging terrorism would be in the years to come.

President Clinton witnessed a considerably high number of terrorist attacks during his presidency, among which he mentions the bomb that exploded in the World Trade Center, in February 26, 1993, in his autobiography. Injuring more than a thousand people and killing six, this terrorist attack was engineered and carried out by a Middle Eastern terrorist group, among which many were captured and detained. Only two days later a religious cult killed four agents of the Bureau of Alcohol, Tobacco, and Firearms and injured 16 others in their Waco, Texas compound. Calling themselves The Davidians, or Branch Davidians, they were suspected of illegal firearms violations. David Koresh, their messianic leader, believed that he was the Christ and one day while he was preaching in the Church, he said that he has a new message for the church and presented his book of Revelation. What the agents then found in his compound was a vast stock of food and weapons, which showed that they were prepared to undertake unprecedented actions. Koresh had a huge impact, "hypnotic mind control" as Clinton recalls, over his congregation of men, women, and children. The FBI then took more than two months to make the Davidians surrender, as they were constantly delaying it. The FBI had intelligence that Koresh and his followers were abusing children sexually and that he might be planning a mass suicide. They wanted to raid the compound but there were too many people present, and Clinton feared of the high number of casualties that might occur. Finally, he was convinced by the then-Attorney General of the USA, Janet Reno, and he gave a green light, and on April 19 the raid happened. The raid went terribly wrong. When the FBI entered and fired tear gas, Koresh and his followers started a fire, opened the windows, which let the gas out and the winds in. More than 80 people were dead, among them 25 children, and only 9 people survived. What Clinton called a fiasco got even worse when Reno went on TV and took responsibility and Clinton got the criticism for letting the first woman attorney general take the blame (Clinton 2004: 453–454).

Another similar attack was the Oklahoma City bombing, which was carried on April 19, 1995, on the second anniversary of the Koresh raid. Many news outlets immediately portrayed this as an Islamic terrorist attack, but then it turned out to be a right-wing extremist group who hated the federal government and wanted to carry an attack two years after the FBI raided the Waco compound. It was estimated that 168 people died and more than 680 got wounded in a truck bomb that damaged more than 300 nearby buildings. Most of the dead were employees of the federal government, and there were 19 children present. The terrorists were immediately imprisoned and in two days convicted of terrorism. According to Timothy McVeigh, the mastermind, they chose this date as a symbol among the right-wing extremists, against what they called the abusive power of government in raiding the Branch of Davidians. They wanted to be a law by themselves and hated the federal government. This showed that anti-federal government paranoia was already present in the USA. After the bombing in Oklahoma the right-wing media became more visible, calling people to rise against the government and offering know-how and easy instructions on how to make bombs and oppose the government (Clinton 2004: 615–617). Today there are many right-wing, conspiracy-driven, anti-government organizations, which have established camps in rural areas in different states around the country. They are heavily armed and terrorist attacks committed by these right-wing terrorists supersede all other terrorist attacks committed by terrorist groups in the USA.

Internationally, the most lethal attacks were committed by al-Qaeda in 1998 in Tanzania and Kenya, the American embassies were hit in these two African countries simultaneously, leaving 257 dead, and more than 5000 injured. Among the dead were 12 Americans, most of them diplomats. The attacks were the result of Osama bin Laden's call to "bringing the war home to America". Al-Qaeda cells were activated and there were calls to hit American institutions and interests in the Gulf states and embassies everywhere they had cells (Clinton 2004: 741–743). Fortunately, they were not brought to life. These were the most lethal terrorist attacks that Clinton talks about, among other smaller ones, in his autobiography. Clinton witnessed some terrible terrorist events too, including an Islamic and a Christian terrorist group, among others.

Clinton dared to call terrorist events by their name, terrorism, instead of attributing them to a religious, racial, or ethnic group. When the Oklahoma City bombing happened, many were quick to call it an "Islamic fundamentalist attack", while President Clinton was quick to declare, "this is not a question of anybody's country of origin. This was a murder, this was evil, this was wrong. Human beings everywhere, all over the world, will condemn this out of their own religious convictions, and we should not stereotype anybody" (quoted in NYT, April 21, 1995). In Jakarta he declared, "even though we have had problems with terrorism coming out of the Middle East, it is not inherently related to Islam – not to religion, not to the culture" (Clinton 1994c). But he also made sure to put a stance against "the dark forces of terror and extremism" that threaten the Arab-Israeli peace process (Clinton 1994a). Among Clinton's top foreign policy advisers, Anthony Lake, Robert Pelletreau, and Timothy Wirth stated that Islamic extremists use religion to mask their lust for political power; thus terrorism and Islam should not be confused, as the problem for the USA is not Islam or the Muslims; instead it is "the use of violence by any person, regardless of religion, national origin or ethnicity" (quote in The Future of U.S. Anti-Terrorism Policy; see also Lake 1994; Pelletreau 1994). Lake furthermore rejected the notion that "the United States, as the sole remaining superpower in search of the new ideology to fight, should be bent on leading a new crusade against Islam" (Lake 1994). These were the best responses given to those who were advocating for securitizing Islam and equating Islam to terrorism and terrorists. This line of discourse can be seen during the whole Clinton presidency, challenging those who claimed that Islam was to be blamed and that there is a clash of civilization.

By analyzing Clinton's discourse toward Islam, we can see a consistency and correctness toward Islam, at least in rhetoric. In practice, these are symbolic actions that reached out to Muslim communities in the USA and to Muslim countries abroad. He rejected stereotypes against Muslims and Islam (Gerges 1999: 95) and tried to bring Islam and Muslims on board for democratic enlargement. President Clinton wanted to understand the Muslims and Islam to be able to make a policy toward them. For this purpose, his administration held a one-week seminar, in February 1993, to discuss points by which they should address the question of Islam, Muslims, and politics (Economist 1995). President Clinton wisely prevented the securitization of Islam and in fact he desecuritized it to bring it to the platform of working together for the Wilsonian ideals of democracy promotion, which was not the case during his predecessors, Reagan and Bush. President Clinton and most of his administration were careful not to associate Islam with hostile keywords, although sometimes they did refer to "Islamic terrorism" or "Islamic extremism" (Gerges 1999: 111), which is a result of many years of association of these keywords with Islam, so it could not be changed overnight or over the course of the two terms of the Clinton presidency. The desecuritization or non-securitization of Islam worked well during Clinton's presidency, where the US international image was the highest, terrorists threats the lowest, and more countries advanced toward democracy.

As expected, President Clinton started his presidency with focusing on domestic politics rather than foreign policy. The first couple of years were devoted mainly to improving domestic social and economic policies. When his administration saw that engagement in the foreign policy is inescapable, they worked on promoting the term "democratic enlargement" and took very cautious steps toward it. It is important for this work to note that these cautious steps were not taken to win new enemies or construct new enemies. Democratization was the main goal in discourse, but crusade for democracy was not an option. America led the military interventions in Yugoslavia, by succeeding to bring on board other countries to take these steps together. They convinced European and NATO powers to intervene, first diplomatically and then militarily, to resolve the Yugoslavian conflicts.

As far as Islam is concerned, there were no serious statements that Islam needed to be combated, that Islam is a threat, or that Islam needed to change to be able to bring democracy. In the Balkans, Islam was only mentioned when there was a need for public support, abroad and in America. Similarly, in the limited engagement in the Middle East, Islam was brought on board to promote human rights, free speech, and democracy. Islam was only mentioned for supporting the US policies, rather than a differentiating phenomenon. It entered very cautiously into political discourse, and despite some attempts to securitize it, Clinton and his administration were successful in repelling those claims.

The Clinton presidency is a very important period for understanding the difference between the politicization and the securitization of Islam. This also explains one of this work's two regions, which has resulted in a successful American policy, rather than the other one, which has not been successful. In the next chapter we analyze the next presidency to understand if Islam played a role, if Islam was securitized, and what were the implications if that was the case. The next chapter will show the role, if any, of Islam in these successful and unsuccessful US foreign policies.

This chapter has shown how the US administrations have dealt with Islam in their foreign policy after the Cold War, especially during the Clinton administration. The pre-Clinton administrations had different approaches toward Islam, and while Islam never became a security issue, acts like the Iranian Revolution and the hostage crises eventually triggered such debates. During the presidency of Bill Clinton there were actors who wanted to make Islam into a security issue, as a threat to the west, but Clinton wisely rejected such claims and decided to leave Islam in the social and political discourse. He was very careful when he spoke about Islam to keep it as a religion and to use the discourse of Islam only when he needed support to make his arguments.

This chapter has concluded that Islam was not successfully securitized, despite some attempts before the Clinton administration and during Clinton's presidency. The next chapter will analyze how the Bush administration handled the situation, especially after the 9/11 terrorist attacks, and how the war on terror campaign resulted in a debacle in the Middle East.

References

AbuKhalil, As'ad. 2002. *Bin Laden, Islam, and America's New "War on Terrorism".* New York: Seven Stories.
Acheson, Dean. 1969. *Present at the Creation: My Years in the State Department.* New York/London: W. W. Norton & Company.
Allison, Graham, and Philip Zelikow. 1999. *Essence of Decision: Explaining the Cuban Missile Crisis.* New York: Addison-Wesley.
Ambrose, Stephen E., and Douglas G. Brinkley. 1997. *Rise to Globalism.* New York: Penguin.
Andrew, Christophe. 1995. *For the President's Eyes Only: Secret Intelligence and the American Presidency from Washington to Bush.* New York: HarperCollins.
Appleby, R. Scott. 1995. Democratization in the Middle East Does Not Threaten the West. In *Islam: Opposing Viewpoints,* ed. Paul A. Winters. San Diego: Greenhaven Press.
Beinart, Peter. 2008. *The Good Fight: Why Liberals – And Only Liberals – Can Win the War on Terror and Make America Great Again.* New York: HarperCollins.
Berger, Samuel R. 2000. A Foreign Policy for the Global Age. *Foreign Policy,* November/December. http://www.foreignaffairs.com/articles/56625/samuel-r-berger/a-foreign-policy-for-the-global-age. Accessed 28 Nov 2014.

Blair, Tony. 1999. *Speech by Prime Minister, Tony Blair*. Chicago, US. April 22. http://www.pbs.org/newshour/bb/international-jan-june99-blair_doctrine4-23/. Accessed 16 Oct 2014.

Brzezinski, Zbigniew. 1997. *The Grand Chessboard: American Primacy and Its Geostrategic Imperatives*. New York: Basic Books.

Bulliet, Richard W. 1994. Rhetoric, Discourse, and the Future of Hope. In *Under Siege: Islam and Democracy*. New York: The Middle East Institute of Columbia University.

Cameron, Fraser. 2002. *US Foreign Policy After the Cold War: Global Hegemon or Reluctant Sheriff?* London/New York: Routledge.

Carter, Jimmy. 1977. *Address at Commencement Exercises at the University of Notre Dame*. May 22. http://www.presidency.ucsb.edu/ws/?pid=7552. Accessed 28 Nov 2014.

Clinton, Bill. 1992. Democracy in American. *Speech Delivered at the University of Milwaukee*. October 2. http://www.presidency.ucsb.edu/ws/index.php?pid=85226. Accessed 28 Nov 2014.

———. 1994a. *Remarks to the Jordanian Parliament in Amman, Jordan*. October 26. http://www.presidency.ucsb.edu/ws/?pid=49373. Accessed 6 May 2015.

———. 1994b. *The President's Remarks at White House Welcoming Ceremony for King Hussein of Jordan and Prime Minister Yitzhak Rabin of Israel*. Washington, DC. July 25. https://www.gpo.gov/fdsys/pkg/WCPD-1994-08-01/pdf/WCPD-1994-08-01-Pg1548.pdf. Accessed 8 Nov 2017.

———. 1994c. *The President's News Conference in Jakarta*. Jakarta: November 15. http://www.presidency.ucsb.edu/ws/?pid=49491. Accessed 6 May 2015.

———. 1995a. *Remarks by President Clinton and King Hassan of Morocco upon Arrival at the White House*. Washington, DC. March 15. http://clinton6.nara.gov/1995/03/1995-03-15-president-and-king-hassan-of-morocco-upon-arrival.html. Accessed 6 May 2015.

———. 1995b. *The President's News Conference With King Hassan II of Morocco*. Washington, DC. March 15. http://www.presidency.ucsb.edu/ws/?pid=51106. Accessed 6 May 2015.

———. 1995c. *The President's News Conference With Prime Minister Benazir Bhutto of Pakistan*. Washington, DC. April 11. http://www.presidency.ucsb.edu/ws/?pid=51220. Accessed 6 May 2015.

Clinton, William J. 1999. *Remarks at the Legislative Convention of the American Federation of State, County, and Municipal Employees*. March 23. http://www.presidency.ucsb.edu/ws/?pid=57294. Accessed 8 Nov 2017.

———. 2004. *My Life*. New York: Random House.

Coll, Steve. 2004. *Ghost Wars: The Secret History of the CIA, Afghanistan, and Bin Laden, from the Soviet Invasion to September 10, 2011*. New York: Penguin Books.

Cox, Michael. 1995. *US Foreign Policy After the Cold War: Superpower Without a Mission?* London: Printer/Royal Institute of International Affairs.

———. 2000. Wilsonianism Resurgent? The Clinton Administration and the Promotion of Democracy. In *American Democracy Promotion: Impulses, Strategies, and Impacts*, ed. Michael Cox, G. John Ikenberry, and Takashi Inoguchi, 218–239. New York: Oxford University Press.

Economist, The. 1995. A Wobbly Hand of Friendship: America and Islam. (Clinton Administration's Policy Towards Muslim Nations). *The Economist*, August 25. http://www.highbeam.com/doc/1G1-17261241.html. Accessed 6 May 2015.

Esposito, John. 1999. *The Islamic Threat: Myth or Reality?* New York: Oxford University Press.

Fouskas, Vassilis. 2003. *Zones of Conflict: US Foreign Policy in the Balkans and the Greater Middle East*. Sterling: Pluto Press.

Fuller, Graham E., and Ian O. Lesser. 1995. *A Sense of Siege: The Geopolitics of Islam and the West*. Boulder: Westview Press.

Gerges, Fawaz A. 1999. *America and Political Islam: Clash of Cultures of Clash of Interests?* Cambridge: Cambridge University Press.

Hadar, Leon. 1995. Political Islam Is Not a Threat to the West. In *Islam: Opposing Viewpoints*, ed. Paul A. Winters. San Diego: Greenhaven Press.

Hippler, Jochen. 1995. The Islamic Threat and Western Foreign Policy. In *The Next Threat: Western Perceptions of Islam*, ed. Jochen Hippler and Andrea Leug. Boulder: Pluto Press.

Holsti, Ole R. 2000. Promotion of Democracy as a Popular Demand? In *American Democracy Promotion: Impulses, Strategies, and Impacts*, ed. Michael Cox, G. John Ikenberry, and Takashi Inoguchi, 151–180. New York: Oxford University Press.

Hulsman, John C. 1997. *A Paradigm for a New World Order*. Basingstoke: Macmillan Press.

Huntington, Samuel. 1984. Will More Countries Become Democratic. *Political Science Quarterly* 99 (2): 193–218.

———. 1991. Religion and the Third Wave. *The National Interest* 24 (Summer): 29–42.

———. 1993. The Clash of Civilizations? *Foreign Affairs* 72 (3): 22–49.

Ikenberry, John G. 2000. America's Liberal Grand Strategy: Democracy and National Security in the Post-War Era. In *American Democracy Promotion: Impulses, Strategies, and Impacts*, ed. Michael Cox, G. John Ikenberry, and Takashi Inoguchi, 103–126. New York: Oxford University Press.

Jones, Bryan, ed. 1995. *The New American Politics: Reflections on Political Change and the Clinton Administration*. Boulder: Westview Press.

Kennedy, John F. 1961. *Inaugural Address*. January 20. http://avalon.law.yale.edu/20th_century/kennedy.asp. Accessed 28 Nov 2014.

Kennedy, Robert F. 1966. *Thirteen Days*. London: Macmillan.
Kissinger, H. 1979. *White House Years*. Boston: Little, Brown.
Knutsen, Torbjorn L. 1999. *The Rise and Fall of World Orders*. Manchester: Manchester University Press.
Lake, Anthony. 1993. From Containment to Enlargement. *Remarks of Anthony Lake*. Johns Hopkins University: School of Advanced International Studies. Washington, DC. September 21.
———. 1994. Building a New Middle East: Challenges for U.S. Policy. *Washington Institute for Near East Policy*. Washington, DC. May 17. http://dosfan.lib.uic.edu/ERC/briefing/dispatch/1994/html/Dispatchv5Sup07.html. Accessed 6 May 2015.
Layne, Christopher, and M. Lynn-Jones. 1998. *Should America Promote Democracy?* Cambridge: MIT Press.
Leffler, Melvyn P. 1984. The American Conception of National Security and the Beginnings of the Cold War, 1945–48. *American Historical Review* 89 (2): 346–381.
Lewis, Bernard. 1993. *Islam and the West*. New York: Oxford University Press.
Miller, Judith. 1993. The Challenge of Radical Islam. *Foreign Affairs* 72 (2, Spring): 43–56.
New York Times. 1995. Terror in Oklahoma: The President; Clinton Vows a Relentless Pursuit of Bombers and Hopes to go to Oklahoma. April 21. http://www.nytimes.com/1995/04/21/us/terror-oklahoma-president-clinton-vows-relentless-pursuit-bombers-hopes-go.html. Accessed 6 May 2015.
Pelletreau, Robert. 1994. Current Issue in the Middle East. Address to the Harvard Law School: Islamic legal studies Program in Cambridge. April 11.
Perlmutter, Amos. 1992. Wishful Thinking About Islamic Fundamentalism. *Washington Post*, January 19.
Pipes, Daniel. 1994. Same Difference: The Islamic Threat Part I. *National Review*, November 7.
Powell, Colin with Tony Koltz. 2012. *It Worked for Me: In Life and Leadership*. New York: Harper Collins.
Quoyle, Dan. 1990. *Text of Remarks by the Vice-President, Commencement Address, Graduation and Commissioning Ceremony for the Class of 1990, U.S. Naval Academy, Annapolis, Maryland*. Washington, DC: Office of the Vice-President.
Reagan, Ronald. 1980. An Interview with Ronald Reagan. *Time*, November 17. http://content.time.com/time/magazine/article/0,9171,950485,00.html. Accessed 6 May 2015.
———. 1986. *Address on U.S. Air Strike Against Libya*. April 14. http://www.reagan.utexas.edu/archives/speeches/1986/41486g.htm. Accessed 6 May 2015.
———. 1990. *An American Life: The Autobiography*. New York: Pocket Books.

Rice, Condoleezza. 2000. Campaign 2000: Promoting the National Interest. *Foreign Affairs* 79 (1): 45–62.
Robin, Wright. 1995. Islamist's Theory of Relativity. *Los Angeles Times*, January 27. http://articles.latimes.com/1995-01-27/news/mn-25033_1_muslim-reformation. Accessed 8 Aug 2017.
Shin, Doh Chull. 1994. On the Third Wave of Democratization. *World Politics* 47 (1): 135–170.
Shipoli, Erdoan. 2010. *International Securitization: The Case of Kosovo*. Saarbrucken: Lambert Academic Publishing.
Smith, Tony. 2000. National Security Liberalism and American Foreign Policy. In *American Democracy Promotion: Impulses, Strategies, and Impacts*, ed. Michael Cox, G. John Ikenberry, and Takashi Inoguchi, 85–102. New York: Oxford University Press.
———. 2009. Wilsonianism After Iraq: The End of Liberal Internationalism? In *The Crisis of American Foreign Policy: Wilsonianism in the Twenty-First Century*, ed. John G. Ikenberry et al., 53–88. New Jersey: Princeton University Press.
Talbott, Strobe. 1996. Democracy and the National Interest. *Foreign Affairs* 74 (6): 47–63.
Voll, John, and John Esposito. 1994. Islam's Democratic Essence. *Middle East Quarterly* 1 (3): 3–11.
White House. 1996. National Security Strategy of Engagement and Enlargement. February. http://www.fas.org/spp/military/docops/national/1996stra.htm. Accessed July 2014.
Zoellick, Robert B. 2000. Campaign 2000: A Republican Foreign Policy. *Foreign Affairs*, January/February.

CHAPTER 6

Securitization of Islam in US Foreign Policy: The Bush Administration

Unlike President Clinton, Bush decided to use Islam in most of his foreign policy and security speeches, especially after the 9/11 terrorist attacks. In addressing Islam and the Muslims as the "other", Bush developed his narrative for the war on terror and what was to come afterward.

Through fear and with the help of the media, President Bush heightened the alert of security, placing it deeply within the context of religion through language such as "crusade" and claims of a "call from God". Once religionized, it became easy to turn Islam into a security issue and threat. Bush did not securitize Islam directly; rather, Islam became securitized through association as the opposite of what America, democracy, and the "civilized world" stand for.

Bush did not have a single speech on Islam. Although Bush talked about Islam in most of his foreign policy and security speeches, we analyzed his "Axis of Evil" speech as the primer speech on his doctrine on Islam as this was the speech that nailed Islam as a permanent agenda associated with security. Many other speeches of Bush were superficially analyzed for this purpose as well.

6.1 George W. Bush Administration

The George W. Bush administration is well remembered for its multi-front wars under the war-on-terror flag. Terrorism has been the symbol of President Bush's America, which was not constructed all by Bush himself, but was inherited from his predecessors, and was developed largely during his years of presidency. It was Bush that tackled this issue directly, and it was during these years that many of the policies backfired, ignited more terrorism against the USA, and changed global political order.

Even though many consider the war on terror as something new, in fact it is not. America has been dealing with terrorism for a long time; nevertheless, this time terrorism directly hit her soil and her interests. The USA has been "fighting" terrorism for a very long time, starting with the bombing of Libya in 1986 to fight terrorism; CIA's assassinations in the Middle East, among which the Beirut car bomb that missed the target, a Shi'ite leader, but killed more than 85 and injured more than 185 people; bombing of Lebanon in the 1980s to fight terrorism; Nicaragua mining of harbors in the 1980s, again on pretext of terrorism; support of Israel with the pretext of defending an ally against terrorists (AbuKhalil 2002: 83); and also, the biggest operation, to arm, finance, and train fundamentalists in Pakistan and Afghanistan, against a common enemy (Coll 2004), which has arguably backfired on the USA.

In a CIA report in the beginning of 2000, about how the world will look by 2020, it is estimated that fear will be driving world politics, and America should and will respond with "security measures" (Woodward 2002). One can look at the twenty-first-century terrorist attacks in this perspective, where terrorist attacks cultivate fear and world politics is driven by this fear, where there have been mini-terrorist cells that threaten sovereign countries more than countries threaten each other. After 9/11 we saw that these estimates were true. All the policies that were adopted afterward were products of fighting fear with security measures. These attacks have affected the US counterterrorism policy widely, resulting in the Antiterrorism and Effective Death Penalty Act, based on four points: bringing terrorists to justice for their crimes, pressuring the states that sponsor terrorism, offering no concessions to terrorists and making no deals, and seeking support and assisting allies in fighting terrorism (Cameron 2002: 141). Likewise, many other regulations, acts, and laws have passed, which ultimately limited the rights and liberties of Americans, alienated minorities, and frightened others.

But were the 9/11 attacks at all unexpected? For months prior, there was credible intelligence that al-Qaeda might be preparing an attack on American soil. In fact, one cannot think of the opposite taking in consideration that the USA has the most sophisticated intelligence and technology in human history. Intercepts, informants, foreign intelligence services, and bin Laden himself told a Pakistani journalist that he was planning such an attack. Nevertheless, the Bush administration did not believe it would be possible and did not take these threats very seriously (Eichenwald 2012: 7). When the 9/11 terrorist attacks happened, the world changed forever. This time, America became reactionist to the agenda led by a terrorist group in the mountains of Afghanistan and Pakistan, who inflicted fear and damaged the world's sole superpower and the most sophisticated military in human history.

After the 9/11 attacks President Bush vowed to track down terrorists anywhere in the world and claimed that the USA cannot sit and watch what is happening in the world. Bush followed a policy of trying to establish broader coalitions to tackle terrorist threats. In a speech made by former president, H. W. Bush in Boston on September 14, 2001, he called for multilateralism asserting that:

> Just as Pearl Harbor awakened this country from the notion that we could somehow avoid the call to duty and defend freedom in Europe and Asia in World War II, so, too, should this most recent surprise attack erase the concept in some quarters that America can somehow go it alone in the fight against terrorism or in anything else for that matter. (Bush 2001a)

This is a change of mind from Bush junior's campaign claims, where he asserted that he doesn't think to be as engaged as his predecessor in world politics, that the USA cannot commit troops everywhere it is needed, and that he will be selective. At the beginning of his administration, Bush signaled that he would establish his own policies in the interest of the USA without referring to international partners. Just in the first months in the office, Bush and his administration rejected many international treaties, claiming that the USA should lead and others should follow, and that the USA will decide upon its own interests and not be engaged in humanitarian work.

Furthermore, Bush claimed that the USA will not continue to engage in the peace process in the Middle East and Northern Ireland; that there will be no new troops, but rather a decrease in the number of troops, in the Balkans; that the USA will be committed to go on building national missile defense, regardless of what others think; and that the Kyoto treaty on climate was dead (Cameron 2002: xi–182). Many analysts were reluctant to Bush's foreign policy from the beginning, accusing him of antagonizing old friends and of turning potential partners into adversaries

(Cameron 2002: 30–32). Just before becoming president, Bush gave an interview that signaled how he wanted America to be viewed in the world, "If we are an arrogant nation, they will resent us. If we are a humble nation, but strong, they will welcome us" (PBS 2000). Nevertheless, in his first visit to Europe as the US president he gained so many adversaries that European headlines read: "The Texas Executioner", "Bomber Bush", "Bush Rejects Kyoto", and "US Says No to World Court" (Cohen 2001). Criticism of Bush's international engagement grew harshly at home in the beginning of 2001 accusing him of "not reflect[ing] American principles and ideas" (Cameron 2002: 30–32), to which Bush's administration's National Security Advisor, Condoleezza Rice, answered that the Bush administration was "one hundred percent internationalist", but she criticized the general opinion that "internationalism somehow becomes defined as signing on to bad treaties just to say that you have signed a treaty", and she defined the new Bush administration policies as the "new realism" (Cameron 2002: 30–32).

But after the 9/11 attacks everything changed. Bush divided the world between "us" and "them". This division worked to Bush's advantage in setting the national political agenda outside of his cabinet. It has been stated in this book many times, and other works earlier, that the 9/11 terrorist attacks were a wake-up call. For one, it stopped the criticisms of Bush's foreign policy, and for another it changed his foreign policy. Bush was attracting a lot of criticism from both democrats and republicans. At the beginning of his presidency, even the congressmen from his party were accusing Bush's foreign policy of being a continuation of his predecessors' and of lacking a strategy. On March 7, 2001, the Republican chairman of the House of International Relations Committee, Henry Hyde, voiced his concern:

> The principal problem, the one that concerns me the most, is that we have no long-term strategy, no practical plan for shaping the future ... the fall of that [Soviet] empire took with it the central organizing principle of our foreign policy for the last half century. ... Instead of a firm course, I see drift. Instead of shaping the evolution of events in pursuit of long-term objectives, we have been busy responding to problems as they arise, guided by an agenda that has been more thrust upon us by circumstance than one we have ourselves constructed for our own purposes. (Hyde 2001)

6.1.1 The USA After 9/11

In his eight-minute speech after the 9/11 attacks, Bush expressed condolences for the victims but also delivered the message that America had been threatened and that this was a serious security issue. From his first speech, he built the case for the securitizing act that would follow. He referred to freedom and the US way of life as threatened when he claimed that "Today, our fellow citizens, our way of life, our very freedom came under attack in a series of deliberate and deadly terrorist acts", and he argued further for the extraordinary means that will be used to secure the USA, "we will make no distinction between the terrorists who committed these acts and those who harbor them", and asked Americans to unite in the "monumental struggle of good versus evil ... [where] good will prevail" (Bush 2001c). Furthermore, Bush called this conflict a "crusade". For the draft of the speech on the occasion of the start of the military campaign, there were many discussions of how to word the campaign that Bush was about to take and finally they came up with "Eliminate terrorism as a threat to our way of life, and to all nations that love freedom" (Eichenwald 2012: 55–56). President Bush committed his entire presidency and his legacy to this "crusade". He wanted to become the president of education, with the "no child left behind" campaign, but he said that on 9/11 he immediately understood that he would be a president of war (Bush 2010: 276). In these discussions, it is obvious that they wanted to securitize the American way of life, but for a campaign as the one that was about to come, something bigger must happen, and the second part of the sentence "and to all nations that love freedom" included a global reach.

After the 9/11 attacks, America and the world were in shock. Americans responded to the 9/11 attacks with fear, paranoia, and exaggerated patriotism. Whatever happened and whosever fault it was, Americans wanted revenge. It was obvious that US policymakers had underestimated the non-state actors. It was clear during the Clinton administration that there had been a rise of non-state actors, especially in terrorism, and even Clinton had described terrorism as a force beyond governments' control. Similarly, Richard Clark, a holdover from the Clinton administration, warned about the threats of al-Qaeda at the beginning of 2001, but Paul Wolfowitz argued that too much credit is given to bin Laden and that even though al-Qaeda bombed the World Trade Center in 1993 it had done it through the help of a state, Iraq. Rumsfeld also argued that Saddam Hussein was a bigger threat than bin Laden, and it should come to no surprise that after the 9/11 the focus of the US intelligence, military, and politics was on Iraq and how to bring down Saddam Hussein, rather than recognizing the terrorists as an independent entity (Beinart 2008: 143). When Bush was a governor, there were reports brought to him that suggested that in the near future Americans would be threatened by non-state terrorist groups. According to those reports the worst one was al-Qaeda, which had a vast network and the means to acquire nuclear and chemical weapons. They would not need much to make a lot of damage, a briefcase of such weapons could be easily put in a crowd and be detonated with fatal results. Attorney General John Ashcroft stated that Bush did not want him to mention anything about bin Laden or al-Qaeda, as there was nothing he could do about it (Eichenwald 2012: 2–9) because the only actors they recognized were states.

Not only individual leaders, US institutions also had difficulties comprehending the new threats. The counterterrorism center in the USA was financed by Congress and the White House from time to time, but not continuously. When an attack happened anywhere in the world, this center would attract a lot of funds and then the finances would fade when the attacks were forgotten. Before 9/11 the counterterrorism center was underfinanced; however, no one doubted that after these attacks the center would have unlimited financial resources (Eichenwald 2012: 37), although it was already very late. American foreign and security policy mindset worked only with states and institutional actors. They had difficulties comprehending the necessity to adopt policies, strategies, and mindsets against non-state and unofficial actors.

After the attacks, some administrators in the Bush administration were faster than others to understand that a war against a hybrid entity does not have a certain country or territory; in Defense Secretary Rumsfeld's words "terrorism is by its very nature something that cannot be dealt with by some form of massive attack or invasion. It is much subtler, nuanced, difficult, shadowy set of problems" (quoted in Cameron 2002: 135), which makes it more difficult for us to understand the rationale behind the invasion of Afghanistan and Iraq soon after. The result was an open-ended war on terror, which brought fundamental changes to global politics, individual rights, and relations between state and non-state actors.

Before 9/11, the Bush administration claimed that it lacked the authority to take the risks to stop USA's enemies and he demanded more authority. When 9/11 happened, Bush suddenly had carte blanche on structuring the foreign policy he wanted. As he claimed, "I've told the American people, we would have deficits only in the case of war, a recession, or a national emergency. In this case, we've got all three" (Bush 2002b). Now he had a free hand to abandon a balanced budget. He passed policies to limit citizen rights, because security was the first prerequisite for freedom, and the protection of the country comes before the protection of its citizens (Eichenwald 2012: 58). Certainly, some jihadists became the threat that the USA needed to define its strategy. But this time it was different. A particular government, a universal religion, or a high-tech-rich group did not direct this threat (Beinart 2008: 191). Rather, it was a hybrid group, headed by people that lived in remote non-urban areas, who had hijacked a religion through a radical ideology.

The response of the 9/11 attacks affected many parts of life in America and the world. On the domestic front, George W. Bush brought new and previously unseen measures to strengthen the "homeland". Coordination between the White House and law enforcement agencies was established, including the State, Defense, Justice, and other departments, but also established a new one: the Department of Homeland Security. Congress passed the famous Patriot Act six weeks after the attacks, giving the government extraordinary powers and tools with which to fight terrorists, including wiretapping, seizing phone and email records, business, banking, educational and medical records, and also searching homes of the suspected, without a warrant. No one knows how these rights were used, but the FBI's demand on wiretapping people's phones, emails, and financial records has increased a hundredfold since the Patriot Act, and this could have been used for anything, from drugs to white-collar crimes to political and trade competition. After the Patriot Act the government detained 1200 foreign nationals, without charging them with crimes, without informing their families, and without warrants. The National Security Agency (NSA) has spied on thousands of Americans, and created parallel secret prisons in many places around the world, where America has been accused of holding suspects for months, and even years, with no information and without due process (Beinart 2008: 109). The carte blanche that the Patriot Act gave to the Bush administration was a cornerstone of the new redlines to which American presidents could go. These extraordinary powers given to the government were considered as necessary because "we are at war and we have to do things differently" to quote the Attorney General John Ashcroft and Olson (2002). Although there was much debate and criticism, Congress had only one answer, that of the "sunset clause" which gave this act only five years and would expire afterward (Cameron 2002: 145–146). The Patriot Act produced many unclear actions of the government, with many controversies.

Before 9/11, the allegations of private prisons and torture by the USA were unthinkable; today they are hardly contested (Beinart 2008: 109–110). After the first Patriot Act, the Bush administration turned into a rule-breaking machine. Bush openly informed that America would not be abiding any international treaty, or world opinion; rather it would be abiding only its own rules and moral sense. The administration refused compliance even with the International Convention on Torture, which was signed and ratified by the USA, and when the Red Cross examined America's prison facilities in Iraq, the USA hid what they called the "ghost detainees" and the CIA-run "ghost facilities", that no one knows anything about, their whereabouts, or destiny (Beinart 2008: 136). The enhanced interrogation techniques that were utilized at these "ghost facilities" are considered to have been torture. Even the CIA director, Leon Panetta, has acknowledged that despite the information they got, these techniques should have never been used, because that information could have been taken by other more efficient means. Most of the information came out of fear, so most of them were false anyway, and there was no tangible information such as the address of bin Laden or similar information (Panetta 2014: 223–224). Contrary to the claims made only recently, the Bush administration established secret relations with Syria and Libya, allies were threatened with devastations, and the national security was reexamined (Eichenwald 2012: 17). The new doctrine became one where the USA is positioned above other countries, institutions, global system, or above the rules. The USA was providing the standard of security and order enforcement. The new security doctrine asserted that America's role and rule in the world is associated with the use of force to find and fight terrorists anywhere in the world, and as Bush claimed, "no nation can be neutral in this conflict" (Shapiro 2007; Daalder and Lindsay 2003). The previously followed Powell Doctrine, which set out preconditions to the use of military forces, including clear military and political objectives, reasonable expectation from the Congress and the American public, costs of the military action, and exhausted means of peaceful resolution of the situation (Powell 2012), died with this new strategic mindset.

As if this was not enough, the government obtained another Act called Domestic Security Enhancement Act, or what some have called Patriot Act II. In 2003 the Center for Public Integrity got their hand in this Act and its executive director, Charles Lewis, explained that with this Act the government gained many times more powers than it had with the Patriot Act I. The government had now the power to strip native-born Americans of their citizenship and imprison them indefinitely if they gave any support, violent or nonviolent, to groups considered to be terrorist groups by the USA (Beinart 2008: 110). These kinds of powers are open to misinterpretation and misuse, and they were used in the USA for other purposes. But most importantly, having these powers given to the security forces constitutes a security environment, boosts fear and panic among the public, and brings them to the point that they can give up their liberties for the security threat that has been told to them exists.

6.1.2 War on Terror: From Weapons of Mass Destruction (WMDs) to Democracy Promotion

The war on terror involved individuals that were already familiar with what was happening in the Middle East and who had been involved with the Middle East for a long time. It involved Bush administration's high-level foreign policymakers, who were inherited from his father's presidency. The complex with the Middle East, and especially with Saddam, was an old one for people like Paul Wolfowitz, who was arguing that W. Bush should finish what H. W. Bush could not.

With the shock that the 9/11 attacks caused in America, both Democrats and Republicans backed Bush to invade Afghanistan. Although the methods were being questioned, not much opposition was voiced from the Democrats. Democrats were as much pressured to back Bush's efforts to fight terrorism, including invading Afghanistan, as were the Republicans. They considered America to be in a state of war with terrorism and supported the administration to tackle this enemy by any means. In congress too, Democrats supported Bush in military buildup and spending on homeland security and foreign aid (Beinart 2008: 172). During the 2008 election campaigns one can find no top-ranked Democrat saying that the USA had a misguided strategy of "freeing" people around the globe (Smith 2009: 79–82). The most supportive Democrats for Bush's intervention in Iraq were Clintonian Democrats, such as Sandy Berger, Madeleine Albright, and Richard Holbrook, who had been the masterminds of the victory in Kosovo, but had a long-standing frustration with Saddam Hussein, from the 1990s (Beinart 2008: 173). Among others, liberal writer Peter Beinart considered the interventions in Afghanistan and Iraq to be a higher goal because defeating Islamist totalitarianism, according to him, was liberalism's "north star". There was no partisan line difference in supporters and critics of Bush's Afghanistan and Iraq policies.

The Bush administration linked the attacks to American values. Bush's first words after the 9/11 were "Freedom, itself, was attacked this morning by faceless cowards ... and freedom will be defended" (Bush 2001c). In those first hours Bush acknowledged that the USA was at war, that someone else declared it against the USA, and this would demand actions and decisions that would involve a lot of risks, which he was ready to take. Soon after the attacks the administration started constructing a new era where the world was changing once and for all and the USA was not going to be tolerant and be patient; it was about to take lead and solve problems like Saddam (Beinart 2008: 152–153). The 9/11 terrorist attacks provided a great opportunity not to be missed. Top Bush administration officials prepared the public for the hard days ahead. Bush himself claimed that the USA was at war with a merciless enemy, against whom America must fight not only in Afghanistan but also in Iraq, Syria, and Iran, because this was a war where the governments around the world must choose sides (Eichenwald 2012: 51). Secretary of State Colin Powell argued that this was a highly risky move that would not be a guaranteed solution if Saddam is toppled (Cameron 2002: 16), but that America should persist.

Bush immediately ordered the invasion of Afghanistan, where allegedly al-Qaeda leaders, including bin Laden, were hiding. But Bush was not going to stop with Afghanistan. Simultaneously the campaign to invade Iraq was happening and ultimately, the "war on terror" resulted in the invasion of Iraq, which began as a campaign to find those responsible for breeding terrorism, those who "hate us because of who we are", and to bring them to justice, as well as to demolish Saddam Hussein's WMDs. Bush could also be considered a mastermind in using the media, and the CNN effect, as it is widely called today. Conservative media lost no opportunity after the 9/11 terrorist attacks to advocate for the war in Iraq, associating Saddam Hussein with al-Qaeda and bin Laden, as well as the weapons of mass destruction. There was war hysteria in America (Gottschalk and Greenberg 2008: 94; Halper and Clarke 2004). Liberal newspapers, such as the *New York Times* and the *Washington Post*, also supported the war in Iraq, and it was only after the failure to find the WMDs that these two newspapers publicly apologized, but others did not. Continuous television coverage of the terrorist attacks on the World Trade Center ensured a massive support for actions against the perpetrators

(Cameron 2002: 107) and brought trauma to the public, rooting fear in the minds and hearts of the American public.

Although Secretary Powell warned about the campaign in Iraq, claiming that it will not be an easy task and that even when Saddam is toppled the work would not be done, the war in Iraq was not taken seriously in the USA. Fox News's host Bill O'Reilly bet that the war in Iraq would not last a week; Bill Kristol of the Weekly Standard claimed that it was misinformation that Shi'a and Sunni cannot get along and that there had been no evidence for this; and also, Fred Barnes, another Fox host, claimed that the war was the hard part, bringing democracy is challenging but much easier than winning the war (Zogby 2010: 123). Nevertheless, nearly two decades after there is still neither peace nor democracy in Afghanistan or Iraq.

For the war on terror campaign, the whole administration played a role in convincing the public for the wars in Afghanistan and Iraq. Most notable was Vice President Cheney who consistently pushed the policy to bomb several countries in the Middle East. His intentions are well known and now documented in the biographies of his colleagues. Secretary Gates recalls that all of the cabinet of the president were looking for ways to block Iran's and Syria's nuclear programs, including negotiating with them. Only Cheney wanted and advocated for attacking Iran and Syria, and this was the only option for him (Gates 2014). Similarly, Colin Powell talks about how Cheney and his team had pushed for his notorious UN speech on Iraq's weapons of mass destruction, which was based on false intelligence. Powell's UN speech on Iraq, the weapons of mass destruction, and war, is the biggest failure of US intelligence. Powell expresses his regrets that he has to live the rest his life with this shame but takes the responsibility for his own speech. In his autobiography, he explains how Bush asked him to present the case against Iraq to the international community in only five days, making the case of Iraq's weapons of mass destruction, violations of UN resolutions, human rights violations, and support for terrorism. Powell argues that this was just a play, which he understood afterward, because Bush and his team had already made up their minds to invade Iraq, and they had never consulted the National Security Council, either before the speech or afterward. Powell also argued that the intelligence presented to him was debatable about the amount of the weapons of mass destruction, but no one doubted that Saddam Hussein had them and continued to build them after the Desert Storm. For the incoherent case on the WMDs, Powell makes it very clear:

Sometime later in the day of my January 30 meeting with the President, my staff received the WMD case the NSC staff had been working on. It was a disaster. It was incoherent. Assertions were made that either had no sourcing or no connection to the NIE. I asked George Tenet, Director of Central Intelligence (DCI), what had happened. He had nothing to do with it, he told me. He had provided the NIE and raw material to National Security Advisor Condoleezza Rice's office. He had no idea what happened to it after that.

I learned later that Scooter Libby, Vice President Cheney's chief of staff, had authored the unusable presentation, not the NSC staff. And several years after that, I learned from Dr. Rice that the idea of using Libby had come from the Vice President, who had persuaded the President to have Libby, a lawyer, write the "case" as a lawyer's brief and not as an intelligence assessment. (Powell 2012: 219)

Because Powell was not satisfied with this report, as it was written from a lawyer on the "guilt and innocence" dichotomy, instead of "fact-based" intelligence, he decided to redo the whole report together with Tenet's staff, his staff, Rice, and some other officials. Nevertheless, Vice President Cheney still pushed to inject some of his thoughts, not based on intelligence, especially the ones that argued the links between Iraq and 9/11. Secretary Powell made the speech, which he thought went well; then America invaded Iraq, but no WMDs were found, as according to Powell "there were none" (2012: 221). Finally, he says that it is hard for him to forget this, and most likely he will never forget it, but "as we move on, we must make sure the lessons learned are never forgotten or ignored" (2012: 224), which is what this work argues: that mistakes have been made and there are some people who take responsibility, but most importantly one should learn from the mistakes so as not to repeat them.

While we are taking lessons, we must mention that most of the officials involved in making the case for Saddam's WMDs were consultants to Republican presidential candidates in 2016. Paul Wolfowitz, Deputy Defense Secretary, was Jeb Bush's foreign policy expert; John Bolton, US ambassador to the UN, was advising Ted Cruz; Marco Rubio had Elliott Abrams, William Kristol, and Cheney's advisor Eric Edelman (Walcott 2016).

On January 24, 2016, Politico's John Walcott published an article about a report by the Joint Chief of Staff (JCS) that made it to Donald Rumsfeld's desk, Bush's former Secretary of Defense. The document that Walcott spoke of reveals gaps of intelligence related to Iraq's WMDs, as well as how Rumsfeld hid what he knew from the others. It is of no surprise that Rumsfeld is mostly known for his obsession with "known unknowns". For him there were many unknowns, and this report has shown that knowledge on various aspects of Iraq's WMD program ranged from 0% to 75%. Moreover, the report acknowledged that "Our knowledge of the Iraqi (nuclear) weapons program is based largely—perhaps 90%—on analysis of imprecise intelligence". The JCS report said that they cannot confirm any Iraqi facilitates that produces, tests, fills, or stores biological weapons. The author reports that according to a September 5, 2002, memo by Major General Glen Shaffer, Joint Staff's intelligence director, to Rumsfeld unveiled that "We don't know with any precision how much we don't know" and that "Our assessments rely heavily on analytic assumptions and judgment rather than hard evidence. The evidentiary basis is particularly sparse for Iraqi nuclear programs". This was five months before Secretary Powell made his UN speech about Iraq's WMDs. The uncertainty did not prevent President Bush from claiming in Cincinnati, in October 2002, that America was sure that Iraq was producing thousands of tons of chemical agents, mustard gas, nerve gas, and other chemical agents, because American "surveillance photos reveal that the regime is building facilities that it had used to produce chemical and biological weapons". But, we understand that all the reports spoke the opposite, that they cannot confirm or deny such a process, and that there was no clear evidence of facilities that were being used for the building of these chemical agents or WMDs. Also, what we understand from this report is that the intelligence and defense community had informed the administration that they believed that Saddam was building WMDs, but this is only based on analysis instead of intelligence and evidence and that the precision could range from 0% to 75% the most. This report was not shared with the Congress or other administrators at the White House by Rumsfeld until 2011 when it was declassified; thus, it is no surprise that the alleged WMDs of Saddam were never found.

However, after these weapons were not found, the discourse shifted toward a campaign to overturn tyranny, to expose the pretensions of tyrants, and reward the hopes of the decent. In his second inaugural address, President Bush said, "the peace we seek will only be achieved by eliminating the conditions that feed radicalism and ideologies of murder" furthermore foretelling his future plans "if whole regions of the world remain in despair and grow in hatred, they will be the recruiting grounds for terror, and that terror will stalk America" (Bush 2005). The focus had now shifted from fighting the "evil" to a long-term agenda of overturning tyrants and spreading freedom and democracy.

Promotion of democracy and the American national security have become one and the same, where America becomes the world policeman and where the security of the USA is the best for everyone else (Ikenberry 2009: 8–9). For all those who believe that Bush was bringing to life the vision of Wilson, there is a slight difference: Wilson wanted to make the world safe for democracy, and not go out to hunt for monsters to destroy (Knock 2009: 35), whereas Bush wanted to crusade for democracy (Jervis 2006). In fact, Iraq was just the start of a longer expedition according to the Bush administration rationale. The expedition would continue with Lebanon, Libya, Somalia, and Sudan, until it would finally finish with Iran (Eichenwald 2012: 123). Nevertheless, especially at the beginning, Bush could not ask for public support with the pretext of bringing Saddam down, or to bringing democracy to Iraq, so he was consistently using the arguments that the next attacks in America would be much bloodier than the 9/11 attacks if the terrorists were armed with WMDs and backed up by Saddam Hussein (Beinart 2008: 148–149). Afterward Bush substituted the hunt for WMDs with "bringing democracy", and until he invaded Iraq he and his administration used this argument.

Michael Ignatieff (2004) called George W. Bush's "God's gift to mankind" approach to democracy as the democratic providentialism. To reach his conservative voters, Bush used this rhetoric for his reelection, for the Iraq war, and for justifying the war on terror. This approach argues that America is the driver of democracy and the history of the world, which has shown to be an illusion, according to Ignatieff. No one questions the USA's power to spread democracy, but the world today is much more complicated and America cannot do it alone. Iraqi war exceeded beyond being an American campaign toward a global issue. This is why it is important to understand the ideology behind such an operation. Many analysts consider this a Wilsonian idea, sharing the blame between the conservatives and the liberals. It is true that many liberals supported this war, but the question remains: was the American foreign policy hijacked by a group who was hiding behind the Wilsonian ideology (Ikenberry 2009: 1–2) to justify their acts and plans? It is believed that an American Wilsonian tradition played an important role, for the overall grand strategy, like the safety of American national security and the promotion of democracy. Nevertheless, the viewpoint and the methods were those of the Cold War, which were a result of the Bush senior's staff transferring to Bush junior, who were either officials during the Cold War or experts on Soviet Union.

Many have compared Bush to Wilson, and to be able to understand Bush's democracy promotion we must too. The continuous repetition by President Bush that the security of the USA is dependent on the spread of democracy qualifies him to be compared with Wilson and his ideas of democracy promotion and democratic peace. Bush wanted to leave a trademark in the new global politics after the Cold War (Smith 2009: 53; Ikenberry 2009: 1). They have been compared on the grounds of democracy promotion, but they have been contrasted on the methods. One is sure that the world does not need an isolated America, it definitely needs a Wilsonian America, but one that is properly adopted and practiced in the circumstances of the twenty-first century (Slaughter 2009: 92). President Bush made many speeches referring to Wilsonian ideas, where sometimes he would sound more Wilsonian than Wilson himself, such as in the 2002 National Security Strategy document, where he stated that "In keeping with our heritage and principles, we do not use our strength to press unilateral advantage. We seek instead to create a balance-of-power that favors human freedom" (White House 2002). Wilsonian at his best, the president pledged to use American power for universal rights (Zakaria 2002; Ikenberry 2009: 8). Bush could have not been more Wilsonian than during his second inaugural address in January 2005:

> We are led by events and common sense to one conclusion: *The survival of liberty in our land increasingly depends on the success of liberty in other lands.* The best hope for peace in our world is the expansion of freedom in all the world. ... So it is the policy of the United States to seek and support the growth of democratic movements and institutions in every nation and culture, with the ultimate goal of ending tyranny in our world. (CNN 2005; Bush 2010: 396)

Arguably, Bush saw himself as Wilsonian. He saw his quest in the Middle East, especially Iraq, as the quest for democracy that will make the whole region more peaceful and safer for the next generation, like the democracies America helped build in Germany, Japan, and South Korea (Bush 2010: 393). He wished to win the war so he can win the peace, where war would be replaced by peace (Smith 2009: 54–55). Bush believed in the power of the American military to secure this peace. He praised every American that served this higher purpose and made the American nation safer, made 25 million people live in freedom, and changed the misdirection of the Middle East for the next generation. Bush accepts that wrong things were done, but he argues that the cause was eternally right (Bush 2010: 394). Nevertheless, Bush also contrasted with Wilson in many policies, if not more than he complied with. An important differentiating point was that Wilson highly favored multilateralism instead of unilateralism, which Bush used as his road map (Slaughter 2009: 91). Bush saw no purpose of having international organizations, or international treaties, to limit the USA. Wilson, on the other hand, was a strong believer in the role of the League of Nations for a system of collective security, promise of peace, and balance-of-power politics (Smith 2009: 59–60). The Bush Doctrine too has some clashes with Wilsonianism. While Wilson favored collective security, the Bush Doctrine is based on American military supremacy. Wilson was no pacifist, he was an imperialist on his own, but he favored a more balanced power, where cooperation instead of domination would lead to world peace, unlike Bush who openly advocated for USA's supremacy and individual leadership (Smith 2009: 56–74). The biggest Bush supporters were the neoliberals who were outrageous of being wrong with their liberal ideas and wanted the responsible actors for 9/11 to be accounted in justice.

What Bush, and his administration, wanted to sell was that power without purpose is "ephemeral", while purpose without power is "impotent", to use the exact words of Tony Smith (2009: 54–55). Bush wanted to leave a mark in global affairs on how to conduct international relations, and serve the best purpose of American security, while bringing peace to the world. But, first and foremost he wanted to justify the invasion of Iraq and the fiasco in the Middle East. More than a decade since the invasion of Iraq, neither peace nor democracy came to either Iraq or the Middle East. Clearly, Bush had failed in democracy promotion in the Middle East and elsewhere. His policies only jeopardized democracy at home.

At the end of the day it seems that the debate about Bush being Wilsonian will be continuing for a long time. Political analysts will disagree with each other, some claiming that Wilsonianism was hijacked by Bush, who took the decades-long developed ideas of liberal institutionalists (Smith 2009), and others claiming that bridges have been built to advance collective security and cooperation among democracies (Knock 2009; Slaughter 2009). Nevertheless, John Ikenberry challenges the Wilsonian vision, evolution, and its relevance in the twenty-first century while questioning if Bush had a defined foreign policy character and logic (2009: 2–4).

Whatever the reasons, it seems that there is a consensus among political analysts and scholars that US foreign policy in the Middle East is a mess and it failed in many, if not all, fronts. The public and the elite opinion in the Middle East hit the bottom, and America's place in the world is still to be defined, after so many years in war (Smith 2009: 75–75). Earlier, even though public opinion did not always favor America, the elite of those countries were in favor of the USA. Today, there is hardly any group, let alone political a group in the Middle East that is pro-American. People are suspicious of the USA, its interests, goals, and there are even conspiracies regarding its culture. The USA today arises anger and opposition (Zakaria 2001). First, people in the Middle East accepted American acts as humiliation. While people wanted democracy, a poll made in September 2003 showed that only 5% of Iraqis thought that the USA was there to bring democracy and help the Iraqi people, in comparison to more than 50% who thought that the USA was there for the Iraqi oil (Beinart 2008: 162). US popularity dropped significantly in 2003, in relation to 1999 or 2000. Likewise, in Turkey and Brazil the popularity of the USA dropped by 20%, in Germany by 40%, in Morocco by 50%, and in Indonesia by 60%. Many Muslims feel that they and their religion are threatened by foreign powers, mainly by the USA, and it is documented that people that feel that their religion is threatened are more likely to support the terrorist organizations there.

For the terrorists, American aggression posed an opportunity for recruiting. Misusing the word "Jihad" the terrorists used this to gain support, including youngsters from Western countries who went to Iraq to fight against the invasion. The main reason of support for al-Qaeda in the Middle East has been their opposition of the USA (Beinart 2008: 138–139). Having been covered so much by CNN, al-Qaeda leaders on many occasions expressed their gratitude to the press, claiming that they "beat America at their own game" (Bergen 2012: 57–58). Fear and humiliation are among the most important elements that lead to radicalization and irrational actions. This is what the war on terror has done, and it has fueled radicalization more than it has solved it, due to its incorrect discourse and acts. The Bush administration's failure to think of a post-invasion strategy brought greater chaos. These western Jihadists will ultimately go home, in their European or American homes, and with the war continuing for more than ten years, these citizens are a problem in itself, bearing the risk of terrorizing the society they live in.

Colin Powell claims that the governments in Afghanistan and Iraq fell quickly, but it was the lack of achievable goals, or means to achieve them, that brought the bigger failure, which resulted in continuous commitment of additional forces. In Iraq and Afghanistan, strategy was replaced with wishful thinking (Powell 2012: 207). Not to mention that more than 2,000 Americans killed and more than 15,000 wounded greatly discouraged the American people from supporting their troops. In fact, the situation became exactly what the terrorists wanted: a tired America, without the will to fight (Beinart 2008: 165–166). Had the Bush administration thought of this campaign as a longer one, which would continue beyond the fall of Saddam, where democracy needs to be built, then the invasion would have gone differently, probably better (Beinart 2008: 158). A post-invasion strategy would have prepared the military and the public for the consequences.

Analyzing the general strategy of the USA we can see that all American leaders want the same thing, the security of the USA and its citizens; nevertheless how they want to achieve it changes. Even the anti-imperialists wanted revenge, or at least to punish those responsible and bring down al-Qaeda. These requests were logical, taking in consideration that they also wanted to stop Milosevic in Bosnia and Kosovo. Nevertheless, the problem was that there was no distinction between civilians and terrorists. The terrorists needed to be brought to justice and innocent civilians needed to be protected (Beinart 2008: 171). With committing so much force, and having no clear strategy at hand, the USA was only reactionary to the acts of al-Qaeda terrorists. Lives of innocent people were taken and terrorists were not brought to justice.

Why this book gives this much importance to the "war on terror" is because that bears a great importance on how the public opinion was shaped. The place of Islam in this entire situation will be evaluated below, but to make it clear one must understand that the context on which Islam was securitized after 9/11 was very important. What the Bush administration did is increase the fear and security concerns of the USA, and alert the people.[1] Constructing such an atmosphere of security in the country made people rally around the flag. Then they brought this fight down to civilization, religion, and culture. After this was succeeded, putting Islam at the

[1] For more on the industry of fear in post-9/11 America, see Ali, Wajahat et al. (2011). *Fear Inc.* report. Center for American Progress. https://www.americanprogress.org/issues/religion/reports/2011/08/26/10165/fear-inc/

center was easy. Although Islam was about to be securitized many times before, that did not happen because it was difficult, so this administration needed the proper ground to be able to do that. They did not try to directly securitize Islam, but because the problem was a religious-security nexus problem and because Islam was "the other" in this security atmosphere, Islam has become a security concern, especially after it was associated with different keywords in the same speeches.

6.1.3 *Bringing Back the Cold War and Securitizing Islam*

The new threat of "Islamic extremism/radicalism" was linked to previous threats that the USA won against: either Saddam Hussein or the Soviet Union. One of the biggest mistakes was to consider the post-9/11 era as a Cold War era, and this is where the USA started to securitize Islam. Bush defined the 9/11 attacks as Cold War-like attacks, declaring in front of the Congress only nine days after that "We have seen their kind before, they are the heirs of all the murderous ideologies of the 20th century ... they follow the path of fascism, Nazism, and totalitarianism" (Bush 2001b). One cannot expect less when taking in consideration that the security advisors and decision-makers in Bush administration were all Cold War actors, and none else but Bush's foreign policy teacher, and then his National Security Advisor, Condoleezza Rice, was a Soviet expert, who was the main influencer in Bush's foreign policy agenda. Soon after Bush declared who the attackers were, in the Congress, conservative press started the campaign of association of these attacks with the Cold War: Norman Podhoretz from the Commentary called this the Fourth World War, claiming that the Cold War was the Third World War, and Victor Davis Hanson, from National Review Online, pulled the "iron veil" across the Muslim world (Beinart 2008: 112–113). In many speeches Islam was mentioned in association with terrorism and in association with the Cold War, totalitarianism, fascism, and Nazism.

Bush continuously compared the 9/11 attacks with the attack on Pearl Harbor. But also, he wrote in his autobiography (2010) that it is interesting that Kandahar fell on December 5th, the 60th anniversary of Pearl Harbor. Similarly, he proudly stated that the first movie he screened in the White House was the "Thirteen Day Crisis", a famous movie about the Cuban Missile Crisis (Bush 2010: 273). This shows his two obsessions: the first one with the Soviet Union and the Cold War and the second one with leaving a legacy. Bush saw Iraq exactly as Kennedy had seen Cuba, and he saw the engagements in the Middle East as the continuation of the Cold War. Reading his autobiography, one can easily understand that he was also obsessed with finishing his father's job in the Middle East, to leave a Bush legacy. In fact, it would seem that he subconsciously believes in the symbolism of these dates and events. As a devout Christian and American he believed in a calling to take action, or maybe he was convinced by his aids, who were his father's team: Cheney, Rumsfeld, Rice, Gates, and Powell.

These were the people that started to construct Afghanistan, Iraq, Muslims, and Islam as threats and enemies of the USA. They were ready to use any method to securitize the situation and achieve the consent for the wars in the Middle East. In a speech to the War Veterans, Vice President Dick Cheney talked about the 9/11 attacks, the war in Afghanistan, and bin Laden. Nevertheless, soon after he warmed up in the podium he started making the case that to be able to fight terrorist threats America needs to make sure that those governments are changed. He called Saddam Hussein "the sworn enemy of the US" because he broke the promise he gave to the UN by building up his nuclear arsenal. Chaney argued that there is no doubt that Saddam now has WMD and that this is a multiple-time confirmed information. Furthermore, Cheney said that toppling Saddam would inspire freedom-loving movements to topple other dictators in other lands, and American liberators would be welcomed just as in Afghanistan (Eichenwald 2012: 352–353). But, most importantly Cheney made these remarks when making the case for why the USA should fight Saddam: "extremists would have to rethink their strategy of jihad". It is common for American securitizing actors to use Arab words and phrases in security speeches. It has become the norm to use words like "Jihad" to explain terrorism, to connote a security threat, and to link Islam and Muslims to terrorism, without knowing the real meaning of any of those words.

Cheney was also comfortable with manipulating polls conducted by Zogby International (Zogby 2010: 49–52), so much so that Zogby himself called it "Bent It Like Cheney" (51), to be able to make his point and invade Afghanistan and Iraq. He went further to securitize Islam by associating Islam with the Taliban, against all other religions, first by saying that in Afghanistan they have imposed "an extreme form of Islam on the country, closing schools for girls, forbidding music, and carrying out grisly executions" and then by saying that "Taliban had gotten the world's attention earlier in 2001 by blowing up two monumental sixth-century Buddhas at Bamiyan in central Afghanistan on the grounds that they were idols". In a similar fashion, he explained that the biggest reminder of "the threat Islamist terrorism represented" was the attacks in Madrid (Cheney 2011: 332–352). For Cheney, 9/11 was the doom's day. In his memoir, he clearly states that it was the mission that had to define the coalition, not the coalition to define the mission. He claimed that the USA wanted allies, but America was at war so if America had to stand alone in its mission, America would (Cheney 2011: 331). According to Cheney, America was at war and everything was now legal, extraordinary means were accepted, as he claimed, "We can't do politics on the basis of how we are perceived abroad. Guantanamo did no harm to US, the people who criticize it are doing more harm" (Cheney 2011: 356). He also argued that no American values were abandoned or compromised in these acts, not because torture was not used but because they got important information and those people were neither innocent nor victims, and most importantly "they [the people that interrogated them] made our country safer, and a lot of Americans are alive today because of them" (Cheney 2011: 523) equating here American morals and values with American security.

Tom DeLay, the notorious former House Majority Leader, who was accused of taking large amounts of money and benefits from notorious lobbyist Jack Abramoff, gave a short speech in 2004 where he tackled the Arab world, Islam, and Muslims. In the speech, he used the word "evil" 20 times when talking about the Arab world, among others, "This evil we face today may come in new forms, but it is not new", or "the same evil that terrorized past generations with Holocaust and the Gulag terrorized us with 9/11 attacks", or that "the war on terror is a war against evil". He made sure to declare his support to Bush by reminding the audience that he agrees with the president that "we will not distinguish between the terrorists and those nations who help and harbor them" and that "this war, make no mistake, [is] of good versus evil" (DeLay 2004). If one questions what is good and what is evil for DeLay, one can look at his congressional speech in 2003 where he equates all Arabs with evil, for example, when speaking of Palestinians, he marks them as "violent men" who kill and laugh when Israeli children are killed, and he said, "if this is not evil, nothing is". Furthermore, he asked for continued hunting of the Palestinians who remain enemies of the civilized world; he asked that the Congressmen and Congresswomen join Israel's heroic struggle against evil; and he asked the Palestinian leaders to stand with the civilized world to fight evil and be like their predecessors (DeLay 2003). After the 9/11 attacks, most officials talked about "us" versus "them", about the war of "good" versus "evil", without determining who "evil" was. Nevertheless, when we look at their other speeches, before or after, we can clearly see who they refer to as "evil".

Similarly, Bush's Secretary of Defense from 2001 to 2006, Donald Rumsfeld, recalling that he was a special envoy to the Middle East in 1983 when 241 Americans were killed in Beirut asked for a firm military presence in the Middle East. The pullout of American Marines from Beirut was wrong according to Rumsfeld, because this was perceived by Islamist extremists as American impotence. In this regard, he argued that after the 9/11 attacks America needs "to go and root these guys out. We can't just hunker down again ... we can't reach this time the way we reacted last time" (quoted in Eichenwald 2012: 31). Rumsfeld saw this as an opportunity to do what he couldn't in 1983. He and others advocated for invasion without a long-term strategy. For Rumsfeld, Cheney, Rice, and others who were part of H. W. Bush's administration, this was the opportunity to finish the job they had left unfinished in the Middle East.

Bush also used religious language to justify the wars in the Middle East and securitize Islam. When talking to Jacque Chirac of France, Bush used religious discourse to convince Chirac:

> Jacques you and I share a common faith. You're Roman Catholic, I'm Methodist, but we are both Christians committed to the teachings of the bible. We share one common Lord ... Gog and Magog are at work in the Middle East. Biblical prophecies are being fulfilled. ... This confrontation is willed by God, who wants to use this conflict to erase His people's enemies before a new age begins. (quoted in Eichenwald 2012: 459)

Immediately after the phone call Chirac ordered his staff to get more information on Gog and Magog, which he had no idea about, and inform him. After a long research, they found Thomas R. Mer, an authority academician on Hebrew Scriptures. Mer said that Gog and Magog are mentioned in the Old Testament to describe a future war, an apocalyptic conflict in the time of the Messiah. In the New Testament, it is mentioned again as a future war, although in a different time and a different people from the ones mentioned in the Old Testament. The war will be fought at the end of times with Satan deceiving the people against Christ and His saints. But, in this war the righteous will be victorious and Satan will lose (Eichenwald 2012: 460–461). This is what Bush was referring to when talking to Chirac about his new war in Iraq.

But is this something new in American politics? Many American presidents or high-level administrators have used these kinds of references over time. Ronald Reagan used the same reference when he claimed that the USA will win against the Soviet Union, which has abandon God during the Russian Revolution. Bush must have decided that Gog and Magog are not relevant with the good and the evil of the Cold War, but with the good in the USA and the evil in Baghdad (Eichenwald 2012: 460–461). Although he was trying to be politically correct in most of his speeches, Bush's subconsciousness gave him up.

Bush claimed that his Afghanistan, Iraq, and Israeli-Palestinian mission was a "call from God" and that he was only answering that call. President Bush claimed that he was "driven with a mission from God" according to one of the Palestinian delegates, Nabil Shaath, at the Israeli-Palestinian summit in Egypt in September 2003. Israeli daily *Haaretz* published a transcript containing a version of President Bush's remarks, which authenticate what Mr. Shaath has said:

> "President Bush said to all of us: 'I am driven with a mission from God.' God would tell me, 'George go and fight these terrorists in Afghanistan.' And I did. And then God would tell me 'George, go and end the tyranny in Iraq.' And I did."
>
> Mr Bush went on: "And now, again, I feel God's words coming to me, 'Go get the Palestinians their state and get the Israelis their security, and get peace in the Middle East.' And, by God, I'm gonna do it." (quoted in MacAskill 2005)

In a conference at his ranch in Texas, Bush spoke about global threat of Islamic extremism, taking Islam as a monolithic religion of violence, combining with Reagan language, and even going as forward as referring to a real and profound threat of "Islamo-fascism" (Bush and Rice 2006) and after three days saying it bluntly that "this nation is at war with Islamic fascists" (Bush 2006). This was not the first or the last time that he announced his sympathy for Reagan, who he called as the biggest inspiration in his autobiography. One of the lessons he claimed he got from Roosevelt and Reagan was to lead the public instead of chasing public opinion polls (Bush 2010: 272). Bush's favorite book is Truman's biography. He was highly influenced by Truman and said that he admired his decision to do what he thinks is right despite the people's disapproval, just as he himself took decisions that he thought were correct despite public opinion (Bush 2010: 174–175). In fact, he did lead the public with his discourse and associating the situation that he brought America in with America's biggest fears and historical events. He also wanted to send a message to the American people, and foreign countries, that America is strong and that America should not repeat the mistakes that Clinton and Reagan made by retreating from Somalia and Libya, which made America look weak.

Although George Bush claimed that his government is not against Muslims and Arabs in this "crusade", when he announced the 27 terrorist groups and individuals all of them were Arab or Muslim (AbuKhalil 2002: 85). Even the Irish Republican Army (IRA) was not on that list, who could hold fundraisers in the USA having no fear that the USA would bomb Northern Ireland, or the Basque and Corsican terrorist groups for that matter (AbuKhalil 2002: 85). In 2001 the Bush administration announced a terrorist list of seven countries, out of which five of them were Muslim. Neither Pakistan nor Afghanistan figured on that list, and neither did non-state terrorist groups. The depiction of the list of terrorist states was a continuation of the concept of "rogue states", that has been used in the USA for decades, to define states like Cuba, Iraq (under Saddam), Libya, North Korea, and Iran, which were the states on the State Department's list of terrorist states. In January 2002, the Bush administration made another list, composed of Iraq, Iran, and North Korea, and named it "the Axis of Evil". The USA saw all these "rogue" or "terrorist" states as the same and tried to address them with the same policies, problematic due to their different forms of government, relations with the USA (Litwak 2000; Chomsky 2000), and social and economic situations.

Another securitizing actor among Bush's main team was Attorney General John Ashcroft. He declared in 2002 "Islam is a religion in which God requires you to send your son to die for him. Christianity is a faith in which God sends his son to die for you" (quoted in Salaita 2006: 40–41). Both Bush and Ashcroft advocated for Muslims to restructure their organizations and their faith as "moderate Islam", changing Islamic teachings, practices, and so on. They promoted the "good Muslims", non-practicing, in love with American pop culture, that would suit American interests and understanding of how a Muslim should be. They wanted to form their own Muslim community, *jamaat*, but they ended up having only "Mufti Bush" and "Ayatollah Ashcroft" in that community (Haddad 2004). Declarations like this prepare the public for the existence of good versus evil, and then it was easier to put whomever in one or the other category.

Although the PR campaign for the prestige of the USA in the Middle East was a total failure, when it comes to securitizing Islam, Bush and his aides were very professional in using the media, and PR, in their advantage. There was a media propaganda campaign, with news constantly showing the 9/11 attacks, which helped Bush to bring up the security alert (Fierke 2007). Trauma and fear are very helpful in constructing the threats, needs for securitizing a referent object, and the use of extraordinary means. It works the other way around too. The new president of CNN warned the journalists that covering Afghani death tolls is inappropriate because America is in war right now (AbuKhalil 2002: 15–16). So, the selection of the type of news that was given was a pivotal point in constructing the security climate.

To start the campaign for the war in Afghanistan Bush first appeared in the media and then in front of the Congress, to convince the lawmakers and the American public that the situation is fragile and America is risking its security if we don't deal with the failed states in the Middle East right away. President Bush brought human rights violation and mistreatment of women to the screen. These were all true, but the question remains: why now? Taliban had been in power from the early 1990s, and these violations were present ever since, so why did they become a problem for the USA now, that they need to open war against? What about these violations coming from Pakistan, Saudi Arabia, United Arab Emirates, or other US allies? (AbuKhalil 2002: 86–87). Like this example there were other ideas that were chosen to be put forth, to be able to vilify Afghanistan first and then Iraq, not that they did not exist, but these were carefully chosen to be promoted on the eve of the intervention.

After 9/11 and during the wars that followed, Hollywood did its part. Hollywood managed to depict Arabs and Muslims as public enemy number one, uncivilized, fanatically religious, heartless and brutal, and money-mad people who terrorize westerners, especially the Christians and the Jews (Shaheen 2001: 4; Bakalian and Bozorgmehr 2009: 40). This was an addiction to the continuous stream of videos and images of the 9/11 attacks, which Bush used to increase fear and panic to the public. Most importantly, television promoted American Muslims as enemies within (Spellberg 2013: 280). With reference to the al-Qaeda sleeper cells, the American Muslims have been portrayed as potential terrorists who may commit acts of terrorism anytime (AbuKhalil 2002: 25). After 9/11, hundreds of Arabs have been arrested but not a single one of them has been found to have ties either to bin Laden or al-Qaeda, according to the Department of Justice (AbuKhalil 2002: 26). This profiling and association, either in speech or in visuals, securitized Islam more than the direct securitization by the policymakers. Bush claiming that the terrorists want to send the Christians and Jews out of the Middle East automatically securitizes Islam and Muslims as "they" although it is not directly mentioned. Similarly, having all the bad guys being Arabs, who terrorize Christians and Jews, securitizes Islam and Muslims without mentioning them.

The American media has portrayed a direct link between Islam—violence—and terrorism. When a Muslim terrorist is engaged in violence or terrorism, it is portrayed as Islamic terrorism, but when a Christian terrorist does the same, although he might have been motivated by Christian motives for that act, that person is isolated into an insane, sick, and lone wolf; and the act is attributed to his individuality. In 1995, when two White Americans, one being Timothy McVeigh associated with the supremacist radical Christian Identity Movement, bombed the federal building in Oklahoma, and killed 168 people, most Americans assumed that it was a work of foreign Muslims (Peek 2011: 24). Nevertheless, no Protestant feared for their life or thought of having to condemn the attacks after it was learned who McVeigh was. Muslims, on the other hand, fear for their life and feel that they need to condemn these attacks done by Muslim- or Arab-sounding names (Spellberg 2013: 281). And still, the most common accusation toward Muslim leaders and communities is that they do not condemn terrorist attacks committed in America. This cannot be further from the truth. After every attack, Muslim leaders issue statements in major news outlets. Among other statements on 9/11 they stated that:

> American Muslims utterly condemn what are vicious and cowardly acts of terrorism against innocent civilians. We join all Americans in calling for the swift apprehension and punishment of the perpetrators. No political cause could ever be assisted by such immoral acts. (Peek 2011: 24–25)

When the Jewish Defense League leaders were indicted on charges of plotting to bomb a mosque and the office of an Arab-American congressman (AbuKhalil 2002: 26–27), no one talked about Jewish terrorism. In fact, that should be the standard, that these acts should be taken as they are: terrorist acts. They should not be attributed to any religion, ethnicity, or social group. Instead, they should all be categorized the same way: as terrorist acts. Associating these bizarre acts with a religion, ethnicity, or a social group should not be the standard. The 9/11 attacks killed people from all backgrounds and terrorized everyone. They have gone far from being a terrorist attack of a group and should be called and treated with the name they deserve to be treated: crimes against humanity. Nevertheless, the sanctions on Iraq, which kill more than 5000 children every year according to UNICEF, do not help to solve this crime against humanity, as the invasion of Afghanistan and Iraq did not. The fanatics and fundamentalists of all religions and ideologies are the same: cruel, homophobic, and violent.

Bush's main success was to polarize the world into "with us" and "against us" by connoting the "good and the evil". Even when he made remarks about the Israeli-Palestinian conflict, Bush said that he is for a two-state solution but that all nations need to act and the Palestinians need to elect new leaders, who oppose terrorism because "as I've said in the past that nations are either with us or against us in the war of terror" (Bush 2001b). He even linked the Israeli-Palestinian conflict to the polarization of "with us" or "against us". Soon, the "they" that was meant to mean the masterminds of the 9/11 became very inclusive, including whole countries, religion, and ethnicities (Zogby 2010: 82). This stance of Bush is in perfect alliance with the stance of bin Laden, who claimed that "these events have split the entire world into two adobes: an adobe of belief where there is no hypocrisy; and an adobe of unbelief, may God protect us and you from it" (quoted in AbuKhalil 2002: 84) in his first public appearance after the 9/11. Both reject the third way. What Bush meant by "they" and "them" was Muslims and Islam. Just a week after the 9/11 attacks, in a joint session in the Congress, Bush declared "They want to drive Israel out of the Middle East. They want to drive Christians and Jews out of vast regions of Asia and Africa" (Bush 2001b) and here it is clear that "they" means Muslims and only Muslims. But then he changed the discourse. Bush's later "we are not at war with Islam" does not hide the fact that he had already attributed these attacks to Muslims, despite the fact that Muslims have been the primary victims and target of terrorism.

Mistake after mistake, Bush after a time started differentiating between a good Muslim and a bad Muslim, and the Secretary of State Powell called all the good Muslims to speak against the bad Muslims. This had the wrong impact, implying that there is a problem with the religion itself, as Thomas Friedman of New York Times refers to "a struggle within Islam"

(Friedman 2001). The good and bad debate brought another wider attack toward Islam as it implied that Islam had a problem and needed to be changed to embrace the good Muslims, who were portrayed as American-looking, secular, not practicing, versus the bad Muslims, who were portrayed as Eastern-looking, practicing, religious Muslims.

The wrong policies of the Bush administration toward the Middle East, and Muslims in general, come as no surprise: first, because they thought that securitizing Islam would serve their cause better, which was shown to be wrong, and second, because of who they had as their guide to the Middle East. The Bush administration's guide to the Muslim world, Bernard Lewis, is an orientalist who wrote that the reason why the radical Islamic terrorist groups attack the USA is because the Muslims believe that the USA has become morally corrupt, socially degenerate, and politically and military enfeebled. This pushed many to criticize the weak Clinton policies and favor policies that would build a nation that can distinguish good from evil, not a liberal nation of relativism (Beinart 2008: 133). This was another view of the need to construct the American nation toward more conservative views. These so-called experts on terrorism and the Middle East have found in 9/11 an opportunity to put forth their agenda of military engagement in the Middle East, which they had been writing about for many years.

6.1.3.1 The Axis of Evil Speech
Bush does not have a specific speech where he addressed Muslims and Islam that can be considered as his doctrine toward Muslims, the Muslim majority countries, and Islam, like Clinton's Jordan speech or Obama's Cairo speech. The nearest one is his State of the Union Address in 2002, also known as the "Axis of Evil" speech. Bush does not have a single speech for Muslims and Islam because in most of his speeches he included them, especially the speeches on national and international security. Let's briefly analyze this speech and see where he put Islam, Muslims, and the "Axis of Evil". He named Iraq and Iran and spoke much of Afghanistan as the new "Axis of Evil", included in the same category as North Korea. As it can be understood from the name given to that speech, Bush demonized these countries as evil, and it is interesting that the new ones are both Muslim majority, because North Korea was always on the "rogues state" list, coined earlier by Madeleine Albright. Although one might not consider this speech as Bush's doctrine toward Islam and Muslims, this is an important window to seeing Bush's security mindset.

First, Bush praised his administration on the work they had done in Afghanistan to bring peace and justice, but most importantly he stressed the rights and freedoms that America brought to Afghani women. He praised his war in Afghanistan in that they have "put the terror training camps of Afghanistan out of business", but then he claimed that many other training camps, outside of Afghanistan, are still operative in a dozen of other countries, where terrorists are trained, mentioning Hamas, Hezbollah, Islamic Jihad, and Jaish-i-Mohammed. Bush did not refrain from directly threatening the countries that he thought harbored these cells and reminded them "if they do not act, America will".

In the second part of his speech he focused on targeting the three main countries he was aiming at: North Korea, Iran, and Iraq. He put them in the same category as regimes that sponsor terror and threaten America and its allies with WMDs. For North Korea, Bush focused on mentioning that its citizens are starving while they developed WMD; for Iran, he focused on the oppression of peoples' freedom by an unelected regime, who supports terrorism and pursues WMD; and for Iraq, he focused on the weapons that they used against their people and on what they had to hide from the world. He argued firmly that there is no doubt that the regime is pursuing WMD, anthrax, and nerve gas development.

Bush argued that "states like these, and their terrorist allies, constitute an axis of evil, arming to threaten the peace of the world", while making his case of why indifference by the USA would be catastrophic as they will build WMD-s, which might fall in the hands of their terrorist allies. Bush did not forget to remind that "all nations should know: America will do what is necessary to ensure our nation's security".

As for how far Bush is willing to go, and how fast, it is best to quote him at large:

> We'll be deliberate, yet time is not on our side. I will not wait on events, while dangers gather. I will not stand by, as peril draws closer and closer. The United States of America will not permit the world's most dangerous regimes to threaten us with the world's most destructive weapons.
>
> Our war on terror is well begun, but it is only begun. This campaign may not be finished on our watch – yet it must be and it will be waged on our watch.
>
> We can't stop short. If we stop now [...] our sense of security would be false and temporary. History has called America and our allies to action, and it is both our responsibility and our privilege to fight freedom's fight. (Bush 2002a)

Bush made sure to construct this as a historical moment and a responsibility of America. For Bush, this was a unique opportunity that had been offered to America, to serve something bigger than self, and America will not let this moment pass by. He referred to this transition from "If it feels good, do it" to "Let's roll".

In the budget that Bush mentioned in his speech he focused on three points: win this war, protect the homeland, and revive the economy. As noted, two-thirds of the budget were on defense and military spending. Acknowledging that the USA has spent over a billion dollars a month in the war on terror, Bush suggested that America should be prepared for future operations, marking the biggest budget increase in defense spending in the previous two decades, because "while the price of freedom and security is high, it is never too high. Whatever it costs to defend our country, we will pay". Similarly, President Bush asked to double his budget on homeland security. He said that they would focus on bioterrorism, emergency response, border and airport security, and intelligence. Nevertheless, he did not ask for a considerable increase in the budget for outreach to communities, education, social welfare, health, or other issues that America was facing.

For the Muslim world, Bush asked the American people to "join a new effort to encourage development and education and opportunity in the Islamic World" because America should "overcome evil with greater good [...] to lead the world towards the values that will bring lasting peace". Bush should be given credit for praising "Islam's own rich history" and for bringing the Muslim world back to its great history.

Bush focused only on Islamic terrorist groups, while he never mentioned any other, non-Islamic terrorist group, as Clinton or Obama had. Also, he only mentions the threats that came from outside of the USA, such as direct threats or threats that people from outside might bring to US airports, and infiltrating US communities.

Finally, among many "security keywords" that Bush used, the most commonly used were terror, 36 times; security, 19 times; war, 12 times; danger, 8 times; enemy, 6 times; and evil, 5 times; other keywords were used more seldom in this four-thousand-word speech. These were the words used to denote the "Axis of Evil", namely North Korea, Iran, and Iraq, and legitimize the continuation of the so-called war on terror.

6.1.4 The Result of the War on Terror and the Securitization of Islam

It is hard to believe that the country with the biggest marketing and public relations (PR) industry in the world did an incredibly poor job marketing and PR for itself toward the global audience. The USA was basically responsive to the statements of Osama bin Laden and al-Qaeda. First, they made the mistake of calling this campaign a "crusade", which brought everything downward from the beginning of the campaign. After this word was uttered, people in the Middle East and around the world started to regard American claims as forgery just so they could win the "crusade" against the Muslim world. This is why they regarded even the 9/11 attacks as actions orchestrated by the USA or Israel in order to begin their "crusade". To fight this and market "America", Colin Powell, then Secretary of State, hired top companies and well-known PR experts. Powell hired Charlotte Beers, who headed J. Walter Thompson, Ogilvy and Mather, leading public relations companies, to be undersecretary for public affairs and diplomacy. The administration also hired leading PR companies for advising on America's image abroad (Cameron 2002: 138; Zogby 2010: 1). Considered by Fortune Magazine to be the most powerful woman in America, Beers was the mastermind behind campaigns of Head and Shoulders and American Express, and now she was hired to re-brand the USA in the Middle East (Zogby 2010: 1). This campaign turned out to be a disaster, resulting in the resignation of Beers. She had made the same mistake that most American foreign policymakers make: viewing the Middle East through an American lens. Beers decided to open a London office to manage the PR campaigns in the Middle East, but she never thought to open an office in the Middle East, although she had done that when she was with Ogilvy and Mather. Her campaign of a picture of Osama bin Laden "Wanted Dead or Alive" published in Arab newspapers not only did it not work, but it also gave Osama bin Laden additional free publicity, for which the Arab commentators considered a vulgar language reminiscent of cowboy mentality. Similarly, she made a video campaign of American Muslims saying, "I have never been disrespected because I am a Muslim", but these were paid advertisements, and the perception was that America was buying influence, paying people for propaganda (Zogby 2010: 2–3). Beers refused to acknowledge the local perception, and instead of promoting similarities and favorable views between the USA and the Middle East, she wanted to impose a certain propaganda.

Two years after Beers departed, President Bush and Secretary Powell hired Karen P. Hughes as the Undersecretary of State for Public Diplomacy and Public Affairs at the Department of State and as a counselor to the president. Hughes was the third person to hold this position, after Beers and Margaret Tutwiler, who lasted only five months. She took a tour of the Middle East in 2005 that became known for her assertion that she hoped that women in Saudi Arabia could "fully participate in society" as they do in America, where she was answered by a woman in the audience that "The general image of the Arab woman is that she isn't happy [...] Well, we're all pretty happy" (quoted in Weisman 2005). This is a common misconception in America. Many in the administration had this belief that everyone in the world would live like an America's if they had a chance. The issue of women driving is one of these misconceptions. Hughes made the mistake of bringing it up as "an important part of my life" (quoted in Weisman 2005). But the Arab women in the audience disagreed that this was a matter of great concern for them. Just because it is an important thing in an American woman's life doesn't mean that it would be important for an Arab woman. Looking at the questions of the audience directed to Ms. Hughes in her trip in the Muslim world, we can see the issues that are important for the people there, who have doubts about American leadership and justice. Most of the questions were about Palestine, the prison in Guantanamo, and the stereotypes of Muslims held by Americans after September 11.

Another problem, as with most American policies toward the Middle East, was that these campaigns were at best appealing toward Arab elite, not the average citizens (Zaharna 2001). Three years after 9/11, a report by the Department of Defense stated that the problem with America's image in the world is much more complicated than that of the failure of its communication strategies. The report pointed out that casting the new threat of Islamic terrorism in a way that offended the Muslim population was the core of this problem. The US government and Americans in general think that they need to advertise the USA in the Middle East, to bring the USA to the Middle East. But they miss the fact that the USA is already there, that all US major media outlets are available as long as there is Internet. Instead, there is a need to bring the Middle East to the American audience. Americans need to see and be familiar with Arab and Muslim culture, cuisine, media, and way of life. This way there can be an exchange of ideas and experiences and a mutual understanding between the two.

The money and resources that the US government spent in the Middle East to create the US image there were gone to waste. The aftermath of 9/11 showed that the amount of money is secondary; primary is the fact that the USA refuses to improve even today. They need to listen to Arabs and Muslims and to hear what they have to say, what they think, and what they want.

With these policies of the USA neither the American image nor the understanding of the Middle East in the USA improved. Even today people in America ask: why do they hate us? That is among the first questions that Bush asked and answered himself. The president answered this question to the Congress in the same month of the 9/11 attacks, saying that "they hate what they see right here in this chamber: a democratically elected government. Their leaders are self-appointed. They hate our freedoms: our freedom of religion, our freedom of speech, our freedom to vote and assemble and disagree with each other" (Bush 2001b). But at the same time, he was accusing "them" of wanting to overthrow the same "self-appointed leaders" that he was criticizing just above (Bush 2001b). This question was wrong then and it is wrong today. This answer was and continues to be even worse. The media had portrayed this as a war of liberation, to liberate women from violation and bring prosperity to the Middle East. Nevertheless, the people on the ground did not think the same.

America approached Islam and saw Muslims from a security perspective. This issue caused Muslims, Arabs, Middle Easterners, or even people with common sense to oppose Bush's policies. The reasons were multiple, starting from the anti-Americanism that remained in some parts of the world from the Cold War, the role of the US organizations such as the International Monetary Fund (IMF) or the World Bank, antipathy of the influence of American culture, American imperial ambitions, and most importantly, American support for the corrupt dictators in the Middle East (Eichenwald 2012: 137). This does not mean that everyone in those lands hated America, but among the ones that disliked, or hated, these are some of the reasons that they brought up.

Two American policy experts, former National Security Advisors, Scowcroft and Brzezinski, argue that the USA must reexamine its policies toward the Middle East, toward the support for the corrupt dictators there and for the unconditional support for Israel. In Brzezinski's words, there is no justification "for Israel's indefinite suppression of the Palestinians" and the uncritical support of the USA toward the corrupt

Saudi regime (quoted in Cameron 2002: 137–138). The USA should then begin to think of how they can win the minds and the hearts of the Arabs, especially the American Arabs, who are highly influenced by conspiracies of their own, such as the conspiracy that the 9/11 attacks were the acts of Mossad, and this was why no Jewish person showed up at work that day. There are many Middle Eastern citizens, on the other hand, who hate both, bin Laden for the violent and terrorist acts of al-Qaeda and George Bush for the US policies in the region (Zogby 2010: 121; AbuKhalil 2002: 84). We need to see this as normal because both Bush and bin Laden have asked the people to choose between two options, with us or against us, which does not represent the third, and bigger, camp.

We must note that all of these campaigns, military, political, media, and others, were done in order to keep America safe from terrorists. However, Patterns of Global Terrorism report showed that there was a raise in terrorist incidents against the USA since America military engaged in Afghanistan and Iraq (USDS 2003). This shows that a war without strategy, and the securitization of Islam, had fired back to America and has not made America safe, to the contrary it made America less safe.

The so-called war on terror has cost billions to American taxpayers, but the administration did nothing to secure America domestically. By 2003, the Council for Foreign Relations had estimated in a report that only 10% of the American fire departments could respond adequately to a collapsed building; that most of the public health laboratories in the USA could not detect WMD attacks; and that most police departments could not secure a site after a WMD attack (CFR 2003). The Coast Guard has estimated that it needs $5 billion to minimally secure America's coasts; nevertheless the Bush administration gave only one-seventh of that; also, they have given only one-twenty-fourth to what the American Public Transportation Association asked, to protect the USA against a Madrid-like attack in 2004 (Beinart 2008: 127). In a recent test at Transportation Security Administration's (TSA) checkpoints in America's dozens of the busiest airports, the undercover investigators have managed to smuggle weapons, fake explosives, and other materials. The TSA personnel and technology failed to catch these materials in 95% of the cases (Costello and Johnson 2015). Similar tests made again in 2016 and 2017, at different airports, failed to detect prohibited items with the same 95% rate (Blake 2017). It seems that the war on terror was only planned to be fought abroad and not to defend Americans in America. The war on terror was only considered to go hunting for the perpetrators, or to crusade for democracy, rather than for national security of the USA.

The invasion of Iraq was for Secretary Madeleine Albright the biggest disaster in American politics, because it has ruined America's reputation on a level that could not be reversed. The war in Iraq has put America in a negative position and Secretary Albright claims that it has militarized democracy (quoted in Meyer 2015). She made these comments at a conference at Woodrow Wilson Institute in DC, on "Is the United States Still the 'Indispensable Nation'?", where she argued that an indispensable nation does not stand alone, but engages with partners who have been chosen very carefully. Senator Bob Dole, who was a great advocate for intervention in Bosnia and Kosovo, made similar comments back in 2009, arguing that America is the indispensable nation, and what made America that nation is the multilateral partnership that should be pursued today (Dole 2009). After 9/11 people who have served America for many years have warned against unilateral acts of revenge. None other than the 41st US President, George H. W. Bush, stated that "this most recent surprise attack [should] erase the concept in some quarters that the United States can somehow go it alone in the fight against terrorism, or in anything else, for that matter". His son disagreed, claiming that "At some point, we may be the only ones left. That's okay with me. We are America" (both quoted in Albright 2003) before he went to war in Iraq.

As far as this book's focus is concerned, the Bush administration period was the most vivid time of how Islam was securitized, how Islam was brought to be a security issue in the US foreign policy, and how this backfired on the USA. John Esposito correctly observes that during this time the Muslims were forced to question "What are the limits of this Western pluralism? Who is included or excluded?" (Esposito 2010: 228), a value that the USA and the West have considered as ultimate.

This could be clearly seen during the 2008 presidential elections. In 2008, we saw a great anti-Muslim campaign to degrade Barack Obama by accusing him of being a Muslim. These accusations are not new; the first president who was accused of being a Muslim was Thomas Jefferson, America's third president and one of the founding fathers. But it is important to note that these accusations and the limit of American pluralism from the founding times are present even today, and these accusations give voice to the story of how difficult it is for a Muslim to get elected to office (Spellberg 2013: 9). In the swearing-in ceremony of Congressman Keith Ellison, he affirmed that Jefferson was a visionary man who believed in knowledge and wisdom from all different sources (quoted in Frommer 2007) answering those who claimed that the Qur'an that Ellison was swearing in with was owned by Jefferson because he wanted to know better the Islamic threat and he wanted to consult primary sources of the threat (Boykin and Soyster 2010: 223–224). Campaigns against Keith Ellison became even worse over the years. When he ran for the chairmanship of the Democratic National Committee, he was accused of not being loyal to America, not being a real American, and wanting to destroy it because that is what his religion, Islam, commands him to do.

These depictions are a result of ignorance toward Islam, thinking that it is a religion where every Muslim is and thinks the same, ruling out the fact that so many cultures and people with different backgrounds are part of it, let alone the historical facts of the pluralism of Islam and its prophet, as well as the pluralism of other religions and the prophets before Muhammad, which Muslims must accept. It is no coincidence that one of the most purchased books on Islam after 9/11 was *The Complete Idiot's Guide to Understanding Islam*, a book on the tables of many high-level administrators after the 9/11 (Eichenwald 2012: 46). Unfortunately, this mindset has not improved over the years and we hear the same debates about Muslim politicians and social activists in every election cycle, or during a major social event.

To be able to understand if Islam was securitized it sometimes suffices to follow the speeches of western politicians, American and European, when they cannot find answers to social problems, they usually dress them in religious garments. Muslims in the West have social, political, and economic problems, like everyone else. Most of these problems have nothing to do with religion, rather with policies, economic, social, or political, of that country. When politicians cannot answer their calls, they "Islamize" the problems that are as common for Muslims as they are for non-Muslims (Ramadan 2007).

In this path that the USA chose during the Bush presidency we can see that in relation to Islam, Bush was careful not to publicly securitize Islam as the enemy of the USA directly; nevertheless, Islam had been securitized indirectly by association. It was not securitized by the few direct links that they made to Islam, like Bush, Cheney, Rumsfeld, and Rice talking about "Islamo-fascism" because they were few examples. Rather, Islam was securitized by association. The securitization of Islam, and the speech act, was done through other means than speaking, like masquerading as art and literature, myths, caricatures, and alike. The security atmosphere was constructed primarily through fear. By inflating fear, one can do many things, as best explained by the English professor, George Falconer, a character in the film A Single Man, played by Colin Firth in 2009, as quoted by Nathan Lean (2012: 14):

> Fear, after all, is our real enemy. Fear is taking over our world. Fear is being used as a tool of manipulation in our society. It's how politicians peddle policy and how Madison Avenue sells us things we don't need. Think about it. Fear that we're going to be attacked, fear that there are communists lurking, around every corner, fear that some little Caribbean country that doesn't believe in our way of life poses a threat to us. Fear that black culture may take over the world. [...] Fear of growing old and being alone.

Fear has been inflicted through all the speeches of senior Bush staff, how America was at war, and how America needed to do anything to fight this war. The results were the open-ended Patriot Acts and the unknown practices resulting from them. Bush and his administration gave this security atmosphere a flavor: civilizational and cultural war, mainly rooted in religious differences. When Bush talked about what needed to be done he called this a "crusade" which is clearly associated with religious holy war of the Christians. For this war, he divided the world into "with us" and "with them". It suffices to look at this quote of his to understand who "us" and "them" are: "They want to drive Israel out of the Middle East. They want to drive Christians and Jews out of vast region of Asia and Africa" (Bush 2001b). Although Bush said that America was not at war with Islam, associations like these leave no need for Islam to be directly mentioned as a threat, when uttered in the context of "us" versus "them".

Bush has never refrained from proudly expressing his religious views and devotion. After becoming a devoted Christian, he said that he found a new life. Also, he proudly claims the credit of deciding to start a faith-based organization for prisoners to spread the gospel while president (Bush 2010: 277–281). We do not judge this as right or wrong, but when it comes to reading the world as a religious struggle, then this mentality has led to securitizing religion, or perhaps religionizing security, normally a secular process, and making Islam into the other. Bush's religious references, especially the ones of war, are very much debated: he quoted Christian religious scripts for the war of apocalypse to Chirac; he claimed that his biggest idol was Jesus while writing in his memoir that the story of Moses in the Bible is the story that made him run for president; he believed in a religious mission, claiming that the invasion of Afghanistan and Iraq and an Israeli-Palestinian peace deal were calls from God; and did not refrain from using the word "crusade" to explain the American war in the Middle East. Leaving Islam out of anything that he explained as "us" constructed Islam as the "other". And it was easy to securitize Islam in this security environment, where people were acceptive of authoritarianism, prejudice, and stereotypes due to fear.

When America has a foreign adversary, they tend to denigrate that adversary in all ways possible, as strongly as possible, as was seen during the Cold War, where this adversary could be felt everywhere: in academia, in media, in entertainment, in Hollywood, and in everyday life. One aspect of democracy is that it requires serious work to demonize the enemy to the people, public opinion, and sometimes other nations. Fuller (2010: 8) simplifies this adversarial work as something that should be simplified down to a message that would fit on a bumper sticker. For Fuller, "In today's world, 'Islam' has become that bumper sticker for America, the default cause of many of our problems in the Muslim world. In the past America has fought the anarchists, Nazis, Fascists, communists – today it is 'radical Islam'" (2010: 8). It has been implied that the danger coming from Islam is the danger coming from an extreme ideology, which is hostile to science, education, nation, democracy, modernity, rights, tolerance and is considered as backward, extreme, violent, and intolerant (Gottschalk and Greenberg 2008: 94) and is a security threat. In fact, what the US administration under Bush tried to sell is that the problem is not just with "radical Islam" but with Islam itself. Blaming Islam answers the questions of: Why do they hate us? Why do they hate democracy? Why are they violent? Why do they engage in terrorism? Why don't they accept what is better for them, what the US plans for their bright future? This only denies the reality that others might not be happy or might not agree with American policies.

Another fact that helps us to understand that Islam was securitized is the results that resonated into numbers. The view of the USA in the Middle East was the lowest, because they saw that what America targeted was Islam, and they wanted to change and make Muslims conform to American beliefs. But most important are the many surveys made on the rise of Islamophobia in the country. Interestingly, after 9/11 Islamophobia did not have a rapid rise in America. Some polls showed that it had a slight rise, whereas some showed that it had a slight fall. What was seen as a skyrocketing of Islamophobia and anti-Muslim sentiments was the campaign before the intervention in Iraq and during the election cycle of 2004 and 2008.[2] The raise of Islamophobia in America was a result of the campaign of defaming Islam before the war in Iraq in order to gain support for the invasion. And this is the most important factor that shows that Islam was securitized, by association, as was explained in this chapter. The second highest anti-Islam sentiments were recorded during election cycles, where campaigns and speeches against Islam have become so common.

George W. Bush referred to Islam while speaking about security, using security terms and keywords to create association. Although Bush and his administration would rarely accuse Islam directly, this association effectively securitized Islam. Claims that "they" are our enemy, the ones that are not Jewish or Christian, without mentioning Muslims, asserted that "they" were meant to be the Muslims. Islam was the "other", associated with security keywords opposite of what America stands for. We can certainly conclude that Islam was successfully securitized during the Bush presidency.

Another indicator that Islam was successfully securitized was President Obama's acknowledgment that in America, Islam is viewed as a threat and as the "other". He mentioned this in his speech in Cairo, claiming that he wants to change that narrative. Obama tried to desecuritize Islam, and in the next chapter we can see why he wanted to do so, how he planned to do it, and if he achieved that goal. Nevertheless, whatever success the Obama administration achieved, the election of President Trump in 2016, claiming that he thinks that "Islam hates us [America]", shows that the desecuritization of Islam remained only on Obama's wish list.

---

[2] These polls have helped us vastly in the writing of this book, and they contain important information. The best polls that this book has referred to are the Gallup and Pew reports, but there are many others from the FBI, and Counter Terrorism Task Force (which can be found in the bibliography). Georgetown University's the Bridge Initiative (http://bridge.georgetown.edu/), under the School of Foreign Service's Center for Muslim Christian Understanding, has continued an incredible work on opening exposing Islamophobia called "Super Survey: two decades of American's view on Islam and Muslims", and their Super Survey analyzes the data of the major polls made from 1993 to 2014 on American's views on Islam and Muslims. The Super Survey can be found at: http://bridge.georgetown.edu/the-super-survey-two-decades-of-americans-views-on-islam-muslims/

References

AbuKhalil, As'ad. 2002. *Bin Laden, Islam, and America's New "War on Terrorism"*. New York: Seven Stories.

Albright, Madeleine K. 2003. Bridges, Bombs, or Bluster? *Foreign Affairs*, September/October. https://www.foreignaffairs.com/articles/2003-09-01/bridges-bombs-or-bluster. Accessed 8 Aug 2017.

Ali, Wajahat, Eli Clifton, Matthew Duss, Lee Fang, Acott Keyes, and Faiz Shakir. 2011. *Fear, Inc.: The Roots of the Islamophobia Network in America*. Center for American Progress. https://www.americanprogress.org/issues/religion/reports/2011/08/26/10165/fear-inc/. Accessed 8 Nov 2017.

Ashcroft, John, and Ted Olson. 2002. Interview with John Ashcroft and Ted Olson. *CNN*. http://www.cnn.com/TRANSCRIPTS/0212/17/lkl.00.html. Accessed 12 May 2015.

Bakalian, Anny, and Mehdi Bozorgmehr. 2009. *Backlash 9/11: Middle Eastern and Muslim Americans Respond*. Barkley: University of California Press.

Beinart, Peter. 2008. *The Good Fight: Why Liberals – And Only Liberals – Can Win the War on Terror and Make America Great Again*. New York: HarperCollins.

Bergen, Peter L. 2012. *Man Hunt: The Ten-Year Search for bin Laden from 9/11 to Abbottabad*. New York: Broadway.

Blake, Andrew. 2017. TSA Failed to Detect 95 Percent of Prohibited Items at Minneapolis Airport: Report. *The Washington Times*, July 6, 2017. http://www.washingtontimes.com/news/2017/jul/6/tsa-failed-detect-95-percent-prohibited-items-minn/. Accessed 17 July 2017.

Boykin, William G., and Harry Edward Soyster (eds.). 2010. *Shariah: The Threat to America*. Center for Security Policy. September 13. https://familysecuritymatters.org/docLib/20100915_Shariah-TheThreattoAmerica.pdf. Accessed 28 Nov 2014.

Bush, George H.W. 2001a. Transcript of Former President George Bush's Speech in Boston, Massachusetts, on Tolerance Toward Muslims and How his Son, President Bush, Has Handled the Situation. *Washington Post*, September 13. http://www.washingtonpost.com/wpsrv/nation/transcripts/bushsr-text_091301.html. Accessed 28 Nov 2014.

———. 2001b. *Address to a Joint Session of Congress on the Subject of the War on Terrorism*. Washington, DC. September 20. http://history.house.gov/Historical-Highlights/2000-/President-George-W--Bush-addressed-a-Joint-Session-of-Congress-on-the-subject-of-the-war-on-terrorism/. Accessed 12 May 2015.

———. 2001c. Full Transcript of George Bush's Statement. September 11. http://www.theguardian.com/world/2001/sep/11/september11.usa19. Accessed 10 Nov 2015.

———. 2001d. *Presidential Address: Bush Calls Upon Americans to Unite in 'Monumental Struggle of Good vs. Evil' After Terrorist Attacks*. Sarasota.

September 11. http://library.cqpress.com/cqalmanac/document.php?id=cqal01-106-6369-328078. Accessed 10 Nov 2015.
———. 2002a. State of the Union Address. January 29. http://www.presidency.ucsb.edu/ws/index.php?pid=29644. Accessed 28 Nov 2014.
———. 2002b. Remarks on the National Economy and an Exchange with Reporters in Crawford. April 26. http://www.presidency.ucsb.edu/ws/?pid=63116. Accessed 28 Nov 2014.
———. 2005. State of the Union Address. February 2. http://www.presidency.ucsb.edu/ws/index.php?pid=58746. Accessed 28 Nov 2014.
———. 2006. *Bush: U.S. at War with 'Islamic fascists'*. August 10. http://www.cnn.com/2006/POLITICS/08/10/washington.terror.plot/. Accessed 18 Jan 2016.
———. 2010. *Decision Points*. New York: Broadway.
Bush, George W., and Condoleezza Rice. 2006. President Bush and Secretary of State Rice Discuss the Middle East Crisis. August 7. http://georgewbush-whitehouse.archives.gov/news/releases/2006/08/20060807.html. Accessed 12 May 2015.
Cameron, Fraser. 2002. *US Foreign Policy After the Cold War: Global Hegemon or Reluctant Sheriff?* London/New York: Routledge.
Cheney, Dick. 2011. *In My Time: A Personal and Political Memoir*. New York: Threshold Editions.
Chomsky, Noam. 2000. *Rogue States: The Rule of Force in the World Affairs*. Cambridge, MA: South End Press.
CNN. 2005. Bush: 'No Justice Without Freedom'. (Bush's Second Inaugural Address Full Transcript). January 20. http://www.cnn.com/2005/ALLPOLITICS/01/20/bush.transcript/index.html. Accessed 21 Nov 2014.
Cohen, Roger. 2001. America the Roughneck (Through Europe's Eyes). *New York Times*, May 7. http://www.nytimes.com/2001/05/07/world/america-the-roughneck-through-europe-s-eyes.html. Accessed 28 Nov 2014.
Coll, Steve. 2004. *Ghost Wars: The Secret History of the CIA, Afghanistan, and Bin Laden, from the Soviet Invasion to September 10, 2011*. New York: Penguin Books.
Costello, Tom, and Alex Johnson. 2015. TSA Chief Out After Agents Fail 95 Percent of Airport Breach Tests. *NBC News*, June 1. http://www.nbcnews.com/news/us-news/investigation-breaches-us-airports-allowed-weapons-through-n367851. Accessed 17 July 2017.
Council on Foreign Relations (CFR). 2003. *Emergency Responders: Drastically Underfunded, Dangerously Unprepared*. http://www.cfr.org/terrorism/emergency-responders-drastically-underfunded-dangerously-unprepared/p6090. Accessed 16 Nov 2014.
Daalder, Ivo, and James Lindsay. 2003. *America Unbound: The Bush Revolution in Foreign Policy*. Washington, DC: Brookings Institution Press.
DeLay, Tom. 2003. Israel Resolution Floor Remarks. June 25. House of Representatives Records.

———. 2004. Resist Until the End in the Path of God. February 20. http://www.freerepublic.com/focus/news/1084817/posts?page=3. Accessed 22 Dec 2015.

Dole, Bob. 2009. Bosnia and American Exceptionalism. October 25. http://www.bosniak.org/bob-dole-bosnia-and-american-exceptionalism/. Accessed 3 Aug 2017.

Eichenwald, Kurt. 2012. *500 Days: Secrets and Lies in the Terror Wars*. New York: Touchstone Book.

Esposito, John L. 2010. *The Future of Islam*. New York: Oxford University Press.

Fierke, K.M. 2007. *Critical Approaches to International Security*. Cambridge/Malden: Polity Press.

Friedman, Thomas. 2001. Foreign Policy; The Real War. *New York Times*, November 27. http://www.nytimes.com/2001/11/27/opinion/foreign-affairs-the-real-war.html. Accessed 17 July 2017.

Frommer, Frederic J. 2007. Ellison Uses Thomas Jefferson's Quran. *Washington Post*, January 5. http://www.washingtonpost.com/wp-dyn/content/article/2007/01/05/AR2007010500512.html. Accessed 28 Nov 2014.

Fuller, Graham E. 2010. *A World Without Islam*. New York: Little Brown.

Gates, Robert M. 2014. *Duty: Memoirs of a Secretary at War*. New York: Alfred A. Knopf.

Gottschalk, Peter, and Gabriel Greenberg. 2008. *Islamophobia: Making Muslims the Enemy*. New York: Rowman and Littlefield.

Haddad, Yvonne. 2004. The Shaping of a Moderate North American Islam: Between 'Mufti' Bush and 'Ayatollah' Ashcroft. In *Islam and the West Post 9/11*, ed. Ron Geaves et al., 97–114. New York: Ashgate.

Halper, Stefan, and Jonathan Clarke. 2004. *America Alone: The Neo-Conservatives and the Global Order*. Cambridge: Cambridge University Press.

Hyde, J. Henry. 2001. Reinvigorating U.S. Foreign Policy. http://democrats.foreignaffairs.house.gov/archives/107/hfa066f.pdf. Accessed 23 Nov 2014.

Ignatieff, Michael. 2004. Democratic Providentialism. *New York Times*, December 12.

Ikenberry, John G. 2009. Woodrow Wilson, the Bush Administration, and the Future of Liberal Internationalism. In *The Crisis of American Foreign Policy: Wilsonianism in the Twenty-First Century*, ed. John G. Ikenberry et al., 1–24. Princeton: Princeton University Press.

Jervis, Robert. 2006. The Remaking of Unipolar World. *Washington Quarterly* 29 (3): 7–19.

Knock, Thomas J. 2009. Playing for a Hundred Years Hence: Woodrow Wilson's Internationalism and His Would-Be Heirs. In *The Crisis of American Foreign Policy: Wilsonianism in the Twenty-First Century*, ed. John G. Ikenberry et al., 25–52. Princeton: Princeton University Press.

Lean, Nathan. 2012. *The Islamophobia Industry: How the Right Manufactures Fear of Muslims*. London: Pluto Press.

Litwak, Robert S. 2000. *Rogue States and US Foreign Policy: Containment After the Cold War*. Baltimore: Johns Hopkins University Press.

MacAskill, Ewen. 2005. George Bush: God Told Me to End the Tyranny in Iraq. *The Guardian*, October 7. http://www.theguardian.com/world/2005/oct/07/iraq.usa. Accessed 7 Aug 2017.

Meyer, Ali. 2015. Madeleine Albright: Iraq Is the Biggest Disaster in American History. *CNSNEWS*, May 15. http://www.cnsnews.com/news/article/ali-meyer/madeleine-albright-iraq-biggest-disaster-american-history#.VxdMO-0EotM.twitter. Accessed 3 Aug 2017.

Panetta, Leon. 2014. *Worthy Fights: A Memoir of Leadership in War and Peace*. New York: Penguin Press.

PBS. 2000. Presidential Debate Excerpts: Gov. George W. Bush vs. Vice President Al Gore. October 12. http://www.pbs.org/newshour/bb/politics-july-dec00-for-policy_10-12/. Accessed 28 Nov 2014.

Peek, Lori. 2011. *Behind the Backlash: Muslim Americans After 9/11*. Philadelphia: Temple University Press.

Powell, Colin with Tony Koltz. 2012. *It Worked for Me: In Life and Leadership*. New York: Harper Collins.

Ramadan, Tariq. 2007. *Europe and Its Muslims: Building a Common Future*. Doshisha University. July 24. http://tariqramadan.com/english/2007/07/24/europe-and-its-muslims-building-a-common-future-japan-33/. Accessed 22 Dec 2015.

Salaita, Steven. 2006. *Anti-Arab Racism in the United States: When it Comes from and What it Means for Politics Today*. London: Pluto Press.

Shaheen, Jack. 2001. *Reel Bad Arabs: How Hollywood Vilifies People*. New York: Olive Branch.

Shapiro, Ian. 2007. *Containment: Rebuilding a Strategy Against Global Terror*. Princeton: Princeton University Press.

Slaughter, Anne-Marie. 2009. Wilsonianism in the Twenty-First Century. In *The Crisis of American Foreign Policy: Wilsonianism in the Twenty-First Century*, ed. John G. Ikenberry et al., 89–117. Princeton: Princeton University Press.

Smith, Tony. 2009. Wilsonianism After Iraq: The End of Liberal Internationalism? In *The Crisis of American Foreign Policy: Wilsonianism in the Twenty-First Century*, ed. John G. Ikenberry et al., 53–88. Princeton: Princeton University Press.

Spellberg, Denise A. 2013. *Thomas Jefferson's Qur'an: Islam and the Founders*. New York: Knopf.

U.S. Department of State (USDS). 2003. Patterns of Global Terrorism 2002. April. http://www.state.gov/documents/organization/20177.pdf. Accessed 6 Oct 2014.

Walcott, John. 2016. What Donald Rumsfeld Knew We Didn't Know About Iraq. Politico. January 24. http://www.politico.eu/article/what-donald-rumsfeld-knew-we-didnt-know-about-iraq/. Accessed 8 Aug 2017.

Weisman, Steven R. 2005. Saudi Women Have Message for U.S. Envoy. *New York Times*, September 28. http://www.nytimes.com/2005/09/28/world/middleeast/saudi-women-have-message-for-us-envoy.html?_r=0. Accessed 27 Oct 2015.

White House. 2002. *The National Security Strategy of the United States of America*. September 2002. http://nssarchive.us/NSSR/2002.pdf. Accessed 21 Nov 2014.

Woodward, Bob. 2002. *Bush at War*. New York: Simon & Schuster.

Zaharna, R.S. 2001. American Public Diplomacy in the Arab and Muslim World: A Strategic Communication Analysis. Foreign Policy in Focus. November 1. http://fpif.org/american_public_diplomacy_in_the_arab_and_muslim_world_a_strategic_communication_analysis/. Accessed 10 Nov 2015.

Zakaria, Fareed. 2001. The Politics of Rage: Why Do They Hate Us? *Newsweek*, October 15. http://www.newsweek.com/politics-rage-why-do-they-hate-us-154345. Accessed 6 Oct 2014.

———. 2002. Our Way: The Trouble with Being the World's Only Superpower. *New Yorker*, 14 October.

Zogby, James. 2010. *Arab Voices: What They Are Saying to Us, and Why It Matters*. New York: Palgrave Macmillan.

CHAPTER 7

Desecuritization and Resecuritization of Islam in US Foreign Policy: The Obama and the Trump Administrations

President Obama tried to bring the narrative outside of the box that President Bush drew, but when President Trump came into power he continued the old Bush way, even stronger. President Trump bashed the same media that President Bush used, and he gave voice to alternative, far-right, conspiracy-driven media such as Breitbart and InfoWars.

Obama's Cairo speech and his speech at the mosque in Baltimore have been analyzed for the same purpose as we analyzed Clinton's Jordan speech and Bush's Axis of Evil speech. His speech in Cairo was his first speech abroad where he laid down the principles of his administration toward Islam and Muslims. His speech in Baltimore is among his last speeches, and we have analyzed it to understand how Obama and his administration approached Islam while he was in office. Another speech that we briefly touch upon is his speech on the occasion of the killing of the 9/11 mastermind, Osama bin Laden. This was important because he chose not to associate this victory of capturing America's most wanted terrorist with Islam.

As far as the Trump administration is considered, we have included his campaign speeches in regard to Islam and Muslims while analyzing his first year of presidency. Nevertheless, because this is only his first year and because he keeps the issue of Islam and Muslims constantly on the daily agenda, we have focused more on how he and his administration see Islam and Muslims and what they know about Islam and Muslims. As this is only

© The Author(s) 2018
E. A. Shipoli, *Islam, Securitization, and US Foreign Policy*,
https://doi.org/10.1007/978-3-319-71111-9_7

the beginning of the Trump administration, it will be impossible to assess how the administration has exactly approached Islam. However, it is of utmost importance to touch upon what we know: campaign debates, speeches of key people in the administration, and the present remarks of the President Trump toward Islam. We have not focused on any particular issues or debates because those change daily and might be irrelevant by the end of his presidency.

7.1 Obama Administration

The fear of Muslims and Islam is not something new. Since the 1700s, many Americans have feared a Muslim becoming a president, but not only a Muslim, also a Jew, or a Catholic. Nevertheless, the founding fathers made it clear that America was being built for the millions who are yet to come, and at that a Papist or a Mohametan could become a president (Spellberg 2013: 290). Similarly, as was the case with the election of Senator Barack Obama to the Presidency of the USA, the opponents' tendency to label someone as a "Muslim" is not new either, they did it with Thomas Jefferson when he ran for president. This charge is not limited to the president, any Muslim American citizen who ran for office in the twenty-first century got this reaction, such as the first elected congressman Keith Ellison. The aim is to discredit legitimate candidates as non-American or anti-American, questioning their trustworthiness and their loyalty toward America. Fortunately, these campaigns rarely succeed, as Muslims are being elected to different offices, and those charged with being hidden Muslims have been elected as presidents, both Jefferson and Obama. Nevertheless, this use of religious differences as a political weapon to deny the civil rights of Muslims, granted by the founding fathers, is worrying because it is still present in the twenty-first century (Spellberg 2013: 271). The defenders of these liberties are not few either. New York City's mayor, Michael Bloomberg, defended the building of the Islamic complex in lower Manhattan in 2010, referring to the clear principles of the constitution and arguing that not letting the Muslims build this complex would be a denial of the right to build houses of worship on a private property, which might happen in another country but not in the USA (Lisberg 2010). These controversies have gained ground more than ever and they continue to grow.

Analyzing the situation that the USA is in, we can see that while the USA is the only superpower in the world today, not many countries, including very close and traditional allies, want to follow Washington's lead in global politics, especially in the Middle East. This is a result of the eight years of determinacy on questionable foreign policy issues (Holsti 2006: 20) and mistakes that resulted in the complex foreign policy and unrest in the Middle East, including the inability of America to act in conflicts such as Syria. Nevertheless, the latest administration's incapability to articulate its policies clearly, align with allies, and distance itself from Russia, has put into question US leadership in the world.

Obama wanted to change the image of the USA, and that was the notion that the USA is not at war with Islam. The Republican majority congress did not help Obama's presidency, and his room for change remained very limited, but he tried to bring this issue in his first visit abroad and whenever he talked about his policy in the Middle East. One issue that left President Obama behind in foreign policy was the Healthcare Bill, which consumed most of his time, most of his energy, and most of his image.

President Obama lost many chances to form his doctrine in foreign policy and democracy promotion during his presidency, and one of them was during the military coup in Egypt. With what has happened in the world since the beginning of this century, one would expect an American response against unlawful coups. President Clinton had evolved the responsibility to intervene as a responsibility-to-protect doctrine, where the USA, together with its allies, would protect the innocent population from atrocities and violence committed by their own governments. Obama could evolve this even further into the responsibility to protect from unlawful military coups against the elected governments and the people of a country. This was a good opportunity for Obama, but it slipped from his hand.

From the beginning of his presidency, Obama made efforts to improve understanding between the USA and the Muslim world. Sometimes with symbolic gestures, like calling key Arab leaders in the first day in office, to promise them that the USA will be re-engaged in the region, especially in the Arab-Israeli conflict; appointing George Mitchell as a special envoy to the Middle East; and giving the first interview to Al Arabiya; Obama tried to communicate to the American people that Muslims are the same as Americans who want development and prosperity but also to communicate to the Muslims that "Americans are not your enemy" (Obama 2009a).

7.1.1 Obama's Approach Toward Islam

On many occasions Obama tried to promote the idea that Islam is not America's enemy and that America is not the enemy of Muslims. Unlike his predecessor, Obama did not associate Islam and Muslims with evil in his speeches, and he included Muslims in the list of victims of terrorism. He showed this in speeches and we are going to analyze three which we think are the most important. First is the Cairo speech, because this was his first speech abroad and because he chose to address the Muslim world from the stage of Cairo University. This is the most important speech in understanding Obama's approach toward Muslims, Islam, and the Muslim world. Second, the speech he made after the killing of bin Laden, which was a great victory for him, and an opportunity to take credit, and he chose to remain on his message that Islam and America are not in war with each other and that Muslims are Americans too. Finally, one of his last speeches, and certainly the last one toward the Muslims, is his speech at a Baltimore mosque, where he addressed the Muslim congregation, ensuring them that America is their country. This time he chose to address Muslims from "home", and this had a great symbolic meaning as well.

7.1.1.1 The Cairo Speech

President Obama's first visit abroad included Turkey and Egypt. Addressing the Muslim world from the podium of Cairo University was a very strong message to the Muslim world in particular and to the whole globe in general—the message that America this time is putting things right, moving away from past failures, and setting a new approach toward unilateralism and the Middle East. His remarks raised hopes so much that this speech was referred to when the prestigious Nobel Peace Prize was awarded to Obama.

The symbols in the discourse of presidents are very important. In his first trip abroad, in Istanbul, the President used Islamic symbolism to give a message that Islam was not alien to America and Americans. In a town hall meeting with students, he said that he would be with them and take questions until the call for prayer; while in Cairo he greeted the audience at the Cairo University with the Arabic greeting *Asselaamu Aleykum*. Obama's Cairo speech was a declaration of his policy toward Islam and Muslims.

His remarks in Cairo challenged both Muslim and western audiences worldwide, accepting failures and giving hope for the future. In his Cairo speech, Obama accepted the securitization of Islam and Muslims by the USA, claiming that this is not something new but is a result of centuries-long debates and tensions of the denial of rights and opportunities to Muslims, and disregarding their aspirations. Furthermore, he argued that the 9/11 attacks were not the cause of these misunderstandings and stereotypes, but rather the misunderstanding and fear are the ones that have defined Arab-American relations, where violent extremism only exploited this situation. Acknowledging the securitization of Islam, President Obama said that extremism and violence "has led some in my country to view Islam as inevitably hostile not only to America and western countries, but also to human rights". This is a direct acknowledgment that even the US president saw that Islam had been securitized in America.

Obama's Cairo speech was not only the first move to recognize the securitization of Islam but rather to desecuritize it as well. He called for diplomacy, dialogue, and a relationship built on trust. He also called for the end of the relationship dictated by misunderstanding and violence. In his own words:

> So long as our relationship is defined by our differences, we will empower those who sow hatred rather than peace, and who promote conflict rather than the cooperation that can help all of our people achieve justice and prosperity. This cycle of suspicion and discord must end. (Obama 2009b)

Although some in the USA have accused the president for being too apologetic, President Obama balanced his address to the Muslim world by calling out the stereotypes against Muslims but also reminding Muslims that Americans are also not all the same and do not fit a stereotype, so he called them to end anti-Americanism. He also stated that he will not withdraw from Iraq at once and that America needs to be as careful going out as they were careless going in.

He greeted the crowed by thanking them for their hospitality and brought the goodwill of the American people by focusing on American Muslims. His use of the greeting of peace, *Asselaamu Aleykum*, brought a standing ovation. Obama declared that he was there to represent the American people and that American Muslims were a part of it, despite the questions of whether America was accepting Muslims as Americans or not. He talked about his religion as a Christian and asserted that he feels close to Islam because his father's family was Kenyan and he had lived in Indonesia, where he heard the call of *azaan*. When speaking of his university years, Obama paid tribute to Islam's heritage of civilization that had paved the road to the European renaissance and enlightenment. He then spoke briefly on Islamic innovations, Islamic culture, and religious tolerance, to show his familiarity with Islam, that he said he had gotten to know in three continents (America, Africa, and Asia) before he came to the region where it was revealed. For the Muslims in America, he added that they had enriched the USA, fought in its wars, served in the government, and had contributed to business, sports, culture, architecture, and all fields of life.

The president made sure to mention that an African American with the name Barack Hussein Obama could make his dream come true and become the president of the USA; that nearly seven million American Muslims are present in America today; that the USA respects the freedom to practice one's religion as an inviolable right; that Muslims are above the US average in education and income; that there are mosques in every state in the USA, and over 1200 in the country; and that the women and the girls are allowed to wear the hijab and that whoever denies it is punished; claiming that there is no doubt that Islam is a part of America.

President Obama praised Islam as an example when he talked about religious freedoms, as something that America holds very dear. He said that he had witnessed the tolerance of Muslims firsthand when he was a child in Indonesia, and he also cited Andalusia and Cordoba as examples. He criticized Muslims for the Shia-Sunni violence, while he criticized America for making it harder for the Muslims to give their *zakat* alms (he used this word) and fulfill their religious obligation. He said he will work on easing the charity giving for Muslims, while he also asked some western countries not to dictate what clothes Muslim women should wear. Similarly, for women's issues, he said that he rejects the notion that women who have chosen to cover their hair are less equal, but he asserted that he believes that women who are denied education are denied equality. Nevertheless, he rejected the notion that this is a problem of Islam, because there are so many countries that have had Muslim women leaders, whereas in America they still struggle for equality.

In acknowledging America's negative policies toward Islam and Muslims, Obama acknowledged that Islam was a matter of security for America and that he wanted to change it. "We meet at a time of great tension between the United States and Muslims around the world" stated Obama, claiming afterward that these tensions are rooted in historical ups and downs between Islam and the west, including cooperation, coexistence, conflicts, wars, colonialism, and Cold War policies where Muslim countries' aspirations were not regarded. Mistrust and fear had increased with the rise of extremism, after which Americans started to view Islam as hostile toward America, the west, and human rights.

President Obama continued by stating "I've come here to Cairo to seek a new beginning between the United States and Muslims around the world" based on the idea that America and Islam are not exclusive or in competition and that they can come together in mutual interest, respect, and common values and principles of justice, progress, tolerance, and dignity. This long-standing mistrust cannot go away with one speech, the president claimed, and he acknowledged that time is needed for these wounds to be healed, but he proposed that America and Muslims must say to each other what they have been holding in for so many years. They must listen to each other, they must learn from each other, and respect each other and find common ground. Obama chose the "Be conscious of God and speak always the truth" verse from the holy Qur'an to address the applauding audience and promised that he would be speaking the truth that night. The president vowed that the partnership between America and Islam should be based on what Islam is and not what it is not, and that in his authority he will fight the negative stereotypes against Islam. He asked the same from Muslims, to fight the stereotypes against America, as America is not the stereotype of a self-interested empire; that America has been a great source of progress; and that America is shaped by every culture in the world, in a simple concept of "Out of many, one".

The president talked about the common enemies and issues that everyone must confront together. The first one he mentioned was violent extremism, but when he started to talk about this he asserted, once again as he had in Turkey, that America is and will never be at war with Islam and that America stands with all the faiths in rejecting the killing of innocents, because as the president it is his duty to protect the American people.

When talking about Afghanistan, he said that there might be debates about America's engagement, but that everyone should remember that al-Qaeda claimed credit for the 9/11 terrorist attack and killed more than 3000 innocent people. These extremists have killed people all around the world, but more than any other they have killed Muslims. The acknowledgment that Muslims have been the biggest victims of jihadi terrorism is something that differentiates Obama and Bush. The president again decided to quote the holy Qur'an, on that whoever kills an innocent is as if he has killed all of mankind and whoever saves a person, it is as if he has saved all of mankind. Differently from President Bush, who claimed that these terrorists wanted to kill Jews and Christians, Obama argued that Islam is not the "other" because Muslims have suffered more than anyone else from these terrorists. He acknowledged that some in America think that Islam is part of the problem of extremism, whereas he thinks that Islam is part of the peacemaking, and in this way he made the move to desecuritize Islam.

Unlike Afghanistan, Obama claimed that Iraq was a war of choice and that it had sparked many debates in America. He admitted that it was wrong, quoting Thomas Jefferson "I hope that our wisdom will grow with our power, and teach us that the less we use our power the greater it will be". He assured the Iraqi people that America has no interest in its territory or resources and that most of the troops would be removed from there in a couple of months.

As far as the 9/11 trauma in the country, President Obama said that he prohibited torture and had signed for Guantanamo to be closed. Despite acknowledging that these horrible acts have happened in the USA, it turned out that he could not close Guantanamo during his presidency.

One of the most fragile issues in the Arab world is the Israeli-Arab conflict. President Obama touched upon that issue too in the Cairo speech. After explaining how dear US-Israeli relations are for America, he said that threatening the existence of Israel is wrong and unacceptable. But, he continued by saying that the suffering of Muslim and Christian Palestinians must stop. For 60 years they have been in search for peace and security, the President acknowledged, but what they received was humiliation and occupation. This suffering was intolerable for his administration, and according to what he said in Cairo, America will support the two-state solution, and he would do anything in his power to make sure that there is a peaceful solution. It is interesting to note that throughout his speech he referred to Jews, Christians, and Muslims together—even when he talked about the Israeli-Arab conflict. Instead of referring to the responsibilities of Muslims and Jews only, he referred to Christians living there too, a marked change from his predecessor.

Obama's speech would not be completed without mentioning the weapons of mass destruction, which he said was a common problem for all, while supporting Iran's peaceful nuclear power and referring to the Non-Proliferation Treaty for nuclear weapons.

President Obama talked much about democracy too. When he started talking about democracy, the first thing he said was

> I know there has been controversy about the promotion of democracy in recent years, and much of this controversy is connected to the war in Iraq. So let me be clear: No system of government can or should be imposed by one nation by any other [sic]. (Obama 2009b)

Then he continued as a Wilsonian that this rule does not lessen his commitment that governments should reflect the will of the people. He said he personally believes that all people seek the ability to speak about the way they want to be governed; that people want to have confidence in the rule of law and justice; that people want transparent and uncorrupt governments; that people want the freedom to live as they choose; and he vowed that he would support these rights everywhere, because the governments that support these rights are more stable, successful, and secure.

For the solution of the conflict between Islam and the west, as some have named it, Obama finally addressed it as follows:

> It's easier to start wars than to end them. It's easier to blame others than to look inward. It's easier to see what is different about someone than to find the things we share. But we should choose the right path, not just the easy path. There's one rule that lies at the heart of every religion – that we do unto others as we would have them do unto us. (Applause.) This truth transcends nations and peoples – a belief that isn't new; that isn't black or white or brown; that isn't Christian or Muslim or Jew. It's a belief that pulsed in the cradle of civilization, and that still beats in the hearts of billions around the world. It's a faith in other people, and it's what brought me here today. (Obama 2009b)

The Cairo speech of President Obama was nothing if not a declaration of his administration's foreign policy toward the Middle East, the Muslim world, and Islam. It touched upon most of the topics that are important to the Muslim world and most of the questions that were in the heads of Muslims in America and abroad. What Obama did with his speech in Cairo is not only that he made a move to desecuritize Islam, but he de-religionized security in order to be able to desecuritize Islam, similar to when Bush religionized security to be able to securitize Islam. The end of Obama's Cairo speech, where he quoted the three holy books, showed that he did not take Islam alone but decided to de-religionize security as a whole. This also shows that in fact the George W. Bush administration had not only securitized Islam per se but had brought the security process to the religion as an institution. It is important to quote the end of Obama's speech at length:

> We have the power to make the world we seek, but only if we have the courage to make a new beginning, keeping in mind what has been written.
> The Holy Koran tells us: "O mankind! We have created you male and a female; and we have made you into nations and tribes so that you may know one another."
> The Talmud tells us: "The whole of the Torah is for the purpose of promoting peace."
> The Holy Bible tells us: "Blessed are the peacemakers, for they shall be called sons of God."
> The people of the world can live together in peace. We know that is God's vision. Now that must be our work here on Earth.
> Thank you. And may God's peace be upon you. (Obama 2009b)

7.1.1.2 The Killing of bin Laden

Another very important event during the Obama administration, in relation to Islam, the Muslim world, security, and Muslims in general, was the killing of the al-Qaeda chief terrorist, Osama bin Laden. In his speech on the death of Osama bin Laden, President Obama made sure to choose his words so as not to associate anything else with bin Laden and al-Qaeda, but with terrorism only. In his speech, he mentioned Islam only in one paragraph and religion in two. Because this was a security speech, on the occasion of the killing of America's enemy, a terrorist, President Obama chose not to associate religion as an institution or Islam as a religion, with this matter of security. He reaffirmed once again that America is not and will never be at war with Islam, saying "I've made clear, just as President Bush did shortly after 9/11, that our war is not against Islam". But unlike his predecessor, who in the same speech where he said that the USA was not at war with Islam asserted that they [the terrorists] were killing Jews and Christians, in this way otherizing Islam and associating the terrorists with Islam, Obama went further by acknowledging that in fact it is the Muslims who suffer most from these terrorists. Obama made sure to acknowledge the truth, "Bin Laden was not a Muslim leader; he was a mass murderer of Muslims. Indeed, al-Qaeda has slaughtered scores of Muslims in many countries, including our own." He said that "his

[Osama's] demise should be welcomed by all who believe in peace and human dignity" (Obama 2011).

Another great distinction is that Obama did not make this a religion-associated speech. He did not mention that "he got a call from God, or that this 'crusade' was won"; he did not make religious statements in a speech that was about security. The only time he mentioned religion in this speech was when he said that Islam was not who America is fighting; another occasion is when he said that on 9/11 "no matter where we came from, what God we prayed to, or what race and ethnicity we were, we were united as one American family" to clear the differences between different religions, races, and ethnicities; at the end, he again mentioned God when he said "may God bless you, and may God bless the United States of America" (Obama 2011). In such an important speech, a speech of great victory, Obama decided to mention religion only slightly, and to mention Islam only once, to ensure that he sees Muslims as victims of terrorism instead of claiming that others, not Muslims, are victims of the terrorists.

7.1.1.3 Obama's Speech at the Baltimore Mosque

After analyzing two important speeches of President Obama as related to Islam, it is useful to analyze Obama's last speech toward the Muslim public, which he gave at the Islamic Society of Baltimore on February 3, 2016. This was the first time that President Obama visited a Mosque in the USA while president. If we were to summarize the speech in three words, it would be Islam, security, and America. These were the most focused topics for the president. Analyzing this speech at length will be beneficial to understanding how Obama perceived his success on what he had set forth in Cairo, in the context of America's relationship with Islam and Muslims.

Obama started his speech with "This mosque, like so many in our country, is an all-American story", to tackle the "us" versus "them" rhetoric that Muslim and non-Muslim Americans feel. In the following words, he called on Americans who have never visited a mosque to do so, assuring them that a mosque would be as familiar as their church, synagogue, or temple. We can see in the first minutes of Obama's speech how he wanted to let the Muslim community know that in his view they are all Americans. The beginning of his speech was devoted to the synchronization of American and Muslims, which breaks the formerly constructed rhetoric of Muslims being the "other". Obama got a standing ovation when he said that "the first thing I want to say is two words that Muslim Americans don't hear often enough – and that is, thank you". He thanked Muslims for serving the community, for helping their neighbors, and for keeping America strong and united as a family. In his speech, Obama acknowledged the generations of Muslim Americans who had built this nation, who were farmers, merchants, workers at Henry Ford's assembly line, and designers of Chicago's skyscrapers, but most importantly, Muslims in America were neighbors, teachers, doctors, scientists, entrepreneurs, sports heroes, police officers, firefighters, members of homeland security, armed forces and the intelligence community, and people who gave their lives in America and abroad to keep America safe.

Out of thanking the Muslims for their contribution, President Obama made the case of Islam and security discourse, which he followed during most of his speech. He said he recognized that this time has been very difficult for Muslim Americans, first because, as all Americans, they fear terrorist attacks and the threat of terrorism, and second because the entire Muslim community is often blamed and targeted for the actions of a few. For this he also recognized that most Americans didn't know Muslims and what Muslims think, and the distorted media unfortunately had shaped their mindset. As if this was not enough, the recent political rhetoric during the presidential campaigns had affected this distorted impression, argued the president. The fear that Muslims feel today, the president expressed through examples he gave of Muslims he met and told him this, of mothers who wrote to him on this issue, and of a 13-year-old girl who wrote him a letter. He said he felt responsible because no one needed to feel like this in America, as "We're one American family. And when any part of our family starts to feel separate or second-class or targeted, it tears at the very fabric of our nation". This, for him, was a challenge of America's values.

As in his Cairo speech, Barack Obama expressed on many occasions his familiarity with Islam. He talked about the meaning of Islam as a word, which is peace; about the greeting that Muslims say to one another when they meet: *Asselaamu Aleykum*, which means peace be upon you; and even quoted the Prophet of Islam in "let him treat people the way he would love to be treated" on which he added that as a Christian he finds familiarity, asserting that in Christianity this is what they are also taught. To understand the pressure that Muslims feel in America, sometimes it suffices to see how many times President Obama needed to remind the crowd that he is a Christian during the speech. On many occasions, when speaking about Islam he added "Christians like myself", "my fellow Christians", because of the pressure he felt for so long on the accusation that he was a hidden Muslim. He even made a joke by saying that they suggested that Jefferson was a Muslim too, so he is not the first one. This, many argue, is one of the reasons he hasn't visited a mosque in America for seven years since his presidency.

In this speech, President Obama acknowledged that Muslims and Islam had been securitized, and there is no better statement of that fact than "our television shows should have some Muslim characters that are unrelated to national security", comparing to the times when there were no black people on American TVs. Furthermore, Obama claimed that by trying to show that Islam is the root of the problem, not only does it divert the truth, but it also alienates Muslim Americans, who have been important members of the American family, betrays American values, hurts people, helps the enemies of America to recruit, and, most importantly, makes America less safe. He also argued that engagement with Muslim American communities must not be led by surveillance and profiling and that America "can't securitize [her] entire relationship with Muslim Americans", dealing only through the lens of law enforcement. He also acknowledged that this process, of fighting terrorism together with Muslims and law enforcement, has sometimes gone bad, and this made everyone less safe, so rather than securitization, this process should be built on mutual trust and respect.

For terrorism, the president of course acknowledged that there are terrorist groups that perverted the interpretation of Islam, like Islamic State of Iraq and the Levant (ISIL) and al-Qaeda, but he argued that they are not the first to misuse God's name, and this time these groups twist Islamic texts to justify their terror against America and the west, wrongly claiming that they are at war with Islam. He said that this type of extremism is real, and is dangerous, but it mostly hurts law-abiding Muslims. So, this cannot be a burden on the Muslim community only, or any one faith community, because everyone is responsible for bringing a solution. He then suggested some principles for this goal: firstly, Americans should understand that all are God's equal children, who will need to fight those who try to divide them among religious and sectarian lines. As children of Abraham, tolerance is not enough, and we should embrace our common humanity, quoting the holy Qur'an "O mankind, we have made you peoples and tribes that you may know each other". Secondly, Americans need to stay true to their core American values, including the freedom of religion, which was established by American's founding fathers. This freedom will protect religious faiths, as well as protecting the state from those who want to take it over, using religious means, as in some other countries. He added that everyone should speak up when any of the religious communities is under attack, be them Christians in the Middle East, Jews in Europe, or Muslims in America. Thirdly, we should not give legitimacy to these terrorist organizations and should not play according to their rhetoric. Correctly, the president claimed that groups like ISIL are desperate for legitimacy as religious leaders and holy warriors of Islam. He said he refuses to give them this legitimacy and that everyone should too, because they definitely don't speak and don't defend neither Islam nor Muslims because "the vast majority of the people they kill are innocent Muslim men, women and children".

Another legitimacy the president refused to give was to the ones that claim that America is at war with Islam, because all of the world's religions are a fabric of the USA, its national character, so one cannot imagine for America to be at war with itself. The way he proposed to fight terrorism was to stop giving these groups legitimacy, show that America does not suppress Islam, and uncover the lies that they propagate. Showing that Islam is the root of this problem will only alienate Muslim Americans, it is hurtful, helps the enemies to recruit, and makes America less safe. By bringing these issues to the fore, Obama already acknowledges the existence of these problems.

Finally, President Obama called all the Muslims around the world to reject extremist ideologies that are trying to penetrate Muslim communities, while amplifying the voices who have condemned terrorism, and who are not small in number but who are being prosecuted for what they did. This is needed because this is a war of hearts and minds, where Americans can be an example of faithfulness to Islam and membership of a pluralistic society, cutting-edge science, and believers in democracy. In this sense, the president rejected the clash of civilizations between the west and Islam.

President Obama concluded his speech by calling on Muslim communities to stand up for the future they believe in, in which America will be their partner, to promote peace and pluralism, to fight extremist threats, and to expand healthcare and education. He said that the administration will reach out to young Muslims around the world to encourage them to work on their potential in entrepreneurship, science, and technology. He argued that America's values should guide America in her engagement with Muslims, not surveillance and profiling. The president made a call to the youngsters who are asked, by many factions in society, to choose between identities, in this case Muslim or American, not to listen to those voices, as everyone can and should have multiples identities that coexist together, and as far as being a Muslim and fitting in America, Barack Obama said that as the president of the USA he says it clearly: you fit in here, right here where you belong, as part of America, not as Muslim or American, but as Muslim and American. Finally, President Obama gave examples of how non-Muslims in America stood for Muslims and how Muslims stood for their non-Muslim compatriots, which will not make the news but are very important examples.

As we can understand from this analysis, President Barack Obama acknowledged the securitization of Islam and that it had not been desecuritized even by the end of his two-term presidency. As another push toward that goal he tried to break the barrier of "us" versus "them" between Americans and the Muslims; tried to desecuritize Islam and Muslims by giving examples of Muslims outside the security sphere; and asking Muslims to engage their faith and their community to promote democracy, pluralism, education, healthcare, and making America safer. It is in this regard that this speech can be considered as a speech on Islam, America, security, and democracy.

7.1.2 Obama's Practice in What He Preached

When we think about the gap of what President Obama preached and what he practiced, the first thing that comes to our mind is the closure of Guantanamo prison. This was Obama's first order when in office, but it hadn't closed even when he left. Obama understood his limitations in this case. Even during his second term he couldn't achieve this goal despite the pressure he was putting on his administration. In an exchange with Defense Secretary Chuck Hagel, Obama urged him to move faster on the issue of Guantanamo, whereas Secretary Hagel tried to explain that this is a difficult task and told the president that he had been advocating for this even before Obama was a Senator and suggested that "maybe you need a new defense secretary" (quoted in Thrush 2016). It is no secret that Obama's biggest challenge was to restore the relationship with the Republican majority congress, who opposed most of what the White House was proposing. National security situation and increasing terrorist attacks around the world did not make Obama's life easier either. These challenges greatly affected his inability to succeed in the case of Guantanamo.

Criticisms aside, Obama succeeded to work against all odds and pass the Healthcare Bill. Making this his administration's most important policy, he managed to pass the Affordable Care Act (ACA) in a Republican majority congress. This was a huge step toward the dream of every Democratic president, to try to improve the dysfunctional American healthcare system. Nevertheless, Obamacare was criticized for being too messy, difficult to understand, and needed to be amended (Grunwald 2016). But, with all its problems, the Affordable Care Act that came to be known as Obamacare covered millions of the uninsured and became a hope for improving American healthcare system.

Another pressing issue for Obama was education, especially the student loan program. While his supporters called it "another historic piece of legislation", his opponents considered it to be another job-killing law, in John Boehner's words "today, the president will sign not one, but two job-killing government takeovers" (quoted in Grunwald 2016). Obama's student loan program was bad news for private lenders such as Sallie Mae, who were charging enormous fees with very less risk (Grunwald 2016), but his educational reform wasn't only student loans program. He imagined a tuition-free community college education, not finalized when he left the office, although some community colleges had begun implementing such a policy.

As far as domestic policies and the Muslims are concerned, Obama had a hard time practicing what he promised in his Cairo Speech, or in his speech at the mosque in Baltimore. Muslim Americans had difficult times during the Obama presidency. The FBI continued to intimidate Muslims and Islamic institutions, sending their agents to make the case of radicalism and spying on mosques. Some cases that involved FBI informants radicalizing people in mosques so they can imprison them have been widely discussed, and some of them made it to the big screen. CUNY Law School started a project called CLEAR (Creating Law Enforcement Accountability and Responsibility) and in 2014 filed an appeal against the FBI, on behalf of Muhammad Tanvir, Jameel Algibhah, and Naveed Shinwari. These three American Muslim men were placed on No-Fly List by the FBI, although they had no criminal records. The agents told them that they could get off that list if they agreed to be FBI informants in the Muslim communities. In 2015 the US government sent them letters that they were removed from that list because they never posed a security threat, but that the FBI had listed them because they were interested in collecting information on Muslim Americans. CLEAR, together with the

Center for Constitutional Rights, filed for an appeal to request damages remedied for the harm they had undergone. But, for CLEAR and the Center for Constitutional Rights, this is more serious. Shayana Kadidal, CCR's Senior Managing Attorney, stated that "Unless there are consequences for constitutional violations, there is nothing to prevent them from recurring in the future [...] Though our lawsuit forced the government to undo our clients' abusive placement on the NoFly List, removing people from the list alone cannot repair the harms they suffer while on it" (quoted in CCR 2016). For the practice of using Muslim Americans to spy on their communities, CLEAR's Staff Attorney Naz Ahmad explains "FBI agents target vulnerable American Muslims on a regular basis, including those with financial, immigration, or criminal issues [...] Because our clients had none of those vulnerabilities, FBI agents had to create one before they could exploit it." These practices started during President Bush and only intensified during the Obama presidency.

When it comes to foreign policy, Obama's lack of experience in politics, especially in foreign policy, played its role. There were two camps of advisors in the Obama administration: the experienced "hawks" and the Internet-savvy "entrepreneurs". Especially at the beginning, the president sided with the "entrepreneurs" who were more idealist. Nevertheless, the America that Obama inherited needed more realism and a tougher administration.

Although they didn't call it "democracy promotion", the Obama administration started their White House journey with this policy in mind. It was reflected in Obama's Cairo speech, as well as his speech in accepting the Noble Peace Prize. Asked about how he saw himself, President Obama told Jeffrey Goldberg of The Atlantic:

> I am very much the internationalist. ... And I am also an idealist insofar as I believe that we should be promoting values, like democracy and human rights and norms and values, because not only do they serve our interests the more people adopt values that we share – in the same way that, economically, if people adopt rule of law and property rights and so forth, that is to our advantage – but because it makes the world a better place. And I'm willing to say that in a very corny way, and in a way that probably Brent Scowcroft would not say. (quoted in Goldberg 2016)

Nevertheless, the 2017 Freedom House report shows the opposite. 2016 marked the 11th consecutive year that global freedom had declined. Interestingly, the worst governments on freedoms were those countries that Obama tried to do politics with: China, Russia, Iran, Cuba, and especially Turkey, a NATO ally that Obama considered a role model.

Secretary of Defense, Robert Gates, thought that acknowledging the mistakes of the USA in the Middle East was a good move, only because great countries do that, and it raised America's image among the Arab people (2014). The problem that Gates missed was that expectations had been raised very high, starting from expecting the USA to stop Israeli settlements, or recognizing the Palestinian state. Nevertheless, Obama's political stance toward the Middle East, especially Sisi's Egypt and Assad's Syria, disappointed many Arabs. The most pressing case, full of challenges and opportunities, was Egypt. The USA was caught on a tightrope, and even though it was saying that it was not involved in the situation in Egypt, the USA was accused of orchestrating the whole situation. The Muslim Brotherhood accused the USA of supporting Mubarak and Sisi, while Mubarak supporters accused the USA of supporting the Muslim Brotherhood. Secretary Clinton in her biography admits that she did not know how to treat this situation (Clinton 2014: 347). The main reason for this conspiracy was that the USA was always engaged in the world, so it was common for people to think that the political situation in Egypt was another US orchestration. The USA's reputation had superseded its power. The USA under Obama acknowledged and accepted, if not supported, the military coup of Sisi, which left Obama's commitment in Cairo only in speech.

American political leaders had a hard time digesting the new trend of large protests in the Arab world in 2010. After Tunisia's dictator was toppled, people filled Cairo's Tahrir Square, trying to topple longtime dictator Hosni Mubarak. Tunisia was an easy bite, but Egypt was not. While Obama tended to side with the youngsters who demanded democracy, 82-year-old Mubarak was a longtime vital US ally. Internet-savvy Obama advisors such as Rhodes and Power urged the president to side with the revolutionists, but the established political icons, such as Clinton, Gates, Donilon, and Biden, thought that these advisors had only been "swept up in the drama and idealism of the moment" (Clinton 2014: 283). Nevertheless, the Rhodes team won this time, and Obama told Mubarak to step down on February 11. In the elections of June 2012 Mohamed Morsi, a leader of the Muslim Brotherhood, became the new president of Egypt. His immediate power struggle with the judiciary made Obama uncomfortable (Crowley 2016). The people of Egypt also felt uncomfortable with Morsi's policies and in 2013 they came back to Tahrir Square, this time to topple Morsi.

General Abdel Fattah al-Sisi saw this as an opportunity and seized the power from Mohamed Morsi by military coup on July 3, 2013. The White House had no policy on how they should proceed. Calling it a coup means that the USA should cut off military ties with Egypt, by law. Up until August 3 no clear statement was made, and even then, the White House spokeswoman Jen Psaki announced, "We have determined that we do not have to make a determination" (quoted in Crowley 2016) adding more confusion than clarity. On August 14, Sisi massacred a thousand pro-Morsi protestors and imprisoned around 16,000 more, including Mohammed Morsi. Obama was pushed to make an immediate partial freeze of US military assistance to Egypt. Sisi's furious reaction was immediate "You turned your back on the Egyptians, and they won't forget that" (interview for Washington Post: Waymouth 2013). This was the beginning of the harsh rhetoric between the USA and Egypt that tested Obama's limits of standing by his policies and America's values versus America's geopolitical and security interests.

At the beginning of the brutal crackdown, President Obama made it clear "We can't return to business as usual. … We have to be very careful about being seen as aiding and abetting actions that we think run contrary to our values and ideals" (quoted in Crowley 2016). He halted the planned military assistance to Egypt, including helicopters, missiles, F-16 fighter jets, and hundreds of millions in cash transfers. In the months to come, both the President and the Secretary of State talked to Sisi multiple times, pushing him to respect human rights, while asking for his help in countering emerging ISIS in Syria and Iraq. As we understand today, Sisi did neither.

The breaking point was when Obama decided to move forward with delivering the military assistance. On July 30 and 31, eight F-16 fighter jets were delivered to Cairo, which marked "Obama's capitulation to a dictator" (Crowley 2016). The decision was not taken easily; there were many debates, threats, and bluffs. Finally, President Sisi was right to feel triumphant against an American president. But in America, the people that worked in the administration felt the loss too. Politico quotes an anonymous official saying, "We caved", while Robert Ford, US Ambassador to Syria, is quoted saying "It seems like we are swinging back to the idea that we must make a choice between supporting dictators or being safe" (quoted in Crowley 2016). Obama lost a great chance to constitute his foreign policy legacy on the basis of democracy promotion, respecting human rights and elected governments, and opposing military coups.

Another debacle in Obama's foreign policy was Syria. Syria was a particularly challenging situation because Assad used all the means he had at his disposal against Syrian civilians, but the rise of the so-called Islamic State, ISIS, had made any intervention unlikely. In fact, Obama had ordered to work with the Kurdish army in the region to fight ISIS, while remaining indifferent to Assad for such a long time. Some administrators, particularly Secretary Kerry, have advocated for an intervention. At the beginning of the conflict Obama himself set his redline at chemical weapons, saying "We have been very clear to the Assad regime … that a red line for us is we start seeing a whole bunch of chemical weapons moving around or being utilized. That would change my calculus. That would change my equation" (quoted in Goldberg 2016). But the US president never acted on these statements. In 2011, he called Syrian President Assad to step down, but refused to follow up on that. There were many reasons for this inaction: firstly, many politicians expected Assad not to last as long as he did; secondly, Obama had been focused on finishing the two wars America was in, before acting on another one; thirdly, he saw no chance for the rebels to win against a Syrian army backed by two big powers, Iran and Russia, and he did not want to get involved in a war on the side that he was likely to lose; fourthly, Obama was an "over-calculator" trying to calculate every move and its effects; fifthly, there was a lack of consensus among European allies on striking Syria; and finally, Obama believed that the Middle East should not be the center of US interest, and that if he diverts USA's focus in Asia and Pacific, he would let the Middle East handle itself and get America out of that mess. Whatever the reasons, Obama's inaction in Syria angered US allies in Europe and in the Middle East, as well as in Washington DC. Moreover, he lost a great opportunity to be on the right side of history, and now he is remembered for a doctrine of weak foreign policy and minimal stands against oppression, both in Syria and Egypt. Today, Obama's redlines are mocked as being only bluffs. Russia was very comfortable invading Crimea after it was obvious that redlines did not mean much for Obama.

Obama himself was not an admirer of non-intervention, but his doctrine was that if you are going to do something it must be worth it, and it must work. He believed that stretching too thin in the Middle East, like his predecessor had, wasn't smart and this is why he refused to intervene in Syria, or to arm the rebels because they were a group of carpenters, doctors, engineers, who were fighting against an army backed by Russia and Iran. He was much more calculating than Bush and saw that Syria would be a slippery slope. He had a wide range of people in his administration, from those who were against any involvement to the ones that advocated for arming the Syrian rebels like Hillary Clinton and Samantha Powers. Nevertheless, him putting a redline in Syria (about the chemical weapons) and then not doing anything about it after that line was crossed damaged America's and Obama's personal image around the world, as well as in America. While he had the chance to build his doctrine on the responsibility to protect and be on the right side protecting values that American leaders claim their own, he decided to stay still and overturn his threats if the redline is crossed. Obama feared of being trapped by "Washington's Playbook" as he called it, that his allies and adversaries were pressing him to make quick decisions when it comes to military engagement (Goldberg 2016). This must have been at the level of paranoia for him if it stopped him from delivering what he said he would if the redline was crossed.

After ISIS beheaded three Americans in Syria, Obama decided that defeating the terrorist organization is more pressing than overthrowing Assad (Goldberg 2016). To be able to understand how Obama saw the latest events in the Middle East, it is best to quote The Atlantic's Jeffrey Goldberg, who wrote a 65-page piece on Obama's doctrine:

> Advisers recall that Obama would cite a pivotal moment in The Dark Knight, the 2008 Batman movie, to help explain not only how he understood the role of ISIS, but how he understood the larger ecosystem in which it grew. "There's a scene in the beginning in which the gang leaders of Gotham are meeting", the president would say. "These are men who had the city divided up. They were thugs, but there was a kind of order. Everyone had his turf. And then the Joker comes in and lights the whole city on fire. ISIL is the Joker. It has the capacity to set the whole region on fire. That's why we have to fight it." (Goldberg 2016)

Obama also wanted to distance himself from the Middle East as much as he could, although we cannot say that he was very successful. He eyed the Asia Pacific, as he saw the region in terms of its relationship to the future of the US interests.

Despite these debacles, there have been very little changes of the US engagement in the Middle East, some increasing interventions and some decreasing. Obama had not been reluctant in intervening in new wars; he was waging war on six Muslim countries at a certain point of time. In his intervention, he resembles his predecessor Bush more than his co-partisan Clinton. While it took two years for Clinton to intervene in Bosnia, Obama needed only two weeks to intervene in Libya. The drone attacks had increased during his presidency. From the first week in office Obama had resumed drone attacks in Pakistan, increasing drone attacks tenfold from that of Bush, while tripling Bush's boots on the ground (Bergen 2012: 112–121). Outside the Middle East, the Obama administration considered it a priority to be engaged in other regions too (Clinton 2014): in Africa; Russia; Europe, with the Paris agreement; or Latin America, with restoration of diplomatic relations with Cuba. In Europe, the USA's approval rates had gone down drastically during the Bush administration. European people and leadership were at odds with the USA on the invasion of Iraq. The most disturbing situations in these relationships were Bush's with-us-or-against-us rhetoric and Rumsfeld's naming of France and Germany as the "old Europe" during the Iraqi war in 2003. In Bush's eight years, approval of the USA in the UK and Germany had decreased from 83% to 78% and from 53% to 31%, respectively (Clinton 2014: 205). The Obama administration had started their job acknowledging this and working hard to bring better results for America, but the damage that was done was already great, so it was impossible to bring America's approval rates to the pre-Bush era.

The same goes with securitization. Once an issue is successfully securitized, like Islam was during the Bush administration, then it takes much more effort and time to desecuritize it, thus Obama's inability to desecuritize Islam in America, but he had made some progress with the speeches we analyzed above.

Obama started his presidency with a historic electoral win. President Obama managed to make considerable changes in energy policies, healthcare, education, financial policies, law enforcement, and in LGBTQ (lesbian, gay, bisexual, transgender, and queer). rights. How President Obama handled the Ebola crisis was very successful on its own. He trusted fully in science and didn't let fear determine either his policies or the national agenda. In foreign policy, he successfully made an opening to Cuba and negotiated a nuclear deal with Iran. He put into practice what President Clinton had started. But they were overshadowed by the national security agenda that had consumed the attention of American public. Obama's opponents have used his reforms to call him out and polarize society. At the end of his presidency America was a more divided society than when he started his presidency. This is not unexpected because Obama had embraced very controversial issues such as the Black Lives Matter movement, Muslims, the LGBTQ community, or the controversy over the Confederate flag, all issues long overdue, while angering the other side, who were comfortable with discrimination, racism, and homophobia.

What we can say about Obama's foreign policy doctrine is that he overcalculated everything and wanted to work only on issues that he could have an impact on, only on those that he knew he could certainly change without much trouble and engagement. Obama is an idealist, he believes in the ideas of democracy promotion and liberal values, but he definitely is not a crusader for them. What we understand from his doctrine so far is that he wanted to share the responsibility with other liberal allies, spend less energy and resources on foreign policy and more on domestic policies, pull America back from Bush's crusades around the world, give it a shot only when it was worth it, and also decrease risks in foreign policy by not spreading too thin and thinking everything through before committing to any action. This doctrine has not played very well, neither for his legacy nor for America. But the president believed that inaction in Syria and some other places has done a favor to America, who would have found itself in deeper trouble in the Middle East.

7.2 Trump Administration

To write about the securitization of Islam during the Trump presidency is already difficult, as we are only in the first year of this administration. Islam was never absent from his speeches as a candidate and as president. It is difficult to choose the most important speech related to Islam and security, or the speech that we can consider as the speech where he securitized Islam the most, because he did this in most, if not all, the speeches and we believe that he will continue to do so during his whole presidency. The same goes with his policies. He signed an executive order for a "Muslim ban" and then went to Saudi Arabia and celebrated with the Muslim leaders. It is very difficult to predict how it will play out, but we have looked at the people he has employed at his administration, and their views toward Islam, to try to draw a picture between American foreign policy, security, and Islam. Some of these people have already been fired, like Michael Flynn and it is possible that all of these positions might have changed when you read this book, but their influence in the administration will not be gone with them, and their hiring shows that Trump didn't mind their stance toward Islam, and even agreed with them. Trump hired the most anti-Islam and anti-Muslim people in America, who openly professed it, calling Islam a cancer, and calling for a crusade against Muslims. Whatever Obama had done to desecuritize Islam in eight years, Trump had managed to erase even before his inauguration. Moreover, he has gone so much further than Bush that Muslims began to ask for the return of Bush's administration. We must also remember that the Trump administration still refers to Islam as an ideology rather than a religion, trying to construct it outside constitutional religious rights.

It has become common in DC circles to accuse political scientists of not warning, or predicting, the coming of Trump, or what that would mean for American politics. But this cannot be further from the truth. Hundreds of American political scientists issued a statement of concern about Donald Trump and what was changing in American political discourse. They stated that while they seek to understand politics instead of engaging in politics, they are driven by their professional commitment to issue this statement because for them "peace is preferable to war, freedom to tyranny, justice to injustice, equality to inequality, democracy to authoritarianism". Despite their political and partisan differences, they issued and signed this statement to voice their concern about Donald Trump as president because he repeatedly questioned and attacked institutions that make America a democracy and that make democracy work in America, which is unprecedented among American presidential candidates. They voiced nine reasons for concern:

1. He has cast doubt on the validity of the election process, without any supporting evidence.
2. He has stated that he may reject the outcome of a free election if he does not win.
3. He has encouraged supporters to engage in voter suppression and intimidation.
4. He has threatened to jail the leader of the opposition party.
5. He has questioned the independence of the judiciary and the impartiality of judges based on their race, ethnicity, religion, and parentage.
6. He has impugned the loyalty of citizens and other persons in the United States on the basis of race, ethnicity, religion, and country of birth.
7. He has endangered freedom of the press by intimidating individual journalists, banning major news organizations from his rallies, and promising to change libel laws.
8. He has called for the proliferation of nuclear weapons.
9. He has threatened to destroy the strategic basis of NATO, the most important security alliance of the last seventy years, by questioning the commitment of the United States to regard an attack on any member state as an attack on all.[1]

[1] Political Scientists' statement on Donald Trump https://drive.google.com/file/d/0B7l0lh4nmE3OSkpCWjJJNGVoNXc/view (last accessed: August 17, 2017).

Although these are all important issues to tackle in American politics and security, we will focus on the securitization of Islam in the USA during the first year of the Trump administration. Because this is only the beginning of the administration, we will focus on individuals and their public stance toward Islam and Muslims, rather than speeches alone. At the end, we will analyze briefly his "National Security and Terrorism" speech from when he was only a candidate, but it will not be as deeply analyzed as the previous presidents' speeches. This speech is only one example, and there will be more speeches about Islam that he will give during his presidency. Nevertheless, it is important to note that the stance of his administration and himself, toward Islam, is more important. We had to analyze the other presidents' stances from their speeches and see how they securitized or desecuritized Islam, where we understood that it was during the Bush administration that Islam was securitized. This is the first time that a US president has hired people in his cabinet who publicly securitize Islam even while they are in office. Bush and his administration securitized Islam indirectly, by association. Trump and his administration securitize Islam directly.

America's Islamophobia industry have aided the election of Donald Trump to US president, by promoting his anti-Muslim statements and policies, by promoting anti-Muslim and anti-immigration conspiracy theories, and by calling people to support his election. On the other hand, they were awarded with positions at the White House. This is why it is important to analyze who these supporters are that became White House aides. Again, the first six months of the Trump administration has shown to be very unstable, where many people were fired and new people hired. The people we will talk about were hired by Trump, but some of them resigned, some were fired, and others might resign and get fired by the time the reader gets this book, but the important issue here is that this ideology had elected Trump and they've already influenced Trump's and his administration's views toward Islam and Muslims, as well as his policies against Muslims, such as the Muslim ban. Their commonality is that they share anti-Muslim, anti-Islam sentiments. A thorough report on the Trump administration has been published by The Bridge Initiative, of Georgetown University. The report finds that:

1. The Trump campaign capitalized on the already present anti-Muslim sentiment in the country.
2. The campaign's rhetoric brought the ideas of the far-right and fringe movements into mainstream society by publicly declaring that "Islam hates us".

3. Members of Trump's administration have a history of promoting anti-Islam and anti-Muslim views. Some have also made a career of promoting Islamophobia while many others are connected to anti-Muslim activists and organizations.
4. Actions taken by the administration demonstrate that it is committed to implementing many positions that would impact Muslim lives and civil liberties it campaigned on.
5. The future for American Muslims is uncertain. It is expected that there will be additional legislation that would undermine American Muslims' civil liberties. (The Bridge Initiative 2017)

This shows that Islam will be securitized even further during this administration, even more than during the time of George W. Bush. This can be understood from his many speeches, but let's analyze his campaign speech after the Orlando attack that was among his first speeches to directly tackle Islam, Muslims, national security, and terrorism, aptly called by his campaign the "Speech on National Security and Terrorism".

7.2.1 National Security and Terrorism Speech

Candidate Trump made the speech on June 13, 2016, in the wake of the terrorist attacks in Orlando. This was a speech devoted to national security and terrorism, where he spoke only on Islam, Muslims, immigrants, and radical Islamic terrorism. This speech, as others before and after, was marked with blaming his opponents, statements not based on fact, anti-immigration rhetoric, and an anti-Islamic narrative. Correctly, Trump condemned the terrorist attack in Orlando, but it is interesting that while condemning it as a "strike at the heart and soul of who we are as a nation … an assault on the ability of free people to live their lives, love who they want and express their identity" he has since banned transgender Americans from serving in the army, and the LGBTQ community are being targeted by the hate speech of his supporters.

Trump used this event to slam American immigration policies and push for immigration ban. He stated that the killer's parents immigrated to the USA from Afghanistan and that his father had thought of running for president of that country, asserting he was not a real American. He also called out the male terrorist of San Bernardino, who was of Pakistani descent and who brought his "terrorist wife" from Saudi Arabia: "The bottom line is that the only reason the killer was in America in the first place was because we allowed his family to come here", simplifying the issue by relating terrorism in America to immigration, which is false and misleading.

More interestingly, Trump called out the wife of the San Bernardino terrorist, who had come from Saudi Arabia, and that the 9/11 attackers all had visas to enter the USA, to make a point of the lack of screening of people while they are granted visas. But even though the wife of the San Bernardino attacker and most of the 9/11 terrorists came from Saudi Arabia, Trump's Muslim ban did not include Saudi Arabia, a longtime US ally and one of the first countries Trump visited after he was elected president.

Trump loves to talk about radical Islamic terrorism, but it is not clear what he means by it. Is it only terrorists, a particular sect or group within Islam, or Islam in general? Nevertheless, whatever he means by it he claims that "many of the principles of radical Islam are incompatible with Western values and institutions", unclear of which principles of radical Islam and which western values and institutions. Like Bush, Trump claims that this is not only about terrorism, but this is about the way of life because "they" hate "our" way of life. Again, like Bush, Trump points out how Jews and Christians are being targeted and killed by these radical Islamic terrorists, but determinately refuses to acknowledge that like Christians and Jews, Muslims are also targeted in terrorist attacks in the west. In fact, we know of no event that the terrorists asked if there were Muslims in the crowed before they attacked. They do not choose specifically churches, synagogues, or temples to attack, they choose populated places. Moreover, if Trump meant to call out terrorists as part of "radical Islam", then he should know and acknowledge that Muslims are their biggest targets in the Middle East. They have killed more Muslims than any other religious, ethnic, or other identity groups.

Interchangeably using radical Islamic terrorism and radical Islamic immigration, Trump continued to make Islam and Muslims his target. Claiming that Hillary Clinton's immigration policies would bring more "radical Islamic immigration to this country, threatening not only our security but our way of life", Trump quoted an unknown Pew Research poll that allegedly says that 99% of Afghanis support what Trump called "oppressive Sharia Law". Furthermore, he argues that "when it comes to Radical Islamic terrorism, ignorance is not bliss – it's deadly", criticizing the Obama administration's intelligence gathering and law enforcement strategies for being politically correct. The president equated Syrian refugees with a "better, bigger version of the legendary Trojan Horse" in this speech as a candidate. Thus, calling for more screening on immigrants, "We have to screen applicants to know whether they are affiliated with, or support, radical groups and beliefs" and stop them from forming large pockets of radicalization in America. As he did in many other speeches, Trump alienated Muslim Americans and put conditions for them if they want to work with his administration. In this regard, he was clear:

> I want us all to work together, including in partnership with our Muslim communities. But Muslim communities must cooperate with law enforcement and turn in the people who they know are bad – and they do know where they are.
> ... In San Bernardino, as an example, people knew what was going on, but they used the excuse of racial profiling for not reporting it.
> We need to know what the killer discussed with his relatives, parents, friends and associates.
> We need to know if he was affiliated with any radical Mosques or radical activists and what, if any, is their immigration status.
> We need to know if he travelled anywhere, and who he travelled with.
> We need to make sure every single last person involved in this plan – including anyone who knew something but didn't tell us – is brought to justice.
> If it can be proven that somebody had information about any attack, and did not give this information to authorities, they must serve prison time.

Trump criticized President Obama's and Secretary Clinton's political correctness, calling for them to use the term "radical Islamic terrorism" and asking them to be tougher. As a president, we can see that political correctness is not Trump's strongest suit. In fact, if we see his attack on media, his belief in "alternative facts", and support for hate groups, we can understand that correctness in general is not his strongest suit. In this speech, presidential candidate Trump criticized Hillary Clinton for refusing to use the words "radical Islamic terrorism" and for stating that "Muslims are peaceful and tolerant people, and have nothing whatsoever to do with terrorism". On the other hand, he defended gun ownership and said that he will meet with the National Rifle Association (NRA) to talk about "how to ensure Americans have the means to protect themselves in this age of terror". Nevertheless, when the pro-gun Trump supporters are asked about their right of gun ownership, they very rarely claim that they own guns because they feel threatened by terrorists. Most of them claim that they have the right to own guns against government interference. So, gun ownership in the USA is understood as safety against the government rather than against terrorists. Moreover, there has been no case where a gun owner has stopped a terrorist attack in America.

7.2.2 Making Islamophobia Great Again

What Faiza Patel and Rachel Levinson-Waldman from the Brennan Center for Justice at New York University School of Law called "The Islamophobic Administration" is composed of the highest number of Islamophobic appointees in American history. Before coming to the White House, these individuals have advocated policies and made statements against Muslims and Islam, together with the whole anti-Muslim and Islamophobia industry. First, they've pushed the discourse that Islam is not a legitimate religion but a dangerous political ideology; second, that the west, led by America, is in war with Islam; and third, that all American Muslim organizations are part of the Muslim Brotherhood, itself a very loosely defined movement that has never been designated as a terrorist organization in the USA. This discourse justifies American military action in the Middle East and surveillance and profiling of Muslim Americans.

First of all, we must start with the president himself. Appearing on CNN as a presidential candidate, Trump told Anderson Cooper "I think Islam hates us" claiming that although his war is against radical Islam, "it's very hard to define. It's very hard to separate. Because you don't know who's who" (CNN 2016). His spokeswoman, Katrina Pierson, asserted that although he should have used "radical Islam", Trump stood by the sentiment that many Muslims sympathize with ISIS (CNN 2016). In the same interview, Trump said that he is also willing to reinstate waterboarding and even go further than that. This is not the only time that he has shown anti-Muslim bias and Islamophobic sentiments. Before, he said that he would support a Muslim database and that there were major problems with Muslim integration (Hasan 2017; Gabriel 2015). Donald Trump's election campaign rhetoric was based on "Making Islam and Muslims the Enemy" (The Bridge Initiative 2017).

Donald Trump's campaign was overwhelmingly anti-Muslim. He proposed the surveillance of mosques, referring to similar practices of NYPD after 9/11, which were later challenged constitutionally in three lawsuits (Patel and Levinson-Waldman 2017); he repeated the non-factual claim that Muslims in New Jersey cheered when the World Trade Center buildings fell on 9/11 (Carroll 2015); and he continuously claimed that Muslims do not report terrorists, although FBI statements claim the opposite (Cooke and Ax 2016).

Looking at his appointees and campaign rhetoric, the Muslim ban comes as no surprise. A week into his presidency Trump wanted to deliver on his campaign promise of "complete shutdown of Muslims entering the United States" (Trump 2015). He signed an executive order to ban the entrance of seven Muslim-majority countries' citizens, as well as stopping the entry of Syrian refugees indefinitely. After federal courts stopped the implementation of this order a second version was issued on March 6, 2017, exempting green card and visa holders and dropping Iraq from the list of the banned countries. Hawaii and Maryland courts have challenged this executive order as well and the US Supreme Court has ruled that it is unconstitutional.

Trump and his aides have constantly claimed that this was not a Muslim ban, not targeting a particular religious or ethnic group, but rather a national security-driven order. But, if we look at the statements of the president and his staff, it is not difficult to see that it was a Muslim ban:

> Donald J. Trump is calling for a total and complete shutdown of Muslims entering the United States. (Trump 2015)

> ... we're having problems with the Muslims, and we're having problems with Muslims coming into the country. (quoted in Hensch and Byrnes 2016)

> The Muslim ban is something that in some form has morphed into extreme vetting from certain areas of the world. ... It's called extreme vetting. (quoted in Strauss 2016)

> When [Mr. Trump] first announced it, he said, 'Muslim ban'. He called me up. He said, 'Put a commission together. Show me the right way to do it legally.' (Rudi Giuliani quoted in Wang 2017)

Even in the case of the Muslim ban Trump showed how obsessed he was with Obama. In a misleading statement, he claimed:

> My policy is similar to what President Obama did in 2011 when he banned visas for refugees from Iraq for six months. The seven countries named in the Executive Order are the same countries previously identified by the Obama administration as sources of terror. (Trump 2017)

This was misleading on at least five points: Obama's vetting procedure was much narrower in focus and applied only to the refugees who were citizens of Iraq; it was not a ban on visas and refugees still continued to come, but they were more thoroughly vetted. And for what is worse refugees don't even travel on visas, whereas this vetting procedure was made only to Iraqi refugees; this policy came out of a specific threat, after two Iraqi refugees were arrested in Kentucky on terrorism charges; it was an orderly, planned, and organized process, coming after many meetings, plans, and calculations with many agencies and institutions; and finally, there is far stronger vetting today than there was in 2011, even without the Muslim ban (Finer 2017).

President Trump appointed a very controversial individual, *General Michael Flynn*, as National Security Advisor. General Flynn had been caught up in scandals during the Obama administration, which caused Obama to fire him in 2014 from his position as the head of the Defense Intelligence Agency. Nevertheless, the scandals did not stop. He became the center of the Trump campaign—Russia scandal—hiding from Vice President Pence that he met with a Russian envoy and businessmen. Flynn was also accused of not disclosing a lucrative lobbying deal with a Turkish businessman with alleged ties to the authoritative Turkish President Erdogan to write newspaper articles and lobby against Fethullah Gülen, an imam in a self-imposed exile in Pennsylvania, who Erdogan blamed for the failed coup in 2016 and for opposing his authoritarian government. Only after leaving the government did he disclose this deal. Flynn called Islam "a cancer" and called the Muslim world leaders to "declare their Islam ideology sick". In February 2016, Flynn tweeted a link to a YouTube video entitled "Fear of Muslims is RATIONAL," asking his followers to "Please forward this to others". The narrator in the video that Flynn tweeted states, "Please keep in mind that the term 'Islamophobia' is an oxymoron, since having a phobia means having an irrational fear. … Fearing Islam, which wants 80 percent of humanity enslaved or exterminated is totally rational and hence cannot be called a phobia" (Kaczynski 2016; Crowley and Toosi 2016).

The most controversial name regarding Islam, hate, and white supremacy is Trump's appointee Stephen Bannon, who was the executive chairman of the white supremacist Breitbart News Network before he joined the Trump administration as a strategic counselor. While Bannon was heading Breitbart from 2012 to 2016, the news outlet portrayed Muslims as a threat to the USA. In his SiriusXM radio show he hosted anti-Muslim champions like Pamela Geller of "Stop Islamization of America", who he interviewed seven times, and Frank Gaffney, who he hosted for 29 times and called him "one of the senior thought leaders and men of action in this whole war against Islamic radical jihad" who is "doing amazing work, doing God's work. … Just fantastic" (Crowley and Toosi 2016; Mindock

2017; Shane 2017). In an interview for the online right-wing radio show "Western Word Radio with Avi Davis", Bannon commented that "Islam is not a religion of peace. Islam is a religion of submission. Islam means submission" (quoted in Kaczynski 2017) and criticized Bush for trying to be politically correct toward Islam and the Muslims. Bannon has also claimed that "the Judeo-Christian West [is in a] very brutal and bloody conflict … an outright war against jihadist Islamic fascism" (quoted in Hasan 2017). On his SiriusXM radio show, Bannon referred to Islam as "the most radical religion" and asserted that it is much darker and dangerous than Hitler and the Nazis (Harkinson 2017; Reilly and Heath 2017). Although Bannon got fired in August 2017, it was he that played a major role in advising Trump in his stand against Muslims and toward white supremacists. He allegedly helped Trump to draft the "Muslim ban", as well as Trump's comments on white supremacists after the Charlottesville events in August 2017.

Perhaps as controversial as Bannon, Sebastian Gorka is another figure that has led the anti-Muslim discourse in America. He is appointed as deputy assistant in Trump's White House. He argued that it would be "national suicide" to admit Muslim refugees in America and that Islam and the Qur'an are the sources of much of terrorism (Stampler 2017; Kirkland 2017). He called the profiling of Muslims "common sense" (Jilani and Emmons 2016) and the Muslim Brotherhood as the "grandfather of modern jihadism" in a tweet in 2016. Sebastian Gorka argues that the USA's enemy is neither terror nor violent extremism, but "the global jihadi movement, a modern totalitarian ideology rooted in the doctrines and martial history of Islam" (Gorka 2016). He too has appeared and is associated with Breitbart, the Center for Security Policy, and other anti-Muslim outlets. Sebastian's wife, Katherine Gorka, is also a member of the Homeland Security team at the White House. She writes for Breitbart and has advocated for anti-Muslim legislation (The Bridge Initiative 2017).

Another important actor in Trump administration is Michael Anton. He is a Bush alumnus and now a staffer in Trump's National Security Council. During the presidential campaign, Anton worked as an "anonymous booster of the then-candidate Trump" promoting Trump's anti-Islam, anti-immigration policies in right-wing websites, under the name Publius Decius Mus (the name of a self-sacrificing Roman consul), which The Weekly Standard later revealed was Anton (Schulberg 2017). Among other things, Anton wrote that Islam was violent and incompatible with the west. He claimed that the west has no power to change Muslims and that when Muslims come to the west they change it for the worse; thus they needed to be stopped. He also called diversity "a source of weakness, tension and disunion" (quoted in Schulberg 2017).

Another person that allegedly authored the Muslim ban was Stephen Miller. Miller is known for rallying at university campuses against "Islamofascism". Miller is a senior advisor to President Trump, contributing to the president's speeches, executive orders, and addresses. Together with Bannon, he contributed to the president's inaugural address, where the president stated: "We will unite the civilized world against Islamic terrorism, which we will eradicate from the face of the Earth" (The Bridge Initiative 2017), bringing up the clash of civilizations doctrine. Miller was the first national coordinator of the Terrorism Awareness Project, an initiative of his mentor David Horowitz, whose aim was to make "students aware of the Islamic jihad and the terrorist threat, and to mobilize support for the defense of American and the civilization of the West" (Frontpagemag 2017). Miller stated that "[Islamic terrorists] have declared a death sentence on every man, woman and child living in this country" (Miller 2006). Activities of the Terrorism Awareness Project include ads in college campus newspapers on "What Americans Need to Know About Jihad" claiming that "Jihad is a war against Christians", distorting the meaning of jihad and ignoring the condemnation of terrorism by Muslim authorities.[2] Moreover, the project calls on its supporters to "evaluate the Islamic or Mideast Studies departments of their campuses" (Frontpagemag 2017) to monitor them for spreading sympathy for terrorism, equating the study of Islam and the Middle East with terrorism. After graduating college, Miller started working for Alabama Senator Jeff Sessions, the Trump administration's Attorney General, particularly on anti-immigration bills (The Bridge Initiative 2017). Together with Bannon, Gaffney, Gorka, Sessions, and others, they form the White House's viewpoint toward Muslims. They are all related to American Islamophobic organizations that we have analyzed below.

Mike Pompeo, the new CIA Director, has falsely claimed that "Islamic advocacy organizations and many mosques across America [are] poten-

---

[2] Heraa Hashmi, a Muslim student at the University of Colorado, has made a list of the Muslim authorities who have condemned terrorism, "Worldwide Muslims Condemn List". She updates it frequently and you can reach it as a document at https://docs.google.com/spreadsheets/d/1e8BjMW36CMNc4-qc9UNQku0blstZSzp5FMtkdlavqzc/edit#gid=0 (last accessed: August 17, 2017).

tially complicit [in] extremism" when he spoke at a congressional hearing in 2013 (Pompeo 2013). He too subscribes to the clash of civilizations doctrine, claiming that war on terror is actually a war between Muslims and Christians (Fang 2016). He argued that he sees no problem with torture, due process violations, and being imprisoned without charge or trial. He called them humane and lawful and vowed support to Trump's idea to not close the infamous Guantanamo and fill it with "some bad dudes" (Wise 2016; Lipton et al. 2016; Welna 2016). Pompeo has appeared numerous times in radio shows of Frank Gaffney and has advocated to designate the Muslim Brotherhood as a terrorist organization, when he was a congressman (The Bridge Initiative 2017). He also spread the false conspiracy that most US Islamic institutions have ties to the Muslim Brotherhood.

Other anti-Muslim Trump administrators and advisors include Attorney General Jeff Sessions, who referred to Islam as a "toxic ideology" (Warrick and Hauslohner 2016); Secretary Ben Carson, who advocated that Muslims should not be allowed to run for president in the election campaign in 2016; Secretary Rex Tillerson, who equated the Muslim Brotherhood with al-Qaeda, arguing that both are agents of radical Islam, in his confirmation hearing; Walid Phares, Trump's foreign policy advisor, who was involved in Lebanon's right-wing Christian Maronite militia, responsible for the 1982 massacres of Palestinian and Lebanese civilians in Shatila refugee camps. Previously, he had been associated with the anti-Muslim Clarion Project as an expert on Islam and Muslims. He sits in the board of ACT for America and writes for the FrontPage Magazine (The Bridge Initiative 2017). Phares promotes the belief that "Muslims are plotting a secret takeover of American institutions with the end goal of imposing Sharia" (Coppins 2011).

These and other Trump appointees are people who argue that the root cause of terrorism is Islam and have contributed in one way or another to Trump's Muslim ban.

Islamophobic Trump staff are not the lone Islamophobes. As we discussed in a previous chapter, Islamophobia is an industry in America, consisting of influential people, non-profits, charities, corporations, and media. This industry is headed by far-right trolls such as Pamela Geller, Frank Gaffney, Steve Bannon, Breitbart, InfoWars, Steve Emerson, Alex Jones, and others. They have promoted Muslim stereotypes, have amplified the conspiracy theories that Muslims want to take over America and the world, and have spread false information about Islam. Bill Maher of HBO is among them. He claimed that "civilization begins with civilizing the men; talk to women who've ever dated an Arab man. The results are not good", "Islam is the only religion that acts like the Mafia that will fucking kill you if you say the wrong thing", "The Muslim world has too much in common with ISIS", and "People who want to gloss over the difference between Western culture and Islamic culture and forget about the fact that the Islamic culture is 600 years younger and that they are going through the equivalent of what the West went through with our Middle Ages, our Dark Ages", among other things (quoted by Johnson 2017). Bill Maher is in a different category from people like Pamela Geller. He is part of the "new atheists" together with Sam Harris and Richard Dawkins who will work with anyone that is against Islam and thus contribute to the Islamophobia industry.

Among the most noticeable is David Horowitz, of the David Horowitz Freedom Center, whose main goal has been to raise a generation of "political warriors" against the Washington establishment. Before Trump's immigration policy, the wall, or Muslim ban, it was Horowitz's Freedom Center that had rallied "warriors" against immigrants, Islam, and claims of global warming. It has labeled the Clintons as evil, Obama as a secret communist, and the Democratic Party as USA's enemy (O'Harrow and Boburg 2017). What they've self-labeled as a "School for Political Warfare", the Freedom Center is a network of charities linked by ideology, personalities, funds, websites, for-profits, and not-for-profits, including Breitbart News and Trump administrators such as Bannon, Miller, and Sessions. Together with Stephen Miller, Horowitz launched "Students for Academic Freedom" to "balance" the left in high schools and college campuses, but what they really do is attack left-leaning, liberal academics and students, in the name of free speech. The Freedom Center has also sponsored the "Islamofascism Awareness Week" on college campuses, to raise awareness against Islamist militant terror and Jewish hatred in US campuses (O'Harrow and Boburg 2017). David Horowitz also worked closely with the anti-Muslim group headed by Robert Spencer, Jihad Watch.

These are all allies that spread false news and propaganda against President Obama. Nevertheless, the election of President Obama in 2008 was very lucrative for them. The donations from right-wing conservative donors had increased tenfold in the matter of a year. They've spread the propaganda that the left has declared war on America, collaborating with

American enemies abroad. Nevertheless, one of Horowitz's protégées, Steve Bannon, proudly claimed he was a Leninist, who "wanted to destroy the state, and that's my goal, too. I want to bring everything crashing down, and destroy all of today's establishment" according to Ronald Radosh (2016), who claims he had this conversation with Bannon at an event that Bannon organized in his house in DC, for Horowitz. Horowitz's organization has also funded many websites that published articles attacking climate change, immigrant policies, Muslims, Obama, and Hilary Clinton. Such news sites include Breitbart and Frontpagemag.com, but are not limited to them. They have played a great role in making Trump's election propaganda and attacking the Democratic Party, framing them as America's enemies. This has led Sessions, Bannon, Pence, Priebus, Conway, Miller, and many others to enter the White House, according to Horowitz (O'Harrow and Boburg 2017). Although some of them have changed, the point here is that this is the ideology that has brought Trump to power, and although a few actors might change from time to time, the driving force is the same.

Another organization that has been at the forefront of boosting anti-Muslim rhetoric is ACT for America. Led by Brigitte Gabriel, ACT for America was founded in 2007 "to establish a means for all American citizens to provide a collective voice for the democratic values of Western civilization and against the threat of radical Islam" as explained in their Internal Revenue Service (IRS) filing. They claim to be an advocacy group having hundreds of chapters nationwide, and the Southern Poverty Law Center has identified them as "the largest anti-Muslim grassroots group in the United States" (SPLC 2017). They are known for their anti-Sharia rallies and campaigns, opposing Muslim organizations, mosques, refugees, and politicians that have sympathetic views toward Muslims or refugees; and they've supported campaigns and policies against anything Muslim or Islamic. ACT is known for projects and campaigns they conducted with law enforcement against "Global Islamic Movement" and radicalism, against high school and college textbooks, and courses that they deem sympathetic to Islam. They've advocated for designating the Muslim Brotherhood as a terrorist organization. But, if one wonders about their reach to the White House, it is worth quoting a fact sheet prepared by Georgetown University's The Bridge Initiative, an initiative to promote pluralism and counter Islamophobia:

ACT has celebrated its "direct line" to the White House through advisor Walid Phares, CIA director Mike Pompeo, and former National Security Advisor Michael Flynn. Phares and Flynn have served on ACT's board, and Pompeo has spoken at ACT conferences and hosted them on Capitol Hill. In February 2016 during the presidential campaign, ACT head Brigitte Gabriel met Donald Trump at his Mar-a-Lago resort where her group says she gave a national security briefing. After Trump was elected, she met with White House staff in March 2017. (The Bridge Initiative 2017)

Bannon, Flynn, Pompeo, Sessions, and Gorka are closely related to Frank Gaffney of the Center for Security Policy (CSP), which is another organization that promotes anti-Muslim rhetoric, anti-Sharia legislation, and advocates for designating the Muslim Brotherhood as a terrorist organization (Harkinson 2016; Kirkland 2017; Piggot 2016; Bump 2016; Elliott 2011). Gaffney claims that Islam is only a totalitarian ideology and not a religion, thus not entitled to constitutional protection (Posner 2011; Beinart 2017). The Center for Security Policy promotes the conspiracy that America is under the threat of Islamic law and Islamization, as the Muslim Brotherhood has infiltrated the US government and that a number of US politicians have ties with this group. At the Center for Security Policy, Gaffney publishes reports that Muslim Americans support Islamic supremacists' doctrine of Shariah and Jihad and that the Islamic doctrine of Shariah approves the extremists' actions. All these reports have flawed methodologies to serve the propaganda of Gaffney and CSP (ADL 2017). They've been conducted by the company of Kellyanne Conway, Trump's campaign manager, now his counselor at the White House. Gaffney has opposed the opening of mosques and accused imams and mosque board members for promoting "a program that is at odds with our freedoms, our form of government, our Constitution. … You have stealth jihadists at work, trying to advance the situation" (quoted in ADL 2017). He has named many US politicians and political activists as having ties to the Muslim Brotherhood, including Grover Norquist, Suhail Khan, Huma Abedin, Andre Carson, Hillary Clinton, Barack Obama, John Brennan, and many others, in right-wing media outlets such as Breitbart and FrontPage, and Washington Times. During the presidential campaign, candidate Ted Cruz hired Gaffney as his campaign advisor. He supported Trump's statements such as "Islam hates us" and has consistently published reports affirming that what Trump said was true in America, such as the threat of immigrants and Islam. Frank Gaffney was also part of

Trump's transition team. Norwegian terrorist Anders Breivik repeatedly cited Gaffney and CSP in the manifesto he left behind.

Nevertheless, it is not only the right-wing media that has contributed to the present situation of the Islamophobic climate. The mainstream media also played a role, especially because they have all contributed to making terrorism a unique phenomenon of Muslim violence, disproportionately covering the al-Qaeda and ISIS spectacle, and comparing Islam with atheist liberals (Johnson 2017). Fairness and Accuracy in Reporting (FAIR) has conducted much research on how terrorism coverage has singled out Muslims. For example, while the media has not called the January 30 attack on a Quebec mosque, by a white supremacist Alexandre Bissonnette, as terrorism, they've immediately called the October 2014 attack on Ottawa's Parliament Hill by Muslim Michael Zehaf-Bibeau as terrorism and was covered six times more than the Quebec mosque attack in US media, even though the attack at the mosque killed three times more people than the Ottawa Parliament Hill terrorist attack. As was the case under President George W. Bush, the "war on terror" has depicted Muslims as the "other" and the "enemy", which opened the way to today's atmosphere under Trump. Adam Johnson of FAIR called this meta-terror, "not informed by actual terrorist activity, but rather … the fear caused by the coverage of terrorism, unconnected from any actual threat". He identified five manifestations of meta-terror, where there is no actual act of terrorism, only threats, plots, to infame anti-Muslim prejudice:

1) the media disseminating ISIS threats in the form of video or audio;
2) reports about speculative terror attacks (e.g., LA Times, "A Freeway Terror Attack Is the 'Nightmare We Worry About', Law Enforcers Say", 12/21/15);
3) media treating "ISIS plots" manufactured by the FBI as actual ISIS plots, despite the fact that no one in ISIS was actually involved;
4) FBI and DHS "terror alerts" that never precede any actual attacks; and
5) the whole-cloth creation of fake ISIS stories. (Johnson 2017)

Meta-terror is not new. As Johnson (2017) rightly reports, since 2014 the media would publish unthinkable things about ISIS, including that they are building training camps in Mexico, ISIS caliphate maps, female genital mutilation, attacks that never took place, FBI-planned terror plots as actual attacks that really happened, and how more than 100 Americans have joined ISIS (this one was stated by Defense Secretary Chuck Hagel) only to be correct by FBI Director James Comey two days later that the number is not 100 but 12.

Vox's Alvin Chang has conducted a research on the biased coverage of Trump's anti-Muslim statements and Clinton's emails. The most-covered stories were when Trump attacked the Muslim judge and the Khan family, but even those two stories were put away quickly. Not only anti-Muslim statements but his business dealings, treatment of women, lies, healthcare plan, tax plan, building a wall, the Muslim ban, and climate change statements did not get the attention of the American media as much as Clinton's emails. In this study Chang (2016) found that:

> From the beginning of 2016 to late October, the three major networks – CBS, ABC, and NBC – spent 100 combined minutes of their newscasts covering Clinton's emails. They spent 32 minutes on every other policy issue, and no time on climate change, health care, poverty, and trade. This focus on her emails made it relevant throughout the election, peaking right before Election Day. Often, it was a small development that provided little new information, like FBI Director James Comey sending a letter to Congress saying the bureau had more emails to look at – and then saying it didn't change the original decision that she hadn't done anything criminal.

So basically, the American people and American media were more interested in what Clinton wrote in the emails she sent to other people than how Trump is actually going to change their lives.

These actions explain that Trump's anti-Muslim stand that led to the Muslim ban did not happen in a vacuum, and everyone has a part in it, including the far-right Islamophobia industry as well as the corporate media outlets. During the election campaign debates, Hillary Clinton stated also that "we need American Muslims to be part of our eyes and ears, on our frontlines", asserting that Muslims are only good when they are on the frontlines (Shipoli 2016). Associating Islam and Muslims with security has become a very casual narrative that it is done even unintentionally. But, it is important to also know how the subjects of this discourse feel.

It is interesting to see how Muslims feel the change of the administration. Although no such project or survey has been conducted yet, Rumana Ahmed, an American Muslim working for the Obama administration, penned an op-ed for The Atlantic that is worth analyzing to be able to understand how she, a hijabi American Muslim child of immigrants, lived through the transition. She managed to survive in the Trump White House for only eight days. She was working at the National Security Council under Ben Rhodes, and when the Obama administration left she shared an office space with Michael Anton, who was an anti-Islam promoter during Trump's presidential campaign for several newspapers and online platforms. For how Rumana felt and why she decided to leave the White House in eight days, it is best to quote her at length on what she told her anti-Islam, anti-immigration office mate Michael Anton:

> I told him I had to leave because it was an insult walking into this country's most historic building every day under an administration that is working against and vilifying everything I stand for as an American and as a Muslim. I told him that the administration was attacking the basic tenets of democracy. I told him that I hoped that they and those in Congress were prepared to take responsibility for all the consequences that would attend their decisions. (Ahmed 2017)

American Muslim youngsters were inspired by President Obama, by his achievements and his words. Rumana remembers President Obama's Baltimore speech as the antithesis of what Trump stands for: "we're one American family, and when any part of our family starts to feel separate … it's a challenge to our values" (quoted in Ahmed 2017). She nostalgically remembers that working for Obama proved her previous thoughts that the government was inherently corrupt and ineffective, wrong.

Rumana Ahmed is only one voice that amplifies what Muslims felt during the presidential race and elections of 2016. For them it was post-9/11 again. She shares stories of her fifth-grade students at a local Sunday school she volunteered at, about how they were bullied by their classmates and how they fear they will be deported by Trump; how she was almost hit by a car at Costco, by a white man laughing; how another man followed her to the metro and insulted her and her faith, claiming that Trump will send them all back. The worst was that these sentiments were publicly and directly endorsed and promoted by people in power, unlike post-9/11.

The securitization of Islam has already been shown to be devastating. Research by the Center for the Study of Hate and Extremism at California State University showed that in 2015 political rhetoric has fueled anti-Muslim hate crimes in the USA to the highest point since the 9/11 attacks in 2001. Similarly, since Trump proposed the Muslim ban as his campaign promise, Google searches like "kill all Muslims" have risen constantly (Levin 2016: 5–26). FBI reports show similar patterns of raising anti-Muslim hate crimes with the start of the presidential election campaigns in 2015 and 2016. The current White House administration has legitimized Islamophobia and racism, this is why we can see and will be seeing more racist sentiments in the public. Trump has not been shy to show his sympathy for the alt-right, the Ku Klux Klan (KKK), and Nazi supporters. It took him three days to make a statement against the alt-right attacks in Charlottesville, only to claim next day that both alt-right and alt-left groups shared the blame. It took him one week to denounce post-inauguration incidents at Jewish cemeteries and community centers. He has never denounced the anti-Semitic chants of the protestors or the bomb attack at a mosque in Minnesota few days before the Charlottesville events.

In contrast with even the W. Bush administration, the Trump administration securitizes Islam directly. They've identified Islam as the enemy by claiming that "Islam hates us"; they propagate that Islam is not a religion but an ideology, bringing back the Cold War mentality of America fighting a foreign ideology, and also the clash of civilizations doctrine that Islam is incompatible with the west; and that America has to be ready to use any means, especially military, to fight this enemy.

President Obama's views on Islam were closer to those of Bill Clinton than those of George W. Bush. He rejected that America was at war with Islam, and he vowed to desecuritize Islam by de-religionizing security. Nevertheless, Islam was not fully desecuritized, but a major road had been taken, especially in the discourse of the administration. It doesn't mean that the prejudices toward Islam and the Muslims in rhetoric have been nullified during the Obama presidency, because they have not, but they have improved in comparison to that of his predecessor. Otherwise, Obama's answer "I am not nor have I ever been a Muslim" to his opponents' "accusation" of him being Muslim makes a supposition that being a Muslim is indeed something bad (Esposito 2010: 18).

Finally, although it is too soon to predict how this will end, the securitization of Islam during the Trump administration's first 200 days is at another level. Trump's picks for cabinet and administrative positions include people who are known for their anti-Muslim, anti-immigration, and white supremacist views. They have directly securitized Islam as America's antithesis and as an ideology that America needs to destroy by any means.

The next chapter will analyze why Islam was securitized in American foreign policy. It will also bring together the securitization of Islam and democracy promotion, comparing the Balkans during the Clinton presidency and the Middle East during the Bush presidency. For this chapter, we cannot analyze the Trump administration's drives of why they are securitizing Islam directly because it is still very early, but we can argue that the intentions might be the same as with the George W. Bush administration.

References

Ahmed, Rumana. 2017. I Was a Muslim in Trump's White House. *The Atlantic*, February 23. https://www.theatlantic.com/politics/archive/2017/02/rumana-ahmed-trump/517521/. Accessed 17 Aug 2017.

Beinart, Peter. 2017. The Denationalization of American Muslims. *The Atlantic*, March 19. https://www.theatlantic.com/politics/archive/2017/03/frank-gaffney-donald-trump-and-the-denationalization-of-american-muslims/519954/. Accessed 17 Aug 2017.

Bergen, Peter L. 2012. *Man Hunt: The Ten-Year Search for bin Laden from 9/11 to Abbottabad*. New York: Broadway.

Bump, Philip. 2016. Meet Frank Gaffney, the Anti-Muslim Gadfly Reportedly Advising Donald Trump's Transition Team. *Washington Post*, November 16. https://www.washingtonpost.com/news/the-fix/wp/2015/12/08/meet-frank-gaffney-the-anti-muslim-gadfly-who-produced-donaldtrumps-anti-muslim-poll/?utm_term=.b61fc6d8e1dd. Accessed 17 Aug 2017.

Carroll, Lauren. 2015. Fact-Checking Trump's Claim That Thousands in New Jersey Cheered When World Trade Center Tumbled. Politifact.com, November 22. http://www.politifact.com/truth-o-meter/statements/2015/nov/22/donald-trump/fact-checking-trumps-claim-thousands-new-jersey-ch/. Accessed 17 Aug 2017.

Center for Constitutional Rights (CCR). 2016. *American Muslims Who Refused to Become FBI Informants File Appeal Over No-Fly List*, July 29. https://ccrjustice.org/home/press-center/press-releases/american-muslims-who-refused-become-fbi-informants-file-appeal-over?utm_content=buffer2a79f&utm_mediu. Accessed 8 Aug 2017.

Chang, Alvin. 2016. I Looked at 2 Years of Front Pages. Trump's Muslim Ban Got Far Less Attention than Clinton's Emails. *Vox*, November 15. https://www.vox.com/policy-and-politics/2016/11/15/13564522/trump-muslim-ban-front-pages. Accessed 17 Aug 2017.

Clinton, Hillary Rodham. 2014. *Hard Choices*. New York: Simon and Schuster.

CNN. 2016. Donald Trump: 'I Think Islam Hates Us', March 9. http://www.cnn.com/2016/03/09/politics/donald-trump-anderson-cooper-primaryflorida-ohio/index.html. Accessed 17 Aug 2017.

Cooke, Kristina, and Joseph Ax. 2016. FBI to Trump: You're Wrong About Muslims Reporting Extremist Threats. *Reuters*, June 16. http://www.businessinsider.com/r-us-officials-say-american-muslims-do-report-extremist-threats-2016-6. Accessed 17 Aug 2017.

Coppins, McKay. 2011. Mitt's Muslim Problem. *The Daily Beast*, October 12. http://www.thedailybeast.com/mitt-romneys-new-adviser-sparksislamic-uproar. Accessed 17 Aug 2017.

Crowley, Michael. 2016. The Obama Issue: We Caved. *Politico Magazine*, January/February. http://www.politico.com/magazine/story/2016/01/we-caved-obama-foreign-policy-legacy-213495. Accessed 8 Aug 2017.

Crowley, Michael, and Nahal Toosi. 2016. Trump Appointees Endorsed Link Between Islam and Radicalism. *Politico*, November 18. http://www.politico.com/story/2016/11/trump-appointees-islam-radicalism-231647. Accessed 17 Aug 2017.

Elliott, Andrea. 2011. The Man Behind the Anti-Shariah Movement. *New York Times*, July 30. http://www.nytimes.com/2011/07/31/us/31shariah.html?smid=pl-share. Accessed 17 Aug 2017.

Esposito, John L. 2010. *The Future of Islam*. New York: Oxford University Press.

Fang, Lee. 2016. Trump CIA Pick Mike Pompeo Depicted War on Terror as Islamic Battle Against Christianity. *The Intercept*, November 23. https://theintercept.com/2016/11/23/mike-pompeo-religious-war/. Accessed 17 Aug 2017.

Finer, Jon. 2017. Sorry, Mr. President: The Obama Administration Did Nothing Similar to Your Immigration Ban. *Foreign Policy*, January 30. http://foreignpolicy.com/2017/01/30/sorry-mr-president-the-obama-administration-did-nothing-similar-to-your-immigration-ban/. Accessed 17 Aug 2017.

Frontpagemag. 2017. Introducing the Terrorism Awareness Project. *FrontPage Magazine*, January 31. http://archive.frontpagemag.com/readArticle.aspx?ARTID=357. Accessed 17 Aug 2017.

Gabriel, Trip. 2015. Donald Trump Says He'd 'Absolutely' Require Muslims to Register. *New York Times*, November 20. https://www.nytimes.com/politics/first-draft/2015/11/20/donald-trump-says-hed-absolutely-require-muslims-to-register/. Accessed 17 Aug 2017.

Gates, Robert M. 2014. *Duty: Memoirs of a Secretary at War*. New York: Alfred A. Knopf.

Goldberg, Jeffrey. 2016. The Obama Doctrine: The U.S. President Talks Through His Hardest Decisions About America's Role in the World. *The Atlantic*, April. https://www.theatlantic.com/magazine/archive/2016/04/the-obama-doctrine/471525/. Accessed 17 Aug 2017.

Gorka, Sebastian. 2016. Defeating Jihad: The Winnable War. Amazon. https://www.amazon.com/Defeating-Jihad-Winnable-Sebastian-Gorka/dp/1633899861. Accessed 17 Aug 2017.

Grunwald, Michael. 2016. The Obama Issue: The Nation He Built. *Politico*, January/February. http://www.politico.com/magazine/story/2016/01/obama-biggest-achievements-213487. Accessed 15 Aug 2017.

Harkinson, Josh. 2016. Campaign CEO Was a Big Promoter of Extremists. *Mother Jones*, September 15. http://www.motherjones.com/politics/2016/09/stephen-bannon-donald-trump-muslims-fear-loathing. Accessed 17 Aug 2017.

———. 2017. The Dark History of the White House Aides Who Crafted Trump's "Muslim Ban." *Mother Jones*, January 30. http://www.motherjones.com/politics/2017/01/stephen-bannon-miller-trump-refugee-ban-islamophobia-white-nationalist/. Accessed 17 Aug 2017.

Hasan, Mehdi. 2017. Don't Be Fooled by Trump's Saudi Arabia Speech. He's Still an Islamophobe. *The Washington Post*, May 22. https://www.washingtonpost.

com/news/global-opinions/wp/2017/05/22/dont-be-fooled-by-trumps-saudi-arabia-speech-hes-still-an-islamophobe/?utm_term=.f08639597d0a. Accessed 17 Aug 2017.

Hensch, Mark, and Jesse Byrnes. 2016. Trump: 'Frankly, We're Having Problems with the Muslims. *The Hill*, March 22. http://thehill.com/blogs/ballot-box/presidential-races/273857-trump-frankly-were-having-problems-with-the-muslims. Accessed 17 Aug 2017.

Holsti, Ole R. 2006. *Making American Foreign Policy*. New York: Routledge.

Jilani, Zaid, and Alex Emmons. 2016. Former Donald Trump Advisor Calls Racial Profiling "Common Sense". *The Intercept*, June 30. https://theintercept.com/2016/06/30/former-donald-trump-adviser-calls-racial-profiling-common-sense/. Accessed 17 Aug 2017.

Johnson, Adam. 2017. How Corporate Media Paved the Way for Trump's Muslim Ban. *FAIR*, February. http://fair.org/home/howcorporatemediapavedthewayfortrumpsmuslimban/. Accessed 17 Aug 2017.

Kaczynski, Andrew. 2016. Michael Flynn in August: Islamism Is a 'Vicious Cancer' in Body of All Muslims That 'Has to Be Excised'. *CNN*, November 22. http://www.cnn.com/2016/11/22/politics/kfile-michael-flynn-august-speech/index.html. Accessed 17 Aug 2017.

———. 2017. Steve Bannon in 2010: 'Islam Is Not a Religion of Peace. Islam Is a Religion of Submission'. *CNN*, January 31. http://www.cnn.com/2017/01/31/politics/kfilebannononislam/index.html. Accessed 17 Aug 2017.

Kirkland, Allegra. 2017. How Did Sebastian Gorka Go from e Anti-Muslim Fringe to White House Aide? *TalkingPointsMemo.com*, February 9. http://talkingpointsmemo.com/dc/sebastian-gorka-washington-experts-dc-anti-islam-ties. Accessed 17 Aug 2017.

Levin, Brian. 2016. Special Status Report: Hate Crime in the United States. *Center for the Study of Hate & Extremism*. San Bernardino: California State University. http://www.documentcloud.org/documents/3110202-SPECIAL-STATUS-REPORT-v5-9-16-16.html. Accessed 8 Nov 2017.

Lipton, Eric, Charlie Savage, and Michael S. Schmidt. 2016. Donald Trump's Team Shows Few Signs of Post-Election Moderation. *The New York Times*, November 18. https://www.nytimes.com/2016/11/18/us/politics/donald-trump-transition.html?r-%20ref=collection%2Fbyline%2Fcharliesavage&action=click&contentCollection=unde-%20fined®ion=stream&module=stream_unit&version=latest&contentPlacement=1&pg-%20type=collection. Accessed 17 Aug 2017.

Lisberg, Adam. 2010. Mayor Bloomberg Stands Up for Mosque. *New York Daily News*, August 3. http://www.nydailynews.com/blogs/dailypolitics/mayor-bloomberg-stands-mosque-blog-entry-1.1679892. Accessed 28 Nov 2014.

Miller, Stephen. 2006. Unpatriotic Dissent. *The Chronicle*. http://www.dukechronicle.com/article/2006/02/unpatriotic-dissent. Accessed 17 Aug 2017.

Mindock, Clark. 2017. Steve Bannon Allegedly Said He 'Believes the West Is at War with Islam'. *Independent*, February 14. http://www.independent.co.uk/news/world/americas/steve-bannon-war-islam-muslims-alt-right-donald-trump-a7580336.html. Accessed 17 Aug 2017.

O'Harrow, Robert, Jr., and Shawn Boburg. 2017. How a 'Shadow' Universe of Charities Joined with Political Warriors to Fuel Trump's Rise. *The Washington Post*, June 3. https://www.washingtonpost.com/investigations/how-a-shadow-universe-of-charities-joined-with-political-warriors-to-fueltrumps-rise/2017/06/03/ff5626ac-3a77-11e7-a058-ddbb23c75d82_story.html?utm_term=.84c316a8238d. Accessed 17 Aug 2017.

Obama, Barack. 2009a. Interview with Hisham Melhem. *Al Arabiya*, January 29. http://www.alarabiya.net/articles/2009/01/27/65087.html. Accessed 13 May 2015.

———. 2009b. *Remarks by the President on a New Beginning*. Cairo: Cairo University, June 4. https://www.whitehouse.gov/the_press_office/Remarks-by-the-President-at-Cairo-University-6-04-09. Accessed 13 May 2015.

———. 2011. *Osama Bin Laden Dead*, May 2. https://www.whitehouse.gov/blog/2011/05/02/osama-bin-laden-dead. Accessed 12 Jan 2016.

———. 2016. *Remarks by the President at the Islamic Society of Baltimore*. Baltimore. February 3. https://obamawhitehouse.archives.gov/the-press-office/2016/02/03/remarks-president-islamic-society-baltimore. Accessed 5 Nov 2017.

Patel, Faiza, and Rachel Levinson-Waldman. 2017. The Islamophobic Administration. Brennan Center for Justice, April 19. http://www.brennancenter.org/publication/islamophobic-administration. Accessed 17 Aug 2017.

Piggot, Stephen. 2016. Trump's National Security Advisor's Twitter Account Shows Extent of Anti-Muslim Beliefs. *Southern Poverty Law Center*, December 20. https://www.splcenter.org/hatewatch/2016/12/20/trumps-national-security-advisors-twitter-account-shows-extent-anti-muslim-beliefs. Accessed 17 Aug 2017.

Political Scientists' Statement on Donald Trump. https://drive.google.com/file/d/0B7l0lh4nmE3OSkpCWjJJNGVoNXc/view. Accessed 17 Aug 2017.

Pompeo, Mike. 2013. CIA Director Mike Pompeo, Speaking on H. 3258, on June 11, 2013, 113th Cong., 1st sess. Congressional Record 159.

Posner, Sarah. 2011. Welcome to the Shari'ah Conspiracy Theory Industry. ReligionDispatches.org, March 8. http://religiondispatches.org/welcome-to-the-Shariah-conspiracy-theory-industry/. Accessed 17 Aug 2017.

Radosh, Ronald. 2016. Steve Bannon, Trump's Top Guy, Told Me He Was 'a Leninist'. *Daily Beast*, August 22. http://www.thedailybeast.com/steve-bannon-trumps-top-guy-told-me-he-was-a-leninist. Accessed 17 Aug 2017.

Reilly, Steve, and Brad Heath. 2017. Steve Bannon's Own Words Show Sharp Break on Security Issues. *USA Today*, January 31. https://www.usatoday.com/story/news/2017/01/31/bannon-odds-islam-china-decades-us-foreign-policy-doctrine/97292068/. Accessed 17 Aug 2017.

Schulberg, Jessica. 2017. Trump Aide Derided Islam, Immigration and Diversity, Embraced an Anti-Semitic Past. *Huffington Post*, February 8. http://www.huffingtonpost.com/entry/michael-anton-trump-essay-publius-decius-mus_us_589ba947e4b09bd304bff3c8. Accessed 17 Aug 2017.

Shane, Scott. 2017. Stephen Bannon in 2014: We Are at War with Radical Islam. *New York Times*, February 1. https://www.nytimes.com/interactive/2017/02/01/us/stephen-bannon-war-with-radical-islam.html. Accessed 17 Aug 2017.

Shipoli, Erdoan. 2016. Making Islamophobia Great Again. *HuffPost*, November 11. http://www.huffingtonpost.com/entry/making-islamophobiagreat-again_us_57fce10de4b090dec0e71c9e. Accessed 17 Aug 2017.

Spellberg, Denise A. 2013. *Thomas Jefferson's Qur'an: Islam and the Founders*. New York: Knopf.

Stampler, Laura. 2017. Trump's Deputy Assistant, Sebastian Gorka, Has Frequently Denounced Islam. *Teen Vogue*, February 22. http://www.teenvogue.com/story/trumps-deputy-assistant-sebastian-gorka-has-frequently-denounced-islam. Accessed 17 Aug 2017.

Strauss, Daniel. 2016. Trump Defends Proposal for Muslim Ban as Call for 'Extreme Vetting'. *Politico*, October 9. http://www.politico.com/story/2016/10/2016-presidential-debate-donald-trump-muslim-ban-extreme-vetting-229468. Accessed 17 Aug 2017.

The (ADL) Anti-Defamation League. 2017. Frank Gaffney Jr. and the Center for Security Policy. https://www.adl.org/education/resources/profiles/frank-gaffney-jr-and-the-center-for-security-policy. Accessed 17 Aug 2017.

The (SPLC) Southern Poverty Law Center. 2017. https://www.splcenter.org/fighting-hate/extremist-files/group/act-america. Accessed 17 Aug 2017.

The Bridge Initiative. 2017. A New Era in American Politics: The Trump Administration and Mainstream Islamophobia, June 23. http://bridge.georgetown.edu/a-new-era-in-american-politics-the-trump-administration-and-mainstream-islamophobia/. Accessed 17 Aug 2017.

Thrush, Glenn. 2016. Obama's Obama. *Politico*, January/February. http://www.politico.com/magazine/story/2016/01/denis-mcdonough-profile-213488. Accessed 8 Aug 2017.

Trump, Donald J. 2015. *Donald J. Trump Statement on Preventing Muslim Immigration*, December 7. https://www.donaldjtrump.com/press-releases/donald-j.-trump-statement-on-preventing-muslim-immigration. Page Deleted on 9 May 2017.

———. 2016. Transcript: Donald Trump's National Security Speech. June 13. http://www.politico.com/story/2016/06/transcript-donald-trumpnational-security-speech-224373. Accessed 17 Aug 2017.

———. 2017. President Donald J. Trump Statement Regarding Recent Executive Order Concerning Extreme Vetting. January 29. https://www.whitehouse.gov/the-press-office/2017/01/29/president-donald-j-trump-statement-regarding-recent-executive-order. Accessed 17 Aug 2017.

Wang, Amy. 2017. Trump Asked for a 'Muslim Ban,' Giuliani Says – And Ordered a Commission to Do It 'Legally'. *Washington Post*, January 29. https://www.washingtonpost.com/news/the-fix/wp/2017/01/29/trump-asked-for-a-muslim-ban-giuliani-says-and-ordered-a-commission-to-do-itlegally/?utm_term=.dbf43b05604f. Accessed 17 Aug 2017.

Warrick, Joby, and Abigail Hauslohner. 2016. Trump's Security Picks Deepen Muslim Worries About an Anti-Islam White House. *The Washington Post*, November 18. https://www.washingtonpost.com/world/national-security/trumps-security-picks-deepen-muslim-worries-about-an-anti-islamicwhitehouse/2016/11/18/d7796cc6-add6-11e6-8b45-f8e493f06fcd_story.html?utm_term=.089d2f640f82. Accessed 17 Aug 2017.

Waymouth, Lally. 2013. Rare Interview with Egyptian Gen. Abdel Fatah al-Sisi. *Washington Post*, August 3. https://www.washingtonpost.com/world/middle_east/rare-interview-with-egyptian-gen-abdel-fatah-al-sissi/2013/08/03/a77eb37c-fbc4-11e2-a369-d1954abcb7e3_story.html?utm_term=.cd23387ab93b. Accessed 15 Aug 2017.

Welna, David. 2016. Trump Has Vowed to Dill Guantanamo with 'Some Bad Dudes' – But Who? *National Public Radio* (NPR), November 2016. http://www.npr.org/sections/parallels/2016/11/14/502007304/trump-has-vowed-to-fill-guantanamo-with-some-bad-dudes-but-who. Accessed 17 Aug 2017.

Wise, Lindsay. 2016. Trump CIA Pick Mike Pompeo on Torture, Muslims, Terror, Iran, NSA Spying. *McClatchy DC Bureau*, November 18. http://www.mcclatchydc.com/news/politics-government/election/article115635853.html. Accessed 17 Aug 2017.

CHAPTER 8

US Democracy Promotion

We have talked about the debates among the biggest IR theories and their effect on the US foreign policy legacy. We have given an alternative opinion on what better explains the US foreign policy toward Islam, in discourse and practice. The previous three chapters have also put this into the context of the recent US presidents' administrations, in comparison. Nevertheless, one of the most used and discussed policies among US foreign policies is democracy promotion. This work will be incomplete without a discussion on the US democracy promotion abroad to be able to complete an important part of how Islam was seen and why it was securitized. The securitization of Islam was completed during the Bush administration, but to understand why, this chapter will analyze the democracy promotion during the three recent administrations.

Democracy promotion, or what the politicians like to call the "promotion of freedom", is not a recent topic of discussion in American politics. Since the 1970s, this role of the USA and the vision of America have included the promotion of freedom, later transformed to democracy, as a duty of the USA. It was in this culture that millions of American citizens fought in Vietnam (Hunt 2009: 170) for the good of the Vietnamese people and world peace. Nevertheless, since the Cold War, this mission of the USA has been defined and conceptualized to being what is known today as democracy promotion. Exploring foreign markets and expanding American markets abroad have always been a US policy. Americans still firmly believe that domestic wellbeing

© The Author(s) 2018
E. A. Shipoli, *Islam, Securitization, and US Foreign Policy*,
https://doi.org/10.1007/978-3-319-71111-9_8

is very much related to economic expansion abroad (Cox et al. 2000). Democracy promotion was always present in the discourse of US leaders, from Theodore Roosevelt's "national mission" (Quinn 2013) to Wilson's engagements in Europe and Latin America (Thompson 2003), to Franklin D. Roosevelt's "four freedoms" (McCulloch 2004), to Jimmy Carter's "age of limits" (Dumbrell 2013). But after the Cold War it gained even more momentum, from Clinton's "democratic enlargement" (Bouchet 2013) to Obama's "stepping back" and "stepping up" (Carothers 2004). Sometimes it was present only in discourse but sometimes it was also practiced. Carter, for example, focused on an ethical foreign policy to make up the damage that was done to the prestige of the USA after Vietnam, by supporting human rights. He was also doing this in order to prevent the revolutionary acts of Nicaragua and Iran (Dumbrell 2013). George W. Bush, on the other hand, with his democratic crusade, or what he called "enforcement", made very doubtful alliances with non-democratic countries for the US interests (Lynch 2013). In general, all of American presidents are faced with challenges in pursuing a "democratic promotion" foreign policy, or an "interest promotion" foreign policy. This is what some scholars (Wolff et al. 2013; Wolff and Spanger 2013; Grimm and Leininger 2012) have called the "conflicting objectives" or the dilemma between "norms" and "interests". But, in discourse, all US leaders claim to be committed to "promotion of democracy".

8.1 Development of the Democracy Promotion Policy in the USA

Majority of American leaders, and people, believe in the special responsibility that the USA has in spreading values, that Americans call their own, that will contribute to world peace. In the mid-1980s, approximately 80% of Americans believed that the USA has a "messianic" responsibility and that the "US era" is still to come (Hunt 2009: 188–189; Kissinger 1994: 33–34; Cameron 2002: 3–6). These values include freedom, independence, democracy, market economy, and human rights, and most importantly they argue that they should be promoted by all means. Woodrow Wilson best articulated this duty in his last speech in support of the League of Nations, in Colorado on September 25, 1919:

There is one thing that the American people always rise to and extend their hand to, and that is the truth of justice and of liberty and of peace. We have accepted that truth and we are going to be led by it, and it is going to lead us, and through us the world, out in pastures of quietness and peace such as the world never dreamed of before. (Wilson 1919)

The feeling of this responsibility is not new, as other powers before such as France, Britain, or Germany have self-declared this duty as well. All great powers need great ideas. With the end of the Cold War, the USA was the sole great power and it needed a great idea, where the democracy promotion would suit best, bridging its norms at home and discourse abroad (Travis 1998: 253–254; Beinart 2008; Ikenberry 2000). Since the end of the twentieth century, democracy promotion has been the most promoted policy by the USA, and this policy is very rarely questioned, although the methods are debated. Some think that democracy promotion is the best policy, or idea, that reflects America's historical traditions (Cox et al. 2000: 5–6; Kissinger 1994; Holsti 2000), while others think that academic discussions in the USA have led the US policymakers to adopt democracy promotion as an American grand strategy (Chan 1997; Nau 2000).

The USA was mostly led by the idea of democracy promotion abroad but was reluctant at external expenditures for this cause, as it was reluctant about her image abroad. In the 1990s debates among the realists and what they called the supporters of this idea, "the idealists", became very heated with one side (the liberals) defending the "right and smart" thing to do and the other side (the realists) rejecting this "idealistic, non-realist" idea and defending the USA's focus on its self-interest (Cox et al. 2000: 5–6; Travis 1998: 253; Talbott 1996; Smith 2000b: 85). This changed after the 9/11 terrorist attacks, which heated the ongoing discussions on how much should the USA engage in the promotion of democracy abroad.

Democracy promotion is not a unified idea either; different people and different leaders understand it differently. Some support it merely because every human has some rights, others because democracies do not fight with each other, whereas many others in America look at this policy from the US national interest lens only (Talbott 1996; Cox et al. 2000: 7–8), where the USA is safer when there are more democracies in the world, and the US economy is better-off when the global markets are open. President Bush substituted American interests with "making the world a safer place for democracy" when seeking support for the war in Afghanistan and Iraq, which was the same discourse that President Wilson used when asking support to replace the system of balance of power with the community of powers and organized peace.

Democracy plays a very important role in the USA's relations with other countries, but where most other countries—democracies, semi-democracies, developing democracies, weak democracies—differ with the USA is the understanding of democracy and the democracy assistance that the USA provides (Nau 2000: 136). Ikenberry categorized US foreign policy and democracy promotion into five main strategies: democracy and peace; free trade, economic openness, and democracy; free trade, economic interdependence, and peace; institutions and the containment of conflict; and the community and identity. These goals, he argues, are not misguided idealism, they reflect pragmatism, evolvement, sophistication, in claims to create a stable and peaceful world: because first, democracies are more likely to live in peace with each other rather than make war; second, there is a correlation between democratic rule and economic prosperity; third, democracy is correlated with interdependence, which produces stability and is both economically and politically preferable; fourth, democracies respect international organizations, norms, and international rule; and finally, in terms of identity, democracy promotion is very important in creating a common identity and culture (2000: 111; 1999: 58–64).

Although what is meant by democracy promotion might change from person to person, and time to time, what most American leaders and scholars agree is that peace and democracy in the world help America feel more secure and that free trade and economic openness serve the interdependence of these countries, which paves the way for further democratization, making conflicts very costly. This interdependence leads to more peace, resulting in more security for the USA, because when the ideas of peace, interdependence, and democracy are institutionalized, then conflicts become unlikely, and even if it comes down to that it is usually contained by the developed institutions. Democratic identity and culture are also very important because such an identity will spread more democracy and cooperation, which results in America having more friends and fewer enemies to feel threatened by.

The early supporters of democracy promotion were advocating mostly on the norm that to be able to promote democracy and freedoms, the USA should master them domestically. There was a widely accepted view that the USA should master these values at home rather than intervene abroad. This changed not too late after, and the norm that the USA is acting for all of humanity began to take its place in American political debates. The main argument was that what the Americans have been blessed with may have been denied to others. In a matter of time the American politicians and scholars, the supporters of democracy promotion, began to argue that the ends justify the means (Kissinger 1994: 33–34). This was the argument that is used even today for forceful promotion of democracy and the US hostility toward other countries from time to time.

Liberals argue that the promotion of democracy is perfectly consistent with American values, Declaration of Independence, and the Bill of Rights. In the words of Jimmy Carter, "I believe that we can have a foreign policy that is democratic, that is based on fundamental values, and that uses power to influence for humane purposes. We can also have a foreign policy that the American people both support and understand" (Carter 1977). Today, neoliberals are the biggest advocates of this policy. They advocate on the idea that the enlargement of the zone of democratic countries would serve both: the peace in the world and the US national interest and national security.

But democracy promotion was developed during a long period with many debates. This policy was never, even today, supported by everyone. Critics of this policy accused the supporters on the basis of moralism, idealism, and utopianism, especially in the beginning of the twentieth century. Since the Versailles in 1919, liberals have been the targets of American failures in global affairs, by mainly realist authors such as Lippmann, Morgenthau, Niebuhr, and Kennan, from overtrusting the power of international institutions to underestimating the importance of the use of force to solve political issues (Smith 2000b: 86–88; 1994; Ruggie 1996). Many adverse events occurred after the Versailles and the League of Nations, where only Czechoslovakia emerged as what President Wilson imagined, but the depression, bolshevism, and fascism that followed made Wilson and the liberals targets of criticisms.

Critics of Wilsonian liberalism in the USA can be divided into the hardliners who think that talking about the promotion of democracy is nonsense and those, like Kissinger, who take liberalism as a serious identity of the US foreign policy, but who focus mainly on the damages that such an ideology can do to Americans and the people where America will promote democracy (Smith 2000b: 89).

Even in America, not everyone considers democracy promotion the same. Today the credit for this policy is mainly given to Woodrow Wilson, but this policy has a longer history. Wilson included it among the American war aims, in his Fourteen Points speech in April 2, 1917, when he requested the Congress to declare war against Germany (Holsti 2000: 151–152). Zionists, Armenians, Africans, South Europeans, or Irish politicians quote Wilson when they argue for the need of national self-determination, and they have criticized the USA for not extending to them this opportunity (Smith 2000b: 90). Wilson was among the first leaders to see the collapse of the Austro-Hungarian, Russian, and the Ottoman Empires, and he felt that America should do more to embrace the states that want national self-determination. He believed that democratic states, rather than sovereign states, are the building blocks of the peaceful order. He also believed that international institutions should regulate the interactions of states given the political history of the world. Wilson believed that America should be prepared for playing a leading role in this new global order, and he designed what can be called the "national security liberalism" (Smith 2000b: 93) for America. Wilson did not pass by the economic integration that the world needed for the promotion of democracy. While liberals and realists disagree on many issues after Wilson, what they agree on is that Wilson was a great American figure whose main goal was to make the world more democratic, because America is as secure as the enlargement of the democratic zone (Cox 2000: 235; Robinson 2000: 313–314). Below is a brief compilation of how Democrat and Republican presidents, the former known to be more liberal and the latter more realist, might disagree on many issues, including on how this policy should come to life, but they agree on the need to enlarge the zones of democracy.

Wilson was highly criticized after the failure of the League of Nations and the Versailles treaty, but the support for his ideas was not absent during the Cold War. Although there were clashes among conservatives and liberals on where should democracy be promoted, there was no doubt that this policy should be followed. While conservatives argued that the promotion of democracy should be limited to the countries in the Soviet bloc, liberals argued that democracy should be promoted among US allies and countries that were taking support from the USA as well (Holsti 2000: 151–152). This policy quickly became a standard in US foreign policy and a much-discussed topic in domestic politics. Later, presidents such as Reagan, Truman, Kennedy, and Clinton championed these ideas in their foreign policy. Truman called on the US Congress to "support free peoples who are resisting subjugation by armed minorities or by outside pressures" (Truman 1947), and this became later known as the Truman Doctrine; in his inaugural address Kennedy announced that the USA "shall pay any price, bear any burden, meet any hardship, support any friend, oppose any foe, in order to assure the survival and the success of liberty" (Kennedy 1961); Carter declared in Notre Dame, "I believe that we can have a foreign policy that is democratic, that is based on fundamental values, and that uses power and influence for humane purposes. We can also have a foreign policy that the American people both support and understand" (Carter 1977); Reagan called on US allies to "begin a major effort to secure the best – a crusade for freedom that will engage the faith and fortitude of the next generation. For the sake of peace and justice, let us move toward a world in which all people are at least free to determine their own destiny" (Reagan 1982); President Bush, in October 1990, addressed the UN General Assembly by saying that "calls for democracy and human rights are being reborn everywhere. And these calls are an expression of support for the values enshrined in the Charter. They encourage our hopes for a more stable, more peaceful, more prosperous world" (Bush 1990). President Clinton continued this trend by making the enlargement of democratic states the main foreign policy of his administration.

Solid realists such as Kissinger also accept the need for America to continue with the democracy promotion policy, but he notes that:

> the singularities that America has ascribed to itself throughout its history have produced two contradictory attitudes towards foreign policy. The first is that America serves its values best by perfecting democracy at home, thereby acting as a beacon for the rest of mankind; the second, that America's values impose on it an obligation to crusade for them around the world. (Kissinger 1994: 18)

8.2 Tools, Methods, Types, and Controversies of Democracy Promotion

Secretary Madeleine Albright, the first female Secretary of State to hold this position, teaches a class on America's National Security Toolbox at Georgetown University's School of Foreign Service. While she was the US Secretary of State, the wars in Yugoslavia emerged, and she had to take measures to insure American security and interests in the world. For her class at Georgetown University, her national security toolbox includes bilateral diplomacy, multilateral diplomacy, international institutions, aid, development and security, trade and foreign direct investment, sanctions, economic interdependence, coercive diplomacy, use of force, arms control, humanitarian intervention, peace operations, intelligence, covert actions, cybersecurity, counterterrorism, natural resources, and pursuit for influence in the developing world as tools for American national security.

American government uses different tools and methods to promote democracy abroad and pursue influence in the developing world. We can categorize the tools of US democracy promotion into "sticks" and "carrots" to use a very common political science and international relations comparison. First, there are the different types of aids. The USA gives different types of democracy aids, including aids for political processes, governing institutions, civil society, educational programs, and different training programs. Then there are secondary, indirect, aids such as economic or social aid programs. The USA usually uses United States Agency for International Development (USAID), National Democratic Institute (NDI), United States Information Agency (USIA), the State Department, the Department of Defense, the Department of Justice, and other non-governmental organizations that the US government funds, to deliver these aids. Working in many fronts, the USA has a great problem of strategy and identifying the ends of these aids. The USA has been behind defining the kind of democracy it is promoting and how to identify the ends. Free and fair elections, constitution, rights, and separation of power are all needed but not enough.

Aids for democracy programs fall under the "carrots" category. The US government spends over $500 million a year for democracy assistance in over 50 countries of the world. Democracy assistance, designed to solely promote democracy abroad, has been a priority in US foreign policy since the 1980s, where through government agencies, semi-governmental agencies, or non-governmental agencies, the US government sponsors a wide range of programs to stimulate and help democracy promotion in countries as different as Mongolia, Bulgaria, Afghanistan, Kosovo, Serbia, Haiti, Turkey, Guatemala, Macedonia, Egypt, Malawi (Carothers 2000: 181), and a whole range of other countries. These aids are usually distributed through governmental agencies, and governmental programs in those countries, but they are also given to non-governmental organizations who promote democracy. The biggest challenge is to ensure that this money goes to the right place and for the right cause. There are concerns that these aids are misused by local authorities, but more than that there are debates of whether supporting projects of increasing voter turnout in a country where the voting turnout is two to three times that in the USA will help that country's democracy, where people do not have jobs and where local politicians are millionaires.

Another "carrot" that the USA uses very often are the diplomatic favors, which are used by the USA as encouragements for transitional countries. High-level official contacts, official praises, state visits and state-of-the-art hosting of the new leaders, and awards at different high-level meetings are only a few diplomatic favors that the USA uses for the transitional country leaders. Invitation to the White House for the political candidates of a country is very important, which signals the US support for a particular candidate of that country, and in some countries that is the ultimate support that a candidate needs. Other "carrots" include economic rewards, as one of the most commonly used by the USA. As after the elections in Romania in 1992 (Carothers 2000: 187), so after the fall of Slobodan Milosevic, the USA has moved Romania and Serbia, respectively, in the favorable countries for investment.

As far as "sticks" are concerned, the USA is very keen in using this method too. Putting diplomatic pressure, maintaining "cold" diplomatic relations, not inviting those countries' leaders to Washington DC, and lower level of diplomatic contact, to name a few, are some of the "sticks" that the USA uses. In fact, the "sticks" are the mirror views of the "carrots" the USA uses when it wants to give a message. They include economic pressures, denying trade and commercial benefits, denying the favored nation status, working on cutting off the loans from the international financial institutions, or even imposing economic sanctions. The extreme "stick" can be considered the military intervention (Carothers 2000: 186) that the USA rarely used, but is present in the US foreign policy toolbox. In the ten-year period of the Yugoslav wars, Milosevic and his administration were advocating in large for "sticks" to be transformed into "carrots", as can be seen in many diplomatic correspondences.

These methods are all feasible in international relations and are not contrary to international law, but the USA has also been caught up in unfavorable situations multiple times. From supporting dictators in the Middle East to engineering political appointments in the Balkans, these acts have been conflicting with the US interests and values.

The main challenges that remain are the divide between the promotion of democracy as an American value versus a capitalist interest; the contradictory support of the USA for the non-democratic regimes abroad; and the type of democracy that the USA wants to promote that many today call it a "low-intensity democracy" (Gills 2000: 327). Well-known political scientist Robert Dahl claims that according to the experience and data that is present for the period of post-Second World War, the capacity of democratic countries to bring democracy in other countries will remain rather limited (Dahl 1989: 317).

The USA has been in the center of criticism of its mission to promote democracy and this has endangered what the US political elite want to secure by promoting democracy: its national security. If the USA fails to understand the limits of its power, it will get involved in a chaotic situation that it tries to avoid (Cox et al. 2000: 10–11). Many political scientists who criticize US democratic promotion in the Middle East or the Balkans do not question US democratic promotion or the need to do so; what they question are the methods and if the ends justify the means (Smith 2000a, b; Ikenberry 2009; Cox et al. 2000). The first question is, is it worthwhile? The answer to this question is that it is always worthwhile as long as US national security is not endangered more than it is now.

There are many who still doubt the wisdom under the democracy promotion as an objective (Dahl 1989; Gills 2000; Robinson 1996; Smith 2000a, b; Gramsci 1971; Ralph 2000; Carothers 1995). They point to America's historical records of conflicts between what American leadership says about democracy promotion and what they've practiced. The USA has promoted and supported political despots, both in the Middle East and Latin America, for economic interests (Smith 2000a: 65) and because of the lack of alternative powers that would ensure the US security interests in those regions (Ralph 2000: 208).

Another challenge for democracy promotion is that sometimes democracy promotion is understood as "Americanization" or "Westernization" of non-American, or non-Western, countries (Barber 1996, 2003). This makes the task even more difficult because democracy promotion is equated with only a certain way of life. The elite of many non-democratic countries usually support democracy promotion. Most of them are western educated and are the better-off of the countries where the USA wants to pursue this policy. Nevertheless, in most of these countries that elite does not encompass a majority and the priorities on the ground might be different. With the latest actions in the Middle East even the elite of the developing democracies, from the Balkans to the Arab world, have been reluctant in their open support for the democracy promotion policy of the USA, which is an important phenomenon that the US decision-makers should take into consideration.

First thing that the USA should do is to identify the democracy type it wants to promote. Democracy is a big house, with many rooms. It is important that the promoted democracy addresses the issues and concerns of the country it is to be promoted, and this can be adjusted due to the many rooms of the big house of democracy. There are two ways to promote democracy: either the "bottom-up", stressing on the importance and aiding the civil society, political participation, and education on democracy; or the "top-down", stressing on the political aid, targeting the electoral system, political parties, constitution, and judicial reform (Carothers 2004). The type of democracy promotion that is pursued should address the issues that the hosting country is struggling with the most. Promoting democracy only because of the democratic peace might look good in theory but in practice one needs to make sure that the peace persists in the future (Ralph 2000: 217).

The USA has pushed for the liberal market democracy model, focusing on the limited role of the state in economy, open to international exchange, and driven by market principles. Although not openly stated, the standards required for loans by international institutions are designed to strongly favor this model. The election model, where fair and free elections are fostered, is another model that the USA has pursued, but it was soon understood that free and fair elections are not enough for the development of democracy. Nevertheless, although difficult to practice and install, the strong/responsive state model, which works for an accountable state model, is the most stable and promising democracy model (Sorensen 2000: 297–301; Zakaria 1997; Huntington 1992; Kaplan 2003; Lipset 1996; Barber 2003; Diamond 1995; Carothers 2003, 2004). Not everyone agrees that these are the only models that the USA focuses on. Many associate US democracy promotion with promotion of polyarchy, considering it as a fundamental step toward democracy. Polyarchy is a state system where a group of competing elites govern and where mass participation in decision-making elects the leaders among these elite (Dahl 1971). This definition is developed in the post-Second World War America, as "another theory of democracy" where power (cratos) and the people (demos) are redefined (Schumpeter 1942). There is a considerable literature written on this system by scholars in the USA, especially in constructing the democracy to be promoted in Latin America, under the concepts of "democratization", "transition to democracy", "consolidating democracy", or alike (Robinson 2000: 310) that today is very much present in the literature of democracy not limited to Latin America.

The promotion of free market and polyarchic democracy complement each other. Opening the markets to the world for financial and capital investment opportunities has always been a foreign policy priority of the capitalist countries to widen international markets and serve their business elite (Robinson 2000: 313). Woodrow Wilson saw this as an important policy, claiming "Concessions obtained by financiers must be safeguarded by ministers of state, even if the sovereignty of unwilling nations be outraged in the process. Colonies must be obtained or planted, in order that no useful corner of the world may be overlooked or left unused" (delivered in a speech at Columbia University in 1907, as quoted in Parenti 1995: 40; Williams 1972: 72). This mentality has led the USA to push for privatization of businesses and media, equating democracy with capitalism as undivided pair of two (Carothers 1995: 23; Smith 2000a: 68).

Another very much used phrase for the democracy type that the USA promotes abroad is "low-intensity democracy". It focuses on a checklist of the USA prepared democracy instead of a broader political participation and stronger civil society. The lack of focus on social and economic problems that the country faces is one of the features of the low-intensity democracy. This type of democracy best serves the US economic interests, where the government and state have minimal, if any, control over the state's economy (Gills and Rocamora 1992; Robinson 1996; Smith 2000a, b). To quote Robinson:

> The impulse to "promote democracy" is the rearrangement of political systems in the peripheral and semi-peripheral zones of the "world system" so as to secure the underlying objective of maintaining essentially undemocratic societies inserted into an unjust international system. ... Just as "client regimes" and right-wing dictatorships installed into power or supported by the United States were characteristic of a whole era of US foreign policy and intervention abroad in the post-World War II period, promoting "low-intensity democracies" in the Third World is emerging as a cornerstone of a new era in US foreign policy. (Robinson 1996: 6)

For Gramsci, this is a promotion of hegemony where the hegemon wants other classes to internalize their logic and their worldview, usually through pressure by the dominant fundamental groups toward the civil society (Gramsci 1971: 21). These authors have been criticizing US democracy promotion, arguing that it has become less of a goal of foreign policy and more of a tool for economic hegemony. Although one might not agree with all these criticisms, it is obvious that the US decision-makers should seriously give more attention to these criticisms.

There must be a reason why democracy promotion has not been as successful as expected, taking into consideration that it has been a priority in American foreign policy. The number of functioning democracies that have come as a result of US engagement is limited, and in some instances the conditions got even worse, like in the Middle East. The USA needs a thorough analysis and creative thinking to regain ground on this important issue for the US foreign policy (Carothers 2003; Kaplan 2003; Barber 2003). Although there are many suggestions, it is only common sense that the USA needs to put more importance on building bridges between democratization struggles, political solidarity, and the present resistances—national, local, regional, and global—despite the globalization of economic power (Gills 2000: 342). It is similarly important that the USA understands the important divide between "democratization" and "spread of democracy" and then to support the democratic parties to determine their own political future, as Wilson suggested, democratic government is built on strong foundations of national self-determination (Slaughter 2009: 97). Nevertheless, the key point is that Washington DC needs to understand its boundaries and limits, the limits of the democracy promotion ideology that liberal agenda is not the prior policy of other countries (Smith 2000b: 88; Ruggie 1996) and that liberalism is neither a monolithic system nor the only serious option in the table of other countries. American leaders should be more realistic and acknowledge the limits of democracy promotion, the skepticisms that others have, and also their history in order to continue with their idea, updated and improved. According to Danish political scientist Georg Sorensen, the west and especially the USA should not escape the legitimate criticism and should think over them. He argues that there are at least three important and legitimate criticisms that can be made for US democracy promotion in Africa: the failure to appreciate nationalism and political community; too much faith in economy and political liberalism; and the support for the elite domination (Sorensen 2000). The most important lesson is that democracy needs a local support and the USA cannot impose it (Smith 2000b: 101; 75–76). The USA should work with the locals to firmly root the democratic values and adjust a unique democracy in the countries in which it wants to promote democracy and adjust it to the culture, history, traditions, and also address the issues that the local people have.

Every democracy must be culturally, ethnically, and historically specific to every country, instead of a one-size-fits-all democracy, failing to recognize the role of cultures and traditions (Smith 2000b: 67–69).

Democracy and the system of governance in general are like a song. When it is translated into different languages and cultures it loses most of its meaning, effect, and message. American democracy promotion is committed to promote a one-way, single-type, American democracy that worked in the USA and cannot be translated in another system (Carothers 2000: 194). A very common argument in academia is that the spread of liberty is not enough. Usually economic problems, booming population rise, and other issues have left many countries behind and unable to provide services to people, such as education and healthcare, which let radical ideological or religious groups gain prestige by providing educational, economic, or healthcare services (Beinart 2008: 192).

For the USA to continue with its democracy promotion policy it needs public support, to be able to dedicate funds, labor, and become more engaged. This can only be achieved if the national interests are put forward, and the USA has done well so far in bringing on board the general US public, but has done a lesser job in getting the support of the public abroad. The USA has shown that it can support non-democratic regimes when it is in the national interest of the USA, and this has affected in the lack of support abroad. Anthony Lake and Strobe Talbott have both defended the thesis that the support for democracy abroad needs to be balanced against other strategic interests, to ensure the national interest of the USA, and sometimes this can mean that support for democracy is not the ultimate goal (Talbott 1996: 52), as in Clinton's own words "make trade a priority element of American security" (Clinton 1993). The USA is more interested in maintaining the global hegemony than in the promotion of democracy per se (Sanger 1997), so it can control foreign markets and impose US national interest. In other words, the US policy of promotion of democracy abroad is part of a larger liberal grand strategy for a stable, legitimate, and secure international order, which will ensure and serve American interests and most importantly American national security.

8.3 Democracy Promotion for Post-Cold War America: Clinton's Balkans and Bush's Middle East

The US democracy promotion, reasons, methods, and many other aspects can lead to unlimited discussions; nevertheless, the US decision-makers believe in the promotion of democracy as means of its national security. Sometimes it is framed as the promotion of American values, as a moralist and idealist act, but it is always the national security that lies in its core. Even the debates where the democracy promotion is discussed as an American value, it is the national security that is given reference to. Clinton and his administration liked to view this as "two sides of the same coin", which was necessary if America wanted to compete economically, and if it wished to promote a stable international system (Clinton 1991), taking into consideration that Clinton, as most American presidents, considered a stable international system as an important element to American national security. What the USA has achieved, especially by using academics such as Huntington, is to set democracy as the golden standard, as the norm of the international system (Fukuyama 1992: 39–51; Cox 2000: 226). In short, the USA understands that it is better-off to pursue its interest and secure the national wellbeing when other states are democracies than non-democracies, and this is the real driving force for the US foreign policy in the post-Cold War America (Ikenberry 2000: 103–104). US decision-makers also acknowledge that diplomacy without power usually fails, whereas power without diplomacy is dangerous, and thus for America there is no substitute for power (Cox 2000: 230) or diplomacy. Nevertheless, what has been learned from many lessons, especially at the beginning of this century, is that another force that is added to power and diplomacy is the public support, which is the ultimate ingredient that should be taken in consideration for American grand strategy.

With the end of the Cold War we see a change in the US discourse where "Democracy Promotion" is more directly addressed instead of the "National Security" discourse that was more present during the Cold War, meaning the same thing (Ralph 2000: 205). This change of discourse is a result of the association of American national security with the American quest for democracy promotion. Considering the results of the Cold War it is easy for the supporters of the democracy promotion to argue that democracy promotion is what brought America as the sole superpower out of the Cold War. The change of this discourse is what this work is interested in, because this discourse has brought democracy promotion to the level of national security.

Nowhere is this shift better seen than in American foreign policy toward the Balkans and the Middle East after the Cold War. These are very different regions that were handled differently, but they are the regions that the USA got mostly involved with after the Cold War. It is also important to note that both of these regions have Muslim populations. Balkan population is not Muslim-majority as a whole, but the countries the USA has intervened have Muslim-majority populations, and the USA has intervened to help them. After the Cold War the USA aimed at the re-unification of these small, divided countries into unions, where economic and social prosperity is more likely and thus the democracy promotion is easier (Fouskas 2003: 95). One of the main limits of the US policy might be the decline of nation-states and the question is if there can be a promotion of democracy where there is a decline of nation-state (Guehenno 1995: 17). The rise of the "McWorld" and the "Jihad World", over the nation-states, is an important point that signals the challenge of the nation-states.

By the end of the Cold War and the 1990s there was a considerably high focus on the enlargement of the democratic zones. Clinton administration made this a primary foreign policy goal throughout its two terms. Although at the beginning it was more about the promotion of the US economic interests rather than democracy (Smith 2000a: 64–67), later, especially in his second term, economic promotion became another tool of the greater vision of democracy promotion in general. Clinton's presidency is important in many aspects. Being the first president elected after the Cold War, his presidential focus at the beginning was more on domestic affairs rather than international affairs. He needed to solidify his base at home and therefore he vowed to focus on the main issue that brought him to the White House: economy. The fact that the voters did not let George H. W. Bush to continue for the second term was perceived as a sign that Americans want someone who will deal with domestic issues rather than be preoccupied with global issues like Bush did. Thus, at the beginning of his presidency Clinton's engagement with global affairs was minimalist and even those engagements that were present were being handled with extra caution (Cox 1995; Brinkley 1997). Nevertheless, the situations in which the world was going through in the 1990s could not be ignored and the Clinton administration needed to show American leadership in world affairs while also maintaining low-profile rhetoric. Alternative to phrases such as "clash of civilizations" and the possible negative foreign policy news that the administration was keen to stay away from, the Clinton administration decided on the doctrine of "democratic enlargement", which had a considerable positive sound and meaning (Cox 1995, 2000; Brinkley 1997; Jones 1995). It is considered that this discourse started in autumn 1993 and it soon became widely used in the speeches of President Clinton, Secretary Christopher, National Security Advisor Lake, Secretary Albright, and other officials (Cox 2000: 224). Clinton is considered a master of transition from one policy to another, according to the need of the times and the American public. At the beginning of the Yugoslav wars, Clinton promoted territorial integrity of Yugoslavia and non-involvement in its affairs; nevertheless in a couple of years he became the leading figure of change in that territory and a hope for the people of Bosnia and Kosovo.

This shift from a realist policy was, as expected, very much argued and criticized by Clinton's opponents and questioned by friends. The argument that the US security can be affected by other countries' government type was new and unrealistic to post-Cold War Americans (Layne and Lynn-Jones, 1998). The administration answered these doubts by claiming that enlargement of the democratic zones contributed to global security and global stability, especially in the second and third world countries that are transforming from communism to liberalism (Carothers 1997). In a significant speech before reelection, Clinton claimed that democracies do not support or sponsor terrorist acts; they are reliable trading partners; they abide international law; they protect the environment; and the USA must support them because the USA cannot be indifferent about how others governed their countries because ultimately wars were caused by dictators, and democracies do not go to war with each other, which was the closest we'll ever get to a political science empirical truth (Clinton 1991). These were the fundamentals of the Wilsonian ideology and they became the road map of Clinton's democracy promotion arguments in pursuing this strategy and conducting his foreign policy.

Bill Clinton never accepted to be a crusader for democracy. In fact, he very wisely mounted the democracy enlargement policy into a broader American grand foreign policy strategy and even larger into the American democratic tradition. This was a policy that Clinton was very careful with as to not oversell it. In his election rallies in 1992 he accused Bush of poor democratic promotion record and lack of support for the American liberal values. Nevertheless, while accusing Bush for the poor democracy promotion record, Clinton always added that he was not advocating for isolating China, or cutting the relations with the non-democratic countries, but he was advocating for American values on the basis of common sense, as after all there are some countries and cultures who have a long way to go to democracy (Clinton 1992). When in the White House, Clinton did not refrain in praising the ideals of the followers of the great American values, and among others he often paid homage to Wilson, Truman, Kennedy, and others who were very committed to democracy promotion, but who also were masters on the balance of power with Soviet Union. As Clinton's aide, Anthony Lake, later argued, the Clinton administration was building its legacy upon Wilson's, but the real inspiration came from the post-1945 period, constructing a stable world between the conservative realist and liberal Wilsonian, but it was not being either as naïve as Wilsonian or as realist as conservatives (Lake 1994). In this fashion Clinton continued his struggle for democracy promotion and the belief for democracy promotion in the Clinton administration can be summarized in Secretary Albright's words, "It is not only the right thing to do, it is the smart thing to do", on the occasion of President Clinton's trip to Africa to promote trade, human rights, and democracy on March 23, 1998, and reinforced her view on the keynote address to the National Summit on Africa in February 2000 (Albright 2000). The Clinton administration argued on the basis of "right" and "wrong" about the support for other countries and democracy promotion, instead of an American ideal that needed to be crusaded for. This led to a milder reaction by other countries and to a wider acceptance instead of imposition.

The best example that the US foreign policy of democracy promotion is a long-standing policy that has been followed by nearly all the US administrations in the White House is George W. Bush administration. While expecting to be more realist, opposite of the Clinton administration, during the years of George W. Bush the proactive democracy promotion policy was a priority like never before. President Bush campaigned on the idea of less engagement on the world affairs, more focus on domestic politics, and opposition to Clintonian foreign policy. Nevertheless, Bush got engaged in countries that Clinton was avoiding and put the global leadership in his priorities list. Different from Clinton, Bush supported the idea that this policy should be pursued by any means, including force. A new national security doctrine started to be articulated where Americans would start to know more about the "coalitions of the willing", the "struggle between liberty and evil", the "preventive use of force", or the "American global dominance". After the 2003 invasion of Iraq, Bush very commonly used liberals' ideas to justify his actions, as he proclaimed in his second inaugural address, "We are led, by events and common sense, to one conclusion: the survival of liberty in our land increasingly depends on the success of liberty in other lands" (Bush 2005a). Bush certainly wanted to take his part in history, besides Wilson, Truman, and Kennedy, as a president that advanced the cause of freedom and democracy in the world.

Bush did take a remarkable place in the American political history—a conservative president, who campaigned for office on the grounds of a return to realist foreign policy, but who made a U-turn into the liberal internationalist ideas to justify his very expensive foreign policy full of controversial wars and foreign policy acts (Ikenberry 2009: 5). Doubtfully, this was how President Bush wanted to leave a remark in US history, but it surely showed how democracy promotion is a policy that sees no difference between the two camps in US foreign policy, and it becomes a priority even though it might be highly opposed at the beginning.

The promotion of democracy in the Balkans was a long policy of the USA. It saw the Balkans as the divide between the communist Russia and the liberal Europe, so in no way could the USA remain neutral over the region.

Democracy promotion was more natural in Eastern Europe than it is today in the Middle East or than it was in Central Asia and Latin America. Starting from the 1990s political pluralism, rule of law, and civil society started promoting democracy on their own, but with the help of European Union and America it developed much faster.

America and Europe have been involved in the Balkans since the beginning of the 1990s. The establishment of "presence" of the Organization for Security and Co-operation in Europe (OSCE) and NATO forces in Bosnia, Albania, Macedonia, and Kosovo was only the security and military engagement of the western powers, mostly led by the USA; but, in fact many governmental and non-governmental, civilian-led efforts were involved too, to assist, promote, and consolidate democracy and democratic institutions. One of the main focuses was the civil society (Brown 2009). As for the US involvement in the 1990s, it was very clear that America will be very much involved in the region. From January 1991 to June 1991, US Secretary of State James Baker and his Ambassador in Yugoslavia, Warren Zimmermann, brought up the issue of democracy whenever they met with Yugoslav leaders. What they pointed out many times was that they support both democracy and unity of Yugoslavia; nevertheless they would prefer democracy if they had to make a choice (Woodward 2007). That is when the dissolution started, Slovenia got her independence, and now is a full member of the EU; Croatia followed and lately became a member of the EU, with Macedonia, Montenegro, Serbia, Bosnia and Herzegovina, and Kosovo as prospective candidates to the EU.

Nevertheless, the most discussed region that the USA is engaged in is without doubt the Middle East. With all that has happened in the twenty-first century, the Middle East is a priority, but at the same time it has been a headache for the US foreign policy. America's engagement in the Middle East or the Balkans was not something new; the relations that have gone up and down are as old as history itself. The USA has tried to include both the Middle East and the Balkans in the democratization process ever since it became a priority in US foreign policy and security. Although the post-9/11 era gained momentum in US engagement in the Middle East and stopped the ups and downs in their relations substituting them with downs only, during the Cold War the USA had a relatively balanced relationship with the Middle East, as can be understood from both the Eisenhower Doctrine (1957) and the Carter/Reagan Doctrine (the late 1970s to the 1980s). These relations were based on the principles of securing the survival of Israel; keeping away the USSR influence on the Arab states by accommodating divergence of Arab interests; elimination of the different views of the NATO members toward the Middle East; and also preventing the Arab states from using the "oil weapon" and blackmailing the economy of the western countries (Fouskas 2003: 69). These policies have served their purpose and they've prevented escalation of US relations with the region.

Democracy promotion has become a multi-million-dollar industry, involving governments, contractors, non-governmental organizations, advocates, lobbyists, service providers, and professionals from all around the world. USAID-like organizations had a big place in this industry (Brown 2009). The formal US organizations that provide aid in the Balkans and the Middle East range from government to semi-government institutions and civil society organizations. The United States Agency for International Development (USAID) is on the top of the list, having the widest scope of activities and, especially, promoting democracy in every country of these two regions. USAID is followed by the Bureau for Democracy, Human Rights, and Labor (DRL), which is an initiative of the Department of State supporting elections, civil society, human rights, rule of law, and media, among others. Programs they have supported range from helping to establish and fund civil society and non-governmental organizations; training and providing for the electoral processes; trainings on the role of government; international leadership programs for students; providing speaker series on different topics such as free media or good governance; training for media; training against corruption (DRL 2010a, b, c); and other smaller, more specific initiatives, such as South East European Youth Leadership Initiative (SEEYLI) or the Middle East Partnership Initiative (MEPI), and many other initiatives, which are programs of the US State Department specific to development of youth leaders and democracy promotion in

South Eastern Europe (SEE) and the Middle East and North Africa (MENA). They focus on leadership capacity building, political and economic reform, transparency, awareness, and participation. The work they have done so far includes programs on funding businesswomen organizations, anti-corruption organizations, campaigns on the awareness of rule of law, media outlets, and online activism. They have funded and implemented trainings on banking, anti-corruption, media, and rule of law as well.

The story of the US democratic promotion in the Balkans and Eastern Europe in general has been told by different authors (Smith 1994; Creed and Wedel 2000; Carothers 1999, 2004; Guilhot 2005; Traub 2008), but there is more space to talk about, because it is far underwritten in comparison to the democracy promotion in the Middle East, Western Europe, or Latin America.

Looking at it from the perspective of the American grand vision of democracy promotion and the idea of enlarging the zone of democracies to ensure that the USA has less threats, as democracies do not fight with each other, H. W. Bush and Clinton administrations have worked hard on the expansion of the zone of democracies, and in the 1990s they placed this foreign policy high in their agendas, signaling that this will be the agenda of the US post-Cold War era. In fact, during the time of both presidents the number of democratic states increased, from the ex-Soviet Union to South Eastern Europe, but they were all the results of local efforts, and the USA played a role in promoting or helping those efforts to prevail (Holsti 2006: 12). As part of H. W. Bush and Clinton's policy toward the Eastern European and Soviet countries' transition away from communism, American democracy aid expended very rapidly. Since 1989 the USA has provided vast amounts of democracy aid to Eastern European countries as part of the Eastern European Democracy Act of 1989 and to the former Soviet Union countries as part of the Freedom Support Act of 1991 for the election programs, parties, rule of law, and civil society programs (Carothers 2000: 185). These were fundamental elements for the American win of the Cold War and the spread of "market democracy" from Belgrade to Bishkek (Rutland 2000: 243). President George H. W. Bush called for the promotion of democratic governments in the whole of Eastern Europe, by promoting freedoms and institutions, respect for minority rights, and civilian control of the military. The Clinton administration advocated for the idea that failure to promote these values would result in exclusion of these developing democracies from international economic organizations and liberal regimes such as the European Union or North Atlantic Treaty Organization (Smith 2000b: 95). Positive compliance with this agenda, on the other hand, resulted in the inclusion of Poland, Czech Republic, and Hungary into the North American Treaty Organization during his administration, as part of a collective security regime, a dream come true for the Wilsonian ideals of pre-First World War era. At her Wilsonian best, Czech descent Secretary Madeleine Albright stated that:

> American security and prosperity are linked to economic and political health abroad ... we must take advantage of the historic opportunity that now exists to bring the world together in an international system based on democracy, open markets, law and a commitment to peace. Today the greatest danger to America is not some foreign enemy; it is the possibility that we will fail to heed the example of [the postwar] generation; that we will allow the momentum toward democracy to stall, take for granted the institutions and principles upon which our own freedom is based, and forget what the history of this century reminds us: that problems, if left unattended, will all to often come home to America. A decade or two from now, we will be known as the neo-isolationists, who allowed tyranny and lawlessness to rise again, or as the generation that solidified the global triumph of democratic principles. (Albright 1997)

The US engagement in the Yugoslav wars is very important for a number of reasons. First, it was a last touch in defeating Soviet communism; second, the revival of the Wilsonian ideas of international organizations and their roles; and third, promotion of democracy and transformation of the South Eastern European countries to democracy. But, most importantly for America it was a lesson that the USA cannot go alone and it needs both European and Russian support to establish hegemony in Eurasia and enlarge the democratic territory (Nye 2002). This pattern is vivid in comparing Kosovo and Bosnia. While the USA was more reluctant in Bosnia and did not take the lead, Bosnia remained in the hands of European powers, who divided Bosnia to be able to manage it, while making it a non-functioning federation of different cantons. Seeing these mistakes, the USA wanted a chair at the table together with France, Britain, Germany, and Italy. Kosovo's territory was divided into five, among the abovementioned, for the location of their troops and basis. In rebuilding of Kosovo, the USA worked closely with Turkey, due to closer cultural ties between Turks and Albanians, to be able to understand the needs and the expectations of the Kosovars. As a result, Kosovo is one country and has a functional government, although with many problems. Fourth, the USA found a good chance to position itself in the center of the Eurasian conflict zones, to enlarge the democratic territory.

In the Balkans Kosovo plays a central role in explaining democracy promotion and US engagement. First, unlike in Bosnia, in Kosovo America was fully aware and clear that it will intervene, and this time it intervened on time. Being late in Bosnia has led to many complications and unwanted results. Second, the Kosovo intervention was the first full-scale intervention in the name of NATO as a transatlantic organization. Bosnian intervention was very limited and much smaller in scale, limited to the targets in Bosnia, whereas for the Kosovo intervention the time frame was much longer and the whole Federation of Yugoslavia was included in the airstrikes. Finally, the USA considers Kosovo to be a success story. Although Bosnia was a success story too, the belated intervention raised some doubts. This is important to keep in mind when comparing the US intervention in the Balkans with that of the Middle East, which can be argued to be an American (un)success story.

The W. Bush administration made it clear from the election campaigns that the US focus would be more on uncompromising military power instead of the foreign policy developed under Clinton, to which they referred to as "international social work" (Mandelbaum 1996). They have suggested that the US forces would be withdrawn from both Bosnia and Kosovo, as the US military would no longer be used to "escort girls to school". These were times that the promotion of democracy abroad was at the bottom of foreign policy polls (Holsti 2006: 12–13), but what was meant is not that the USA would not "promote" democracy abroad; rather it was a "promotion by hard power" instead of "soft power". Talking on democracy promotion, the Bush administration claimed that they believed that democracies do not fight each other and that the authoritarian regimes bread radical extremism (Baker 2001), so this is why democracy promotion should be pursued at any cost. Furthermore, they claimed that the USA should play a pivotal role in aiding these countries transform to democracy. These claims were based on data such as the Pittsburgh University's findings that "US democracy aid was the only statistically significant factor affecting the pace and success of democratic development" in the period of 1990–2003 (Finkel et al. 2008: Calabresi 2011).

The US foreign policy toward the Middle East changed considerably after 9/11. The USA engaged more but this time it backfired and the American people were caught outside of what they have been told they would. They have been under extensive media and political propaganda that engaging in the Middle East will bring more stability, security, and fewer threats to the USA, whereas it has brought less stability and security and more threats.

Although the USA has woken up with the 9/11 attacks, there have been a considerable high number terrorist attacks targeting US citizens and property before 9/11. In Saudi Arabia, one of the most reliable allies of the USA, there have been two bombings, in 1995 and 1996; in the US embassies in Tanzania and Kenya in 1998; and the bombing of the USS Cole navy ship in 2000 (USDS 2003). A State Department annual report "Patterns of Global Terrorism 2000" pointed out that the vast number of terrorist acts against America has taken place in foreign lands and around 47% of worldwide terrorist attacks were committed against or were targeting American citizens or American property. The same report pointed out that the casualties of terrorism have increased from 233 in 1999 to 405 dead in 2000 (USDS 2001). Traditionally, the USA has approached the combat against terrorists based on the "Antiterrorism and Effective Death Penalty Act": bringing terrorists to justice for the crimes they have committed; pressure on the states that sponsor terrorism; no deals with and no concessions to terrorists; and assist allies as well as seek support from them, to fight terrorism (Cameron 2002: 141). The terrorist acts have had many implications both in US foreign policy and in domestic policy. Internationally, President Bush argued that "as long as the Middle East remains a place where freedom does not flourish, it will remain a place of stagnation, resentment, and violence ready for export" (Bush 2003), signaling his future policies on democracy promotion in the Middle East as a tool to fight terrorism, as stated in his State of the Union Address in 2005 "the best antidote to radicalism and terror is the tolerance and hope kindled in free societies" (2005b).

What was the response to the 9/11 attacks? This response was felt in all the spheres of life in America, and abroad, including changes in the State, Judiciary, Treasury, and Commerce departments. Changes have happened in homeland security, law enforcement agencies, foreign and security policies, expenditures, and alike. President Bush established a new cabinet-level post for Homeland Defense, to coordinate the war on terror and all of the changes that have happened as a response to 9/11. The Congress passed the USA Patriot Act in 2001, giving new powers to the government that have never been given before, to deal with the terrorist threats, including wiretapping, seizing telephone, email, medical, banking, educational and business records, as well as searching the homes of the suspects, and the establishment of military courts to try foreign residents in the USA for terrorist acts (Cameron 2002: 145–146). Interestingly both Democrats and Republicans backed the Bush administration alike and they considered the USA to be at war (Beinart 2008: 172). Bush used anything, and anyone, to push his agenda in what followed 9/11, including legal reforms and the invasion of Afghanistan and Iraq.

President Bush and his administration repeatedly worked on the thesis that the national security of the USA depends on the spread of democracy in the Middle East, and this in fact makes the Iraqi invasion a product of this propaganda, asserting that it is the American interests that have been served by this war (Smith 2009: 53). The Tampico incident of Wilson was compared to the Iraqi invasion of 2003 by Bush, and the invasion of Iraq has been legitimized accordingly. Nevertheless, there are many differences, as there are similarities between the two, but the most important one is the force used in Iraq and the bloodshed, which was not the same thing in Mexico, although Wilson claimed that his job in Mexico was "to teach the South American Republics to elect good men" too (Knock 2009: 34–35; Ikenberry 2009: 14).

It is true that the Balkans, specifically Bosnia and Kosovo, have not transformed into full democracies. There is still a very long road to go, and the conflicts have not been halted altogether. Corruption, lack of efficiency, and high crime rates are all things to worry about when looking at democracy in the Eastern Europe in general and South Eastern Europe in particular. There is something that is not working when it comes to improving the life of the people in the Balkans. The development professionals, western states, foundations, banks, and agencies failed to carry out an effective economic development program. The biggest problem is that these institutions still do not accept that they failed and that they do not know how to improve this. The money invested in the Balkans comes from thousands of miles away from where it is spent (Brown 2009); there is no strict transparency; and because it has become an industry, the same people or institutions have been involved. The worst is that those few organizations that have been involved and had a certain degree of success are sometimes blinded with the messianic complex of "we know it all" (Paddock and Paddock 1973: 299–300). But, at least the situation has improved, there are no active wars at the moment, democratic institutions are being built, and the region is far more stable than in the Middle East, especially in Afghanistan and Iraq, where America intervened.

Before identifying the main differences between the Balkans and Middle East, we must recognize that the biggest advantage of democracy promotion in Balkans was that the policy goals were very clear: first, the goal was to have leaders that are as moderate as possible, in terms of nationalism; second, all the policies that were followed by the government should be Euro-Atlantic oriented; and third, minorities should be protected and positively identified while also promoting multiculturalism (Woodward 2007). But, one cannot claim that these have been easy and reachable goals so far. Ultranationalist-leaning politicians from the Macedonian side have governed Macedonia for many years, and they have been creating a coalition with ultranationalist Albanians. In Serbia, Tadic lost the elections to ultranationalists Vucic and Nikolic. In Bosnia, Dodik has remained the most important actor for many years. Kosovo has been quite another story. No Albanian party has had nationalist discourse, whereas Turkish and Serbian parties have applied their own, but they are in the minority. Only recently, in June 11, 2017 elections, the nationalist "self-determination movement" gained considerably more votes to become the second political force in the country, without any pre-election coalition agreement as other parties had. An important factor for this is the high presence of European and American influence in politics, such as the appointment of the Kosovo president, Atifete Jahjaga, by the US ambassador.[1] This has been a very controversial move, but the US administration, by their ambassador, showed a top-down approach when it came to promoting democracy, that according to the then Ambassador Christopher Dell,[2] she is a moderate (non-practicing) Muslim woman, bound to democratic values and US interests, which can serve as an example of how "democratic" leaders should be.

[1] What is called "the election by envelope", this scandal brought to the Kosovo presidency a policewoman that has never been in Kosovo politics. The US Ambassador to Kosovo, Christopher Dell, mediated this decision between the major parties in Kosovo, which brought up a lot of controversies. For more see http://www.economist.com/blogs/easternapproaches/2011/04/kosovos_new_president and http://www.dw.com/en/kosovo-elects-female-police-chief-as-new-president/a-14974933 and http://www.b92.net/eng/news/politics.php?yyyy=2011&mm=04&dd=08&nav_id=73689.

[2] After his term finished as the US Ambassador to Kosovo, Christopher Dell started working for Bechtel, a construction firm who took the bid for the building of the Tirana-Prishtina highway, the most expensive bid/investment in Kosovo so far. This has caused many controversies. For more see http://www.theguardian.com/world/2014/apr/14/us-ambassador-kosovo-construction-contract-firm-highway and http://foreignpolicy.com/2015/01/30/steamrolled-investigation-bechtel-highway-business-kosovo/.

There are many similarities and many differences between US engagement and democracy promotion in the Balkans and the Middle East. But we believe that the most important differences include unilateral versus multilateral intervention; invasion versus liberation and rebuilding; and the result: a view toward America and terrorism.

International intervention has been the prime target of the critics of US involvement in the Balkans and the Middle East. After the military intervention in Bosnia and Herzegovina, the international community has been accused by academics of "faking democracy", failing to bring justice, and setting up a "European Raj" (Chandler 2000; Knaus and Martin 2003). One of the most voiced critiques is that the top-down political engineering has only helped the nationalist fractions in the Balkans, who appeal only to ethnic votes, while in ex-Yugoslavian republics the superpower has been centered in the international community-appointed Higher Representatives (Brown 2009; Smillie and Todorovic 2001; Sali-Terzić 2001).

The main difference of US actions between the two regions is that in the Balkans the USA acted together with other powers, even trying to bring Russia on board as much as possible, whereas in the Middle East the USA decided to go unilaterally, not being able to convince even the closest US allies. We discussed this topic in the previous chapters. America's campaign in the Middle East lacked a very important Wilsonian element and in fact went against it: multilateralism (Slaughter 2009: 109). Going without the UN or Security Council consent is not new for the USA, as it happened in Kosovo as well, but unlike in Kosovo where NATO and its members gave support, in Iraq the USA had minimal support. It is very important to note that the original Wilsonian vision included multilateralism and the belief in international organizations, whereas Bush openly defamed the UN and other international organizations for not being able to make any decisions and openly declared that the USA will not wait for anyone to take action, but when the USA does, one is either "with us" or "against us".

American engagement and diplomacy in NATO resulted in the first large-scale operation under NATO command. This intervention was also the last among the wars in the ex-Yugoslavia. After the war in Kosovo there were some smaller ethnic conflicts in Southern Serbia and Macedonia that luckily did not escalate to full-scale wars. Precautions taken beforehand helped to maintain these conflicts while they were in the initial state of armed struggles. The intervention in Kosovo has a history and a background. The breakout of the war in Yugoslavia with the succession of Slovenia brought the Balkan region once again to the focus of US foreign policy. Followed by Croatia, Yugoslavia became the main point of focus for American foreign policy in the late 1980s' protests and conflicts erupted in Yugoslavia. While the West was negotiating with Milosevic in Dayton, Ohio, the pacifist Albanian leadership was hoping to be included in the negotiations. Serbia would not approach any deal that included Kosovo, and the exclusion of Kosovo from the Dayton Agreement angered, divided, and frightened the Kosovar Albanians, who pushed them to get organized and start fighting (Clark 2001; Shipoli 2010). Not being included in the Dayton negotiations was a push for Kosovar Albanian fighters to take up arms. Kosovo was not absented from the focus of the west, who were following the situation very closely and issuing statements from time to time.

Going a little away from the Dayton Agreement, the most important statement by US officials was the so-called Christmas warning, uttered by President H. W. Bush in 1992, stating, "in the event of conflict in Kosovo caused by Serbian action, the United States will be prepared to employ military force against Serbians in Kosovo and Serbia proper" (as quoted in NYT 1999; Clark 2001: 108; Coll 2004: 131). The main accelerator of the US and NATO engagement in Kosovo was the massacre of Srebrenica, which illustrated what the west did not want to see again in the headlines (Shipoli 2010; Clark 2001). Mistakes and lack of swift engagement in Rwanda, Somalia, and Bosnia led to unforgettable genocide, which put pressure to act faster in Kosovo, as stated by President Clinton in 1998: "we did not act quickly enough after the killing began. We did not immediately call these crimes by their rightful names: genocide" (Clinton 1998). This explains a lot about why the US and NATO engagement in Kosovo acted faster than what many expected.

America advocated for NATO's enlargement and just before the Kosovo campaign in 1999, NATO included three important Eastern European countries under its umbrella: Poland, Czech Republic, and Hungary. With the enlargement of NATO into the territories that previously were under the influence of Russia, NATO was transformed from a pact into a political organization (Fouskas 2003: 13–15), and NATO had become an important international political organization that will be used in the years to come as both a stick and a carrot for the American and western policies in the Balkans and the Middle East.

During the war in Kosovo, NATO played a crucial role not only in military intervention but during political negotiations as well. It was under the NATO flag that the western powers talked to the Serbian and Albanian leaders. At Rambouillet, it was NATO that asked for three conditions from Serbia so that they would halt the bombing campaign. But the most important point that defined the new role for NATO was the permission for the deployment of NATO forces anywhere in remaining Yugoslavia (Macintyre 1999). As part of the new role of NATO and the engagement of America in the post-Cold War order, President Clinton drew a very clear picture in his speech during the war of Kosovo to the US troops in Macedonia, on June 24, 1999, "We can then say to the people of the world, whether you live in Africa, Central Europe, or any other place, if somebody comes after innocent civilians and tries to kill them en masse because of their race, their ethnic background or their religion, and it is within our power to stop it, we will stop it" (Clinton 1999). It is important to note that for Clinton's Kosovo policy there was no considerable difference between the Republicans and the Democrats in the US Congress (Cameron 2002: 67). Senator Joe Biden, Senator John McCain, Congressman Elliot Engel, and Congressman Joseph DioGuardi were among the prominent lawmakers, from both parties, that pushed the administration to act on Kosovo.

After 9/11, on the other hand, the Bush administration felt no obligation and no need to bring on board either allies or international organizations. This was a big shift from previous US engagements in world security, either in the Balkans or in Africa. Traditionally, the term "rogue states" in American politics has connoted states such as Cuba, Iraq, Libya, North Korea, Iran, and alike, who were on the State Department's terrorist list. While Clinton's Secretary of State, Madeleine Albright, tried to be more sensitive and call them "countries of concern" in 1998, President Bush referred to them as the "Axis of Evil" in his State of the Union Address in January 2002, referring to Iraq, Iran, and North Korea. Furthermore, his administration publicly advocated for regime change in the "rogue states" (Litwak 2000; Chomsky 2000).

Instead of convincing the allies, or the international organizations, to intervene in Afghanistan and Iraq, the Bush administration chose to condition them as "you are either with us or against us", which didn't go very well for the USA. The administration had decided to construct threats in order to legitimize its policies. The Bush administration fed the Congress and American people with false claims of weapons of mass destruction in

Iraq. When they were shown to be fabricated, Bush then flipped the focus to the Wilsonian promotion of democracy. He claimed, as did Wilson, that the world must be safe for democracy, but unlike Wilson who had not gone to the opposite side of the world to search for monsters to destroy in the most volatile regions in the world, Bush did (Knock 2009: 35). Only after the occupation of Iraq did the world, and the American public, understand the Bush administration's foreign policy of democracy promotion, which was ranked at the bottom of 18 goals of Bush administration in 2002. Many supporters of Iraqi invasion, such as Beinart, have accepted that they were proven wrong for believing the fabricated propaganda of the Bush administration and he claimed that "I not only overestimated America's capacities, I overestimated America's legitimacy" (2008: xiii). Similarly, Slaughter argues that they should have looked closer at the available evidence before giving their support to Bush's Iraqi campaign (Slaughter 2009: 109). Secretary Powell (2012), on the other hand, has publicly declared that he is ashamed of himself for not looking deeper into the intelligence for weapons of mass destruction in Iraq and that he made the speech at the UN General Assembly on Iraq's weapons of mass destruction.

In analyzing the prewar and the postwar discourse on Iraq, one can see that the prewar discourse was about containment, WMD, and terrorism; the postwar discourse, however, was more about democracy and freedoms. In his second inaugural address, W. Bush mentioned "freedom" 25 times, "liberty" 12 times, and "democracy" or "democratic" 3 times (Bush 2005a). Democracy made up only a tiny part in the President Bush's prewar speeches, which were filled with notions of weapons of mass destruction and Iraq's terrorist ties. Even when discussing the Taliban, Bush argued that the USA has no responsibility to figure out what kind of government that country should have. The greatest claim by the Bush administration was that they were pursuing liberation and not occupation (Beinart 2008: 152–158). Soon it was understood that Iraq was not a quick exit job and the USA was deeply embedded with over 150,000 troops.

During the discussions of the war in Iraq many scholars, such as, Kaplan, Sanger, Judis, Hirsh, Ikenberry, and Knock, have linked Bush to Woodrow Wilson. Some have argued that he is more Wilsonian than Wilson himself and have argued that he wants the expansion of the zone of democracies, while others have accused him of Wilsonian utopian ideas that can never bear fruit, while Knock and Ikenberry have brought up similarities between

Wilson's war in Mexico and Bush's war in Iraq. Nevertheless, when one looks at the discourse that Bush used in the campaign, such as "the expansion of freedom", "the ultimate goal of ending tyranny in our world" that substituted the "quest for the weapons of mass destruction", one sees that analysts are not completely wrong to link Bush to Wilson (Kaplan 2003; Sanger 2005; Judis 2004: 7–9; Knock 2009: 27). These discussions have lead Michael Hirsh (2002) to call for "the need of new Wilsonianism", which argued that domestic safety is linked to the reduction of national armaments to the lowest possible point. Ikenberry also called for a "New Grand Strategy", stressing the unipolarity of the Bush's policies, the increase of the impulse of global hegemony, and a nuclear policy that has encouraged proliferation. According to Ikenberry the problem is the belief during the Bush administration that American sovereignty is politically sacred (Ikenberry 2002). In his autobiography *Decision Points*, President Bush said that he felt a great sympathy for Ronald Reagan and that Reagan's politics influenced his way of conducting foreign politics. As for the intervention in Kosovo and the invasion of Iraq, the support for both administrations was bipartisan.

How the White House constructed the conflict was very important. In Bosnia and Kosovo, the USA claimed that they were there to stop a potential genocide of ethnic hatred. In Afghanistan and Iraq, on the other hand, revenge for the 9/11 terrorist attacks was promised, while war was declared on terror. In the Balkans, there was no terrorism, whereas in the Middle East there were non-state groups who vowed to destroy the USA and had seriously challenged US security on September 11, 2001.

Terrorism is not something new for America, but until its engagement with the Middle East the general public was mostly unaware of many terrorist attacks that included the USA, US interests, or US citizens. Terrorism is portrayed and presented to the American public as a new phenomenon that did not exist before 9/11. Although there is no universal definition of terrorism, this book considers that terrorism includes any act of inflicting fear, terrorizing someone or a group of people. The same is with international terrorism, there is no universally accepted definition, but in the USA and the world generally it is accepted that international terrorist acts are the acts that involve citizens or property of more than one country. A terrorist group, on the other hand, is a group that professes and is involved in the acts of terrorism. Sometimes terrorist acts are limited, especially by the US definition, to the politically motivated acts against non-combatant targets (Cameron 2002: 141). However we define these concepts, there were many acts of terrorism that have included US citizens, US soil, and US interests. Some have been toward non-combatants and some have been toward combatants as the US military is present in more than 50 countries of the world.

Promoting democracy and fighting terrorism were big challenges for Bush. The challenge of fighting terror meant that the USA needed to work with authoritarian regimes in Pakistan, Kazakhstan, Egypt, as well as their longtime ally Saudi Arabia, and democratic reform demands were not a matter of discussion. In the fight against terrorism, autocracies became favorable for the economic and security interests of the USA, overriding promotion of democracy. Democracy promotion became a policy of fighting terrorism, instead of the other way around, destroying USA's credibility. Bush presented a split personality on the balance between democracy promotion and the war on terror (Carothers 2003).

The war on terror pushed America to violate its own values. With the treatment of al-Qaeda suspects in Guantanamo, the president's non-negotiable demands on values have all been violated: the respect for human rights, the rule of law, and the religious freedoms. The campaign did not, in any way, bring more democracy to the Middle East, and it only supported the Arab autocratic regimes in Saudi Arabia, Egypt, Syria, and elsewhere; it only widened the gap between the USA's rhetoric and actions (Carothers 2003, 2004; Cameron 2002: 147), up until the Arab Spring. Most importantly, these campaigns did not bring more freedom and security to America and American people, as was intended. These campaigns limited American freedom and increased the threats, which in the end made American citizens feel less secure.

The result of the "war on terror" is thousands of Americans dead, tens of thousands wounded, a wounded American army and population, the breeding of international cynicism, and most importantly an unsafe America with a population unwilling to fight and a confused American liberalism (Beinart 2008: 165–166). Today, no single political group in the Middle East has remained pro-American; the suspicion of American interests, values, and even culture has skyrocketed (Zakaria 2001). The USA has shown that it is willing to limit its democracy and freedom at home to "fight for the democracy" of a distant country or region. Supreme Court Justice Sandra O'Connor has warned that the world must see the most severe limitations of the US civil liberties ever, and journalists and pundits across the USA have called to reconsider American civil liberties. USA Today polls have shown that around 49% of American people support the idea of issuing special IDs to people with Arab descent; police were on the hunt for Arab-looking men, and many of these profiles were not accepted to fly on planes, including a secret service agent from the president's own security team, who was kicked off a plane (AbuKhalil 2002: 82). These and other profiling examples have limited civil liberties in the USA. They have alienated a certain group of American citizens and have made those involved to distance themselves from the USA.

For a country with the largest and most sophisticated marketing industry in the world, the USA has done a devastating job in public relations, and they have lost the public relations war with the terrorists. The US government was always in defensive mode in its public relations during the war on terror. From the mistake of describing the war against terror as a "crusade", to attacks against and calls to close the Al-Jazeera news station that was broadcasting Osama bin Laden video statements, to regarding Osama bin Laden as the Che Guevara of the Islamic world (Zaharna 2001; Cameron 2002: 138), these non-democratic requests and measures were mistakes that had negative PR and other consequences. Despite the huge amount of money that the USA has spent in the Middle East, the Bush administration didn't try to listen to the Arabs. The 9/11 and its aftermath showed a need to listen and learn more about and from the Arabs and the Muslims (Zogby 2010). The US Department of State started spending vast amounts of money in hiring PR experts for appealing to the Arab world, including Hollywood producers to promote their messages, but they were targeting the Arab leadership instead of the average Arab citizen.

In less than a month, the State Department hired Charlotte Beers, a marketing icon and Fortune's most powerful woman in America, in efforts to improve communication in the Arab world (Zogby 2010: 1–3). Beers went on a trip to the Arab world, to come back to the USA and establish a London-based company to manage the operations in the Middle East. She then tried to re-brand al-Qaeda and the USA, which was the last push downward. This was perceived in the Arab world as an effort to buy influence by the USA, and the prestige of the USA in the Middle East decreased even further (Zogby 2010: 2–3). Beer's failure brought Karen Hughes on board this time, a longtime trusted adviser to President Bush from the days he was the Texas governor. When she decided to visit the Arab countries, she made the same mistake: talk instead of listen. She went on this trip to "lecture to the Arab people, especially the women". Once, a female student spoke up, saying, "the general image of the Arab women is that she isn't happy ... well, we're all pretty happy" (Weisman 2005). Once again, the image created for the Americans was that they like to "talk at" not "talk with" Arabs (Zogby 2010: 121).

The problem of terrorism was not present in the Balkans, one of the reasons being that America did not act alone in the region, so America was not the target of dissatisfaction. The question that arose in the American public after 9/11 was: why do they hate us? While after the 9/11 Americans were asking for revenge, they also started to ask about the reasons that the USA had aroused such hatred for someone to commit September 11-like attacks. In the speeches, articles, and discourse there are two types of people that ask the question of "why do they hate us?": the first ones are those who question US foreign policy and the second are those who do not bother to try to find out why "they hate us?" and instead just blame "them" for hating American because "they hate freedom", and "they hate the American way of life". What they miss is the fact that there is a history between the USA and the Middle East before "they" started to hate "us", and the USA did not hear about the Middle East for the first time with the September 11 attacks. In this pattern, Secretary Rice claimed that "We had a very rude awakening on September 11th, when I think we realized that our policies to try and promote what we thought was stability in the Middle East had actually allowed, underneath, a very malignant, meaning cancerous, form of extremism to grow up underneath because people did not have outlets for their political views" (Rice 2005) when she was speaking to an audience at American University in Cairo in 2005. These words show how misleading the US administrators were in trying to understand the real reasons of what was happening in the Middle East vis-à-vis the USA.

Americans in the first group are the ones that are digging in the history of relations between the Middle East and the USA, which leads them to the answer of "so much hatred". Usually what can be found in this context are several reasons of why people in the Middle East and many developing countries have unfriendly views toward America. The anti-American propaganda during the Cold War is one of the reasons; the antipathy of the global influence of American culture and the death of small cultures is the second; the third is the leading American role, and hegemony, in the institutions that profess a globalized world, seen as nothing more than global domination, such as the IMF, the World Bank, or the WTO; fourth, and most importantly, the US support of the corrupt and antidemocratic regimes in some places of the world, especially in the Middle East (Cameron 2002: 137–138). This leads to a fifth, the conflict between the discourse of western values and practices in the ground. This list can go on. After the 9/11 terrorist attacks the common intuitive was that people without basic democratic rights and freedoms express their grievances through violence. Nevertheless, it was later understood that they did not hate "western freedoms", in fact they wanted them for themselves, but they were frustrated by the western and especially American support for the region's most repressive regimes, injustices in the region, and lack of will to help the people to resolve their social problems (Hamid and Brooke 2010; Krueger and Laitin 2004; Krueger 2008; Krueger and Maleckova 2003).

Although anti-Americanism exists in the Middle East, one must note that the western-educated elite in fact welcomes the "Americanization", but the mass population usually sees this elite as corrupted and as the ones that are being backed up by the USA. One must also note that this dichotomy is not present in the whole of the Muslim world, including all of the Muslim-majority countries, and this is one of the most important messages of this work. From Bosnia to Bangladesh, from Kosovo, to Nigeria, to Turkey, Indonesia, or Malaysia, most of the Muslims view the USA with sympathy, especially before the Afghanistan and the Iraqi invasions by the USA. Although the post-9/11 actions of the USA have brought questions in these areas as well, it has not escalated into "hatred".

With the invasion of Afghanistan and especially the invasion of Iraq, the USA has increased the hatred that has existed in these two countries and in the region. By 2003, polls showed that only 5% of Iraqis believe that the USA was there to assist the Iraqi people, whereas around 50% believe that the USA was there to "rob" the Iraqi oil (Beinart 2008: 162). The invasion of Iraq has affected the region. People of the region felt humiliated, and this has discouraged some educated, western-minded Arabs, from defending the democracy in their country. Another effect was the many European and American Arabs willing to go and fight against the west, and this has been a side effect of the humiliation that has arisen from the US invasion (Beinart 2008: 165–166). Raised and educated in Europe and the USA, some people were so humiliated that they agreed to leave behind the comforts of the west to go and fight in the mountains of the east.

The question of "why do they hate us?" can also be asked from the perspective of "why do we hate them" or even "why do we hate us" where Americans have started hating their own liberties, their own people, their own compatriots. Moreover, the USA has been exposed to different criticisms from both inside and outside, criticizing its lack of democratic values, American imperialism, and also its acts on breeding the terrorists that have turned against America. It has been claimed that Osama bin Laden, the head of the al-Qaeda terrorist organization, was receiving CIA training and aid to fight the Soviets, which resulted in the formation of al-Qaeda itself (Beinart 2008: 169–170; Coll 2004). How true these allegations are will always be unknown for sure, but even if the USA did not directly help bin Laden or al-Qaeda in their fight against the Soviets, indirectly there were many ways they were linked.[3] But, the most important issue is how the US administration handled this after they turned their back against the USA. The discourse and the acts have not made anything easier and better, neither abroad nor in the USA, and this has damaged the USA's grand strategy. If only the Bush administration had decided that democracy needs to be built and not forced, before the invasion of Iraq, the invasion would have gone far better (Beinart 2008: 158), the damage would have been much lower, and the situation today would be very different. If only the administration had handled the discourse differently, the situation would have also been very different today, and there would have been less polarization. The primary and unfortunate result of the increase of hate was the rise of terrorism. Sometimes people make the mistake of considering the rise of terrorism as the reason for why westerners and Middle Easterners hate each other, but that is the result instead of the cause. Understanding "why they hate us and why we hate them" is very important to being able

---

[3] Although this is very much debated, today this issue is well documented. We decided to refer to it as allegations because it is officially accepted by the American officials. The USA did in fact arm and train the Afghan freedom fighters against the Soviets, among whom was Osama bin Laden Further reference can be found at: http://www.nbcnews.com/id/3340101/t/bin-laden-comes-home-roost/; https://en.wikipedia.org/wiki/Operation_Cyclone; https://www.globalsecurity.org/intell/ops/afghanistan.htm. It is certainly worth noting that the issue came to the fore in American media shortly after 9/11, as did the USA's past relationship to Saddam Hussain during the run-up to and during the invasion of Iraq.

to understand the rise of terrorism and the consequences of the rise of hate speech and hate sentiments.

Although many have argued that the USA should have hired intercultural specialists for improving its image in the Middle East and elsewhere in the world, a study made by Pentagon, three years after 9/11, came to the conclusion that the problem with America's image in the world is much more complex than the failure of communication strategies. They have criticized the administration for portraying Islam as a threat, which offended a large population living in the Muslim world (US Department of Defense 2004). Unwise actions as a response to the terrorist attacks have wounded America, and one of its most important mistakes was to demonize the Islamic religion, to defame it as a religion that needs to change, and bringing the USA face to face against Islam. This has offended many people, abroad and in the USA, and has raised the chances for terrorist organizations to recruit, by giving them the argument that America sees Islam as an enemy that needs to be handled in one way or another.

A very much debated question on the issue of democratization, which is very much related to this book, is whether some cultures, civilizations, or religions are particularly repellant toward democracy. The supporters of this idea, such as Huntington and Stackhouse, claim that democracy is characterized by western, protestant/Christian culture, as the origin of democracy, while others, such as Sen, Schifter, Esposito, and Vanhanen, disagree by providing many theoretical and historical examples. Different models have worked in many places and have failed in many others. The ultimate lesson to be taken from these experiences is that the features of these models, and others, must sometimes be combined in different countries. A free and open market economy does not make a big difference to the 2 million population of the Republic of Kosovo, while the promotion of human rights and freedoms, religious tolerance, and interethnic dialogue might make a much greater impact overall.

The strongest advocates of democracy promotion, neoliberal internationalists, such as Will Marshall, Larry Diamond, Daniel Benjamin, Graham Allison, James Blaker, Anne-Marie Slaughter, Melissa Tryon, Jan Mazurek, and others, have been talking more about the "duty to intervene" instead of the "right to intervene" as a "responsibility to protect". This can be seen in Rwanda and the Yugoslavian conflicts, but the main challenge lies on the institutions who have the "duty to intervene" as the United Nations has proven inefficient, and NATO has taken on this responsibility. Perhaps when there is, finally, the "zone of democracies" acting as an international organization? Nevertheless, what they have identified as the target to intervene against is an ideology, instead of a country (like in ex-Yugoslavia). The president of Progressive Policy Institute (PPI), the self-declared think tank of the Democratic Party, Will Marshall, edited a book on the strategy of America to defeat jihadism as a manifesto of dealing with terrorism. In *With All Our Might: A Progressive Strategy for Defeating Jihadism and Defending Liberty*, 19 writers, known neoliberals, advocate for five main imperatives of the US national security: master all the strengths of the USA; rebuild the USA's alliances; champion liberal democracy; renew US leadership; and implant a new spirit of national unity and shared sacrifice to the American people (Marshall 2006). Strangely, this discourse was widely used by neoconservatives later.

Larry Diamond, a contributor to this book and a member of the PPI, dedicated another book about the war in Iraq "to my students, may they learn from our mistakes" (Diamond 2005), where he doesn't criticize the Bush Doctrine for invading Iraq, in fact he criticizes Bush for not being able to continue to the end. Looking back at Marshall, in his own words, "Democrats must reclaim, not abandon, their own tradition of muscular liberalism as exemplified by Presidents Truman, Kennedy, and Clinton. [...] violent jihadism, like fascism and communism, poses both a threat to our people's safety and a moral challenge to our liberal beliefs and ideals" (Marshall 2006: 9).

Another manifesto of American Democrats is the book of Peter Beinart *The Good Fight: Why Liberals—and Only Liberals—Can Win the War on Terror and Make America Great Again*. After writing that the USA is dealing with a "totalitarian Islam", Beinart argued that America must focus on defeating totalitarianism, while finally he wrote what he meant was that the USA must fight, "Islamist totalitarianism ... must be liberalism's north star" (Beinart 2008).

This was another shift in the USA's discourse in foreign policy from interventions in the Balkans to the interventions in the Middle East. The USA has acted under the idea of spreading the values of democracy for ensuring national security in the Yugoslav wars, especially the Kosovo campaign, as a primary cause. Other secondary causes may have included the ideological message of not seeing Islam as a threat, or the fact that the US base built in Kosovo is the largest US military base outside the USA, after Vietnam, built by Halliburton and then managed by Dick Cheney who became Vice President under George W. Bush (Fouskas 2003: 24–25). Acting in preventing the Kosovo War became a matter of value for the USA and the promotion of democracy in the Balkans was an opportunity to bring down Soviet communism and defeat a threat to US security.

Some argue that the US-led campaign in Kosovo was a campaign to counterbalance the campaigns toward the Muslim countries in the Middle East and the pro-Israeli policy in the Middles East, by showing that America defended the Muslims in Kosovo (Fouskas 2003), but this analysis turns a blind eye to the fact that the war in Kosovo, unlike the war in Bosnia, was never portrayed as a religious conflict. In the conflict of Bosnia, the main differentiating pattern between the Bosnians, Serbians, and Croats was religion, because they all have Slavic roots and speak the same language, whereas in Kosovo the main differentiating pattern was ethnicity, where Christian and Muslim Albanians had non-Slavic roots with a very different language. The Albanian leadership wisely chose not to divide the population—composed roughly of 90% Muslim and 10% Christians in Kosovo but 70% Muslim to 30% Christian among the Albanians in general—on religious basis, and this was another idea of obtaining western support. The point here is that even if the US administrators had used the Kosovo campaign as a pretext for "defending", "saving", or "helping" the Muslims, that was not the primary cause. The message that was intended to be given was that whoever is in need, Muslims or non-Muslims, the USA will intervene to stop another human catastrophe.

This is an important point for this work because the USA has had very different experiences in engagement in these two regions, and one of the reasons is that in the Balkans America did not involve the securitization or even politicization of Islam, rather it involved values, whereas in the Middle East Islam was involved as an issue to be dealt with when promoting democracy, generally as an obstacle to democracy promotion.

Moreover, democracy promotion is very important to being able to understand the justification that the USA uses to engage abroad and prioritize its foreign policy. Equally important for this work is the fact that the USA has changed the narrative from national security to democracy promotion, which directly involves cultural, religious, and ethnic components of the regions that the USA is involved in. Especially after the quest for weapons of mass destruction converted to democracy promotion, Islam was highly involved as an ideology that needs to change in order to promote democracy in the Middle East, and this is how Islam became an obstacle to national security. It is important to understand that this is the biggest difference between engagement in the Balkans and the Middle East, because even though Bosnians and Kosovar Albanians were majority Muslims, the USA did not talk about how Islam is an obstacle, rather it approached the region from the values perspective. In the Middle East, the USA chose to tackle Islam as a security issue, which prevents democracy promotion, and saw how it fired back. The second difference between the two examples is that in the Balkans, civil society was the primary target of support, whereas in the Middle East the USA worked more with the political fractions, which proved to be much more open to corruption than the civil society. Third, in the Balkans, and especially in Kosovo and Bosnia, European Union and NATO were very important actors. America did not work alone, and this made a big difference in sharing the responsibilities. In the Middle East, the USA worked alone, proving much harder to navigate and experiment with democracy, especially taking into consideration that the region was much harder.

In the previous chapters, we saw that Islam was securitized, especially during the W. Bush administration. In this chapter, we saw that USA's national security became synonymous with democracy promotion; the quest for terrorists in Afghanistan and the weapons of mass destruction in Iraq were transformed into the quest for democracy promotion. This quest for democracy promotion was framed as the solution against "their" ideology, way of life, rules, and mentality, which makes "them" hate "us", who "we" are, and "our" way of life. Bush securitized Islam by association instead of direct securitization, the "they and them" is obvious, and the "us, our, and we" is also obvious.

The American policy of democracy promotion, under W. Bush administration, has failed in the Middle East. One of the reasons it failed was that the administration had not learned from their mistakes and continued to ignore them, thus exacerbating the problem. The acknowledgment of mistakes remained only in the discourse, as a rhetorical tool, for intervention and fighting terrorism (Hamid and Brooke 2010), whereas in policy-making they were not considered. The result of the invasion of Iraq was conflicting strategies, expedient decision-making, departmental infighting, and policy incoherence (Allawi 2007: 110) instead of a democratic government that was supposed to succeed Saddam Hussein's. Democracy promotion was instrumentalized for the pursuit of national interest and war on terror, which made the USA look hypocritical and unserious on security, economic, and democracy promotion concerns (Fukuyama and McFaul 2007; Carothers 2003, Allawi 2007; Hunter and Malik 2005).

This priority issue in US foreign polices was overshadowed by the lust for intervention and terrorists hunting, filled with wrong methods and messages, constructing untrusted allies and wrong enemies.

By the time the democracy promotion in Iraq blurred, people in Egypt, Libya, Tunisia, and other countries in the MENA region started believing that they had been deceived, especially after President Obama's 2008 State of the Union Address where he singled out Cuba, Belarus, and Burma, as priorities for democracy promotion. Despite the failures in the Middle East, this should not discourage the responsibility to protect or the responsibility to intervene when it is needed. After all, if the USA had not intervened in Kosovo, in the way that it did without UN consent, Milosevic's war machine would have committed another slaughter in Europe's own backyard (Slaughter 2009: 116). Instead, a lesson should be taken on the rules of interventions and the responsibilities: the multilateralism and the strategy; otherwise the USA would have a post-Vietnam syndrome of isolationism, which would be bad for the USA and would jeopardize any semblance of world peace at a time when there is no shortage of wars and conflicts, from Macedonia to Sudan, from Syria to Myanmar.

We have analyzed the main theoretical approaches to US foreign policy, the democracy promotion as a priority in US foreign policy, and the place of Islam in US foreign policy during the three latest presidents. It is time to put the findings into a conclusion, and then it will be useful to suggest the next steps to solving a part of the democracy promotion and the engagement of Islam in problematic US foreign policy. The conclusion part holds both.

References

AbuKhalil, As'ad. 2002. *Bin Laden, Islam, and America's New "War on Terrorism"*. New York: Seven Stories.

Albright, Madeleine. 1997. *Harvard University Commencement Address*. June, 5. http://www.ucg.org/news-and-prophecy/excerpts-madeleine-albrights-commencement-address/. Accessed 28 Nov 28 2014.

———. 2000. *Keynote Address at the National Summit on Africa*. Washington, DC. February 17. http://1997-2001.state.gov/www/statements/2000/000217.html. Accessed 27 Oct 2015.

Allawi, Ali. 2007. *The Occupation of Iraq: Winning the War, Loosing the Peace*. New Haven: Yale University Press.

Baker, Kevin. 2001. The Year in Ideas: A to Z.: American Imperialism, Embraced. *New York Times*, 9 December.
Barber, Benjamin. 1996. *Jihad vs. McWorld*. New York: Ballantine Books.
———. 2003. *Fear's Empire: War, Terrorism and Democracy in an Age of Interdependence*. New York/London: W. W. Norton.
Beinart, Peter. 2008. *The Good Fight: Why Liberals – And Only Liberals – Can Win the War on Terror and Make America Great Again*. New York: Harper Collins.
Bouchet, Nicolas. 2013. Bill Clinton. In *US Foreign Policy and Democracy Promotion: from Theodore Roosevelt to Barack Obama*, ed. Michael Cox, Timothy J. Lynch, and Nicolas Bouchet, 159–177. London/New York: Routledge.
Brinkley, Douglas. 1997. Democratic Enlargement: the Clinton Doctrine. *Foreign Policy* 106: 111–127.
Brown, Keith. 2009. Do We Know How Yet? Insider Perspective on International Democracy Promotion in the Western Balkans. *The National Council for Eurasian and East European Research*. University of Washington. January 26.
Bureau of Democracy, Human Rights, and Labor (DRL). 2010a. *Egypt*. Advancing Freedom and Democracy Reports, May. Department of State. http://www.state.gov/g/drl/rls/afdr/2010/nea/129790.htm
———. 2010b. *Libya*. Advancing Freedom and Democracy Reports, May. Department of State. http://www.state.gov/g/drl/rls/afdr/2010/nea/129796.htm
———. 2010c. *Tunisia*. Advancing Freedom and Democracy Reports, May. Department of State. http://www.state.gov/g/drl/rls/afdr/2010/nea/129802.htm
Bush, George. 1990. *Address Before the 45th Session of the United Nations General Assembly in New York*. October 1. http://www.presidency.ucsb.edu/ws/?pid=18883. Accessed 28 Nov 2014.
Bush, George W. 2003. *Remarks by President George W. Bush at the 20th Anniversary of the National Endowment for Democracy*. November. http://www.ned.org/remarks-by-president-george-w-bush-at-the-20th-anniversary/. Accessed 27 Oct 2015.
———. 2005a. *Second Inaugural Address*. January 20. http://www.npr.org/templates/story/story.php?storyId=4460172. Accessed 15 Aug 2015.
———. 2005b. *State of the Union Address*. February 2. http://www.presidency.ucsb.edu/ws/index.php?pid=58746. Accessed 28 Nov 2014.
Calabresi, Massimo. 2011. Post-Mubarak: How the U.S. Plans to Aid Democracy in Egypt. *Time*, February 11. http://www.time.com/time/nation/article/0,8599,2048622,00.html#ixzz1Odw86H2e. Accessed 27 Oct 2015.
Cameron, Fraser. 2002. *US Foreign Policy After the Cold War: Global Hegemon or Reluctant Sheriff?* London/New York: Routledge.

Carothers, Thomas. 1995. Democracy Promotion Under Clinton. *The Washington Quarterly* 18 (4): 13–25.
———. 1997. Democracy Without Illusions. *Foreign Policy* 76 (1): 85–99.
———. 1999. *Aiding Democracy Abroad: The Learning Curve*. Washington, DC: Carnegie Endowment for International Peace.
———. 2000. Taking Stock of US Democracy Assistance. In *American Democracy Promotion: Impulses, Strategies, and Impacts*, ed. Michael Cox, G. John Ikenberry, and Takashi Inoguchi, 181–199. New York: Oxford University Press.
———. 2003. Promoting Democracy and Fighting Terror. *Foreign Affairs* 82 (1).
———. 2004. *Critical Mission: Essays on Democracy Promotion*. Washington, DC: Carnegie Endowment for International Peace.
Carter, Jimmy. 1977. *Address at Commencement Exercises at the University of Notre Dame*. May 22. http://www.presidency.ucsb.edu/ws/?pid=7552. Accessed 28 Nov 2014.
Chan, Steve. 1997. In Search of Democratic Peace: Problems and Promise. *Mershon International Studies Review* 41: 59–91.
Chandler, D. 2000. *Bosnia: Faking Democracy After Dayton*. London: Pluto.
Chomsky, Noam. 2000. *Rogue States: The Rule of Force in the World Affairs*. Cambridge, MA: South End Press.
Clark, Wesley K. 2001. *Waging Modern War: Bosnia, Kosovo, and the Future of Combat*. New York: Public Affairs.
Clinton, Bill. 1991. A New Covenant for American Security. *Speech Delivered at the Georgetown University School of Foreign Service*. Washington, DC. December 12.
———. 1992. Democracy in American. *Speech Delivered at the University of Milwaukee*. October 2. http://www.presidency.ucsb.edu/ws/index.php?pid=85226. Accessed 28 Nov 2014.
Clinton, William J. 1993. *American University's Centennial Convocation*. http://www1.american.edu/media/speeches/1993centennial.htm. Accessed 27 Oct 2015.
Clinton, Bill. 1998. *Remarks to the People of Rwanda*. March 25. http://millercenter.org/president/speeches/speech-4602. Accessed 15 Aug 2015.
Clinton, William J. 1999. *Remarks to Kosovo International Security Force Troops in Skopje*. June 22. http://www.presidency.ucsb.edu/ws/?pid=57770. Accessed 15 Aug 2015.
Coll, Steve. 2004. *Ghost Wars: The Secret History of the CIA, Afghanistan, and Bin Laden, from the Soviet Invasion to September 10, 2011*. London/New York: Penguin Books.
Cox, Michael. 1995. *US Foreign Policy After the Cold War: Superpower Without a Mission?* London: Printer/Royal Institute of International Affairs.
———. 2000. Wilsonianism Resurgent? The Clinton Administration and the Promotion of Democracy. In *American Democracy Promotion: Impulses,*

Strategies, and Impacts, ed. Michael Cox, G. John Ikenberry, and Takashi Inoguchi, 218–239. New York: Oxford University Press.

Cox, Michael, et al. 2000. Introduction. In *American Democracy Promotion: Impulses, Strategies, and Impacts*, ed. Michael Cox, G. John Ikenberry, and Takashi Inoguchi, 1–17. New York: Oxford University Press.

Creed, G., and J. Wedel. 2000. *Sociology After Bosnia and Kosovo: Recovering Justice*. Lanham: Rowman and Littlefield.

Dahl, Robert. 1971. *Polyarchy: Participation and Opposition*. New Haven: Yale University Press.

———. 1989. *Democracy and Its Critics*. New Haven: Yale University Press.

Diamond, Larry. 1995. *Promoting Democracy in the 1990s*. New York: Carnegie Commission on Preventing Deadly Conflict.

———. 2005. *Squandered Victory: The American Occupation and the Bungled Effort to Bring Democracy to Iraq*. New York: Times Books.

Dumbrell, John. 2013. Jimmy Carter. In *US Foreign Policy and Democracy Promotion: From Theodore Roosevelt to Barack Obama*, ed. Michael Cox, Timothy J. Lynch, and Nicolas Bouchet, 121–137. London/New York: Routledge.

Eisenhower, Dwight D. 1957. *Eisenhower Doctrine*. January 5. http://millercenter.org/president/eisenhower/speeches/speech-3360. Accessed 17 Oct 2015.

Finkel, Steven E., Anibal Perez-Linan, Mitchell A. Seliqson, and C. Neal Tate. 2008. *Democracy Assistance Project*. Phase II (2006–2007). Vanderbilt University and Others, February 26. http://www.pitt.edu/~politics/democracy/democracy.html

Fouskas, Vassilis. 2003. *Zones of Conflict: US Foreign Policy in the Balkans and the Greater Middle East*. Sterling: Pluto Press.

Fukuyama, Francis. 1992. *The End of History and the Last Man*. New York: The Free Press.

Fukuyama, Francis, and Michael McFaul. 2007. *Should Democracy be Promoted or Demoted? Bridging the Foreign Policy Divide*. Muscatine: The Stanley Foundation.

Gills, Barry. 2000. American Power, Neo-Liberal Economic Globalization and 'Low Intensity Democracy': An Unstable Trinity. In *American Democracy Promotion: Impulses, Strategies, and Impacts*, ed. Michael Cox, G. John Ikenberry, and Takashi Inoguchi, 326–344. New York: Oxford University Press.

Gills, Barry, and Joel Rocamora. 1992. Low Intensity Democracy. *Third World Quarterly* 13 (3): 501–523.

Gramsci, Antonio. 1971. *Selections from the Prison Notebooks*. London: Lawrence and Wishart.

Grimm, S., and J. Leininger. 2012. Not All Good Things Go Together: Conflicting Objectives in Democracy Promotion. *Democratization* 19 (3): 391–414.

Guehenno, Jean-Marie. 1995. *The End Nation-State*. Minneapolis: University of Minnesota Press.

Guilhot, N. 2005. *The Democracy Makers: Human Rights and International Order*. New York: Columbia University Press.

Hamid, Shadi, and Steven Brooke. 2010. Promoting Democracy to Stop Terror, Revisited. *Policy Review*. Hoover Institution. February & March. http://www.hoover.org/research/promoting-democracy-stop-terror-revisited. Accessed 27 Oct 2015.

Hirsh, Michael. 2002. Bush and the World. *Foreign Affairs* 81 (5): 18–43.

Holsti, Ole R. 2000. Promotion of Democracy as a Popular Demand? In *American Democracy Promotion: Impulses, Strategies, and Impacts*, ed. Michael Cox, G. John Ikenberry, and Takashi Inoguchi, 151–180. New York: Oxford University Press.

———. 2006. *Making American Foreign Policy*. New York: Routledge.

Hunt, Michael H. 2009. *Ideology and U.S. Foreign Policy*. New Haven/London: Yale University Press.

Hunter, Shireen, and Huma Malik, eds. 2005. *Islam and Human Rights: Advancing a US-Muslim Dialogue*. Washington, DC: Center for Strategic and International Studies.

Huntington, Samuel. 1992. *The Third Wave Democratization in the Late Twentieth Century*. Norman: University of Oklahoma Press.

Ikenberry, John G. 1999. Why Export Democracy? *Wilson Quarterly* 23 (2): 56–65.

———. 2000. America's Liberal Grand Strategy: Democracy and National Security in the Post-War Era. In *American Democracy Promotion: Impulses, Strategies, and Impacts*, ed. Michael Cox, G. John Ikenberry, and Takashi Inoguchi, 103–126. New York: Oxford University Press.

———. 2002. America's Imperial Mission. *Foreign Affairs* 81 (5): 44–60.

———. 2009. Woodrow Wilson, the Bush Administration, and the Future of Liberal Internationalism. In *The Crisis of American Foreign Policy: Wilsonianism in the Twenty-First Century*, ed. John G. Ikenberry et al., 1–24. Princeton: Princeton University Press.

Jones, Bryan, ed. 1995. *The New American Politics: Reflections on Political Change and the Clinton Administration*. Boulder: Westview Press.

Judis, John B. 2004. *The Folly Empire: What George W. Bush Could Learn from Theodore Roosevelt and Woodrow Wilson*. New York: Scribner.

Kaplan, Lawrence F. 2003. Regime Change. *New Republic*, March 3. http://www.newrepublic.com/article/bush-middle-east-conservative-woodrow-wilson-liberalism. Accessed 28 Nov 2014.

Kennedy, John F. 1961. *Inaugural Address*. January 20. http://avalon.law.yale.edu/20th_century/kennedy.asp. Accessed 28 Nov 2014.

Kissinger, Henry. 1994. *Diplomacy*. New York: Simon and Schuster.

Knaus, G., and F. Martin. 2003. Travails of the European Raj. *Journal of Democracy* 14 (3): 60–74.
Knock, Thomas J. 2009. Playing for a Hundred Years Hence: Woodrow Wilson's Internationalism and His Would-Be Heirs. In *The Crisis of American Foreign Policy: Wilsonianism in the Twenty-First Century*, ed. John G. Ikenberry et al., 25–52. Princeton: Princeton University Press.
Krueger, Alan B. 2008. *What Makes a Terrorist? Economics and the Roots of Terrorism*. Princeton: Princeton University Press.
Krueger, Alan B., and David D. Laitin. 2004. "Misunderestimating" Terrorism. *Foreign Affairs* 83 (5): 8–13.
Krueger, Alan B., and Jitka Maleckova. 2003. Education, Poverty and Terrorism: Is There a Casual Connection? *Journal of Economic Perspective* 17 (4): 119–144.
Lake, Anthony. 1994. The Need for Engagement. *US Department of State Dispatch*. 5/49. December 5.
Layne, Christopher, and M. Lynn-Jones. 1998. *Should America Promote Democracy?* Cambridge: MIT Press.
Lipset, Seymour Martin. 1996. *American Exceptionalism: A Double-Edged Sword*. New York: W.W. Norton.
Litwak, Robert S. 2000. *Rogue States and US Foreign Policy: Containment After the Cold War*. Baltimore: Johns Hopkins University Press.
Lynch, Timothy. 2013. George W. Bush. In *US Foreign Policy and Democracy Promotion: from Theodore Roosevelt to Barack Obama*, ed. Michael Cox, Timothy J. Lynch, and Nicolas Bouchet, 178–195. London/New York: Routledge.
Macintyre, Ben. 1999. Clinton Rejected Warnings of fiasco. *The Times*. April 2.
Mandelbaum, Michael. 1996. Foreign Policy as Social Work. *Foreign Affairs*, January/February. http://www.foreignaffairs.com/articles/51618/michael-mandelbaum/foreign-policy-as-social-work. Accessed 28 Nov 2014.
Marshall, Will, ed. 2006. *With All Our Might: A Progressive Strategy for Defeating Jihadism and Defending Liberty*. Lanham: Rowman and Littlefield.
McCulloch, Tony. 2004. Franklin D. Roosevelt. In *US Foreign Policy and Democracy Promotion: From Theodore Roosevelt to Barack Obama*, ed. Michael Cox, Timothy J. Lynch, and Nicolas Bouchet, 69–85. London/New York: Routledge.
Nau, Henry. 2000. America's Identity, Democracy Promotion and National Interest: Beyond Realism, Beyond Idealism. In *American Democracy Promotion: Impulses, Strategies, and Impacts*, ed. Michael Cox, G. John Ikenberry, and Takashi Inoguchi, 127–148. New York: Oxford University Press.
New York Times. 1999. *Crisis in the Balkans; Statements of United States' Policy on Kosovo*. April 18. http://www.nytimes.com/1999/04/18/world/crisis-in-the-balkans-statements-of-united-states-policy-on-kosovo.html. Accessed 27 Oct 2015.

Nye, Joseph. 2002. *The Paradox of American Power: Why the World's Only Superpower Can't Go it Alone*. Oxford: Oxford University Press.
Paddock, W., and E. Paddock. 1973. *We Don't Know How*. Ames: Iowa State University Press.
Parenti, Michael. 1995. *Against Empire*. San Francisco: City Lights Books.
Powell, Colin with Tony Koltz. 2012. *It Worked for Me: In Life and Leadership*. New York: Harper Collins.
Quinn, Adam. 2013. Theodore Roosevelt. In *US Foreign Policy and Democracy Promotion: From Theodore Roosevelt to Barack Obama*, ed. Michael Cox, Timothy J. Lynch, and Nicolas Bouchet, 37–52. London/New York: Routledge.
Ralph, Jason. 2000. 'High Stakes' and 'Low Intensity Democracy': Understanding America's Policy of Promoting Democracy. In *American Democracy Promotion: Impulses, Strategies, and Impacts*, ed. Michael Cox, G. John Ikenberry, and Takashi Inoguchi, 200–217. New York: Oxford university Press.
Reagan, Ronald. 1982. *Address to the British Parliament*. June 8. http://millercenter.org/president/speeches/speech-3408. Accessed 28 Nov 2014.
Rice, Condoleezza. 2005. *Question and Answer at the American University in Cairo*. Cairo. June 20. http://2001-2009.state.gov/secretary/rm/2005/48352.htm. Accessed 27 Oct 2015.
Robinson, William. 1996. *Promoting Polyarchy: Globalization, US Intervention, and Hegemony*. Cambridge: Cambridge University Press.
———. 2000. Promoting Capitalist Polyarchy: The Case of Latin America. In *American Democracy Promotion: Impulses, Strategies, and Impacts*, ed. Michael Cox, G. John Ikenberry, and Takashi Inoguchi, 308–325. New York, Oxford University Press.
Ruggie, John Gerard. 1996. *Winning the Peace: America and World Order in the New Era*. New York: Columbia University Press.
Rutland, Peter. 2000. Russia: Limping Along Towards American Democracy? In *American Democracy Promotion: Impulses, Strategies, and Impacts*, ed. Michael Cox, G. John Ikenberry, and Takashi Inoguchi, 243–266. New York: Oxford University Press.
Sali-Terzić, S. 2001. Civil Society. In *International Support Policies to South-East European Countries: Lessons (Not) Learned in B-H*, ed. Z. Papić, 175–194. Sarajevo: Muller.
Sanger, David E. 1997. Clinton Seeks Power for Trade Deals Congress Can't Amend. *New York Times*, 11 September.
———. 2005. A Speech About Nothing, Something, Everything. *The New York Times*. January 23. http://www.nytimes.com/2005/01/23/weekinreview/23sang.html?_r=0. Accessed 28 Nov 2014.
Schumpeter, Joseph A. 1942. *Capitalism, Socialism and Democracy*. New York: Harper and Row.

Shipoli, Erdoan. 2010. *International Securitization: The Case of Kosovo*. Saarbrucken: Lambert Academic Publishing.

Slaughter, Anne-Marie. 2009. Wilsonianism in the Twenty-First Century. In *The Crisis of American Foreign Policy: Wilsonianism in the Twenty-First Century*, ed. John G. Ikenberry et al., 89–117. Princeton: Princeton University Press.

Smillie, I., and G. Todorovic. 2001. Reconstructing Bosnia, Constructing Civil Society: Disjuncture and Convergence. In *Patronage or Partnership: Local Capacity Building in Humanitarian Crisis*, ed. I. Smillie, 25–50. Bloomfield: Kumarian.

Smith, Tony. 1994. *America's Mission: The United States and the Worldwide Struggle for Democracy in the Twentieth Century*. Princeton: Princeton University Press.

Smith, Steve. 2000a. US Democracy Promotion: Critical Questions. In *American Democracy Promotion: Impulses, Strategies, and Impacts*, ed. Michael Cox, G. John Ikenberry, and Takashi Inoguchi, 63–82. New York: Oxford University Press.

Smith, Tony. 2000b. National Security Liberalism and American Foreign Policy. In *American Democracy Promotion: Impulses, Strategies, and Impacts*, ed. Michael Cox, G. John Ikenberry, and Takashi Inoguchi, 85–102. New York: Oxford University Press.

———. 2009. Wilsonianism After Iraq: The End of Liberal Internationalism? In *The Crisis of American Foreign Policy: Wilsonianism in the Twenty-First Century*, ed. John G. Ikenberry et al., 53–88. Princeton: Princeton University Press.

Sorensen, Georg. 2000. The Impasse of Third World Democratization: Africa Revisited. In *American Democracy Promotion: Impulses, Strategies, and Impacts*, ed. Michael Cox, G. John Ikenberry, and Takashi Inoguchi, 287–307. New York: Oxford University Press.

Talbott, Strobe. 1996. Democracy and the National Interest. *Foreign Affairs* 74 (6): 47–63.

Thompson, Michael J. 2003. Introduction. In *Islam and the West: Critical Perspectives on Modernity*, ed. Michael J. Thompson, 1–4. Oxford: Rowman and Littlefield Publishers.

Traub, J. 2008. *The Freedom Agenda: Why America Must Spread Democracy: Just Not the Way George Bush Did*. New York: Farrar, Straus and Giroux.

Travis, Rick. 1998. The Promotion of Democracy at the End of the Twentieth Century: A New Polestar for American Foreign Policy? In *After the End: Making U.S. Foreign Policy in the Post-Cold War World*, ed. James M. Scott, 253–254. Durham: Duke University Press.

Truman, Harry S. 1947. *President Harry S. Truman's Address Before a Joint Session of Congress*. March 12. http://avalon.law.yale.edu/20th_century/trudoc.asp. Accessed 17 Oct 2015.

U.S. Department of Defense. 2004. *Defense Science Board 2004 Summer Study on Transition to and from Hostilities.* December. http://www.acq.osd.mil/dsb/reports/ADA430116.pdf. Accessed 6 Oct 2014.

U.S. Department of State (USDS). 2001. *Patterns of Global Terrorism 2000.* April. http://www.higginsctc.org/patternsofglobalterrorism/2000pogt.pdf. Accessed 6 Oct 2014.

———. 2003. *Patterns of Global Terrorism 2002.* April. http://www.state.gov/documents/organization/20177.pdf. Accessed 6 Oct 2014.

Weisman, Steven R. 2005. Saudi Women Have Message for U.S. Envoy. *New York Times.* September 28. http://www.nytimes.com/2005/09/28/world/middleeast/saudi-women-have-message-for-us-envoy.html?_r=0. Accessed 27 Oct 2015.

Williams, Williams Appleman. 1972. *The Tragedy of American Diplomacy.* New York: Dell Publishing Company.

Wilson, Woodrow. 1919. Address in Favor of the League of Nations. *Pueblo.* September 25. http://www.presidentialrhetoric.com/historicspeeches/wilson/leagueofnations.print.html. Accessed 15 Aug 2015.

Wolff, J., and H. Spanger. 2013. Democracy Promoters' Conflicting Objectives: The Research Agenda. In *The Comparative International Politics of Democracy Promotion*, ed. J. Wolff, H. Spanger, and H. Puhle, 3–36. London: Routledge.

Wolff, J., H.-J. Spanger, and H.-J. Puhle. 2013. *The Comparative International Politics of Democracy Promotion.* London: Routledge.

Woodward, Susan L. 2007. Is Democracy Possible in the Balkans? *On preconditions and conditions in Bosnia, Kosovo, and Serbia.* The National Council of Eurasian and East European Research. June 26.

Zaharna, R.S. 2001. American Public Diplomacy in the Arab and Muslim World: A Strategic Communication Analysis. *Foreign Policy in Focus.* November 1. http://fpif.org/american_public_diplomacy_in_the_arab_and_muslim_world_a_strategic_communication_analysis/. Accessed 10 Nov 2015.

Zakaria, Fareed. 1997. The Rise of Illiberal Democracy. *Foreign Affairs* 76 (6): 22–43.

———. 2001. The Politics of Rage: Why Do They Hate Us? *Newsweek*, October 15. http://www.newsweek.com/politics-rage-why-do-they-hate-us-154345. Accessed 6 Oct 2014.

Zogby, James. 2010. *Arab Voices: What They Are Saying to Us, and Why It Matters.* New York: Palgrave Macmillan.

CHAPTER 9

Conclusion

This work has analyzed the securitization of Islam in American foreign policy, concluding that Islam was made a security issue in American, especially after the Cold War. Although it has been longer than an eight-year campaign, it was President W. Bush who decided to securitize Islam, contrary to Clinton who refused to let Islam be securitized and Obama who tried to desecuritize Islam, with limited success. Bush decided to make Islam the "other" and securitize it by association, the opposite of what America stands for, and a synchronized campaign of speech acts, media, and visuals. This work has also talked about democracy promotion and why and how important this policy is for America, especially in its foreign affairs. The main drive is that the expansion of the territories of democracy will make America more secure because democracies do not fight with each other. This was the main reason that the Bush administration decided to securitize Islam, because they felt the need for a threat and enemy to justify their campaign of "democracy promotion" in the Middle East, which was equated to US national security. The quest for threats against the USA was later transformed to the quest for democracy promotion, against the ideological threat that is opposite of what America stands for. In the Middle East, this "other" was obviously Islam.

President Clinton has handled this with care, whereas President Bush decided to "religionize security", to use John Voll's phrase, and in this realm Islam as "other" has been securitized and constructed as a threat. Acknowledging that this was wrong, and that it undermined US foreign policy and security, President Obama decided to desecuritize it at the earliest stages, in his first trip abroad to Cairo, Egypt. These actions have occurred through discourse rather than in practice.

No other policy has been more long-standing in US foreign affairs than democracy promotion. All administrations have followed the same goal and policy, but the methods of how they did it changed, some engaging alone; some trying to engage alliances; some trying to perfect the democratic values at home and be an example; some focusing only on democracy promotion abroad; some have tried to find monsters, crusading for democracy promotion abroad; some have securitized an ideology, others engaging that ideology. US foreign policy doyen, Henry Kissinger, explains that Wilsonianism has been a cornerstone of US foreign policy, "Though Wilson could not convince his own country of its merit, the idea lived on. It is above all to the drumbeat of Wilsonian idealism that American foreign policy has marched since his watershed presidency, and continues to march to this day" (Kissinger 1994: 30). One can see this pattern in the speeches analyzed in this book. All discourse has been for the same goal, Wilsonianist democracy promotion, outliving all other policies and major events in world politics.

Similar to global politics, US politics has been directed by different securitized issues. Race was a securitized issue in the USA and so was ethnicity. Different ethnicities were securitized and this reflected in US politics. Nevertheless, communism was the best-securitized issue, and the longest-standing one, which lasted for decades. Not only did it last for many years but it also brought most of the American people together against a common enemy. This enemy, or this securitized issue, was an idea, an ideology, instead of being someone's background or inborn features. Generations of policymakers and students have been raised with this threat and their perspective toward foreign policy was constructed from this viewpoint. With the end of the Cold War, the viewpoint remained as a frame, but there was no communism in the picture.

New changes needed to be made to tackle the remaining world outside communism, and among the most important changes were the changes in discourse. The focus on "National Security" merged with "Democracy Promotion" (Ralph 2000: 205) and they have been used interchangeably to mean the same thing. This merge came as a result of the quest for democracy promotion as a policy of American national security. The Cold

War experts easily justify this merge, as it was democracy promotion that made America the sole superpower and thus secured its national interests. Nevertheless, the side effect of this was that democracy promotion was now at the level of national security, it was a security issue. The perfect summary of this understanding would be the CIA chief's and then Secretary of Defense Leon Panetta's claim that "to be free, we must also be secure" (2014: 332), but to his credit he claimed that "we must not be forced to choose between security and our values. We can and we must preserve both" (2014: 391–392).

After democracy promotion merged with national security policy, US policymakers needed support, funds, and people. The campaign to guarantee this support became the main public relations goal of American policymakers. They did a good job of getting the American public on board, convincing them that democracy promotion is an important national security issue and a policy of common good. But, the USA has done a weaker job of getting the attention and the support of the international public. Supporting non-democratic regimes when in US national interests and working with different factions for securing these interests have raised many questions internationally.

Both Strobe Talbott and Anthony Lake have defended the idea that the support or the promotion of democracy abroad needs to be balanced against other US strategic interests, sometimes changing priority positions among each other (Talbott 1996: 52). Clinton must have agreed with these claims when he said, "make trade a priority element of American security" (Clinton 1993). In many occasions, the USA is more interested in maintaining the global hegemony rather than promoting democracy (Sanger 1997); however, in discourse, democracy promotion is generally the issue that comes to the forefront. One can understand the will of the USA to keep its hegemonic position so that it can control global markets, pursue US national interests, and keep America secure. Basically, for the USA, democracy promotion is part of a larger liberal grand strategy in foreign policy, to ensure a more stable, legitimate, and secure international order, for the purpose of serving US national interest, among the most important being US national security.

The US engagement with Islam can be understood in this framework. After the Cold War, President Clinton tried to stay out of religious discussions. In his discourse, Islam was mostly avoided, or mildly complimented when it could not be avoided, to try to get the support of Muslims for US policies. His most important speech about Islam was the Jordan speech in 1994. He made this speech as his doctrine toward Islam. Trying to show himself and his administration familiar with Islam, he quoted Qur'anic verses and underlined similarities between Islam and America. Most importantly, he refused to equate Islam with security and to associate it with security keywords.

President Bush did not have a one-speech toward Islam. He chose to use Islam in most of his speeches after the 9/11. Understandably, he was as shocked by the 9/11 attacks as the American people. Nevertheless, it was his and his administration's decision to tackle Islam and make it the "other". In many occasions Bush directly claimed that "the US is not in war with Islam" and he went to a mosque in Washington DC in the first week after the 9/11 attacks to show solidarity with American Muslims. But despite that, Bush alienated Islam and Muslims in most of his speeches. When talking about common enemies, he would talk along the lines of "they do not like Christians and Jews" or "they want to kill Christian and Jews". Of course, he was referring to the extremist terrorists, but by not mentioning Islam he was securitizing and "otherizing" it. Not to mention that the greatest victims of radical Islamist terrorists have always been the Muslims themselves.

This research showed that Bush administration decided to bring religion to security discourse. So, in fact it was security as a very secular institution, and securitization as a very secular process, which were religionized first and foremost. In his conversation with French President Jacques Chirac, Bush said he feels that this is the ultimate war of Gog and Magog, referring to the Biblical texts. He said many times that his most inspiring philosopher was Jesus and that he is a "born-again" Christian at 40 years old. He explained the war on terror as a crusade. And he even said that he had a call from God to invade Afghanistan and Iraq and solve the Israeli-Palestinian conflict (MacAskill 2005). When security and securitization was religionized, then Islam as the "other" became the common threat, became the issue that needed to be dealt in security terms. This religionization of security had made many American allies retreat from being on the same side with America. Secretary Clinton recalls that when they were talking about these issues, her European counterparts would still joke in private messages, after many years, defining the period as "since the crusade". Although there is no single speech where Bush addressed Muslims, Islam, and the Muslim world in particular, his "Axis of Evil" speech in the second State of the Union Address in 2002 showed how he viewed Islam, Muslims, and the Muslim world.

Bush linked this new "other" or "enemy" with US national security. Before the invasion of Iraq, President Bush and his administration filled the US public with, what turned out to be, false suppositions of weapons of mass destruction in Iraq. But, when it showed up that these were all fabricated facts, then Bush and his administration flipped to "democracy promotion". At his Wilsonian best, Bush claimed that the world must be a safe place for democracy, but he went many steps further than Wilson, to go in foreign lands and search for monsters to destroy, something that Wilson had opposed (Knock 2009: 35). After the invasion of Iraq, the American public saw the fabricated facts, which resulted in two US invasions in the Middle East, one of the longest-standing and bloodiest wars, a divided society, with many consequences in the USA. Islam and Muslims had become alienated in America, and Islamophobia skyrocketed.

President Obama, on the other hand, decided to tackle this issue in his first trip abroad. When he went to Cairo in 2009, President Obama had already understood that securitizing Islam and religion was a bad idea. He needed to desecuritize it. His administration agreed that religion is a social issue, or at most a political issue, and when it becomes a security issue then it is very dangerous, as ultimately some group is targeted. This is why he decided to address the issue in Cairo, and by doing so creating his first foreign policy doctrine. His practices toward the Middle East, and toward the Muslim inmates in US secret prisons, can be debated, but what this work was looking for is the discourse, and there was a consistency in Obama's discourse and his views toward Islam, which equates to moves of desecuritizing Islam. If one asks whether Islam is successfully desecuritized, the answer is simply "no". It is very difficult to desecuritize an issue at the systematic level. Desecuritizing the Cold War has taken a long time and we cannot say that it was desecuritized successfully, so the desecuritization of Islam will take even longer and take much more effort from all sides. The elections themselves have shown how difficult it is to desecuritize Islam.

The Trump administration has destroyed any progress made by the Obama administration. Even before the inauguration Islam became resecuritized more than ever, and Islamophobia skyrocketed. Administration officials refuse to refer to Islam as a religion, rather they refer to it as an ideology. This serves their purpose of bringing back the Cold War mentality where America is fighting against an ideology. Their foreign policy toward Iran and North Korea or their global warming and trade policies are compiled according to this mentality. But it remains to be seen what the results will be, if this administration will continue with this mentality, and how far they are willing to go.

The power of the presidents and their administrations mostly lies in the agenda setting and pushing for a certain mindset. When President Bush decided to bring Islam and religion as part of security, the US public was ready to accept such a move. Iran has had a very big impact in the negative view of Islam by the Americans. The biggest mistake is that Americans, the public and some political elite, equate Islam with political Islam and with Iran. A majority of Americans think of Islam as monolithic, they see a majority of Muslims who are in fact very different from each other in thought and in practice. Contemporary Islamophobia and the securitization of Islam started with the Iranian Revolution and the hostage crises. Other attacks toward American interests played their role, and the 9/11 secured this image in Americans' mind. The Iranian Revolution happened before President Clinton, but he decided not to use this to securitize Islam. Even during the Cold War when Muslim groups committed any act against American interests, they were explained as communist groups against American interests, rather than Muslim groups (AbuKhalil 2002: 19–20). These behaviors were attributed to communism rather than Islam.

This work has analyzed these speeches and come up with these results, which translate to the argument that securitizing Islam has not made America safer; in fact it has jeopardized America's national security because it has alienated American Muslims. Securitization of Islam has portrayed America as a hegemonic power driven by war, and it has given arguments to the extremists to recruit Muslims against America. Even secretary Clinton argues that the future of the US lies on the USA "making more friends and fewer terrorists" (Clinton 2014: 874–876).

The main contribution that this book has made is related to expanding the securitization theory by taking Islam as an example. It has found that the securitization of an issue happens at different levels, and it has categorized them into three main groups: domestic, international, and systematic, which was the topic of this work. These are different because the actors and the means are different. These differences have been explained in previous chapters, but it will be of benefit if they are put into a comparison table (Table 9.1).

Table 9.1 The comparison of the three levels of securitization

	Domestic securitization	International securitization	Systematic securitization
Securitizing actors	Political elite, governmental officials, local officials, activists, and influential local persons	International political leaders, media, influential international persons, international organizations	Ideologically driven persons, religious and faith leaders, international political leaders, media, influential international persons, international organizations, interest groups
Audience	Public	Public, political leaders of governments (decision-makers), international leaders	Public, ideologically driven masses, faith-based movements, political leaders of governments (decision-makers), international leaders
Securitizing methods	Speech act	Speech act, visual images	Speech act, visual images, long movies, association, long-term campaigns (movies, TV programs, novels, poems, comics, cartoons, computer games)
Referent objects	Local or national objects, nation, state	International peace and security, values	Ideology, faith, international peace and security, values, the whole world
Threats	Local groups, individuals, bad policies	Threats that concern more than one state or nation: countries, transnational groups, viruses	Threats that divided the world into few poles: ideologies, religions

9.1 What Next?

What are the lessons that can be drawn from this research? There are many scenarios in which the US administration can address this issue. President Obama's approach to desecuritize Islam was a positive starting point, but because the damage was already done it is difficult to repair it in the short time of eight years. Although progress has been recorded in relation to US engagement with the Muslims in America and abroad, there is much work to be done. The most important lesson is the one taken from the Yugoslav wars, that religion should not be securitized. During the Yugoslav wars' interventions, the USA did not make much reference to religion, with a few exceptions when Clinton wanted to point out that despite the Muslim-majority population America intervened in Kosovo, and that the case of Bosnia's inaction did not have to do anything with the Bosnians being Muslim.

There are large gaps between the practices and discourse of the American political elite when it comes to Islam, Muslims, and the Muslim world. They are inconsistent and have portrayed America as hypocritical. But also, the USA should understand that they do not know what is best for everyone. Larry Diamond, a former senior advisor for the Coalition Provisional Authority, explained it very well in relation to the democratization in Iraq: "American political leaders need to take a cold shower of humility: we do not always know what is best for other people, even when we think it is their interests we have in mind … in Iraq, it was frequently our interests that were driving decisions we were trying to impose" (Diamond 2005: 333). There have been many talks about the "war of ideas" among the Muslims, the war between the so-called fundamentalists and the so-called moderates. Nevertheless this "war of ideas" has been more present within the USA (Smith 2009: 85) than in the Muslim world. Foreign policymakers in America are more concerned with what makes a "good Muslim" and a "bad Muslim", than the Muslims themselves.

Another very important step is to take responsibility for the mess America caused. Secretary of Defense, Robert Gates, argues that the USA made many mistakes in Afghanistan, disrespecting and hurting the people and their values. First, it was the civilian casualties, which brought a strategic defeat to the USA. Second, it was the USA and allied forces' military visibility on the Afghan roads, which brought fear to the people. Similarly, there were many cases of disrespecting their culture, Islam, and elders. Collaborating with corrupt Afghan officials was another downside of the USA in Afghanistan. Development projects across the country were not being consulted with the local people and they were implemented in a we-know-what-is-best-for-you kind of way, without learning their needs. Gates further explains that most of the money that went to Afghanistan from the USA was used on bribes, payoffs, and other Dubai accounts. The American and other allied governments were paying off officials, tribal leaders, and family members as agents to secure their cooperation. He protests these acts by saying that "Hillary Clinton and I repeatedly objected to this contradictory behavior by the United States, but to no avail" (Gates 2014: 359–360). Secretary Clinton says that America should take responsibility and that she takes full responsibility on the Benghazi issue, but that America cannot retreat from the world politics because of these mistakes. In her own words "wipe our tears, stiffen our spines, and face the future undaunted" (Clinton 2014: 406). In taking responsibility, the USA should learn from mistakes and decide whom they want as allies on their side. During the Cold War, America worked and partnered with Islamists, some of today's terrorists, against the Soviet Union. Now America works and partners with Russia and authoritative regimes in the Middle East, against these terrorist organizations.

The USA should defend, support, and promote values instead of interests. It should voice concerns against violations of those values if it wants to improve its image in the Muslim world and among the Muslims globally. Education of the youngsters should take the place of the parties that are supported by the USA in the Muslim world, who are only good in suppressing alternative voices. Education of Muslim Americans is also very important. While the majority of Muslim preachers and Islamic scholars are foreign-born, or foreign-educated, today there are third and fourth generation Muslims in America. There is a big gap between their worldviews. Very few Muslim American preachers and Islamic scholars have been trained in the West, and in America today there are very few, if any, credible higher education institutions that can train Muslim preachers, imams, or scholars (Bowen 2012: 114–115). While this may take a long time, actions should be taken as soon as possible, because these educators need to understand the pluralism and multiculturalism of the west, while those who understand this remain in the minority and they are neither considered as western scholars nor considered as fully credible eastern/traditional scholars.

When speaking of education, one should be careful not to make the mistakes and in fact do the opposite of what has been tried with terrible consequences. Some educational efforts have backfired due to the lack of planning, strategy, and different intentions toward Muslims and Arabs. In 2006 the White House announced the Less Commonly Taught Languages Program initiative. This initiative provided financial support for Arabic as a second language across the nation. Although interesting from one perspective, it was shown to be a failure when the intelligence agencies went on the hunt for Arabic speakers, to be able to translate the giant volumes of intelligence in Arabic language. In most of the Arab festivals, newspapers, fairs, and alike, one can see the sponsorship of the US Armed Forces, the FBI, the CIA, and other agencies (Howell 2010: 232). The government agencies were competing for Arabic-speaking Muslims, not because they believed in their intellectual capacity or talents but because they needed someone to translate the vast volumes of intelligence cables from the Middle East. In cultural festivals, one could easily spot recruiting agents, and this was a blowback because Muslims and Arabs were feeling that they were being followed, that they or their children were to be recruited, or were simply scared.

The first rule of PR should be applied to American policy to improve its image abroad. That rule is: listen. The USA should listen to what the people they want to influence have to say. Instead of categorizing them as "good" or "bad", according to how they cooperate and think about America, they should listen and accept their ideas. Reform must be demanded, not imposed from the outside. This is the approach that was expected from the Obama administration and this is what they said they would follow, but it was absent in practice. Democracy must remain a goal, but it should be promoted with local needs and conditions, by improving human rights, education, civil society organizations, and employment. These are important issues for the Muslim world (Zogby 2010: 154), and not to forget that delivering on the many promises made to them on the Israeli-Palestinian conflict would have a big impact and make a great change.

As far as the Obama administration is concerned, during the military coup in Egypt, Obama lost a great chance of leaving a mark in global politics. He could have used this situation to bring up the "responsibility to protect" that Clinton had used during his administration. Clinton used this policy to protect people against oppressive governments, or to protect one small country or entity against a bigger country or entity. Obama could have expended this into the responsibility to protect elected governments against military coups, which have remained from the previous dictatorial governments in the Middle East. Caught by surprise by the Arab Spring and then the coup in Egypt, Obama chose a military junta to be America's next ally.

Obama's Syria policy was a total debacle too. It was expected that the USA would lead in efforts to do something for the refugees, stop the conflict, and ensure the conditions for the return to the normal life. The Yugoslav conflicts can be a great lesson on how to do this. President Clinton wrote this for Kosovo but it is relevant for Syria as well (2004: 785–796): among others there is a need to bring the refugees home safety; clear the ground of unexploded bombs and mines; rebuild homes and shelters; provide food, medicine, water, and immediate needs for the ones that come back; demilitarize the groups that have been fighting; create a secure environment for the minorities; build and organize a civilian administration; and restore the economy and assist in development.

Whatever the new steps in US foreign policy toward the Middle East may be, one is for sure: securitizing Islam will not bring more security, it will bring fear and hatred, resulting in terror, and lack of national security for the USA. Religion is a social issue, or at most a political issue, and it should be dealt with as such. Lessons from Yugoslavia should be implemented in the Middle East. Mistakes in Yugoslavia and the Middle East should be taken as lessons not to be repeated.

REFERENCES

AbuKhalil, As'ad. 2002. *Bin Laden, Islam, and America's New "War on Terrorism"*. New York: Seven Stories.
Bowen, John R. 2012. *Blaming Islam*. Cambridge, MA: MIT Press.
Clinton, William J. 1993. *American University's Centennial Convocation*. http://www1.american.edu/media/speeches/1993centennial.htm. Accessed 27 Oct 2015.
———. 2004. *My Life*. New York: Random House.
Clinton, Hillary Rodham. 2014. *Hard Choices*. New York: Simon and Schuster.
Diamond, Larry. 2005. *Squandered Victory: The American Occupation and the Bungled Effort to Bring Democracy to Iraq*. New York: Times Books.
Gates, Robert M. 2014. *Duty: Memoirs of a Secretary at War*. New York: Alfred A. Knopf.
Howell, Sally. 2010. Competing for Muslims: New Strategies for Urban Renewal in Detroit. In *Islamophobia/Islamophilia: Beyond the Politics of Enemy and Friend*, ed. Andrew Shryock. Indiana: Indiana University Press.
Kissinger, Henry. 1994. *Diplomacy*. New York: Simon and Schuster.
Knock, Thomas J. 2009. Playing for a Hundred Years Hence: Woodrow Wilson's Internationalism and His Would-Be Heirs. In *The Crisis of American Foreign Policy: Wilsonianism in the Twenty-First Century*, ed. John G. Ikenberry et al., 25–52. Princeton: Princeton University Press.
MacAskill, Ewen. 2005. George Bush: God Told Me to End the Tyranny in Iraq. *The Guardian*, October 7. http://www.theguardian.com/world/2005/oct/07/iraq.usa. Accessed 7 Aug 2017.
Panetta, Leon. 2014. *Worthy Fights: A Memoir of Leadership in War and Peace*. New York: Penguin Press.
Ralph, Jason. 2000. 'High Stakes' and 'Low Intensity Democracy': Understanding America's Policy of Promoting Democracy. In *American Democracy Promotion: Impulses, Strategies, and Impacts*, ed. Michael Cox, G. John Ikenberry, and Takashi Inoguchi, 200–217. New York: Oxford University Press.
Sanger, David E. 1997. Clinton Seeks Power for Trade Deals Congress Can't Amend. *New York Times*, 11 September.

Smith, Tony. 2009. Wilsonianism After Iraq: The End of Liberal Internationalism? In *The Crisis of American Foreign Policy: Wilsonianism in the Twenty-First Century*, ed. John G. Ikenberry et al., 53–88. Princeton: Princeton University Press.

Talbott, Strobe. 1996. Democracy and the National Interest. *Foreign Affairs* 74 (6): 47–63.

Zogby, James. 2010. *Arab Voices: What They Are Saying to Us, and Why It Matters*. New York: Palgrave Macmillan.

Index[1]

NUMBERS AND SYMBOLS
9/11, v, vi, 8, 16, 17, 22, 25, 31, 41, 77, 95, 102, 105, 114, 117, 118, 123–125, 141, 143, 162, 168–176, 178, 182, 184–188, 191–194, 197–202, 204, 211, 215, 217, 218, 220, 221, 237, 239, 250, 261, 281–283, 287, 289, 291–293, 294n3, 295, 312, 314

A
ACT for America, 244, 246
Afghanistan, vi, vii, 21, 25, 32, 41, 47, 48, 58, 87–89, 95, 103, 126, 138, 141, 168, 169, 172, 175–177, 184, 186, 189–191, 193–195, 200, 203, 217, 218, 236, 261, 266, 283, 287, 289, 293, 298, 312, 316
Al Assad, Bashar, 228, 230, 231
Albania, 116, 124, 277
Albright, Madeleine, 146, 147, 150, 175, 194, 274, 276, 280, 287
Al-Qaeda, v, viii, 21, 87, 117, 121, 138, 141, 159, 168, 171, 172, 176, 183, 184, 191, 192, 197, 200, 217, 220, 223, 244, 248, 290, 291, 294
American grand strategy, 261, 273
Anti-Americanism, viii, 123, 199, 215, 293
Anton, Michael, 242, 249
Arms embargo, 150, 153
Asecuritization, 72
Ashcroft, John, 172, 173, 190
Axis of Evil, 6, 133, 167, 190, 194–196, 211, 287

B
Balkans, 8, 10, 16, 24, 60, 103, 148, 149, 152, 155, 161, 169, 251, 267, 268, 272–299

[1] Note: Page numbers followed by 'n' refer to notes.

© The Author(s) 2018
E. A. Shipoli, *Islam, Securitization, and US Foreign Policy*,
https://doi.org/10.1007/978-3-319-71111-9

321

Bannon, Stephen, 6, 241–243, 245–247
Beers, Charlotte, 197, 198, 291
Benghazi, 316
Bible, 188, 203, 220
bin Laden, Osama, 141, 159, 169, 171, 172, 174, 176, 186, 192, 193, 197, 200, 211, 214, 220, 291, 294, 294n3
 and death of, 220
Blair, Tony, 58, 105, 151, 152
Bosnia, 10, 22, 25, 47, 103, 139, 149–153, 184, 201, 231, 275, 277, 280, 281, 283–286, 289, 293, 297, 298, 315
Bourdieu, Pierre, 76, 84
Breitbart News, 241, 245
The Bridge Initiative, 118, 205n2, 235, 239, 242–244, 246, 247
Bush, George H. W., 22, 30, 56, 57, 140–143, 169, 175, 188, 201, 274, 279, 286
Bush, George W., 2, 3, 13n1, 16, 22–25, 28, 40, 56, 58, 59, 88, 95, 122, 124, 135, 148, 220, 236, 248, 251, 260, 276, 281, 288, 296, 298
 and securitization of Islam, 167–205

C
Carter, Jimmy, 21, 138–143, 260, 263, 265
Catholics, 106, 111, 121, 124, 143
Cheney, Dick, 6, 26, 28, 31, 41, 46, 177, 178, 186–188, 202, 296
China, 38, 57, 95, 124, 146, 148, 228, 275
Chirac, Jacque, 188, 203, 312
Christianity, vi, 105, 109, 112, 134, 190, 222
Clinton, Hillary, 231, 237, 238, 246, 247, 249, 316
Clinton, William J., ix, 3, 6, 9, 10, 16, 21, 22, 24, 25, 27, 33, 44, 45, 56, 57, 103, 134–154, 158–162, 171, 190, 213, 228, 231, 232, 249, 251, 260, 265, 272–299, 309, 311, 312, 314–316, 318
 and Jordan speech, 133, 155–157, 194, 211
CNN Effect, 30–32, 31n2, 93, 176
Cold War, 3, 5, 9–11, 13–17, 20–24, 26, 27, 29, 41–45, 47, 57, 86, 93–95, 103, 116, 121, 125, 135, 137–145, 153, 162, 180, 181, 185–196, 199, 204, 217, 251, 259–261, 264, 273, 274, 278, 279, 292, 310–311, 313, 314, 317
Copenhagen School, 2, 71, 78, 79, 87
Croatia, 277, 286
Crusades, 10, 87–89, 109, 117, 134, 160, 161, 167, 171, 180, 190, 197, 200, 203, 204, 221, 233, 260, 265, 291, 312
Cuba, 138, 185, 190, 228, 232, 287, 299

D
Dayton, 286
Democracy promotion, 2, 3, 8, 10, 11, 46–48, 60, 95, 96, 103, 104, 125, 137, 139, 145–157, 175–185, 213, 227, 229, 233, 251, 259–299, 309–311, 313
Democratic enlargement, 146, 154, 160, 161, 260, 274
Democratic peace theory, 8, 9, 15, 27, 33, 44, 45, 48–60
Democratization, 10, 53, 124, 137, 139, 140, 161, 262, 269, 271, 278, 295, 316
Department of Defense, 7, 29, 136, 198, 266, 295
Department of Homeland Security, 7, 29, 173

Department of State, 7, 198, 278, 291
Diplomacy, 53, 57, 102, 150, 197, 215, 265, 273, 285

E

Egypt, 6, 153, 189, 214, 228–230, 266, 290, 299, 310
  and military coup, 213, 318
Eisenhower, Dwight D., 20, 113, 156
Ellison, Keith, 114, 201, 202, 212
European Union (EU), 44, 140, 277, 279, 298
Extremism, vi, vii, 3, 104, 119, 136, 154, 156, 160, 161, 185, 189, 215, 217, 218, 223, 242, 244, 281, 292

F

Flynn, Michael, 6, 233, 241, 247
Free market, 26, 27, 38, 42, 52, 57, 60, 154, 269
Free trade, 22, 38, 51, 52, 56, 136, 151, 262
Functional actors, *see* Securitization

G

Gaffney, Frank, 125, 241, 243, 244, 247, 248
Gates, Robert, 177, 186, 228, 316
Geller, Pamela, 123, 125, 241, 244, 245
Ghost facilities, 174
Gog and Magog, 188, 189, 312
Gorka, Sebastian, 6, 242, 247
Guantanamo, 187, 198, 218, 225, 244, 290

H

Hobbes, Thomas, 36, 37, 39
Human rights, vii, viii, 21, 24, 26, 50, 54, 57, 58, 73, 102, 117, 136, 137, 139, 140, 148, 161, 215, 217, 227, 229, 260, 265, 276, 278, 290, 295, 318
Hussein, Saddam, 172, 175–177, 180, 185, 186, 298

I

Idealism, 24, 40–42, 46, 48, 137, 228, 262, 263, 310
Identity, *see* Securitization
Imperialism, 19, 26, 45, 56, 294
InfoWars, 211, 244
Intelligence community, 29, 222
Intervention, vii, 2, 4, 8, 26, 46–48, 58, 83, 95, 103, 136, 139, 141, 150–153, 161, 175, 191, 201, 205, 230, 231, 266, 267, 270, 281, 285, 287, 289, 296, 298, 299, 315
Iran, 15, 89, 140, 153, 154, 176, 177, 180, 190, 194–196, 218, 228, 230, 232, 260, 287, 313
  and hostage crisis, 125, 141–143
  and Non-Proliferation Treaty, 218
  and Revolution, v, 117, 141–143, 162, 314
Iraq, vii, xiii, 3, 10, 15, 22, 25, 31n2, 41, 47, 48, 58, 78, 87–89, 95, 103, 118, 124, 126, 154, 171, 172, 174, 175, 177, 179–186, 188, 189, 191, 193–195, 200, 201, 204, 205, 215, 218, 223, 229, 232, 240, 261, 276, 283, 285, 287, 289, 313, 316
  and 9/11, 31, 176, 178
  and Axis of Evil, 190, 196
ISIL (ISIS), v, vi, viii, 78, 223, 224, 229–231, 239, 245, 248
Islamic Society of Baltimore, 221
Islamic terrorism, 161, 192, 198, 236–238, 243

Islamophobia, v, vi, 9, 16, 104, 114, 204, 205n2, 236, 239–242, 244–251
Israel, 136, 154, 155, 157, 168, 193, 197, 199, 203, 218, 278

J
Jackson, Andrew, 19, 24
Jefferson, Thomas, 24, 110, 111, 114, 125, 141, 201, 212, 218
 and Islam, 112, 113, 143, 223
Jihad, 183, 186, 195, 243, 247
Jihad Watch, 245
Johnson, Lyndon, 20, 26, 41
Jones, Alex, 244

K
Kandahar, 185
Kant, Immanuel, 45, 49, 50
Kennedy, John F., 20, 138, 139, 265, 296
Kissinger, Henry, 25, 28, 48, 49, 53–55, 60, 102, 103, 138, 260, 261, 263, 265, 310
Koresh, David, 158
Kosovo, x, 10, 24, 25, 47, 83, 84, 91, 103, 124, 139, 151–153, 266, 275, 277, 280, 281, 283, 284, 287, 289, 293, 295–297, 318

L
Lake, Anthony, 51, 146, 148, 154, 160, 272, 276, 311
Latin America, 16–18, 20, 232, 260, 268, 269, 277, 279
League of Nations, 36, 52, 54, 56, 140, 182, 260, 263, 264
Lewis, Bernard, 13n1, 104, 134, 135, 139, 194

Liberalism, 8, 9, 13–15, 33, 36, 41–49, 60, 91–96, 145, 151, 176, 263, 264, 271, 275, 290, 296
Libya, 140, 142, 154, 168, 174, 180, 190, 232, 287, 299
Locke, 35

M
Macedonia, 266, 277, 284, 285, 287, 299
Macro-securitization, 5, 93
Media, vi, xiv, 5, 7, 10, 28, 30–32, 76, 90, 92, 101, 104, 105, 114, 116, 119, 124, 135, 140, 146, 159, 176, 191, 192, 198–200, 204, 211, 222, 238, 244, 247–249, 270, 278, 282, 294n3, 309
Miller, Judith, 134, 135
Miller, Stephen, 7, 243, 245
Milosevic, Slobodan, 58, 150, 151, 184, 267, 286, 299
Mohammed, Prophet of Islam, 105, 111, 155, 157
Monroe, James, 18, 20
Moralism, 48, 263
Morgenthau, Hans, 24, 26, 34, 37, 38, 263
Mubarak, Hosni, 153, 228
Muslim Americans, 118, 212, 222–224, 226, 227, 238, 239, 247, 317
Muslim ban, 141, 233, 235, 237, 239–245, 249, 250

N
National Security Council, 28, 51, 177, 242, 249
Nazism, 142, 185

New World Order, 22, 42, 103, 136, 138, 139, 145
Non-politicization, 1, 71
North Atlantic Treaty Organization (NATO), 16, 24, 44, 52, 54, 57, 83, 92, 102, 103, 140, 147, 148, 150–152, 161, 228, 234, 277, 278, 280, 281, 285–287, 295, 298

O
Obama, Barack, 2, 3, 10, 23, 114, 125, 133, 134, 141, 155, 196, 201, 205, 212, 213, 215–219, 221, 228–233, 235–242, 244–251, 260, 299, 309, 310, 313, 315, 318
  and Baltimore mosque speech, 6, 214, 221, 223–225
  and Cairo Speech, 194, 211, 214, 222, 226, 227
  and killing of bin Laden, 214, 220
Oklahoma City bombing, 159, 160
OPEC crisis, 143
Orientalism, 104

P
Palestine, 198
Palestinians, 187, 189, 193, 199, 218, 228, 244
Panetta, Leon, 174, 311
Patriot Act, 83, 173, 174, 203, 282
Pax Americana, 26
Pearl Harbor, 169, 185
Polarization, 3, 193, 294
Policy entrepreneurs, 82, 83
Policy window, 82
Politicization, 1, 71, 72, 121, 297
Polyarchy, 269
Pompeo, Mike, 243, 244, 247

Powell, Colin, 31, 41, 134, 149, 150, 174, 176–179, 184, 186, 193, 197, 198, 288
Public opinion, 27, 30, 32, 34, 101, 141, 183, 184, 189–190, 204

Q
Qur'an, 105–110, 113, 125, 201, 223, 242

R
Racism, 17, 114, 116, 232, 250
Radical Islam, 119, 204, 237, 239, 244, 246
Radicalism, 104, 119, 179, 185, 226, 246, 282
Rambouillet, 150, 287
Reagan, Ronald, 21, 56, 57, 138–143, 146, 161, 189, 190, 264, 265, 278, 289
Realism, 8, 9, 13–15, 18, 33–43, 49, 60, 91–96, 137, 170, 227
Religionization of Security, 312
Republican Party, 14, 119
Republicans, 25, 40, 47, 55, 57–58, 116, 123, 148, 149, 170, 175, 213, 225, 226, 264, 283, 287
Rice, Condoleeza, 28, 41, 138, 148, 170, 178, 185, 186, 188, 189, 202, 292
Roosevelt Corollary, 18
Roosevelt, Franklin D., 19, 44, 55–57, 260
Roosevelt, Theodore, 18, 19, 260
Rumsfeld, Donald, 26, 29, 41, 171, 172, 178, 179, 186, 188, 202, 232
Runnymede Report, 115
Russia, 19, 53, 55, 57, 137, 144, 213, 228, 230, 232, 241, 277, 285, 317
Rwanda, 47, 58, 139, 148, 286, 295

S

Sanctions, 157, 193, 265, 267
Securitization, 1, 3, 5–7, 9, 10, 13, 15, 30, 33, 60, 74, 75, 78, 80, 83, 85, 86, 88–91, 94–96, 133–162, 215, 223, 225, 232, 233, 235, 250, 251, 259, 297, 298, 309, 312, 314
  and audience, 4, 11, 81, 82, 84, 93
  and framing, 76
  and identity, 71, 77
  and language, 76, 167
  and referent object(s), 2, 71–73, 79, 87, 92, 93
  and speech act, 71, 75, 79, 84, 92
Securitization theory, 4, 9, 11, 13, 33, 60, 71–96, 314
Securitizing actors, 2, 4, 5, 32, 72, 73, 75–78, 80–85, 92, 93, 95, 186, 190
Securitizing move, 75, 76, 87, 96
Security Studies, 2, 7, 73, 83, 86, 92
  Branch Davidians, 158, 159
September 11, 103, 115, 198, 289, 292
  See also 9/11
Serbia, 266, 267, 277, 284–287
Sessions, Jeff, 243–246
Sharia, 123, 244
Sisi, Abdel Fattah, 228, 229
Soviet Union, 15, 20, 21, 43–45, 50, 57, 121, 137–140, 142, 143, 152, 180, 185, 189, 275, 279, 317
Srebrenica, 150, 286
Syria, 174, 176, 177, 213, 228–231, 233, 290, 299, 318

T

Talbott, Strobe, 42, 43, 137, 147, 261, 272, 311
Taliban, 25, 138, 141, 186, 191, 288
Truman Doctrine, 20, 264

Truman, Harry, 19, 20, 44, 52, 55–57, 139, 140, 145, 189, 264, 275, 276, 296
Trump, Donald, 3, 6, 10, 33, 96, 119, 205, 212–233, 239–242, 244–251, 313
  and National security and terrorism speech, 134, 235–238
Turkey, 20, 30, 56, 74, 88, 89, 124, 153, 183, 214, 217, 228, 266, 280, 293

U

UN General Assembly, 265, 288
United Nations (UN), 19, 23, 24, 52, 54, 56, 57, 92, 102, 115, 136, 139, 146, 147, 150, 157, 177–179, 186, 265, 285, 288, 295, 299
United States Agency for International Development (USAID), 266, 278
Utopianism, 48, 263

V

Versailles, 43, 263, 264
Voltaire, Francois-Marie Arouet, 106, 107, 109

W

War on terror, 3, 8, 10, 17, 76, 77, 84, 93, 114, 122, 124, 143, 162, 167, 172, 175–185, 187, 195–205, 244, 248, 282, 290, 291, 298, 312
Weapons of mass destruction (WMD), 3, 29, 46, 95, 124, 148, 154, 157, 175–186, 195, 200, 218, 287–289, 297, 298, 313
Wilsonianism, 5, 8, 19, 24, 36, 43–45, 48, 52–59, 145, 147, 160,

180–182, 219, 263, 275, 276, 280, 285, 288, 289, 310, 313
Wilson, Woodrow, 2, 8, 9, 19, 24, 42–44, 48, 53–58, 139, 140, 145, 180–182, 201, 260, 261, 263, 264, 270, 271, 275, 276, 283, 288, 313
Woods, Bretton, 139, 151
World War II, 43, 50, 51, 55, 56, 136, 137, 169

Y
Yugoslavia, 11, 22, 42, 48, 140, 145–157, 161, 265, 275, 277, 281, 285–287, 319

Z
Zone of democracies, 279, 288, 295

CPSIA information can be obtained
at www.ICGtesting.com
Printed in the USA
LVOW13*1736110518
576868LV00015B/414/P